W9-BCD-823

THE
HANDY
HISTORY
ANSWER
BOOK

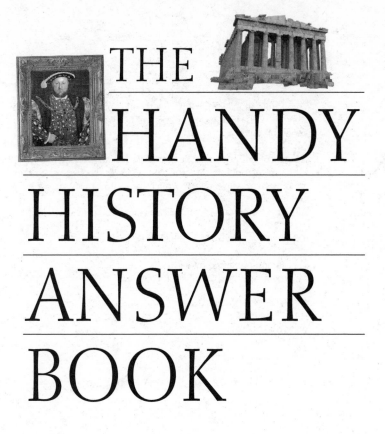

THE HANDY HISTORY ANSWER BOOK

Rebecca Nelson

BARNES
&NOBLE
BOOKS
NEW YORK

THE
HANDY
HISTORY
ANSWER
BOOK

Copyright © 1999 by Visible Ink Press™

This edition published by Barnes & Noble, Inc.,
by arrangement with Visible Ink Press LLC.

2003 Barnes & Noble Books

ISBN 0-7607-4649-4

Printed and bound in the United States of America

03 04 05 06 07 08 MC 9 8 7 6 5 4 3 2 1

Contents

ERAS AND THEIR HISTORICAL HIGHLIGHTS . . . 1

Prehistoric Era . . . Stone Age . . . Copper Age . . . Bronze Age . . . Iron Age . . . Classical Age . . . Mayan Empire . . . Aztec Empire . . . Greek Civilization . . . Mycenaean Age . . . Dark Ages in Greece . . . Greek Gods . . . Golden Age of Greece . . . The Roman Republic . . . The Roman Empire . . . The Renaissance . . . The Industrial Revolution . . . Eras of World Wars . . . The Cold War . . . Post-Communism

EXPLORATION & MIGRATION . . . 41

Leif Ericsson . . . Marco Polo . . . Christopher Columbus . . . Hernando de Soto . . . John Cabot . . . Northwest Passage . . . Sir Francis Drake . . . John Cavendish . . . Lost Colony . . . Hawaii-Loa . . . Captain Cook . . . Lewis and Clark . . . Amelia Earhart . . . Space Exploration . . . Gold & Diamond Mining . . . Exodus from Egypt . . . Trail of Tears . . . Slavery . . . Immigration

WARS, OVERTHROWS & REVOLUTIONS . . . 75

GOVERNMENT, LAW & POLITICS . . . 139

NATURAL, MAN-MADE & OTHER DISASTERS . . . 211

PHILOSOPHY, SCIENCE & INVENTION . . . 251

MEDICINE & DISEASE . . . 309

RELIGION . . . 337

CULTURE & RECREATION ... 353

First Artwork and Alphabet . . . Public Education . . . Montessori Schools . . . U.S. Desegregation . . . Aesop's *Fables* . . . Shakespeare . . . Voltaire . . . Fine Art . . . Leonardo da Vinci . . . Michelangelo . . . Architecture . . . Johann Sebastian Bach . . . Mozart . . . Jazz . . . Balanchine . . . Modern Dance . . . Games . . . Motion Pictures . . . Network Television . . . Cable Television . . . Olympic Games

Introduction

What is the Irish Question? When did people begin to write? *The Handy History Answer Book* will tell you. *Handy History* is your resource for learning, for tracking down fugitive facts, and for brushing up on the events, terms, and history-makers many of us remember from schooldays but somehow can't always neatly define. This book is not intended to be a comprehensive work on history; it can't be done in a single volume. Still, the editors and the other minds who conceived of this book believed that thoughtful people should have a convenient place to go to look up those nagging questions that come up in everyday conversation and in everyday reading. Serious questions like: "What was the Byzantine Empire?", "Why is Shakespeare so widely studied?", and "What exactly happened at Watergate?" And not-so-serious questions like: "What did Shakespeare study?", "Who is Hoyle?", "When was color television invented?", and "Who was more important to rock-and-roll—Elvis Presley or the Beatles?"

While *Handy History* focuses on Western civilization, it's impossible to do so without taking Eastern cultures into consideration. The influences of the East are certainly evident in the West, and vice versa. It turns out that, as the saying goes, our world is indeed a global village. This being so, the reader will find a number of questions and answers regarding Eastern events, ideas, and innovations.

You'll find more than 500 questions and answers in nine chapters: Eras and Their Historical Highlights; Exploration and Migration; Wars, Overthrows, and Revolutions; Government, Law, and Politics; Natural, Man-made, and Other Disasters; Philosophy, Science, and Invention; Medicine and Disease; Religion; and Culture and Recreation. In addition, a Chronology of World Events, which you'll find on page xv, highlights major eras or specific events within the Prehistoric Era; the Classical Age of Greece and Rome; the Middle Ages; the Renaissance, including expansion and reformation; the Enlightenment and the Scientific Revolution; the Revolutionary Era, describing wars and the birth of industry; and the Modern World, which provides a decade-by-decade glimpse of the twentieth century.

The editors of *Handy History* hope that these pages provide you with hours of interesting reading, even if it is intermittent—after all, this is a book that, your question answered, you actually can put down . . . and return to the next time a historical term, event, or person comes up and you'd like to find out a little more about it.

In finding the answers to these frequently asked questions, the editors on this project have made every effort to check a number of different sources—in order to provide a balanced point of view on history as well as to ensure accuracy. It's perhaps a popularly held perception that history is unchanging, but as new information is discovered, interpretations change, and when scant is known of a historical event, scholars have done their best to fill in the gaps with theory. Because of these factors, history is not a closed book. There is always more to be learned and to be discovered.

Acknowledgments

This book would not have been possible if not for the hard work and dedication from the editors at Visible Ink Press. Many thanks go out to Michelle Banks for her efforts at editing the manuscript; Julia Furtaw and Christa Brelin for their leadership and insight on this project; and Michelle DiMercurio for her beautiful cover design work for this book.

Additional thanks must be extended to Sarah Chesney for her photo acquisition work; Pam Reed and Randy Bassett for photo scanning and cropping; Jeff Muhr for his technical wizardry in coding the manuscript; and Marco Di Vita from The Graphix Group for his timely and commendable work with typesetting.

Photo Credits

All photos from AP/Wide World can be found on pages: 247, 275, 306, 330, 368, and 403.

All photos from Archive Photos can be found on pages: 65, 66, 68, 77, 97, 107, 125, 132, 136, 168, 176, 181, 199, 201, 220, 235, 266, 278, 285, 355, 416, and 424.

All photos from Corbis Corporation can be found on pages: 2, 43, 59, 78, 232, 273, 327, 361, and 413.

Photo of Michelangelo's *David* appears courtesy of Susan D. Rock.

Photo of Alexander Graham Bell appears courtesy of U.S. National Aeronautics and Space collection.

Remaining photos, that are not public domain appear courtesy of the Library of Congress.

Cover photo of Henry VIII appears courtesy of Corbis Corporation.

Cover photo of Civil War battle appears courtesy of the Kobal Collection.

Chronology of World Events

Prehistoric Era

2,000,000,00–10,000 B.C.: **The Old Stone Age:** Paleolithic man uses stone tools; humans evolve from their apelike ancestors to modern-looking hunter-gatherers

35,000–8500 B.C.: Earliest forms of art and communication are used

10,000 B.C–2500 B.C.: **The New Stone Age:** Neolithic man learns to produce food rather than collect it—the beginnings of agriculture; communities come into being, laying the foundation for the great civilizations that will follow

3300–2500 B.C.: **The Bronze Age:** Humans begin using bronze metal to make tools

3000 B.C.: Greek civilization begins to flourish: the Minoans, who live on the island of Crete, are Europe's first advanced civilization

2500 B.C.–2000 B.C.: **The Iron Age:** Man learns to melt and cast iron

Egyptian Imhotep becomes history's first physician

The Classical Age

2000 B.C.–A.D. 500: The Classical Age is dominated by the Greeks and the Romans

c. 1450 B.C.: The island of Crete is struck by a two-hundred-foot tidal wave (tsunami), destroying or seriously weakening the Minoan civilization and making way for the rise of the mainland Greek Mycenaeans

c. 1400 B.C.: The Israelites are led by the Hebrew prophet Moses; the first five books of The Bible are written

1200 B.C.: The Trojan War begins when the Mycenaeans attack the city of Troy, considered the key to the profitable Black Sea trade

c. 1000 B.C.: Mayan culture begins to flourish in Central America

The Song of Solomon is written in the Middle East

700s B.C.: The city of Rome is established

600s B.C.: Taoism is established

The Book of Job is written in the Middle East

500s B.C.: Birth of the Roman Republic

The Celts spread across present-day France, Italy, Portugal, Spain, and the British Isles

400s B.C.: Greek civilization reaches its height—called the Hellenic Age

Greek philosopher Socrates lays the foundation for Western thought

300s B.C.: Macedonian king Alexander the Great amasses empire that stretches from Egypt to India, spreading Greek ideas and customs

200s B.C.: Halley's Comet is first spotted

The first Punic War begins in Italy

100s B.C.: The Romans conquer Macedonia

The Punic Wars end; the Romans are victorious over the Carthaginians

Julius Caesar is born

60s B.C.: Caesar is elected consul and the First Triumvirate is formed to govern Rome

40s B.C.: Caesar is murdered by his countrymen

20s B.C.: The Roman Empire is established by the ruler Augustus, and the two hundred years of the *Pax Romana* begins

6 B.C.: Ovid writes *The Metamorphoses*

c. A. D. 30: Jesus is crucified

A. D. 300s: Roman emperor Constantine the Great converts to Christianity and henceforth during his reign, Christians regain freedom of worship and the Christian church becomes legal

Constantine the Great moves the capital of the Roman Empire to Byzantium (later called Constantinople, which is today Istanbul, Turkey), shifting the focus from West to East and paving the way for the Byzantine Empire

Upon the death of Theodosius the Great, the Roman Empire is divided in two—East (centered in Byzantium) and West (centered in Rome)

The Middle Ages

A. D. 400s: Under the leadership of Attila, the Huns rule much of eastern Europe, but after he dies (in 453), their dominance ends

The city of Rome suffers repeated attacks at the hands of various Germanic tribes, and finally falls in 476, marking the end of the West Roman Empire; the East Roman

Empire, which has remained Christian but has been significantly influenced by the East, will survive as the Byzantine Empire

500s: Byzantine Empire, centered in Constantinople (present-day Istanbul, Turkey), grows in strength and influence

600s: Islam is created by Muhammad, who is believed to be a prophet of Allah (God)

700s: Feudal system begins to be established as a way of organizing and protecting communities

800s: Charlemagne is crowned ruler of the Holy Roman Empire, a loose confederation of German and Italian states; but after his death in 814, the empire lapses

During China's Tang Dynasty, the first book is published—*The Diamond Sutra*

900s: Otto I is crowned emperor of the Holy Roman Empire, a confederation of Western European states

1000s: Sea-faring Norseman Leif Ericsson arrives at Newfoundland or Nova Scotia, Canada (in 1001); he will go down in many history texts as the first European to set foot on North American soil but the landing is not authenticated

Pope Urban II announces in 1095 the first of the Christian Crusades to recover the Holy Land (of Palestine) from the Muslims

1100s: Feudalism takes hold in France and spreads into England, Spain, and other parts of the Christian world

Europe's first university is formed at Bologna, Italy (in 1158)

1200s: Genghis Khan amasses his empire in the East

Marco Polo travels to the East (1270), where he remains for some 25 years before returning to his native Venice, bringing back fantastic accounts of his journey

The Magna Carta is signed at Runnymede, England (1215)

The Crusades, a series of nine military expeditions, end; the Christian goal of permanently recovering the Holy Land of Palestine is not realized, but trade routes have been established, new markets opened, and ship-building has been improved

Florentine poet Dante Alighieri writes *The Divine Comedy*

Renaissance, Expansion, and Reformation

1300s: Renaissance takes hold in Europe and will last until the 1600s: Italian artists and writers including Botticelli, da Vinci, Raphael, and Machiavelli create timeless works; the prosperous city-states of Florence, Rome, Venice, and Milan grow in influence; the printing press helps spread the ideas of the Renaissance to other parts of Europe, where Erasmus, Shakespeare, Sir Thomas More, and the van Eycks, among others, produce masterpieces

In central Mexico, the Aztec Indians establish the city of Tenochtítlan (c. 1325) on the future site of Mexico City

The Hundred Years' War begins (1337) between England and France, who will fight intermittently until 1453; England will, during the course of the conflicts, lose all claims to lands on the European Continent

Japanese *No* Drama is created

1400s: European colonialism begins as Spain and Portugal each send explorers in search of new trade routes to India and the Far East

Albert II is crowned emperor (in 1438) of the Holy Roman Empire; he is the first ruler from the Hapsburg family—who will go on to hold power in Europe almost continuously until 1806

The Byzantine Empire falls to the Ottoman Turks (1453)

Gutenberg builds his first printing press (1440s)

Under the sponsorship of Spanish monarchs Ferdinand and Isabella, Italian explorer Christopher Columbus voyages west (in 1492) in search of a trade route to the East, and lands on an island he names San Salvador; alternately called Watlings Island, the area is today part of the Bahamas

1500s: The first authenticated European landing on the North American continent takes place (in 1500) when Portuguese navigator Gaspar de Corte-Real makes landfall and explores the coasts of Labrador and Newfoundland, Canada

Italian explorer Amerigo Vespucci reaches the Western Hemisphere and is later credited for being the first European explorer to realize that he had actually arrived in a New World, which will be named for him: the name "America" is derived from "Amerigo"

The Reformation begins (1517) when theology professor Martin Luther nails his Ninety-Five Theses to the door of the Castle Church at Wittenburg in Saxony, Germany

Michelangelo sculpts *David* (1501–04)

The Spaniards, led by Hernán Cortes, arrive in central Mexico (in 1519) where they find the remarkable Aztec city of Tenochtítlan

The Inca Indians of South America are brought under control of the Spanish (1530s)

The Ottoman (Turkish) Empire becomes increasingly powerful, spreading Islamic culture in the East and into Europe

The Scientific Revolution has its roots in the work of Galileo, who will be credited with no less than establishing the modern method of experimentation

The Enlightenment and the Scientific Revolution

1600s: Galileo advocates the Copernican system of the universe, proposing that the Earth revolves around the Sun (1613)

The Scientific Revolution is in full swing, with Isaac Newton, Joseph Priestley, and Rene Descartes among the prominent thinkers of the era, which will witness key discoveries in astronomy, anatomy, mathematics, and physics

The Ottoman Empire begins its 300-year decline

The Peace of Westphalia (1648) ends the Thirty Years' War, helping establish Protestantism in Europe

Harvard University is chartered (1636) outside Boston, Massachusetts

English philosopher John Locke publishes his ideas on government, which will have lasting impact, even influencing the Founding Fathers of the United States more than a century later

Oliver Cromwell is named (in 1653) Lord Protector of England, interrupting the reigns of the English monarchs

Charles II ascends the English throne (1660), beginning the eight-year period known as the Restoration

The British Parliament compels monarchs William and Mary to accept the Bill of Rights (1689), asserting the crown no longer has absolute power and must rule responsibly through Parliament; England's constitutional monarchy is founded

The advances of the Scientific Revolution have resulted in science courses becoming part of school curricula—from elementary schools to universities

The Revolutionary Era: Wars and the Birth of Industry

1700s: Trained scientists develop new technologies—including complicated farm machinery and equipment for textile manufacturing and transportation

The Industrial Revolution begins in Great Britain with the introduction of power-driven machinery, and soon spreads to Western Europe and America; the populations of these areas begin to move away from their agricultural roots, adopting new, urban lifestyles, with an emphasis on goods and services

Bach begins his career as a composer (early 1700s)

French military engineer Nicolas-Joseph Cugnot builds a steam-powered road vehicle—it is the precursor to the automobile

The Boston Tea Party and other acts of colonial rebellion spark the American Revolutionary War (1775–83)

The Constitutional Convention is convened at Philadelphia (1787); the U.S. Constitution is born

The French Revolution (1789–99) begins with the storming of the Bastille and the Oath of the Tennis Court

France's Reign of Terror under Revolutionary leader Robespierre ends in 1794

Napoleon rises to power (1799)

1800s: The Holy Roman Empire ends (1806) in the Confederation of the Rhine, which brings most of the German states under French domination, precipitating a war with Prussia

xix

The Gold Rush is on in California (1850s)

Sigmund Freud is born (1856)

Charles Darwin publishes *Origin of Species* (1858)

Famine causes widespread Irish emigration from the mid-1800s to the end of the century

The Civil War (1861–65) is fought in the United States

The Red Cross is founded in Switzerland (1863)

Louis Pasteur develops pasteurization (1866)

The Franco-Prussian War is fought (1870–71); with all the other German states joining Prussia, the conflict becomes one between France and Germany; the fighting is ended with the Treaty of Frankfurt, establishing a new German Empire and setting the stage for World War I

The great Chicago Fire rages (1871)

Alexander Graham Bell invents the telephone (1875)

New philosophies spread, including existentialism and Marxism

American Thomas Alva Edison, "The Wizard of Menlo Park," invents (during the late 1800s) the automatic telegraphy machine, stock-ticker machine, incandescent light bulb, phonograph, and kinetoscope

The gas-powered automobile is invented (late 1800s)

The Johnstown (Pennsylvania) Flood kills thirty thousand people in 1889

The Duryea Motor Wagon Company turns out the United States' first production motor vehicle (1896)

French chemists-physicists Pierre and Marie Curie discover *radium* (1898)

American suffragists, determined to win the right to vote, organize

The Modern World

1900s: At Kill Devil Hills, North Carolina, brothers Wilbur and Orville Wright make the world's first flight in a power-driven, heavier-than-air machine—the airplane

1910s: The *Titanic* sinks (1912)

American automaker Henry Ford invents the assembly line (1913), which will revolutionize the manufacturing of consumer goods and helps usher in a new era of capitalism

Austria-Hungary declares war against Serbia in late July 1914, and the European power is soon joined by Germany and Bulgaria, which form the Central Powers

The Allies declare war on the Ottoman Empire in November 1914, after Turkish ships bombard Russian ports on the Black Sea and Turkish troops invaded Russia

World War I, known as the Great War, is fought in Europe (1914–18)

Germany agrees to an armistice and the Central Powers surrender, drawing World War I to a close; ten million lives have been lost in the trenches of Europe

In January 1919, Allied representatives gather in Paris to draw up the peace settlement; in an effort to keep Germany in check, the Treaty of Versailles metes out severe punishment to Germany, intended to diminish its stature in Europe

1920s: As one of the losing Central Powers in World War I, the Ottoman Empire is officially dissolved (1922)

The Roaring Twenties, also called the Jazz Age, is marked by extreme optimism in the United States

U.S. Congress passes (in 1920) the 19th Amendment to the U.S. Constitution, granting women the right to vote

The cultural movement that will come to be called the Harlem Renaissance begins (in 1925)

James Joyce's *Ulysses* is deemed obscene by the U.S. government (1928)

The First Academy Awards ceremony is held in Hollywood (1928)

The U.S. stock market crashes on "Black Thursday" (October 29, 1929): overproduction, limited foreign markets, overexpansion of credit, and stock market speculation have combined to create a financial crisis that will last until 1940

1930s: The Great Depression grips the United States and affects the world economy as well

The Dust Bowl devastates the Great Plains states (1934)

Adolf Hitler rises to power as a staunch nationalist leader in Germany, promising to restore Germany to its pre-war stature

Germany, Italy, and Japan form an alliance, known as the Axis (1936)

World War II begins when Hitler's Nazi troops invade Poland on September 1, 1939

1940s: World War II (1939–45) is fought in Europe, Asia, and the South Pacific

The United States joins the Allies in fighting the Axis Powers after the Japanese bomb Pearl Harbor on December 7, 1942

American General Dwight D. Eisenhower leads the Allied forces in an invasion of Normandy, a region in northwestern France that lies along the English Channel, on June 6, 1944; the Allied victory there is a turning point in World War II

Following eleven months of bloody conflict, Germany surrenders to the Allies on May 7, 1945, ending the war in Europe; U.S. President Harry S Truman, who took office in April following the death of President Franklin D. Roosevelt, declares May 8 V-E Day (Victory in Europe Day)

The United Nations is chartered during the closing days of World War II

The United States drops atomic bombs on Hiroshima (August 6, 1945) and Nagasaki (August 9, 1945)

The Japanese surrender on August 14, 1945, ending World War II; September 2, 1945, is declared V-J Day (Victory over Japan Day)

Israel is decreed a state by the United Nations (1947)

Indian nationalist and spiritual leader Mohandas Ghandi is assassinated (1948)

The Soviet Union explodes its first nuclear bomb (1949)

In a speech given in March 1946, British Prime Minister Winston Churchill warns that "an iron curtain has descended across the Continent"; the statesman's remark is in response to Soviet leader Joseph Stalin's tactics in Eastern Europe, which indicate barriers between East and West

The Cold War begins

1950s: Distrust deepens in the Cold War between democratic Western powers and Communist Eastern bloc countries

The Soviet Union launches the *Sputnik* satellite in October 1957, sparking the Space Race

The polio vaccine is pronounced safe and effective (1955); polio will virtually be eradicated from developed nations as a result of the vaccine

Elvis Presley makes his first commercial recording (1954)

The Montgomery (Alabama) Bus Boycott (1955–56) helps launch the Civil Rights movement, whose aim is to eliminate racial segregation and discrimination in the United States

1960s: The Civil Rights movement gains momentum in the United States; Supreme Court decisions send a clear message that racial segregation and discrimination are unconstitutional

The U.S. government backs the disastrous Bay of Pigs invasion of Fidel Castro–led Cuba in 1961

The Cuban Missile Crisis heightens worries that the Cold War will turn into a "hot" war; the 1962 situation is averted when the Soviets comply with President John Kennedy's demand that the missiles be removed from the island nation

Color television is broadcast for the first time (1962)

The Palestinian Liberation Organization (PLO) is formed (1964) by Arabs in Palestine

The British Invasion (of the American music scene) is highlighted by Beatlemania (1964)

American astronaut Neil Armstrong is the first person to walk on the moon (1969)

More than half a million American troops are sent to South Vietnam to fight in the Vietnam War; in the United States, protesters stage demonstrations against American involvement in the Southeast Asian war

1970s: An April 13, 1970, explosion aboard *Apollo 13* puts its three astronauts in a disastrous situation; America watches and waits as the real-life drama unfolds and ends safely when the module splashes down in the South Pacific

The Watergate scandal causes President Nixon to resign from office on August 9, 1974

The last U.S. troops are brought home from Vietnam (1973)

Microsoft is founded (1975)

1980s: CNN makes its first broadcast in 1980 and MTV in 1981, launching the cable television industry

Mikhail Gorbachev becomes head of the Communist Party and leader of the Soviet Union in 1985, bringing to an end the reign of the old guard of Stalin-trained leaders; Gorbachev institutes policies of openness to the West and economic development in his own country

The Iran-Contra affair shakes the Reagan presidency (1986–87)

Unrest continues in the Israeli-occupied Gaza Strip and West Bank

1990s: The Soviet era draws to a close in Eastern Europe as multi-party elections are held in Romania, Czechoslovakia, Hungary, East Germany, and Bulgaria in 1990

East Germany and West Germany are unified (October 1990)

The Persian Gulf War is fought (1991)

The Soviet Union dissolves (1991–92)

The PLO and Israel sign an accord in May 1994, providing for Palestinian self-rule in the Gaza Strip

The most destructive act of terrorism in American history takes place on April 19, 1995, when a bomb explodes in an Oklahoma City federal building, killing 168 people and injuring more than 500

World Wide Web becomes part of the Internet (1991)

South Africa's system of racial segregation, Apartheid, ends and in April 1994, the country holds its first elections in which blacks are eligible to vote; black South Africans win control of parliament and black leader Nelson Mandela becomes president

Resolution to the ages-old Irish Question appears imminent (1997–98), though protests and violence continue

THE
HANDY
HISTORY
ANSWER
BOOK

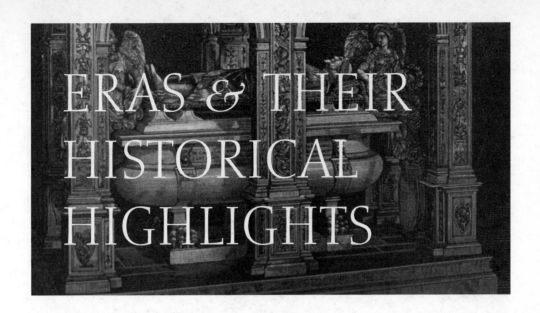

ERAS & THEIR HISTORICAL HIGHLIGHTS

PREHISTORIC ERA (BEGINS 3,000,000 B.C.)

When did **history** begin?

In the simplest terms, history began when man began to document events in writing. Anything prior to the advent of writing is commonly referred to as "*pre*historic." The Prehistoric Era accounts for the periods of man's evolution and development that preceded his ability to document events. Since man began to write about 3,500 years before Christ (or about 5,500 years ago), one could say that this is when history began.

What is the **Prehistoric Era**?

The term Prehistoric Era refers to the time before written history began, so it encompasses the Stone Age (Paleolithic and Neolithic ages), the Bronze Age, and the Iron Age. The Prehistoric Era spans the time from about 2,000,000 B.C. to roughly 2000 B.C., when the Classical Age began (with the rise of the Greek and Roman empires).

What is **Neanderthal Man**?

The term refers to a hominid who walked the earth in the Middle Paleolithic Age (during the Old Stone Age). The term "hominid" generally

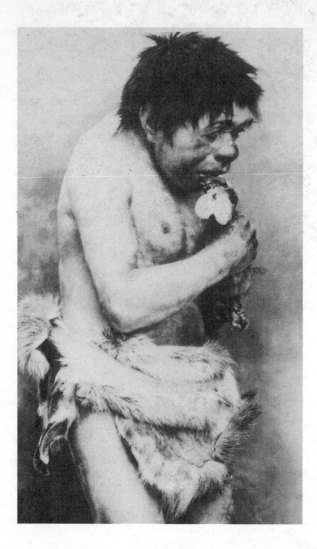

Neanderthal Man.

refers to an erect-walking primate that is an extinct ancestor to man. A hominid can be an ancestor of "true" man (modern man) or a relative, such as a modern primate. (In this context, the term "man" is used to refer to both males and females of the genus Homo.)

Neanderthal Man was discovered in 1856 near Düsseldorf, Germany, when workers came across the skull and skeletal remains of what appeared to be a human. The finding sparked discussion and controversy about the nature of the being. There were two arguments: the skull, markedly different from that of nineteenth-century man, was that of a pathologically deformed human being (an individual who was thought to have suffered from severe bone disease or some sort of congenital malformation); or, the skull belonged to an "early" man. This latter view was supported by the famous English naturalist Thomas Henry Huxley in his book *Man's Place in Nature* (1863).

Another advocate for the argument that the skull belonged to an early man was French surgeon and anthropologist Paul Broca, who accepted Charles Darwin's theory of evolution. In this light, Broca argued that the Neanderthal skull was a key to human evolution.

In 1886, two similar skeletons, along with some stone tools, were found in Belgium. This discovery strengthened the argument of Huxley and Broca—that these remains actually belonged to man's early ancestors. Excavations in 1890–92 on the island of Java (in Southeast Asia) furthered the argument and, for the most part, settled the controversy: A number of fossil remains were found in the banks along the Solo river. Named *Pithecanthropus erectus* by their discoverer, Dutch paleontologist Marie Eugène F. T. Dubois, the findings were popularly known as "Java Man."

Subsequent findings, including that of the so-called "Peking Man" in the summer of 1923 in China, produced evidence that approximately 70,000 to 11,000 years ago, there were groups of the Neanderthal race in Europe, western Asia, and northern Africa. At some point in time they disappeared and were replaced by another type of man; the cause of this disappearance is unknown.

When did **mankind** first walk on the face of the earth?

The discovery of "Lucy" in the 1970s confirmed that it was more than three million years ago that humankind first walked the earth, but in the mid–1990s, scientists found new evidence, which suggested that it was even longer ago—more than four million years ago—that humankind first walked upright.

In November 1974, American Donald C. Johanson made one of paleoanthropology's most widely publicized finds when he discovered a partial skeleton at Hadar, Ethiopia. More than three million years old, the female skeleton was the most complete hominid fossil ever found, but the skull was not recovered. The creature stood three and one-half feet tall and, although apelike, had definitely walked upright. When Johanson officially announced his find in 1979, "Lucy" (named for the Beatles song "Lucy in the Sky with Diamonds," which was popular in the camp at the time the fossil was found) became known as the mother of all humankind. (Her sex was confirmed by the pelvic bones.) Since she was an erect-walker, the finding gave certainty to theories that hominids walked erect at three million years B.C.

Since the discovery of Lucy, two older finds have been made. In 1994, anthropologist Meave Leakey, wife of Richard Leakey, found a bipedal species that is 4.1 million years old, which she named *Australopithecus anamnesis* at Kanapoi, near Lake Turkana in Kenya. Also in 1994, University of California, Berkeley, paleoanthropologist Tim D. White and an international team found fossils of a chimp-like animal dating back to 4.4 million years ago. Named *Ardipithecus ramidus*, it remains uncertain whether this hominid is part of the human family tree, but researchers believe that continued study will provide answers.

FROM THE OLD STONE AGE TO THE CLASSICAL AGE

What is the **Stone Age**?

What people commonly refer to as the Stone Age is actually two ages: The Old Stone Age (begins about two million years B.C. to about 10,000 B.C.) and the New Stone Age (which began c. 10,000 B.C. and ended c. 2500 B.C). It was during these periods that man used stone tools.

During the Old Stone Age, also called the Paleolithic Age, man was evolving from his apelike ancestors to modern-looking hunter-gatherers. Early modern man's progress continued to the end of the Old Stone Age, around 10,000 B.C. Then, as the Ice Age ended and the earth warmed, the hunter-gatherers again revolutionized their way of life. They opted for a more settled existence in which they could exercise greater control over their food supplies. With the coming of the New Stone Age, or Neolithic Age, man turned to agriculture.

The New Stone Age, or the Neolithic Age, brought profound changes in the development of man. Neolithic man learned to produce food rather than collect it. People were no longer dependent on hunting, fishing, and

What is the Bronze Age?

The Bronze Age (c. 3300 B.C.–2500 B.C.) is the period of human culture when man began using bronze metal to make objects—principally, tools. The Neolithic Age slowly came to an end as various cultures in Eurasia that had depended on wood, stone, and bone for tools began to develop the techniques for metallurgy. Bronze proved to be an excellent material for making tools and weapons. People in the Middle East learned to produce bronze by mixing tin and copper (hence, the transition years between the Neolithic Age and the Bronze Age are sometimes referred to as the Copper Age). Bronze had considerable hardness, strength, and density, and proved more reliable and durable than the stone, wood, and bone tools that had been in use.

The Bronze Age lasted until the beginning of the Iron Age.

gathering wild fruit and nuts for subsistence. They learned to cultivate crops, domesticate animals, make pottery, weave textiles from fiber and hair, and produce more sophisticated tools and weapons by hammering, grinding, and polishing granite, jasper, and other hard stone. More substantial houses and communities, even fortified villages, came into being, laying the foundation for the great civilizations that would follow.

Near the end of the New Stone Age, craftsmen in the Middle East learned to make tools and weapons from metal. The world's earliest known man-made copper objects—beads, pins, and awls—were fabricated in Turkey and Iran around 8000 B.C. Archaeological evidence points to copper mining in the Balkans by around 5000 B.C. From there the technology probably spread west, reaching the Alps about a thousand years later and marking the beginning of the Copper Age (4000 B.C.–2200 B.C.).

Was there really such a thing as the **Copper Age**?

Some texts do not refer to a Copper Age, moving directly from the Stone Age to the Bronze Age. In fact, the Copper Age (c. 4000B.C.–2200 B.C.)

overlapped with both the end of the Old Stone Age (the Neolithic Age) and the Bronze Age, and is marked by man's use of copper as a material for tool-making.

What is the **Iron Age**?

The real advent of the Iron Age came not with the discovery of the metal (in 2500 B.C.), but with the invention of the process of casing or steeling it, probably about 1500 B.C. This happened when it was learned that by repeatedly reheating wrought iron in a charcoal fire and then hammering it, it not only became harder than bronze but also kept its hardness after long use. (Wrought iron was discovered accidentally when smiths found that by hammering the small bead-like pieces of iron left as a residue after smelting copper they could form the iron particles into a mass. This kind of wrought iron, however, was good only for decorative purposes, and for more than a thousand years after 2500 B.C., iron remained a precious ornamental metal. Bronze, which was harder and capable of being sharpened to a fine cutting edge, continued to be the functional metal for tools and weapons.)

The next technological improvement, which again meant a further hardening of the metal, was the process of quenching it, that is, a process of repeatedly plunging the hot iron into cold water. It was only after this series of discoveries and inventions that the significant impact of iron on culture and civilization was appreciably felt.

Because bronze was scarce, it was also costly. Consequently, it was not until iron came into use that man extended his control over nature. For this reason, iron has been called the "democratic metal." Widespread use of iron tools meant a general increase in living standards. For example, the use of iron axes brought about the clearing of forests, and therefore new land came under cultivation. Other significant developments included the application of iron tools to sheep-shearing and cloth-cutting, and the invention of the lathe, the most fundamental machine tool.

The Iron Age lasted until the beginning of the Classical Age (c. 2000 B.C.)

What is the **Classical Age**?

The Classical Age refers to the ancient Greek and Roman worlds, roughly 2000 B.C. to A.D. 500. The Classical Age followed the Prehistoric Age and preceded the Middle Ages. During this period, the ancient Greeks and Romans made contributions to literature, philosophy, science, the arts, and letters that are still relevant today.

THE MAYAN EMPIRE

Was the **Mayan Empire** the most advanced early civilization?

In some regards, the Mayas were more advanced than other civilizations. Their development preceded that of the other agrarian civilizations in Central and South America—principally the Aztec and the Inca.

The Mayas were an agricultural people who originated about 1000 B.C. in the Yucatan Peninsula (Central America) and eastern Mexico. There they developed a civilization that was highly advanced: Not only did the Mayas produce remarkable architecture (including the flat-topped pyramids that are visited by tourists) and art (including painting, murals, and sculpture), but they developed their own writing system—probably the first in the Western Hemisphere. They used this system to record time, astronomical events, their history, and religion (they believed in more than 160 gods). They also developed an advanced mathematics as well as a 365-day calendar believed by some to be even more accurate than the Gregorian calendar in use today.

At its peak, the Mayan population numbered some fourteen million. Their history is divided into three periods: the Pre-Classic period began about the time they originated (roughly 1000 B.C.) and extended into A.D. 300; this was the groups formative period. During the Classic period, 300–900, Mayan culture spread throughout the area and they developed city-centers at Copán (Honduras), Palenque and Uxmal (Mexico), and Piedras Negras, Uaxactún, and Tikal (Guatemala). Scholars believe Tikal was home to some fifty thousand people and was not only a center for government, education, economics, and science, but it was also a spiritual mecca for the Maya.

It was in the second half of the Classic period that the Maya made their greatest accomplishments in art and science: Europe would not produce a superior system of mathematics for centuries to come. During the

7

Post-Classic period (900–1546), they were invaded by the Toltecs. However the Maya absorbed these people rather than being conquered by them. Nevertheless, by the time the Spanish arrived in the mid-1500s, the Mayan civilization was in decline. Some historians attribute this to widespread famine or disease while others believe the decline was due to a rebellion of the people against the harsh government. Though they were conquered by the Spaniards and became assimilated into the larger culture that developed in the region, Maya Indians still survive in Mexico and Central America today.

AZTEC EMPIRE

How did the **Aztec** and **Inca Empires** compare with the Mayan?

While all were advanced civilizations that were eventually conquered by the Spaniards, the Inca and Aztec cultures reached their peaks in the fifteenth century—just before the arrival of the Europeans in the New World— while the Maya culture had reached its zenith about five hundred years earlier and was already in decline by the time the Europeans arrived. It's also important to note that each of these groups occupied a different region of the Americas—the Aztecs settled in central Mexico, the Incas in southwest South America (primarily Peru), and the Mayas in the Yucatan Peninsula of Central America. In these regions, each group carved out its own stronghold, and for a time, their civilizations flourished.

The Aztecs founded their central city of Tenochtitlán (the site of Mexico City) about 1325. A poor nomadic people before their arrival in Mexico's central region, the Aztecs believed the Lake Texcoco marsh was a prophetic place to settle. Before they built it into a great city, they first had to fill in the swampy area, which they did by creating artificial islands. In the 1500s, when the Spanish first saw the remarkable city— with its system of causeways, canals, bridges, and aqueducts—they called it the Venice of the New World. In addition to constructing the impressive trade and cultural center of Tenochtitán, the Aztecs were farmers, astronomers, mathematicians, and historians—who recorded the events of their civilization. Their religion was pantheistic—they worshiped many gods. Given that, it's not surprising that when the

Spanish conquistadors arrived, at first the Maya believed they were gods, and even welcomed them with gifts.

The Incas developed one of the most extensive empires in all the Americas. During the hundred years before the arrival of the Spanish, the Incas expanded their territory along the western coast of South America to include parts of present-day Peru, Ecuador, Colombia, Bolivia, Chile, and Argentina. Though it was a vast region, it was nevertheless a closely knit state ruled by a powerful emperor. The government was subdivided down to the local level, but because the emperor required total obedience from his subjects, local rulers were kept in check.

Like the Aztecs in Mexico, the Inca developed an infrastructure that included a network of roads, bridges, and ferries as well as irrigation systems. They, too, built impressive edifices, demonstrating their abilities as engineers. The magnificent city of Machu Puchu was modeled in clay before construction began. The Inca were also skilled craftspeople, working with gold, silver, and textiles. Like the Aztecs, the Incas worshiped many gods. And when the Spaniard Francisco Pizarro (c. 1475–1541) arrived in the region in 1532, he was welcomed as a god at first. However, by 1537, the Inca region was brought under Spanish control.

GREEK CIVILIZATION

How did **Greek civilization** begin?

Ancient Greek civilization began with the Minoans. As Europe's first advanced civilization, the Minoans were a prosperous and peaceful people who flourished on the island of Crete from about 3000 to 1450 B.C. The Minoans built structures from stone, plaster, and timbers; painted walls with brilliant frescoes; made pottery; wove and dyed cloth; cultivated the land (they are believed to be the first people to produce an agricultural surplus, which they exported); constructed stone roads and bridges; and built highly advanced drainage systems and aqueducts. (At Knossos, the royal family had a system for showers and even had toilets that could be flushed.) In short, the Minoans were a sophisticated people who loved music and dance, games, and entertainment.

What is the Mycenaean Age?

The Minoans were either conquered by or succeeded by the Mycenaean, who were mainland Greeks: In about 1450 B.C., Crete was struck by a two-hundred-foot tidal wave, which is thought to either have completely destroyed the island or to have weakened it to a point that it could be overtaken. The Mycenaeans flourished from about 1650 B.C. to 1200 B.C., a time known as the Mycenaean Age, carrying forth the culture and skills they had learned from the Minoans (who had been their neighbors). In addition, the Mycenaean were skilled horsemen, charioteers, and accomplished sailors who ruled the Aegean. Mycenaean culture revolved around their fortified palaces, called acropolises (top cities). Their cities included Argos, Corinth, Sparta, and the then small cities of Athens and Thebes.

In about 1200 B.C., the Mycenaean attacked the city of Troy, which was considered the key to the profitable Black Sea trade, thus launching the Trojan War. After ten years of fighting (a period that is recounted by Homer in the *Iliad*), the Mycenaean were victorious. But soon their period of triumph ended as the Dorian peoples (from the northwestern part of the Greek mainland) overran most of the Peloponnesus (the southern peninsula of Greece). The Dorians, aided by the superiority of the iron sword, flooded southward, where they sacked and burned the great Mycenaean cities and conquered the wealthy sea traders, throwing Greece into the period known as the Dark Ages, or Archaic Period, which lasted from 1100 to about 800 B.C.

What were the **Dark Ages** of **ancient Greece**?

After the Dorians conquered the Mycenaean in 1100 B.C., these nomadic peoples thrust Greece into a period of decline that lasted three hundred years. The Dorians rejected the life of the great Mycenaean cities in favor of their nomadic shepherding and hunting life. A tribal people, they possessed a harsh sense of justice, and the period was marked by feuds between clans. Men typically carried weapons—now made of iron (it was the Dorians who brought the new, more durable metal from the north, ending the Bronze Age in Greece).

During this Dark Age, there is little evidence of Greek civilization: the Linear B script used by the Mycenaean disappeared, and art, which had prospered during the Mycenaean Age, declined. Under Dorian rule, as many as fourth-fifths of the Mycenaean sites were abandoned, and many regions and islands seem to have been depopulated. There is no evidence of trade with other countries. Poverty had overtaken the Greeks.

As the Dorians took possession of the Greek mainland, a few Mycenaean communities survived in remote areas. Many Mycenaeans fled eastward to Athens, which became a haven for those who hoped for a return to the former civilization. Other Mycenaeans crossed the Aegean and settled on the coast of Asia Minor. Most of these refugees spoke Ionian Greek.

A lasting legacy of the Dark Ages of Greece is its mythology: As Ionian Greeks attempted to hold on to the refined civilization of the Bronze Age, they commemorated the greatness of the past in song and verse, including Homer's *Iliad* and *Odyssey*. These epics were combined with eighth-century poet Hesiod's *Theogony*, an account of the creation of the universe and the generations of the gods, to give rise to a new Greek religion based on the god Zeus and eleven other gods who resided on Mount Olympus in northeastern Greece. The Greek gods were later adopted by the Romans and given different names.

Who were the **twelve Greek gods** and who were their **Roman** counterparts?

The Greek civilization regarded their gods as a close-knit family who controlled the fate of mortal man. Zeus (Roman counterpart was Jupiter), was ruler of all the gods on Mount Olympus. He had two brothers: Hades (Pluto), who ruled the underworld; and Poseidon (Neptune), who ruled all the seas and lived underwater. Hestia (Vesta) was the only sister of these three powerful gods. Zeus's wife, Hera (Juno), bore him one child, Ares (Mars), but Zeus, who could not resist the beauty of several young maidens, went on to father many children such as Artemis (Diana), Aphrodite (Venus), Hermes (Mercury), and Apollo. One exception to Zeus's usual parental method was Athena (Minerva), who sprang

11

from Zeus's head fully grown and in full armor. Hera, jealous of Zeus's literal offspring of Athena, bore Hephaestus (Vulcan) on her own.

What was the **Golden Age** of **ancient Greece**?

It is the period of classical Greek civilization that followed the so-called Dark Ages of Greece, which came to an end about 800 B.C. Over time, the Dorians had become more settled and they gradually revived trade and culture on mainland Greece. The self-governing city-state (*polis*) evolved, including the military center of Sparta, and Athens, which became a center for the arts, education, and democracy. This was the beginning of the great Hellenic Age or Classical Greek civilization. Greek civilization reached its height in Athens during the mid–400s B.C., a period of outstanding achievement known as the Golden Age.

What are the **hallmarks** of **Classical Greek civilization**?

The classical Greeks, who called themselves the Hellenes and their land Hellas, influenced the Western world more than any other people. Their contributions to every field of endeavor remain with us today, more than two thousand years later.

Greek thought shaped science, medicine, philosophy, art, literature, architecture and engineering, mathematics, music, drama, language, and politics. The classical Greeks believed in individual freedom, reasoning, truth, and that everything should be done in moderation. They also held that man should find time for both work and play and should balance the life of the mind with the exercise of the body.

The knowledge that became the Greek legacy had its beginnings in the settlements established in Asia Minor after the Dorian invasion of the Greek mainland. The Phoenician alphabet was acquired by the Greeks who adapted it to their language. They began using it to record Homer's oral epics (*Iliad* and *Odyssey*) and the works of other Greek poets and historians.

Among the great Greek philosophers are Socrates, Plato, and Aristotle. Greek literature includes the epic poetry of Homer as well as the passionate love poems of Sappho. The Greeks gave us the tragedies of Aeschylus, Sophocles, and Euripides, which continue to be studied by students today, along with the comedies of Aristophanes and Menander. The classical Greeks loved to speak, and oratory is considered by some to be their highest form of prose. Orators known to the modern world are Antiphon, Lysias, Isocrates, and Demosthenes.

Herodotus, called the "father of history," left the modern world with an account of the Persian Wars and the events that led up to them. The Greeks also gave us the "father of medicine" in physician Hippocrates, who taught that doctors should use reason to determine the cause of illness and should study the patient's appearance, behavior, and lifestyle to diagnose and treat. (The "Hippocratic Oath," still sworn by medical students graduating today, is attributed to Hippocrates.) Greek scientists include Thales and Pythagoras; scientist-philosophers include Leucippus and Democritus. And of course, the Greeks gave us the Olympic Games.

ROMAN EMPIRE

Which came first, the **Roman Republic** or the **Roman Empire**?

The Roman Republic, which for centuries afterward was considered the model form of a balanced government, was established in 509 B.C. The Roman Empire was not established until 27 B.C. when Augustus (63 B.C.–A.D. 14) became its first ruler. In brief, the development of ancient Rome is as follows.

In 753 B.C., the city of Rome was established (legend has it, the city was founded by brothers Romulus and Remus). Since Rome was situated on wooded hills above the Tiber River, about fifteen miles from the sea, it enjoyed the advantages of access to trade routes while having natural protection from aggressors. The city was defensible. Agriculture prospered in the area, as did other economic endeavors including manufacturing and mining.

In 509 B.C., the Republic was established by noblemen. The government was headed by two elected officials who were called consuls. Since they shared power, a certain measure of balance was ensured in that either one could veto the actions of the other. And the posts were brief; each

13

What is the legacy of ancient Rome?

Since the Romans borrowed and adapted the ideas of the Greeks, with whom they had come into contact about 300 B.C. and later conquered (in 146 B.C.), the culture of ancient Rome is sometimes called Greco-Roman. Over the course of centuries, Romans spread their ideas throughout the vast empire.

They also developed a legal code, which outlined basic principles while remaining flexible enough that lawyers and judges could interpret the laws, taking into consideration local customs and practices. The code later became the model for legal systems in Europe and in Latin America. Further, Roman armies built a network of roads, aqueducts, and tunnels, putting in place an infrastructure that outlasted the empire itself. The language of the Romans, Latin, remained the language of educated Europeans for more than one thousand years. And the Latin-based (or Romance) languages of Italian, French, and Spanish took over in everyday communication. The economic system put in place during the height of the Roman Empire, with a centrally controlled money supply, also had lasting effect.

Though the empire had crumbled by A.D. 476, its cultural, social, and economic establishments continued to have validity well into the Middle Ages, when the Roman Catholic Church grew in numbers and in influence.

elected official served for only one year. These heads of state were guided by a Senate, which was made up of senior statesmen. There were also assemblies where the people had a voice.

About 300 B.C., the Romans came into contact with the Greeks, adopting not only some of their ideas, but their mythology as well.

By 275 B.C., Rome controlled most of the Italian peninsula. Their homeland stable, the Romans set their sites on overseas expansion, and between 264 and 146 B.C., fought the Punic Wars in order to gain territory.

In the last century B.C., Rome entered a period that is considered the height of their civilization. But about the middle of that century, the Republic was torn by civil wars. After twenty years of fighting, the Roman Empire was formed in 27 B.C. when Julius Caesar became the first emperor. While vestiges of the Republic were maintained, the emperor held supreme authority, nominating the consuls and appointing senators, controlling the provinces, and heading the army. The civilian assemblies were still in place, but had for the most part lost their voice in government.

The Roman Empire would last for nearly five hundred years. By the third century A.D., Roman armies had conquered so many peoples that the Empire stretched across Europe and included the entire Mediterranean coast of Africa as well as parts of the Middle East. During this time of power and expansion, trade thrived—over a vast network of roads and sea routes, which extended to China, India, and Africa. Coins, made of gold, silver, copper, and bronze, were issued and controlled by the Roman government. In A.D. 476, after suffering a series of attacks from nomadic Germanic tribes, Rome fell.

What was the *Pax Romana*?

The *Pax Romana* was the height of the Roman Empire, a period of peace that lasted from 27 B.C. to A.D. 180, roughly two centuries. During this time, no other country or force was strong enough to challenge the Roman Empire, so citizens turned their attention to commerce, learning, the arts, and literature, all of which flourished.

ANCIENT TRIBES
(VISIGOTHS, HUNS, VANDALS)

What happened to the **Celts** during the **Roman Empire**?

The Celts were an Indo-European people who by 500 B.C. had spread across what is now France, Italy, Portugal, Spain, and the British Isles (where their descendants still live today), and by 200 B.C. had expanded as far as present-day Bulgaria and Greece. When the Romans conquered much of Europe (about 300 B.C.), many Celts were absorbed into the Roman Empire. However, those Celts living in Ireland, Scotland, Wales, southwest England, and Brittany in northwest France were able to maintain their cultures, and it is in these regions that people of Celtic origin still live today.

What is known about the **Celt** peoples **prior** to the **Roman Empire**?

Before Europe was conquered by Rome, Celts, who were themselves divided into smaller tribes, had become rather advanced in many ways: Their society was divided among three classes (common people, the learned, and aristocrats); they formed loose federations of tribes; they raised crops and livestock; they used the Greek alphabet to write their own language; and they were among the first peoples in northern Europe to make iron. They also developed a form of metalwork that most people today recognize as Celtic, called *La Tène*. However, they had never formed one united nation, so that when Roman armies swept across Europe, the Celts were overrun.

Who were the **Huns**?

The Huns were a nomadic central Asian people who, in the middle of the fourth century A.D., moved westward. They first defeated the Alani (a group in the Caucasus Mountains region, between the Black and the Caspian seas), and then conquered and drove out the Goths. Unified by the ruler Attila in A.D. 434, they gained control of a large part of central and eastern Europe by about A.D. 450. The Italian countryside was ravaged in the process. As a result, many people settled on marshy islands—which later became the city of Venice.

With the death of Attila in A.D. 453, the subjects of the Huns revolted and defeated them. The Huns were later absorbed into the various peoples of Europe.

To which tribes does the term **"barbarian"** refer?

The term is used to refer to any of the Germanic tribes that, during the middle of the first millennium A.D. (beginning about 400), conquered the West Roman Empire and divided it into many kingdoms, replacing

What happened to the Visigoths?

When both the Visigoths and Ostrogoths were attacked by the Huns in A.D. 370, the Visigoths fared better, many of them fleeing into a Roman province. In A.D. 378, the Visigoths rebelled against the Roman authorities. On horseback, they fought the battle of Adrianople (in present-day Turkey), destroying a Roman army and killing Rome's eastern emperor, Valens (328?–78). The introduction of the cavalry as part of warfare determined European military, social, and political development for the next thousand years.

After the battle of Adrianople, the Visigoths moved into Italy, and under the leadership of their ruler, Alaric (c. 370–410), they sacked Rome in A.D. 410, an event that signaled the beginning of the decline of the Roman Empire. After the success of the Visigoths, one tribe after another invaded the empire.

The Visigoths continued westward into Gaul (present-day France), and there set up a monarchy that consisted of much of France and Spain and was centered in Toulouse. But they were driven out by the Franks in A.D. 507, and withdrew into the Iberian Peninsula. Toledo (Spain) was established as the capital of the Visigoth kingdom in A.D. 534. In A.D. 587, the Visigoths were converted from Arian to orthodox Christianity. Roderick (or Rodrigo), the last of the Visigoth kings in Spain, was defeated and killed in A.D. 711, during a battle with the Muslims, who invaded from northern Africa. The Muslims (Moors) went on to rule most of the Iberian Peninsula until the mid–1400s.

the strong central and local governments of the Romans. The Germanic tribes included the Goths, the Vandals, the Franks, and the Lombards.

Who were the **Goths**?

The Goths were a group of Germanic tribes who originated in what is now Scandinavia. As early as the third century A.D., the Goths invaded

What is the difference between the Roman Empire and the Holy Roman Empire?

Roughly four and a half centuries separated the two empires, both of which were comprised of vast regions of western and central Europe.

The Roman Empire was established in 27 B.C., when Julius Caesar became emperor, and lasted until A.D. 476, when Rome fell. The Holy Roman Empire began in the mid–900s A.D., when Otto I (912–73) of Germany gained control of most of northern and central Italy. Pope John XII crowned Otto emperor in 962, and in the 1200s, the area of power officially became known as the Holy Roman Empire, which ended July 12, 1806, in the Confederation of the Rhine, which brought most of the German states under French domination and precipitated a war with Prussia.

the eastern provinces of the Roman Empire. During the following century, they divided into two groups—a western group known as the Visigoths (who were north of the lower Danube River, in central Europe) and an eastern group known as the Ostrogoths (those who were north of the Black Sea, between Europe and Asia). Along with other tribal Germanic peoples, the Goths brought the downfall of the Roman Empire in the early part of the Christian era.

What happened to the **Ostrogoths**?

The eastern division of the Goths, the Ostrogoths were overrun and absorbed by the Huns in A.D. 370. When the powerful Hun leader, Attila, died in A.D. 453, subjects of the Huns revolted and the Ostrogoths regained their freedom. Theodoric became the ruler of the Ostrogoths in A.D. 493 and it was under his leadership that the group invaded northern Italy, where they remained. In the middle of the following century, they were overthrown by the armies of the Byzantine Empire. Like other Germanic tribes, the Ostrogoths were absorbed into the various groups of Europe.

Who were the **Vandals**?

Like the Goths, the Vandals were a Germanic people who originated in an area south of the Baltic Sea in what is now Scandinavia. By A.D. 100 they had moved into the southern region of (present-day) Poland. But there they eventually found themselves threatened by the Huns, so they began moving westward late in the fourth century. Early in the fifth century, the Vandals overran Gaul (France), Spain, and northern Africa, where they eventually settled. Between A.D. 428 and A.D. 477, the Vandals were ruled by the powerful king Genseric. In 455, they ravaged Rome. Their pillage was so thorough that the word "vandal" is used to describe anyone who willfully destroys property that is not theirs.

In A.D. 533 and A.D. 534, like the Ostrogoths, the Vandals were defeated by armies of the Byzantine Empire.

Who were the **Franks**?

The Franks were another Germanic people who divided into two branches—the Salians (who settled near the lower Rhine River, near the North Sea) and the Ripuarians (who moved into what is now Germany, along the middle Rhine River).

In A.D. 359, the Franks entered into the Roman Empire as allies, but in 481 Clovis (c. 466–511) gained the Salerian Frank kingship and by 486 he had begun a campaign of aggression, conquering Romans, Gauls, Visigoths, and other groups. Under this cruel and cunning king, the Franks soon controlled all of Europe—from the Mediterranean to the English Channel, and from the Pyrenees Mountains to the Rhine River. Even after Clovis's death, the Franks maintained their stronghold in the region, which is how France eventually got its name.

Though Clovis was a powerful ruler, much later he was succeeded as king of the Franks by the even more powerful Charlemagne, who ruled from A.D. 768 to A.D. 814, creating a vast empire. In 800, Pope Leo III crowned him emperor of the Romans. It was after Charlemagne that the empire of the Franks began to break up, becoming the kingdoms of France, Germany, and Italy.

How were the **Gauls** related to the **Celts**?

The ancient Gauls were a Celtic people who spoke forms of the Celtic language. They occupied Gaul—a region west of the Rhine River (an area that today consists of France, Belgium, Luxembourg, part of Germany, and part of the Netherlands). The Gauls were led by priests, who were called Druids. By 390 B.C., the Gauls had moved southward, across the Alps and into Italy. In the third century B.C., they battled the powerful Romans there and were defeated, becoming subjects of Rome. Later, under Julius Caesar, the Romans conquered all of Gaul, so that by 50 B.C., the region was part of the Roman Empire. Five centuries later, Gaul was overrun by the Franks, for whom the region was named. Thus, French people today are descendants of the Gauls. Also, the Galatians (one of the Christian peoples the apostle Paul wrote while he was in jail) were descendants of the Gauls who settled in Macedonia and Asia Minor.

Who were the **Lombards**?

The Lombards, too, were a Germanic tribe who are thought to have originated on an island in the Baltic Sea. In the last century B.C., the Lombards moved into Germany and gradually continued southward so that by A.D. 500, they were settled in present-day Austria. From 568 to the mid–700s, they controlled much of Italy, posing a serious threat to the papal supremacy so that in A.D. 754, Pope Stephen II appealed to the powerful Franks for help. By this time the Franks were ruled by Charlemagne's son, Pepin (714?–68), who was able to defeat the Lombards. Their influence is still felt today since the northern region of Lombardy is named for them.

MIDDLE AGES/MEDIEVAL PERIOD/ DARK AGES (BEGINS 500)

What was the **Holy Roman Empire**?

The Holy Roman Empire was a loose federation of German and Italian states, originally formed on Christmas of A.D. 800, when Charlemagne

(742–814) was crowned emperor of the Romans by Pope Leo III. But after Charlemagne's death, the empire lapsed and was not fully reinstated until Otto I was crowned emperor. Though the empire was strongly associated with the Roman Catholic Church, disputes between emperors and popes began in the mid–1100s. In 1250, Pope Innocent IV was successful in gaining independence from the empire for the Italian city-states.

Later in the history of the Holy Roman Empire, the House of Hapsburg rose to power, defining the era. The first member of the Hapsburg family to rule the empire was Albert II who became emperor in 1438. With the exception of a five-year period (1740–45), the family continued to hold power to 1806, when Emperor Francis II declared the end of the Holy Roman Empire.

What was **feudalism**?

Feudalism is often confused with manorialism. Both were systems that emerged during the Middle Ages. While feudalism was a military and political system, manorialism was an agricultural system.

After the fall of the Roman Empire, the vast area that had been centrally controlled by Rome was divided by Germanic tribes. Since tribes were loyal only to themselves, disorder ensued, with kingdoms warring against each other. This continued for some three hundred years, until the 700s when order began to be established through the feudal system, in which a lord granted his subjects (who were called "vassals") land, and in return, the vassals would provide the lord with services including military protection. The ties between lord and vassal were strengthened through the taking of oaths and the observance of ceremonies. Since the word feudal is derived from the Latin word *fief*, meaning estate or land, feudalism is sometimes referred to as a system of fiefdoms. Feudalism originated in France and by the 1100s had spread into England, Spain, and other parts of the Christian world. By the 1400s, it began to disappear.

Feudalism did not involve peasants directly in the system, which was based on the relationship between lord and vassal, both of whom were considered aristocrats. Manorialism, on the other hand, did involve the peasants, since it was through this system that the lord of the manor would organize agricultural labor on his land. This labor was provided by peasants, who would work the land in exchange for their own sustenance and protection.

A Viking in traditional dressings. Vikings were known to ransack churches and homes at night during the Dark Ages.

What are the **Dark Ages** and how did they get that name?

The Dark Ages usually refer to the historical period in Europe from about A.D. 500 to 1485, also known as the Middle Ages, or Medieval period (*medieval* is from the Latin *medium aevum*, meaning "middle age"). The Middle Ages followed the collapse of the Roman Empire (in A.D. 476, which signified the end of the Classical Age) and preceded the Renaissance.

This terminology is the legacy of seventeenth-century historians who considered the period a barbaric interruption of a tradition that began in ancient Greece and continued through the European Renaissance. Modern scholars have tried to correct this view, but the popular perception of the medieval period as "dark" still remains.

(The term Dark Ages is also used to refer to a Greek historical period, from about 1100 B.C. to about 700 B.C., which was considered to be a period of decline.)

What are the characteristics of **Medieval times**?

Although the Middle Ages were shadowed by poverty, ignorance, economic chaos, bad government, cruelty, and a contempt for human life, it was also a period of cultural and artistic achievement. For example, the university originated in medieval Europe, the first university having been established in 1158 in Bologna, Italy.

The period was also marked by the belief, based on the Christian faith, that the universe is an ordered world, ruled by an infinite and all-knowing God. This belief persisted even through the turmoil of wars and social upheavals, and it pervades medieval church architecture, the poetry of Dante Alighieri (1265–1321), the philosophy of St. Thomas Aquinas (1226–74), the Gregorian chant, and the music of composers such as Guillaume de Machaut (ca.1300–77).

Were the **Crusades** motivated by more than just religion?

The Crusades were a series of Christian military expeditions during the Middle Ages. While the goal of the religious battles was the recovery of the Holy Land (Palestine) from the Muslims, expansionism was also an objective, since Europe's population was on the rise, precipitating the need for new lands and new trade routes. Yet another objective was the protection of the Byzantine Empire, the Greek-Christian empire centered in southeastern Europe at the city of Constantinople. Byzantium had become an enormously wealthy and powerful region, controlling commerce in the Mediterranean, as well as presiding over East-West trade routes. But the Empire was under siege: the Turks, under the leadership of Seljuq, were rapidly expanding their territory, conquering much of Asia Minor. The Seljuq Turks were a fierce people who had been converted to Islam, and they began to inspire fear among Europeans, who now found it difficult to reach the Holy Land because of Turkish expansionism.

In 1095, the Byzantines appealed to Pope Urban II for help against the Turks. When Urban announced the Crusade in 1095, in Clermont-Ferrand, France, the response was enthusiastic. Although the First Crusade (1096–99) was very successful, ending with the conquest of the Holy Land, subsequent efforts saw mixed results. In 1204, the Fourth Crusade sacked the city of Constantinople, bringing the Byzantine Empire under the control of Western Europe. A children's Crusade, led by a young visionary in 1212, was sabotaged, according to some sources; before the expedition had reached the enemy, the children were sold into slavery.

The Crusades ended, rather ingloriously, in 1291, when the city of Acre (Israel), which was the last Christian stronghold, fell to the Muslims. Nevertheless, Europe emerged from the period of expeditions economically strengthened. It had gained new markets, and its political power remained undiminished.

THE RENAISSANCE (BEGINS 1350)

Why is the **Renaissance** considered a time of rebirth?

The term Renaissance is from the French word for "rebirth," and the period from A.D. 1350 to 1600 in Europe was marked by the resurrection of classical Greek and Roman ideals; the flourishing of art, literature, and philosophy; and the beginning of modern science.

Italians in particular believed themselves to be the true heirs to Roman achievement. For this reason, it was natural that the Renaissance began in Italy, where the ruins of ancient civilization provided a constant reminder of their classical past and where subsequent artistic movements—Gothic, for instance—had never taken firm hold.

How can the **attitude** of the **Renaissance** be characterized?

The artists and thinkers of the Renaissance, like the ancient Greeks and Romans, valued earthly life, glorified man's nature, and celebrated indi-

How did the Renaissance get started?

Social and political developments in the late Middle Ages (A.D. 476–1000) gave rise to the spirit of the Renaissance.

The Crusades (military expeditions undertaken by Christian powers in the eleventh, twelfth, and thirteenth centuries to win the Holy Land from the Muslims) brought Europeans into contact with other cultures and most importantly with Byzantine civilization. The remnant of the eastern Roman Empire, Byzantium had preserved much knowledge from ancient times. In addition, many texts thought to have been destroyed during the ransacking of the western empire remained preserved in various translations throughout the Middle East. So it was during the Crusades that some of these were brought back to Europe, where classical scholars undertook the task of deciphering the West's cultural past.

In northern Italy, a series of city-states developed independent of the larger empires to the north and south of them. These small states—Florence, Rome, Venice, and Milan, among others—gained prosperity through trade and banking, and as a result, a wealthy class of businessmen emerged. These community leaders admired and encouraged creativity, patronizing artists who might glorify their commercial achievement with great buildings, paintings, and sculptures. The most influential patrons of the arts were the Medici, a wealthy banking family in Florence. Members of the Medici supported many important artists of the Renaissance, and as a result Florence became the most magnificent city of the period.

One way patrons encouraged art was to sponsor competitions in order to spur artists to more significant achievement. In many cases, the losers of these contests went on to greater fame than the winners. After his defeat to Lorenzo Ghiberti in the competition to create the bronze doors of the Baptistery in Florence, Filippo Brunelleschi made several trips to take measurements of the ruined buildings of ancient Rome. When he returned, he created the immense *duomo* (dome) of the Cathedral of Florence, a classically influenced structure that became the first great monument of the Renaissance.

vidual achievement. These new attitudes combined to form a new spirit of optimism—the belief that man was capable of accomplishing great things.

This new outlook was the result of the activities of the wealthy mercantile class in northern Italy, who, aside from supporting the arts and letters, also began collecting the classical texts that had been forgotten during the Middle Ages. Ancient manuscripts were taken to libraries where scholars from around Europe could study them. The rediscovery of classical texts prompted a new way of looking at the world. During the Middle Ages, scholars argued that the meaning of life on earth lay primarily in its relation to an afterlife. Therefore, they believed that art for its own sake had no value, and they even frowned on the recognition of individual talent. (For this reason, many of the great works of the Middle Ages were created anonymously or were hidden from view.)

In contrast, Renaissance artists and thinkers studied classical works for the purpose of imitating them. As an expression of their new optimism, Renaissance scholars embraced the study of classical subjects that addressed human, rather than scientific, concerns. These "humanities," as they came to be called, included language and literature, art, history, rhetoric, and philosophy. Above all, humanists (those who espoused the values of this type of education) believed in man's potential to become well versed in many areas. Thus, the "Renaissance man" refers to an individual whose talents span a variety of disciplines.

By taking a critical view toward a broad number of subjects, artists including Michelangelo, Brunelleschi, and da Vinci, came upon ideas that changed the way all others viewed the world. One such discovery was perspective—the visual means of representing three-dimensional objects on a flat canvas.

From the Renaissance on, people in all disciplines began using critical skills as a means of understanding everything from nature to politics.

Which **artists**, **writers**, and **thinkers** are considered the greatest minds of the **Renaissance**?

The great writers of the Renaissance include the Italian poet Petrarch (1304–74), who became the first great writer of the Renaissance and was one of the first proponents of the concept that a "rebirth" was in progress; Florentine historian Niccolo Machiavelli (1469–1527), who wrote what might be the most important work of the period, *The Prince* (1513); English dramatist William Shakespeare (1564–1616), whose works many view as the culmination of the Renaissance writing; Spain's Miguel de Cervantes (1547–1616), who penned *Don Quixote* (1605), a tale that gently pokes fun at medieval codes of conduct; and Frenchman Francois Rabelais, (c. 1483–1553) who is best known for writing the five-volume work *Gargantua and Pantagruel*.

The great artists of the Renaissance include the Italian painters/sculptors Sandro Botticelli (1445–1510), among whose works include *The Birth of Venus*; Leonardo da Vinci (1452–1519), whose *Mona Lisa* and *The Last Supper* are among the most widely studied works of art; Michelangelo Buonarroti (1475–1564), whose sculpture of *David* became the symbol of the new Florence; and Raphael Sanzio (1483–1520), whose *The School of Athens* is considered by art historians to be the complete statement of the High Renaissance.

How did the **Renaissance** spread from **Italy** to the **rest of Europe**?

Eventually the ideas born in Italy during the 1300s spread northward, which is at least in part attributable to German Johannes Gutenberg's printing press (c. 1440–50). Before long, the spirit and ideas that were taking hold in Italy reached France, Germany, England, and the Netherlands, where the Renaissance continued into the 1600s.

One of the most important figures of the northern Renaissance was the Dutch humanist Desiderius Erasmus (1466?–1536), who produced his own translation of the New Testament, and his book *In Praise of Folly* (1509) is a scalding criticism of the clergy, scholars, and philosophers of his day.

Another notable figure of the northern Renaissance was Englishman Sir Thomas More, who was a statesman and advisor to the king. More's *Utopia*, published in 1516, criticizes the times by envisioning an ideal society in which police would be unnecessary, politicians would be honest, and money would cease to exist.

The works of Flemish artist Jan van Eyck (1395–1441), including his groundbreaking portrait *Man in a Red Turban*, demonstrate that the principles of the Renaissance were felt as strongly in northern Europe as they were in Italy.

When did **European colonialism** begin?

Seeking out colonies for economic benefit dates back to ancient times: even the Romans ruled colonies in Europe, the Middle East, and Africa. But colonialism took hold between 1400 and 1600 A.D. when powerful European countries sent explorers to find new lands and forge new trade routes.

Portugal and Spain sought sea routes to India and the Far East. In the process, the Portuguese gained control of what is now Brazil; they also established trading posts in West Africa, India, and southeast Asia. Spain gained control of most of Latin America and areas of what is now the United States. However, the Dutch, English, and French also had influence in these areas. And of course, the English eventually established the Thirteen Colonies in North America. The Netherlands gained control of the Indonesian islands, which became the Dutch East Indies. The English became a strong influence in India and Africa. They also moved into parts of Canada, as did the French.

The results of colonialism were many: While trade was expanded, the colonies were also rife with conflict: indigenous peoples were killed or forcefully displaced from their lands, and foreign powers fought with each other for control of the same areas (the British and French fought four wars in North America between 1689 and 1763 alone). Further, Europeans brought to these new lands their own languages, religions, and systems of government, imposing their culture, beliefs, and ideologies on native peoples.

What was the **Enlightenment**?

The Enlightenment, which is also referred to as the Age of Reason (or alternately as the Age of Rationalism), was a period when European philosophers emphasized the use of reason as the best method for learning the truth. Beginning in the 1600s and through the 1700s, philosophers such as Jean-Jacques Rousseau, Voltaire, and John Locke explored issues in education, law, and politics. They published their thoughts,

Are the Enlightenment and the Scientific Revolution the same?

The two terms describe interrelated and sequential European intellectual movements that took place from the 1500s to the 1800s. Together, the movements shaped an era that would lay the foundations of modern Western Civilization, foundations that required the use of reason, or rational thought, to understand the universe, nature, and human relations. During this period, many of the greatest minds in Europe developed new scientific, mathematical, philosophical, and social theories.

Scientists came to believe that observation and experimentation would allow them to discover the laws of nature. Thus, the scientific method emerged, which required tools. Soon the microscope, thermometer, sextant, slide rule, and other instruments were invented. Scientists working during this time included Sir Isaac Newton, Joseph Priestley, and Rene Descartes. The era witnessed key discoveries and saw rapid advances in astronomy, anatomy, mathematics, and physics. The advances had an impact on education: universities introduced science courses to the curricula, and elementary and secondary schools followed suit. As people became trained in science, new technologies emerged—complicated farm machinery was developed, as was new equipment for textile manufacturing and transportation, paving the way for the Industrial Revolution.

issuing attacks on social injustice, religious superstition, and ignorance. Their ideas fanned the fires of the American and French revolutions in the late 1700s.

Hallmarks of the Age of Reason include the idea of the universal truth (e.g., two plus two always equals four); the belief that nature is vast and complex but well ordered; the belief that humankind possesses the ability to understand the universe; the philosophy of Deism, which holds that God created the world and then left it alone; and the concept of the rational will, which posits that humans make their own choices and plans, and therefore, do not have a fate thrust upon them.

While the Age of Reason proved to be a flurry of intellectual activity that resulted in the publication of several encyclopedias of knowledge, toward the end of the eighteenth century, a shift occurred in which Europeans began to value passion over reason, giving rise to the romantic movement and ending the Age of Reason. (This change in outlook is evident in English novelist Jane Austen's *Sense and Sensibility*.)

Nevertheless, the philosophies put forth during the Age of Reason were critical to the development of Western thought. The celebration of individual reason during this era was perhaps best expressed by Rene Descartes, who refused to believe anything unless it could be proved. His statement, "I think, therefore I am," sums up the feelings of skeptical and rational inquiry that characterized intellectual thought during the era.

What were the **effects** of the **Industrial Revolution**?

The Industrial Revolution began in Great Britain during the 1700s, and by the early 1800s, it had spread to Western Europe and the United States. It had been brought about through the introduction of power-driven machinery to the manufacturing process. Soon, goods that had been made by simple machines or by hand were manufactured in quantity by technologically advanced machinery. Gone were the days of home-based or workshop-based production. Factories were built to house the new machines, causing a population shift from rural to developing urban areas by the mid-1800s, as people went where the work was. As industry grew, it required financial institutions that could provide money for expansion, thus giving birth to a new breed of wealthy business leaders called capitalists. Savvy businessmen, backed by capitalists, built great industrial empires.

Government and policy changes evolved more slowly than did industry itself, resulting in serious problems such as poor and sometimes dangerous working conditions, exploitation of workers (including child laborers), overcrowded housing, and pollution. Reforms were slow to come, but social activism, much of which centered around trade unions, alleviated these problems over time. The rapid development of industry caused sweeping social changes: the Western world, which had long

A young boy at work in the textile mills in the height of the Industrial Revolution.

been an agricultural society, became an industrial society, where goods and services are the primary focus.

THE ERAS OF THE WORLD WARS

What was the **modern world** like prior to the **World Wars**?

After the Industrial Revolution and prior to the Great War, which began in 1914, and would not come to be known as World War I until a second world war broke out, society experienced sweeping changes.

Western culture of the late 1800s to 1945 was dominated by revolutionary changes in scientific thought, primarily in chemistry, genetics, and physics. The idea—which had developed during the Scientific Revolution—that the laws of nature were wholly discoverable and predictable was dismissed. New scientific thought viewed the forces of nature as random, unpredictable, and changeable. Science became involved with

31

examining minute physical forms and properties, and with the unseen world of subatomic particles. The period saw the accomplishments of chemists Marie and Pierre Curie, physicists Max Planck and Albert Einstein, naturalist Charles Darwin, and the founder of psychoanalysis, Sigmund Freud.

The change and unpredictability of new scientific discoveries was reflected in new art forms. Painting became highly representational, geometric, and abstract. Music became atonal, discordant, and highly experimental. Literature emphasized psychological motives and relationships, anxiety, and pessimism. Together these characteristics form what is considered "modern." Painting and sculpture were marked by the works of the Impressionists and Post-Impressionists as well as surrealists Pablo Picasso, Marc Chagall, and Salvador Dalí, and muralist Diego Rivera. Led by Arnold Schoenberg, modern music began to abandon traditional harmony and tonality in favor of abstract mathematical patterns. Claude Debussy and Igor Stravinsky strove to create music that would leave a more naturalistic impression on listeners. Charles Dickens, Thomas Hardy, Gustav Flaubert, and Anton Chekhov penned complex novels that were realistic depictions of life. Playwrights Henrik Ibsen and George Bernard Shaw wrote dramas criticizing society.

The period also saw rapid population growth and the movement of peoples. A rising standard of living and scientific discoveries like the germ theory (Louis Pasteur) and the antiseptic principle (Joseph Lister) caused mortality rates to improve. The population of Europe exploded as a result. Between 1800 and 1900 alone the population had risen from 188 million to 434 million. Exploding population, the Potato Famine in Ireland (1846, 1848, and 1851), and Jewish pogroms (organized persecutions or massacres) led to one of the great migrations in history. By the turn of the nineteenth century, sixty million people had left Europe for places like the United States, Canada, Argentina, Australia, and South America.

In the business sector, capitalism had taken off—promoting private ownership, focus on profit, and the free market economy. Businessmen adopted a laissez-faire philosophy, opposing government interference in the sphere of economics. Industrialization meant urbanization. Factories employed large numbers of people who moved to commercial centers, which at first were unable to handle the sudden influx. There was no public transportation, and parks were nonexistent. The hasty erection of small, densely packed houses led to slum conditions where disease spread rapidly due to a lack of sewage systems and plumbing. City governments planned and built water systems, roads, parks, transportation systems, and public hospitals. Paris was completely transformed by Georges Haussmann in the last half of the nineteenth century with broad boulevards, parks, and streetcars.

Two new classes had emerged—a strengthened middle class and a much larger group of factory workers. The middle class was distinguished by occupations that required mental rather than physical skill. Consequently, education became a prime avenue for social and economic improvement. The upper middle class, who were leaders of industry and banking, imitated the aristocracy by buying country homes and attempting to arrange favorable marriages with the upper classes. The true middle class, composed of successful industrialists and professionals, were clothes-conscious, rented rather than owned their homes, and spent lavishly on dinner parties. The lower middle class was composed of foremen or floor supervisors, most of whom had moved up from the worker position. Rather than dinner parties, they spent money on organized sports events and periodicals.

Women were becoming increasingly aware of the social and political forces that were shaping their lives. They had begun to sense that the limits of hearth and home that had formerly determined women's "sphere" no longer applied. By the late nineteenth century, this heightened awareness had given way to the suffragist movement, led in England by Emmeline Pankhurst. The sometimes radical tactics of British suffragists, which included marches and rallies, chaining themselves to railings, throwing themselves in front of carriages, and self-starvation, finally won them the right to vote in England in 1929.

As for government, after Napoleon's abdication in 1814, the rulers of Europe met at the Congress of Vienna and attempted to work out a peace settlement that would return Europe to stability. Conservatism, or the idea of preserving the traditional ways of doing things, permeated their thinking. This was a reaction to the ideas of the Enlightenment and the sweeping changes and instability that had been brought on by French Revolution. To implement the conservative agenda, former ruling families were put back in power. Instead of establishing a new German nation-state, the German Confederation, an alliance of thirty-nine independent states and dominated by Austria, was organized. In order to maintain a balance of power in Europe, France was restored and its borders were returned to pre-revolutionary status.

Socialism also emerged during the nineteenth century, with adherents arguing that government should rationally organize the economy and not depend on competition, that wealth should be more equally distributed between rich and poor, that private property should be abolished in favor of state ownership, and that the poor should be protected.

After the Franco-Prussian War of 1871, the nations of Europe set about creating a series of diplomatic alliances that effectively divided Europe into two large, opposing camps. Smaller nations were ruled by large powers or empires. As powers competed, they fortified their armies and accelerated an arms race at a pace more rapid than ever before in history—a race that would continue throughout the twentieth century.

WORLD WAR I AND II

How could the world fight two **World Wars** in such close sequence?

World War I was referred to as the "Great War," and understandably so given the enormous effect it had worldwide. The price of World War I was paid in human casualties; it is estimated that more than ten million soldiers died and twenty million were wounded. Civilian casualties were equally devastating, resulting from hunger and influenza epidemics that spread through even neutral countries. It is not surprising that the spirit of the generation immediately following the war was described as "lost." During the 1920s, with the death toll of the World War I a recent memory, the civilized world enjoyed a period of relative peace. Agreements reached during the 1921 Washington Naval Conference and the 1928 Kellogg-Briand Pact reflected a shared desire to make such widespread military aggression a thing of the past.

But beginning in 1929 and lasting for the next several years, a general economic downturn occurred in the world economy, triggered by the United States stock market crash of October 1929. As the vast American economy fell into a dramatic and sustained depression, other industrialized countries—especially Germany—quickly felt the impact. Unemployment jumped to record levels in many nations, and the lack of social welfare programs resulted in many families becoming destitute. Frantic politicians and economists searched for solutions to the spiraling crisis, many turning to isolationist or anti–free trade policies.

The global economic downturn of the 1930s bred significant political and social changes in many nations, but those that took place in Europe and the Far East were particularly important. These political and economic aftershocks positioned the world on a path that eventually led to World War II.

POSTWAR/COLD WAR ERAS
(BEGINS 1945)

When did the **Cold War** begin?

In the years following the conclusion of World War II, the nations of Western Europe and the United States became alarmed by Soviet advances into Eastern Europe, and many Europeans and Americans voiced concerns that Communists, spearheaded by the Soviet Union, were plotting to take over the world. Political leaders in England, the United States, and elsewhere referred to this new menace in grim terms. In March 1946 former British prime minister Winston Churchill warned about the "Iron Curtain" of Soviet totalitarianism that had divided the European continent, and in 1947 U.S. president Harry Truman announced a policy of containment of Communist incursions into other countries. This policy came to be known as the Truman Doctrine, and it remained an integral part of American foreign policy for the next 40 years.

The eroding relationship between the Western powers and the Soviet-led Communist empire was also due in large part to disagreements over Germany. Due to marked differences of opinion, a plan for joint government of Germany by the Allies—the Soviet Union, the United States, Britain, and France—had proved unworkable. By 1948 Germany was in

35

serious economic straits, and the United States, Britain, and France began to discuss uniting their zones. The Soviets responded by ordering a blockade of land and water traffic into the German city of Berlin, control of which had been divided between the Allies after the war (the Soviets controlled East Berlin, while the other Allies controlled West Berlin). Unfazed, Great Britain and the United States ordered an airlift operation to provide supplies and food to the people of West Berlin, and this proved spectacularly successful for the eleven-month duration of the blockade. In 1949 Germany was formally divided into two countries. West Germany, formed by the territories of the West, was allowed to form a democratic government, and it became officially known as the Federal Republic of Germany. The same year, East Germany (also known as the German Democratic Republic) was folded into the Soviet empire.

By 1949, the year that the Soviet Union exploded its first nuclear bomb, the world had been roughly divided into two camps: the American camp, which included the nations of Western Europe and other anti-Communist governments, and the Soviet Union and its satellite countries. These camps were soon girded by formal political alliances. In 1949 a military alliance known as the North Atlantic Treaty Organization (NATO) was formed by twelve nations (United States, Great Britain, France, Italy, Norway, Portugal, Iceland, Denmark, Canada, Belgium, Luxembourg, and the Netherlands). By 1955 NATO had seen three more countries— Greece, Turkey, and West Germany—join its alliance. The Soviet Union responded by creating the Council for Mutual Economic Assistance (COMECON) in 1949 and the Warsaw Pact in 1955. COMECON was an effort to coordinate economic and industrial activities among Communist nations, while the Warsaw Pact was a military agreement between the Soviets and the Communist governments of Eastern Europe.

As the Cold War deepened during the course of the 1950s, distrust on both sides was exacerbated by the shadow of possible nuclear destruction and fears about the shape of the planet's political and economic future. As both the United States and the Soviet Union funneled large amounts of their resources into the development of weapons systems, the situation evolved into an arms race. Deterrence would determine the victor; the race would be won by the nation able to create weapons so powerful that the other nation would be deterred from attacking. Competition for economic and territorial supremacy spilled over into feverish contests in other areas such as athletics, the arts, and the sciences.

In 1957, for instance, the Soviets beat the West into space with the Sputnik launch. Both this event and the Russians' successful manned space launch in 1961 caused great consternation among American and Western European populations. Other events, such as the shooting down of an American U-2 spy plane (1960), the Cuban Bay of Pigs disaster (1961), the building of the Berlin Wall (1961), and the Cuban Missile Crisis (1962), further heightened tensions between the two sides. In fact, the presence of Soviet missiles in Cuba and the resulting standoff between U.S.president John F. Kennedy and Soviet leader Nikita Khrushchev before the missiles were removed found the two superpowers precariously close to war.

POST–COMMUNISM ERA

What led to the **decline** of **communism in Eastern Europe**?

Anti-communist sentiment among Eastern Europeans was bolstered by the actions and policies of Soviet leader Mikhail Gorbachev (1931–). When Gorbachev took office in 1985, the Soviet economy was in decline. In order to reverse the trend, he advocated major reforms to the economy, moving it away from the government-controlled (communist) system toward a decentralized system, similar to those of Western (noncommunist) countries. The power, Gorbachev maintained, should rest with elected officials. But Gorbachev's efforts at modernization of the Soviet Union did not end with the economy; he further proposed a reduction in the power of the Communist Party, which had controlled the country since 1917. Gorbachev's programs for reform were termed *perestroika* (which means "restructuring"). Meantime, Gorbachev opened up relations to the West, which included visits with President Ronald Reagan, who naturally supported the Soviet leader's programs. Gorbachev referred to his policy of openness as *glasnost*. Both terms quickly caught on around the world. And while the reforms to the economy produced a slow and painful change for the Soviet people, and Gorbachev had many detractors (including government officials), he also had many supporters—both inside and outside the Soviet Union.

37

People in other Eastern European countries watched with interest as the Soviet people moved toward a more democratic system. Strikes in Poland had begun as early as 1980, where workers formed a free labor-union called Solidarity. But the following year, the Communist leaders of the Soviet Union pressured the Polish government to put an end to the movement—which it did. After Gorbachev became head of the Soviet Union and initiated sweeping changes, the reform movements in other countries soon realized that the Soviets under Gorbachev would no longer take hard-handed tactics toward anti-Communist efforts in other countries. In 1989, the Polish government ceased to prohibit Solidarity, and the Communist Party lost their influence in Poland. The same was true in Hungary, East Germany, and Czechoslovakia. By the end of the decade, most of the Eastern European Communist governments were overthrown in favor of democratic-oriented governments. The transition was effected differently in each country: the "overthrow" in Czechoslovakia was so peaceful that it was called the Velvet Revolution; while in Romania, a bloody revolt ensued, and hardline-Communist dictator Nicolae Ceausescu was executed.

In 1990, multi-party elections were held in Romania, Czechoslovakia, Hungary, East Germany, and Bulgaria. The non-Communist party that was put in power in East Germany agreed to unification with West Germany, creating one Germany on October 3, 1990. That same year Gorbachev received the Nobel Peace Prize for his contributions to world peace.

How did the **Soviet Union** fall apart?

Soviet leader Mikhail Gorbachev's liberal reforms met with strong opposition from conservative Communist officials. They were angered by the hardships produced by the transition to a free market economy and were dissatisfied with the Soviet Union's loss of influence over neighboring countries where Communism had fallen in 1990. On August 19, 1991, Communists attempted to overthrow Gorbachev as president of the Soviet Union. Though the effort failed in the face of widespread public opposition, it nevertheless weakened Gorbachev's leadership. Soon the fifteen Soviet republics declared independence but indicated their willingness to become part of a loose confederation of former Soviet republics. Though Gorbachev tried to prevent the complete dissolution of the Soviet Union, on December 8, 1991, the republics of Russia, Ukraine, and Belorussia (Belarus) broke away completely from the Soviet Union and formed the Commonwealth of Independent States. All the remaining republics—except Georgia—followed suit. On December 25, Gorbachev resigned as president, and the Soviet Union ceased to exist.

In 1992, with continuing reforms in Eastern Europe and the end of the Soviet Union, the only Communist-dominated countries that remained were (with the exception of Cuba) Asian nations—China, Laos, North Korea, and Vietnam.

NOTABLE EXPLORERS

Were the **Vikings** really the **first Europeans** to reach **North America**?

It is believed that the sea-faring Norsemen, who are alternately called the Vikings, were in fact the first Europeans to see the Western Hemisphere. Norwegian-born Leif Ericsson (c. 970–c. 1020) is generally credited with having been the first European to set foot on North American soil. Ericsson was the son of Erik the Red, who founded the Norse settlement in Greenland. Ericsson moved with his family to Greenland in A.D. 985 or A.D. 986. About that same time, it is believed that another Norseman, Bjarni Herjolfsson, who was driven off course on his way from Iceland to Greenland, was the first European to *sight* North America; however, he did not go ashore. It is believed that Ericsson decided he would follow up on this discovery, and about 1001, he set out from Greenland with a crew of thirty-five men and is believed to have landed on the southern end of Baffin Island. The expedition then continued on, likely made it to Labrador, and later landed on the coast of what is today either Newfoundland or Nova Scotia, Canada. Ericsson made his way back to Greenland with descriptions of a place he called Vinland (Wineland), since he had observed grapes and wild wheat growing there. This sequence of events is relayed in the *Greenlanders' Saga*, written in about A.D. 1200.

The first authenticated European landing was in A.D. 1500 when Portuguese navigator Gaspar de Corte-Real made landfall and explored the coast of Labrador and Newfoundland. A year later, he made a second trip to North America but never returned. The following year, his brother, Miguel, went out on an expedition in search of his lost brother, who was not found.

How old was **Marco Polo** when he traveled to the Far East?

Marco Polo (1254–1324) was only in his teens when he left Venice (about 1270) with his father, Niccolò, and his uncle Maffeo, traveling an overland route to the east. The Polo brothers had made such a trip once before—in 1260 they had traveled as far as Beijing (China), but upon their return home, they learned that Niccolò's wife (Marco Polo's mother) had died. So when the pair of adventurers set out again, they took a young Marco Polo with them.

The Polos traveled from Acre, Israel, to Sivas, Turkey, then through Mosul and Baghdad in Iraq, to Ormuz, a bustling trade center on the Persian Gulf, where they intended to take a ship for the east. Seeing the ships, the travelers determined they weren't reliable transport, so they opted to continue on land, heading north to Khorasan (in Iran), through Afghanistan, and to the Pamirs—a high plateau range in central Asia. It took the Polos forty days to transverse the high-altitude range, finally reaching the garden city of Kashgar (China). From there, the Polos followed a path skirting the Taklamakan Desert and then rested before crossing the Gobi Desert, which they did in thirty days' time, covering some three hundred miles. Stopping in Tun-hwang, the center of Buddhism in China, they then followed a southeast path that would have paralleled the Great Wall. After following the Yellow River, the Polos were met by emissaries of Kublai Khan (1215–94). They continued with their guides on a forty-day trip to Xanadu (Shang-tu), three hundred miles north of Beijing, where they were received by the Great Khan, founder and ruler of the Mongol dynasty and who was grandson of Genghis Khan (c. 1167–1227). It was May of 1275.

Having met the elder Polos on their previous trip, the travelers were again welcomed. Kublai Khan, who was an ardent Buddhist and a patron of the arts, took a liking to the young Marco Polo, who entered into diplomatic service for the ruler. In that capacity Marco Polo traveled to India, and he visited the Kingdom of Champa (what is now Vietnam), Thailand, Malaya, Sumatra, Sri Lanka, and India. The Polos, European

Explorer Marco Polo.

courtiers who were well liked by the Great Khan, stayed in China until 1292, finally returning home by way of Sumatra, India, and Persia, and arriving back in Venice in 1295. By this time, Marco Polo was a man in his forties, having spent most of his life to that point in the East.

How much of the **adventures** of **Marco Polo** are really true?

Most of the tales are accepted as true and accurate by modern scholars. Only those accounts that deal with places where it is not known that Marco Polo traveled (such as Africa) are seen as legend rather than fact.

43

Upon his return to Venice in 1295, Marco Polo took up the family occupation and worked as a merchant. Three years later, he was on board a ship that was captured by a rival Genoese ship. Thus, he was imprisoned in the port city of Genoa, where he met a writer named Rustichello, who was from the Italian city of Pisa. Polo recounted his stories to Rustichello, who wrote them down in the *Book of Ser Marco Polo*. The book was an immediate success. Readers today know the stories as *The Travels of Marco Polo*.

Why did **Spain** authorize **Columbus's expedition** in search of a westward route to the Indies?

When Christopher Columbus (1451–1506), who was Italian, became convinced that the earth was round (he had been studying the writings of Ptolemy) and that he could, therefore, reach the East by traveling due west across the ocean, he first took the idea to the king of Portugal to seek his financial aid in about 1483. The move was a natural one: he had settled in Portugal at the age of twenty-five, had married a Portuguese woman (who bore him one son before she died), and Portugal was the leading seafaring nation of Europe at that time, carrying out southbound voyages with the intent of rounding Africa and reaching the Indies to the east. But Columbus was rebuffed by the Portuguese monarch. In 1484, when he took his plan to the Spanish monarchs, Ferdinand and Isabella, they too refused to back him. But Columbus persisted and in 1492, the king and queen agreed to sponsor the plan. There were two reasons for the decision: the overland trade route to the Indies had long been cut off by the Turks, and the Western Europeans found themselves in need of finding a new route to the lucrative East. Further, Isabella and Ferdinand were devout Christians, as was Columbus, and they all shared a desire to advance the Christian religion. In short, the monarchs saw that there were both material and religious advantages for backing Columbus's expedition.

Where did **Columbus** actually land in the **New World**?

Columbus set sail from Palos, in southwest Spain, on August 3, 1492, and he sighted land on October 12. Going ashore, he named it San Salvador;

Christopher Columbus.

alternately called Watlings Island, today it is one of the Bahamas. With his fleet of three vessels, the *Nina*, the *Pinta*, and the *Santa Maria*, Columbus then continued west and south, sailing along the north coast of Cuba and Haiti (which he named Hispaniola). When the *Santa Maria* ran aground, Columbus left a colony of about forty men on the Haitian coast where they built a fort, which, being Christmastime, they named La Navidad. In January of 1493, he set sail for home, arriving back in Palos on March 15 with a few "Indians" (native Americans) as well as some belts, aprons, bracelets, and gold on board. News of his successful voyage spread rapidly, and Columbus journeyed to Barcelona where he was triumphantly received by Ferdinand and Isabella who bestowed him with honors.

On his second voyage, which he undertook on September 25 of that same year, he sailed with a fleet of seventeen ships and some fifteen hundred men. In November he reached Dominica, Guadeloupe, Puerto Rico, and the Virgin Islands. Upon returning to Haiti (Hispaniola), Columbus found the colony at La Navidad had been destroyed by natives. In December 1493, he made a new settlement at Isabella (present-day Dominican Republic), which became the first European town in the New World. Before returning to Spain in 1496, Columbus also discovered Jamaica.

On his third voyage, which he began in May 1498, Columbus reached Trinidad—just off the coast of South America. On his fourth and last trip he found the island of Martinique, before arriving on the North American mainland at Honduras. It was also on this voyage, in May 1502, that he sailed down to the Isthmus of Panama—finally believing himself to be near China. But Columbus suffered many difficulties, and in November 1504 he returned to Spain for good. He died two years later in poverty and neglect. He had, of course, never found the westward sea passage to the Indies. Nevertheless, the Caribbean islands he discovered came to be known collectively as the West Indies. And the native peoples of North and South America came to be known collectively as "Indians."

Why does **controversy** surround **Christopher Columbus**?

It's due in part to the fact that history wrongly billed Columbus as the discoverer of the New World. The native peoples living in the Americas before the arrival of Christopher Columbus were the true discoverers of these lands. These peoples had migrated thousands of years before: As

How did America get its name?

America is derived from the name of Italian explorer Amerigo Vespucci (1454–1512), who took part in several early voyages to the New World. Vespucci had been a merchant in service of the Medici family in Florence and later moved to Spain, where he worked for the company that outfitted the ships for Columbus's second and third voyages. He then sailed with the Spaniards on several expeditions (in 1497, 1499, 1501, and 1503). Though scholars today question his role as an explorer, in a work by German geographer Martin Waldseemüller published in 1507, the author credited Vespucci with realizing that he had actually arrived in a New World—not in Asia as other explorers (including Columbus) had believed. Thus, Waldseemüller suggested the new lands be named for the Italian-born explorer. For his part, Waldseemüller had been led to believe this by Vespucci himself who had written to Lorenzo de Medici in 1502 or 1503, relaying his discovery of a new continent and vividly describing it. About a year later, the letter was published under the title *Mundus Novus* (New World), which was translated and published in subsequent editions.

The designation was used again in 1538 by Flemish cartographer Gerardus Mercator. Today, the term in the singular refers to either continent in the Western Hemisphere, and sometimes specifically to the United States. In the plural, it refers to all of the lands of the Western Hemisphere, including North and South America and the West Indies.

early as 50,000 B.C., they came across the Bering Strait from Asia and migrated southward, throughout North and South America, reaching Tierra del Fuego by 8000 B.C. Therefore, it is correct to say that Columbus was the first European to discover the New World, and there he encountered its native peoples.

But it was for his treatment of these native peoples that Columbus is a controversial figure today—and he also had become a controversial figure during his own lifetime. Columbus was called back from the New World twice (on his second and third voyages) to be investigated for his dealings with the Indians. The first inquiry (1496–97) turned out favorably for the explorer: His case was heard before the king and charges were dismissed. However, troublesome rumors continued to follow Columbus, and in 1500 he and his brothers (Bartolomé and Diego) were arrested and sent back to Spain in chains. Though later released and allowed to continue his explorations (he would make one final trip to the New World), Columbus never regained his former stature, lost all honor, and died in poverty in the Spanish city of Valladolid in 1506.

Who was **Montezuma**?

Montezuma (or Moctezuma) was the name of two rulers of the Aztec Indians in Mexico. Montezuma I ruled an area that extended from the Atlantic to the Pacific. He is credited with enlarging Tenochtitlán (what is today Mexico City). He died in 1469, but three years earlier had been succeeded by his nephew, Montezuma II, who is the Montezuma most people are familiar with. It was during his reign that the Aztecs came into contact with—and were eventually conquered by—the Spanish, headed by Hernán Cortes. In 1519, Montezuma had tried to persuade Cortes not to come to Mexico City, but Cortes and his troops marched inland anyway. The Aztecs rose up to fight the Spaniards, but Montezuma was wounded as he addressed his warriors. He died a few days later, on June 30, 1520, one year before Mexico City would fall to the Spaniards.

How was **Cortes** able to claim **Mexico for the Spaniards**?

On behalf of the European power, Hernán Cortes (1485–1547) claimed Mexico after conquering its native peoples. In 1519, Cortes landed on the eastern coast of Mexico and founded the city of Veracruz. From there he marched inland, making an alliance with the Tlaxcalan Indians (who had fought wars against the Aztecs in central Mexico). On November 8 of that year, Cortes marched into Mexico City (then named Tenochtitlán) and took the Aztec leader, Montezuma, hostage. Cortes then continued to Mexico's west coast and when he returned to Mexico City in the central part of the country in 1520, he found the Aztecs were in revolt against the Spaniards. Fierce fighting ensued and by the end of

June, Montezuma was dead. This period of warfare is still remembered today by Mexicans as *la noche triste* (the sorrowful night). It was not until the following year, in August of 1521, that Cortes claimed Mexico City and the land after a four-month battle, which they called New Spain, came under control of the Spanish.

Who was **Cabeza de Vaca**?

Alvar Nuñez Cabeza de Vaca (1490?–1557?) was a Spanish explorer who in 1527 joined an expedition to the Americas. Because of his reports that he believed the area north of Mexico might be rich in precious metals, other Spanish explorers were later inspired to explore the region.

After landing in Florida in 1527, Cabeza de Vaca and a few others, including the black explorer Estevanico, became separated from the ships. The men built a barge and sailed from northern Florida to the Texas coast, where they made landfall. They then continued on foot to northwestern Mexico. Cabeza de Vaca is known for having lived with Indians for several years.

In 1540, Cabeza was appointed governor of Paraguay, but he proved to be inept in that capacity and was deposed by the colonists.

What were the **Seven Cities of Cíbola**?

The reference is to an area in present-day northern New Mexico that was thought by early Spanish explorers to contain vast treasures. One expedition in search of these legendary golden cities was that led by Francisco Vasquez de Coronado (1510–54), who sought to claim the riches for Spain. In 1540, he set out from North Galicia (a province northwest of Mexico City) with some three hundred Spanish troops as well as some Indians. They made it into the region where Arizona and New Mexico lie today. They encountered Zuni Indian settlements and believed these to be Cíbola; they captured the Zuni, but of course they found no gold. Separate expeditions set out from there, still hoping to locate riches. They did not find any precious metals, but they did make some discoveries: They were the first Europeans to see the Grand Canyon, to travel up the Rio Grande Valley, and to encounter several native peoples living in the region, including the Pueblo. Coronado was later (in 1546) accused of cruelty in his treatment of these peoples.

49

What areas of the **United States** did **Hernando de Soto explore?**

Spanish explorer Hernando de Soto (1500?–42) ventured throughout the Southeast before he caught fever and died along the banks of the Mississippi River.

Having been part of a brutal expedition that crushed the Inca empire (in what is now Peru), in 1536 de Soto returned to Spain a hero. But he sought to go back to the New World and got his wish when King Charles I appointed him governor of Cuba and authorized him to conquer and colonize the region that is now the southeastern United States.

Arriving in Florida in the winter of 1539, de Soto and an army of about six hundred men headed north during the following spring and summer. In search of gold and silver, they traveled through present-day Georgia, North and South Carolina, through the Great Smoky Mountains, and into Tennessee, Georgia, and Alabama. After defeating the Choctaw leader Tuscaloosa in October of 1540 in south-central Alabama, the Spaniards headed north and west into Mississippi. They crossed the Mississippi River on May 21, 1540, and de Soto died later that same day. Since he had shown no mercy in his conquests against the native peoples, de Soto's troops sunk his body in the river so that it would not be discovered and desecrated by the Indians. Then his army continued on without him; under the direction of Luis de Moscoso, they reached present-day Mexico in 1541 and named it New Spain.

How many trips to **North America** did **John Cabot make?**

Explorer John Cabot (c. 1451–98) probably made it to North American shores just once, in June of 1497—but having done so, he bears the distinction of being the first European to reach the North American mainland after the Vikings.

Cabot's story began in 1493, when Christopher Columbus returned to Spain from his voyages, claiming to have reached Asia. From the accounts of the trip, Cabot, who was himself a navigator (and merchant), believed it was unlikely that Columbus had traveled that far. He did, however, believe it was possible (as did subsequent explorers) to find a route—a northwest passage—that ran north of the land mass Colum-

What became of John Cabot's son, Sebastian?

Sebastian, who was born in Bristol, England, about 1476, and who then sailed—as a very young man of only twelve or thirteen—with his father on his successful expedition to North America the summer of 1497, did not take part in his father's ill-fated venture the following year. Had he done so, the world would have lost another great adventurer, since that expedition was never heard from again. Instead, Sebastian had stayed behind and, as an adult, picked up the cause of his father and other merchant-navigators who were determined to find overseas trade routes to the East.

During his lifetime, Sebastian Cabot drew up maps for both the English and Spanish royalty, and in 1527 he led a Spanish expedition that reached South America's Río de la Plata, and sailed into the Paraná and Paraguay rivers. In 1544, Cabot published an engraved map of the world. And seven years later, under a pension from King Edward VI, he founded the Merchant Adventurers of London. This group sponsored expeditions seeking a northeast passage (around Europe) to establish a trading route to the East. In so doing, the group effected trade with Russia.

bus had discovered, and which would, in fact, reach Asia. In 1495 the Italian Cabot, born Giovanni Caboto, took his family to England, and the following year, in March, appealed to King Henry VII for his endorsement in pursuing the plan. For his part, the king, who was well aware of the claims made by the Spanish and Portuguese who had sponsored their own explorations, was eager to find new lands to rule. And so he granted a "patent" authorizing Cabot's expedition.

Later that year, 1496, Cabot set sail, but problems on board the ship and foul weather combined to force him to turn back. The following spring, on May 20, 1497, he sailed again, in a small ship that had been christened *Matthew*. The crew of twenty included his son, Sebastian. On June 24, they sighted land and Cabot went ashore. While he saw signs of human habitation, he encountered no one. From reports of the trip, scholars believe Cabot had reached the coast of present-day Maine, Nova Scotia, Cape Breton, and probably Newfoundland. He then sailed home, returning to England on August 6. He reported to the king six days later and was given a reward, as well as authorization for a more sizeable expedition, which he undertook in May of 1498. This time Cabot set sail with five ships in his command. But the expedition was not heard from again. Some theorize that Cabot had again reached the coast of Newfoundland, since evidence turned up that subsequent Spanish explorers had knowledge of English discoveries.

What is the **Northwest Passage**?

It's the passage by sea between the Atlantic and the Pacific oceans, which was long sought after by explorers. Though it was eventually found through a series of discoveries, it was not completely navigated until 1903–06, by Norwegian explorer Roald Amundsen.

Nevertheless, convinced of the existence of such a passage, numerous navigators, many of them English and French, attempted to find it during the early years of European westward sea exploration. Their determination led to the discovery of the St. Lawrence River (between Canada and the United States) by Jacques Cartier in 1534–35, of Frobisher Bay (off the coast of Baffin Island, and north of Quebec) by Sir Martin Frobisher in 1576, of Davis Strait (between Baffin Island and Greenland) by John Davis in 1587, and of the Hudson River (in New York State) by Henry Hudson in 1609–11.

When, following centuries of efforts, Roald Amundsen finally completed the first successful navigation of the Northwest Passage in September 1906, it was after a journey that lasted more than three years. The thirty-year-old Norwegian had left the harbor at Oslo at midnight on June 16, 1903, aboard the *Gjöa*, a ship so small it required only a crew of six; Amundsen had bought the vessel with borrowed money. After a harrowing adventure that saw the *Gjöa* and her crew survive a shipboard fire, collision with a reef, fierce winter storms, and ice that had hemmed them in, Amundsen arrived in Nome, Alaska, where the entire town turned out to greet them. The nephew of Norwegian explorer Otto Sverdrup (1855–1930), who was there at the time, played the Norwegian national anthem as the ship pulled into the dock. Amundsen is said to have broken into tears.

How **long** was it before someone **reached the East** by sailing west?

It was not until 1520 that a route was found. Portuguese explorer Ferdinand Magellan (c. 1480–1521) was on an expedition for Spain when in 1520 he found a southwest passage, which took him around the southern tip of South America, through a winding waterway that still bears his name—the Strait of Magellan. Having set out from Spain in September 1519, it was a full year later before Magellan (born Fernão de Magalhaes, and known in Spain as Fernando de Magallanes) reached this point, south of the South American mainland and north of the Tierra del Fuego island chain (today these islands are part of Argentina and Chile). And this was only after he had crushed a mutiny. Nevertheless, Magellan had found a connection between the Atlantic and the Pacific oceans. He sailed on from there, reaching the island we know as Guam on March 6 of 1521. Ten days later, he discovered the Philippines. On the Philippine island of Cebu, he made an alliance with a treacherous native sovereign for whom he undertook an expedition to the nearby island of Mactan. It was there that Magellan met with his death in April of 1521. His expedition continued without him, under the direction of Juan Sebastian de Elcano, who in 1522 returned to Seville, Spain, along with eighteen other survivors of the Magellan expedition. Their cargo, aboard the ship *Vittoria*, included valuable spices—which more than paid for the expense of the expedition.

Who was the **first** to **go around the world**?

By sea, the first to circumnavigate the Earth was the Basque navigator Juan Sebastian de Elcano (c. 1476–1526), though eighteen sailors who made the trip with him also claim the distinction. The trip was completed in 1522 and had taken nearly three years. In 1519, Elcano had set out with Ferdinand Magellan on a Spanish-sponsored expedition that became the first one successful in finding a western route to the East. Having rounded the southernmost point of mainland South America in 1520, and entering into the South Pacific, the expedition reached the Philippines in 1521. When Magellan was killed there, it was Elcano who took leadership of the crew and guided the expedition westward, returning to Spain as the first sea captain to go around the world.

Who was the **first Englishman** to **circumnavigate** the globe?

It was English admiral Sir Francis Drake (1540 or 1543–1596), who set out in 1577 to explore the Straits of Magellan. He did so, investigating the coast of South America (he and his crew plundered coastal Chile and Peru in the process) before continuing up into the South Pacific. He eventually reached the coast of present-day California, which he named New Albion (a name that did not stick), and claimed it for Queen Elizabeth I. He continued sailing northward and is believed to have reached Vancouver—still in search of the Northwest Passage. Not finding it (he was much too far south, explorers would later learn), he sailed westward. He reached the so-called Spice Islands (today they are the Moluccas) in east Indonesia in 1579. Drake also found the Indonesian island of Java before continuing west through the Indian Ocean, rounding the southern tip of South Africa at the Cape of Good Hope, and skirting the coast northward to Sierra Leone, on the west African coast. From there Drake returned home to Plymouth, England, where he landed in 1580, the first Englishman to travel around the world. He was knighted by the queen one year later.

It is also Drake who, along with his fellow countryman Sir Walter Raleigh, bears the now-dubious honor of having introduced tobacco smoking to his homeland: In 1586, Drake returned from another expedition to North and South America, where he did battle with the Spanish fleets for control of lands, before picking up colonists in Virginia, who carried with them potatoes and the materials and implements for tobacco smoking. Drake remained in the service of the queen for his whole life, going on to fight and defeat the Spanish Armada in 1588. On a mission to the West Indies in 1596, Drake died on board his own ship.

What was **John Cavendish's** claim to fame?

English navigator John Cavendish (c. 1560–92) followed in Francis Drake's footsteps. Seeing Drake return from his exploits at sea and against the Spanish, Cavendish was inspired. And it was for good reason:

Who was the first woman to circumnavigate the globe?

It was a young French woman whose name is known only as Bare. In 1766, Louis Antoine de Bougainville (1729–1811), a French naval officer undertook a sucessful around-the-world expedition and returned to France in 1769. But the crew made an interesting discovery en route: When the French came on shore in Tahiti, the Tahitians immediately noticed something the crew had not—that one of the servants on the expedition was in fact a woman. Bare had been hired in before the ships left France by one of the officers, Commercon, who also served as botanist on the expedition. Commercon did not know Bare was a woman. Her secret discovered by the Tahitians, Bare confessed, revealing that she was an orphan who had first disguised herself as a boy to get employment as a valet. Later when she learned about Bougainville's expedition, she had decided to continue the disguise in order to carry out an adventure that would have been impossible if she were known to be a woman. She was the first woman known to have circled the globe.

Drake had earned himself fame, wealth, and the honor of being knighted. So in 1586, Cavendish set out with three ships for Brazil, made it through the Strait of Magellan, and then proceeded to capture Spanish treasure—including their prized ship, the *Santa Ana*. The Kings of Spain later mourned the loss and the fact that the ship had been taken by "an English youth . . . with forty or fifty companions."

Cavendish, now in the Pacific, continued his voyage, which took him to the Philippines, Moluccas, and Java before he rounded the Cape of Good Hope (Africa) and returned home. The journey had taken two years and fifty days, cost him two of his own ships, and made him the third person to circumnavigate the globe.

But his welcome in England was not what he expected: The twenty-eight-year-old was received with acclaim, but was not knighted by the queen. The fame and fortune that had come his way quickly vanished, as he spent most of his new wealth and his renown faded. By 1590, Cavendish thought he would try the journey again. Setting sail with five ships in August of 1591, the fleet was headed for trouble. Having made it to South America, heavy storms separated the ships as they attempted to make their way through the Strait of Magellan. The ship Cavendish captained turned back toward Brazil, attempting to make landfall. But Cavendish himself never made it. He died en route, believing he had been deserted by his mates.

What was the **Lost Colony**?

The term refers to the second English colony established in America: Set up in 1587 on Roanoke Island, off the coast of North Carolina, by 1590 it had disappeared without a trace. Theories surround the disappearance, though it is not known for sure what happened.

Roanoke Island had also been the site of the first English colony, set up in 1585 by about one hundred men who were sent there by Sir Walter Raleigh (1554–1618). Raleigh had perceived it to be a good spot for English warships (that were fighting the Spanish) to be repaired and loaded with new supplies. But the plan was not a success: the land wasn't fertile enough to support both the colonists and the Indians living nearby, and ships couldn't get close enough to the island since the surrounding sea proved too shallow. The colonists returned to England the following year. Meantime, Raleigh had dispatched another group of colonists from England. They arrived at Roanoke days after the original settlers had left. Seeing the site had been abandoned, all but fifteen of the colonists opted to return to England.

In spring of 1587, Raleigh sent yet another group of colonists to America, but these ships were headed for an area near Chesapeake Bay, farther north (in present-day Virginia). Reaching the Outer Banks in July, the ships' commander refused to take the colonists to their destination and instead left them at Roanoke Island. The colonists' leader, John White, who had also been among the first settlers at Roanoke, returned to England for supplies in August. However, the ongoing war between England and Spain prevented him from returning to the colony until three years later. Arriving back at Roanoke in August of 1590, where he expected to be met by family members whom he had left behind as well as the just over one hundred settlers (including some women and children), instead he discovered the colony had been abandoned.

The only clue that White found was the word Croatoan, which had been engraved on a tree. The Croatoan, or Hatteras, Indians were friendly Indians who lived on an island south of Roanoke Island. White set out to see if the colonists had joined the Hatteras Indians, but weather prevented the search and his expedition returned to England instead.

Two theories explain what might have become of the lost colonists: Since the shores of Chesapeake Bay had been their original destination, the colonists might have moved there but, encountering resistance, perished at the hands of the Indians. Other evidence suggests that the colonists became integrated with several Indian tribes living it North Carolina. Either way, they were never seen again by Europeans.

Who was **Hawaii-Loa**?

He was a Polynesia chief who sailed some 2,400 miles of open water from the Marquesas Islands, near Tahiti, to discover the Hawaiian Islands in the A.D. 400s. The islands were rediscovered by Europeans in 1778 when Captain James Cook landed on the island of Kauai and named the islands after John Montagu, who was the fourth earl of Sandwich and first lord of the admiralty. Captain Cook died there at the hand of the natives in a skirmish over a stolen boat.

What were the famous **Captain Cook's discoveries**?

British navigator Captain James Cook (1728–79) was one of the world's greatest explorers, commanding three voyages to the Pacific Ocean and sailing around the world twice. In 1768–71, aboard the ship *Endeavor*, Cook conducted an expedition to the South Pacific, where he landed in Tahiti, and made the first European discovery of the coasts of New Zealand, Australia, and New Guinea, which he also charted. In 1772, Cook set out to find the great southern continent that was believed to exist. He spent three years on this voyage, which skirted the ice fields of Antarctica. On his last voyage, which he undertook in 1776 on a mission of finding a passage around North America from the Pacific, Cook charted the Pacific coast of North America as far north as the Bering Strait. He met his death in 1778 on the Hawaiian Islands. Cook's voyages led to the establishment of Pacific Ocean colonies by several European nations.

What was the goal of the **Lewis and Clark expedition**?

The expedition, which began in 1804 and took more than two years to complete, had three purposes: To chart a route that would be part of a passage between the Atlantic and Pacific oceans; to trace the boundaries of the Louisiana Purchase territory; and to lay claim to the Oregon region.

Thomas Jefferson was president of the United States at the time, and he believed that a route could be found between St. Louis and the West Coast. As early as 1801, Jefferson had conceived of the idea that the Missouri and Columbia rivers might be followed west, leading to the Pacific. The journey would also be a reconnaissance mission, which would collect information about the vast region and endeavor to set up communications with its inhabitants. On April 30, 1803, the United States bought the Louisiana Territory from France. The Purchase extended from the Mississippi River to the Rocky Mountains, and from the Gulf of Mexico to British America (Canada). Jefferson soon picked his private secretary, Meriwether Lewis (1774–1809), to lead a westward expedition. Lewis then chose as his co-leader William Clark (1770–1838), who, as a lieutenant in the U.S. Army, had served General Anthony Wayne on the frontier (1792–96). Beginning in the summer of 1803, Lewis and Clark undertook the necessary preparations for the overland journey. These included studying the classification of plants and animals, learning how to determine geographical position by observing the stars, and recruiting qualified men (mostly hunters and soldiers) for the expedition.

On May 14, 1804, the Lewis and Clark expedition left St. Louis and headed up the Missouri River to its source. They then crossed the Great Divide and followed the Columbia River to its mouth (in present-day Oregon) at the Pacific Ocean, where they arrived in November of 1805—one and a half years after they had set out. They arrived back in St. Louis on September 23, 1806, having gathered valuable information on natural features of the country, including its flora, fauna, and the Indian tribes who lived there.

The expedition had been helped by the addition, in what is now North Dakota, of a Shoshone Indian woman named Sacagawea. Lewis and

Sacagawea guiding explorers Lewis and Clark through the Rocky Mountains.

Clark had hired her husband, French-Canadian trader Toussaint Charbonneau, as an interpreter during the winter of 1804–05. Lewis and Clark thought Sacagawea would be able to help them communicate with the Shoshone living in the Rocky Mountains, which she later did: her brother was their chief.

Lewis was later made governor of Louisiana, a post he served from 1807 to 1809. Clark resigned from the army in 1807 and became brigadier general of the militia and superintendent of Indian affairs for Louisiana Territory. He later became governor of the Missouri Territory.

Who was the **first person** to reach the **North Pole**?

There has been some dispute over this one: The credit usually goes to American explorer and former naval officer Robert E. Peary (1856–1920), who, after several tries, reached the North Pole by dogsled on April 6, 1909, along with Matthew A. Henson and three Inuit companions. Unbeknownst to him, five days before this achievement, another American explorer, Dr. Frederick Cook (1865–1940), claimed that he had reached the Pole a year earlier. Cook and Peary knew each other:

Cook had been the surgeon on the Peary Arctic expedition of 1891–92, which reached Greenland. And for his part, Cook's claim was investigated by scientists, but the evidence he supplied did not substantiate the claim. Thus, Peary has been recognized as the first to reach the northern extremity of the Earth's axis.

Who was the **first person** to reach the **South Pole**?

Norwegian explorer Roald Amundsen (1872–1928) was first to reach the South Pole, in December 1911. Before earning this distinction, he had achieved another first—sailing the Northwest Passage (1903–06).

Amundsen's desire to be an Arctic explorer had been with him almost his entire life. As a teen, he is said to have slept with his bedroom windows open year-round in order to become accustomed to the cold. When he was a young man of twenty-one, he turned his attention away from the study of medicine to making an Arctic passage. He recognized that many of the previous (and failed) attempts to travel to the Arctic shared a common characteristic: "This was that the commanders of these expeditions had not always been ships' captains." He resolved to become an experienced navigator, and soon took jobs as a deck hand on various ships.

In 1897, Amundsen was chosen as the first mate on the *Belgica*, the ship that would carry the first Belgian Antarctic expedition under the command of Adrien de Gerlache (1866–1934). Also on board was the American Frederick Albert Cook, who had been on one of Peary's earlier Arctic expeditions and who would, in 1909, dispute Peary's claim that he was the first to reach the North Pole. This was the same news that Amundsen would hear as he was preparing to reach the North Pole. Upon learning of the success of Peary's 1909 expedition, Amundsen shifted his sights to reaching the South Pole instead and quietly began to lay plans to do so. In fact, it was not until his expedition, which left Oslo in September of 1910, was under way that he telegraphed his announcement back to Norway that he was in fact headed to the South, not the North, Pole. As it turned out, a race was on between the Norwegians and the British: shortly after Amundsen had set sail, naval officer Robert Falcon Scott had left England at the head of an expedition to reach the South Pole.

The Norwegians landed at Ross Ice Shelf, Antarctica, on February 10, 1911. It was not until ten months later—on December 14, 1911, on a

Who was the first climber to reach Everest's summit?

The "first" belongs to New Zealander Sir Edmund Hillary (b. 1919), who was the first person to climb to the summit of Mount Everest, the highest mountain in the world. After numerous climbers made attempts on Everest between 1921 and 1952, it was Hillary who reached the top on May 29, 1953, as part of a British-led expedition; he was followed by fellow climber Tenzing Norgay, a Nepalese. Hillary took a picture of Tenzing at the summit, but Tenzing did not know how to work the camera so there is no picture of Hillary. The "Sir" was added to Hillary's name by Queen Elizabeth II, who took great pleasure in the fact that the triumph on Everest had been achieved by the British. Having been crowned on June 2, 1953, it was one of Queen Elizabeth's first official acts.

The Everest summit was not reached from its more difficult east face until 1983.

sunny afternoon, that the Norwegians raised their country's flag at the spot their calculations told them was the South Pole. Before heading north again, they celebrated their achievement with double rations. When British naval officer Robert Falcon Scott's expedition arrived at the Pole on the morning of January 18, 1912, they found the Norwegian flag flying over it. On the way back they all died due to bad weather and insufficient food supplies. Amundsen's Norwegian expedition arrived safely at their base camp on January 25, 1912.

When was the **first nonstop transatlantic** flight made?

It was in 1927: On May 21, at 10:24 p.m., American Charles A. Lindbergh (1902–1974) landed his single-engine monoplane, the *Spirit of St. Louis*, at Le Bourget Airfield, Paris, after completing the first non-stop solo transatlantic flight. Lindbergh, declining to take a radio in order to save weight for ninety more gallons of gasoline, had taken off in the rain from Roosevelt Field, Long Island, New York, at 7:55 a.m. on May 20. The plane was so heavy with gasoline (451 gallons of it) that *Spirit of St. Louis* had barely cleared telephone wires upon takeoff. Lindbergh covered 3,600 miles (1,000 miles of it through snow and sleet) in 33 hours, 29 minutes, won the $25,000 prize that had been offered in 1919, and became a world hero—hailed as "The Lone Eagle."

When was **Amelia Earhart** last heard from?

American aviator Amelia Earhart (1897–1937?), the first woman to fly across the Atlantic Ocean alone, was last seen on July 1, 1937, and was last heard from on July 2, as she and navigator Fred Noonan (1893–1937?) attempted to make an around-the-world flight along the Equator.

During the early 1920s, Earhart had become interested in aviation, which was very new at the time. She took flying lessons and in 1928 was invited to be the only woman on board a transatlantic flight, which departed from Newfoundland and landed in Wales. She became famous as the first woman to cross the Atlantic by air. She followed that up in 1932 with a solo flight across the Atlantic: Earhart took off from Harbor Grace, Newfoundland, on the evening of May 20, 1932. Her destination was Paris. Within hours, problems began for the aviator: She encountered a violent electrical storm, the altimeter failed, the wings iced up, and finally, the exhaust manifold caught on fire. Earhart decided to land in Ireland rather than attempting Paris. After a fifteen-hour flight, she touched down in a pasture outside of Londonderry in Northern Ireland. Again, notoriety and acclaim were hers, as the first woman to cross the Atlantic in a solo flight. She went on to set speed and distance records for aviation, and soon conceived of the idea of flying around the world along the Equator.

On June 1, 1937, Earhart and navigator Fred Noonan departed from Miami, Florida, and headed for Brazil. From there, they flew across the Atlantic to Africa and then across the Red Sea to Arabia. Then it was on to Karachi, Pakistan, Calcutta, and Burma. They reached New Guinea on June 30 and prepared for the most difficult leg of the journey—to Howland Island, a tiny speck of land only two and a half miles long in the middle of the vast Pacific Ocean. The next day, July 1, they left New Guinea and began the 2,600-mile flight to Howland Island. On July 2, a U.S. Navy vessel picked up radio messages from Earhart: she had reported empty fuel tanks. Efforts to make radio contact with her failed. Though a massive search ensued, no trace of the plane or crew was found and no one knows for certain what happened to them. Speculation surrounds their disappearance. One theory had it that Earhart's true mission in making the around-the-world flight was to spy on the Japanese-occupied Pacific islands. However, this has never been substantiated and, given the circumstances under which they were flying, the likelihood is that the plane crashed into the ocean, claiming both Earhart's and Noonan's lives.

THE SPACE RACE

When did **space exploration begin**?

The "Space Age" began on October 4, 1957, when the Soviet Union launched *Sputnik* (later referred to as *Sputnik 1*), the first artificial satellite. The world reacted to the news of *Sputnik*, which took pictures of the far side of the moon, with a mix of shock and respect. Soviet Premier Nikita Khrushchev (1894–1971) immediately approved funding for follow-up projects. And leaders in the West, not to be outdone by the Soviets in exploring the last frontier, also vowed to support space programs. Four months later, the United States launched its first satellite, *Explorer 1*, on January 31, 1958.

The Soviets followed the success of *Sputnik I* by sending the first animal into space—a dog named Laika, a small female Russian samoyed who traveled aboard *Sputnik 2*, launched November 3, 1957, to become the first living creature to go into orbit. But the trip ended badly for Laika: She died a few days into orbit. Both the Soviets and the Americans needed to prove that animals could survive in outer space before sending humans into orbit. While the Soviets experimented with dogs traveling in space, by the end of 1958, the United States would send a monkey into space. The following spring, two female monkeys, Able and Baker, were launched into orbit by the U.S. and were recovered alive.

Not only had the launch of Sputnik initiated the Space Age, it had also started a Space Race: The Soviet and American programs would continue to rival each other, with one accomplishment leap-frogging the other, for about the next three decades.

Who was the **first person in space**?

The first person into space was Soviet cosmonaut Yuri A. Gagarin (1934–68), who orbited the Earth in the spaceship *Vostok I*, launched April 12, 1961. The flight lasted one hour and forty-eight minutes. The achievement made Gagarin an international hero. President John F. Kennedy announced later that year, on November 25, that the United States would land a man on the Moon before the end of the decade. The first step toward that goal was made by putting the first American into orbit: On February 20, 1962, astronaut John Glenn, Jr. (b. 1921) orbited Earth three times in the spaceship *Friendship 7*.

Who was the **first man** to walk on **the Moon**?

It was American astronaut Neil Armstrong (b. 1930), who on July 20, 1969, stepped out of the lunar module from Apollo 11 and walked on the moon. Armstrong, who was joined by astronaut Edwin "Buzz" Aldrin, Jr. (b. 1930), uttered the famous words, "That's one small step for a man, one giant leap for mankind." (The live voice transmission had dropped the "a" before "man," but it was added in later.)

What impact did *Challenger* have on the U.S. space program?

On January 28, 1986, the space shuttle *Challenger* exploded seventy-three seconds after takeoff. (Please see page 239 for further information about the tragic episode.) The immediate effect on the U.S. space program was that all scheduled launches were scratched, pending the outcome of the government investigation into the disaster. President Reagan acted quickly to establish a Presidential Commission to look into the January 28, 1986, accident, appointing former Secretary of State William B. Rogers as the chair. Rogers conducted a thorough investigation involving public and private hearings, more than 6,000 people, 15,000 pages of testimony, 170,000 pages of documents, hundreds of photographs, and reports of independent technical studies. Additionally, the commission reviewed flight records, film evidence, and the recovered debris.

Edwin "Buzz" Aldrin placing the American flag on the Moon.

On June 6, 1986, the commission released its report, citing the cause of the disaster as the failure of the O-ring seals "that are intended to prevent hot gases from leaking through the joint during the propellant burn." The commission had learned that although both NASA and the O-ring manufacturer Morton Thiokol were concerned about the seals (which had also been used on other shuttles), they had come to regard them as an acceptable risk. The commission went on to say that "the decision to launch the *Challenger* was flawed." The U.S. House of Representatives' Committee on Science and Technology, which had spent two months conducting its own hearings, also concluded that the disaster could have been prevented, citing that "meet-

65

NASA's space programs resume after the *Challenger* tragedy.

ing flight schedules and cutting costs were given a higher priority than flight safety."

After the tragedy, NASA faced an uphill climb to regain their status: They faced the blame for the disaster; public confidence in the agency plummeted; and NASA's own astronauts became concerned that their lives had been put at risk.

However, the commission had also made nine recommendations to NASA, including a complete redesign of the solid rocket booster joints, giving astronauts and engineers a greater role in approving launches, reviewing the astronaut escape systems, regulation of the rate of shuttle flights to maximize safety, and a sweeping reform of the shuttle program's management structure.

A turnover of personnel, which included some astronauts, resulted at the space agency, which spent almost three years rebuilding. It was not until September 29, 1988, that an American shuttle again flew in space.

MAJOR "RUSHES"

MINING

What was the **biggest gold rush**?

The greatest American gold rush began on January 24, 1848 when James Marshall discovered gold at Sutter's Mill in Coloma, California. Within a year, a large-scale gold rush was on. As the nearest port, the small town of San Francisco grew into a bustling city as fortune-seekers arrived from around the world. By 1850, due to the influx, California had enough people to qualify it for statehood. This pattern repeated itself elsewhere in the American West, including the Pikes Peak gold rush in 1859, which effectively launched the city of Denver, Colorado. The gold rush led to the discovery of copper, lead, silver, and other useful minerals. It also spawned related industry. One of the success stories is that of Levi Strauss (1829–1902), a Bavarian immigrant who in 1853 began making and selling sturdy clothing to miners in San Francisco.

In other countries, gold rushes had the same effect on the growth and development of regions: After the precious metal was discovered in Australia in 1851, the country's population almost tripled over the course of the next decade. An 1861 gold rush in nearby New Zealand doubled the country's population in six years time. An 1886 discovery in South Africa led to the development of the city of Johannesburg. Just over a decade later, the infamous Yukon gold rush (in the Klondike region of Canada) spurred development there.

Familes trying to strike it rich during the California gold rush.

DIAMONDS

When did **diamond mining begin** in Africa?

An 1867 discovery of a "pretty pebble" along the banks of the Orange River in South Africa led to the finding of a rich diamond field near present-day Kimberley (the city was founded in 1871 as a result of the mining). Similar to the California Gold Rush roughly a decade and a half earlier, the finding in central South Africa prompted people from Britain and other countries to flock to the area. However, the ultimate outcome was conflict: Since both the British and the Boers (who were Dutch descendants living in South Africa) claimed the Kimberley area, the first Boer War ensued in 1880.

MIGRATION/MOVEMENT OF PEOPLES

When did people first **migrate** to the **Western Hemisphere**?

From Europe's discovery of the American "Indian" at the end of the fifteenth century to the present, the questions of who the native American populations are and how they came to the Western Hemisphere have intrigued scholars, clergymen, and laymen.

Early theories (put forth primarily by clergymen not long after Columbus arrived in the Americas in 1492) posited that the New World's indigenous people were descended from the ten lost tribes of Israel, or that the Indians' ancestors were Welshmen, or even that the natives came from the fabled lost continents of Atlantis and Mu.

However, the advancement of anthropology has yielded some answers: Since no skeletal remains of a human physical type earlier than *homo sapiens* have yet been found in the Americas, it is clear that the continents were settled through migration. Many scholars believe that Asians came to America during two periods: the first, between 50,000 and 40,000 B.C.; and the second, between 26,000 and 8000 B.C. They are believed to have come by way of a great land bridge over the Bering Strait, between Asia and North America. (This causeway was covered by water from about 40,000 to 26,000 B.C. because of a period of melting, which would have prevented passage.)

Most scholars also agree that there were several discrete, and perhaps isolated, movements of various peoples from Asia to the Americas. The migrations might have been prompted by population increases in the tribes of central Asia, which impelled some to move eastward in quest of food sources—animals. (As game moved across the Bering Strait, hunters followed.)

Over time, population growth caused early man to continue southward through the Americas so that by 8000 B.C. there were primitive hunters even in Tierra del Fuego (which forms the southernmost part of South America). Around 5000 B.C., the disappearance of large game animals in both North and South America produced a series of regional developments in certain areas, culminating in the emergence of several great civilizations, such as those of the Inca and Aztec.

Why is the Exodus from Egypt so well known?

The Exodus of the Jews from Egypt, an event recorded in the Bible and corroborated by historical evidence, is well known to Jews and non-Jews alike since the event, which Jews commemorate with Passover, came to symbolize departure from oppressive conditions (the Hebrews had been enslaved in Egypt).

According to the Bible (the Old Testament books of Genesis and Exodus), the ancestors of the Hebrews had settled in the Nile delta of Egypt 430 years before the Exodus, or about the seventeenth century B.C. A change of dynasty caused the Hebrews, because of their growing numbers, to be looked upon with hostility. They were put to work as state serfs in the construction of stone-cities.

The Biblical account tells about a series of confrontations between the Pharaoh and Moses, who had been commissioned by God to lead his people to the Promised Land. The Pharaoh refused to allow the Hebrews to leave Egypt but was later convinced, through a series of divine signs and calamities, to permit them to go. The Promised Land has come to be a symbol for freedom and the realization of hopes.

What is the **Trail of Tears** and when did it happen?

The Trail of Tears was the government-enforced western migration of the American Indians, which began March 25, 1838. More than fourteen thousand members of the Cherokee Nation were forced from tribal lands in Georgia, Alabama, and Tennessee, and were escorted west by federal troops under the command of General Winfield Scott, along an eight-hundred-mile trail that followed the Tennessee, Ohio, Mississippi, and Arkansas rivers to Indian territory west of the Red River.

The journey took between ninety-three and 139 days, and the movement westward was called the Trail of Tears not only because it was a journey the native people did not wish to take, but because an estimated four thousand people—mostly infants, children, and the elderly—died en route. The deaths were brought on by sickness, including measles, whooping cough, pneumonia, and tuberculosis.

Escorted in waves, it was a full year before the Cherokee had been relocated and some had refused to leave their tribal lands in the southeast. The forced migration thus resulted in the fragmentation and weakening of the tribe.

What are the **origins** of **slavery in America**?

The roots of slavery in North America date back to about 1400 when the Europeans arrived in Africa, inextricably linking the histories of all three continents for centuries to come.

At first, the result of African contact with Europeans was positive, opening trade routes and expanding markets. Europeans profited from Africa's rich mineral and agricultural resources, for a while abiding by all local laws governing their trade, Africans benefitted from new technologies and products brought by the Europeans. But the relationship between the two cultures soon turned disastrous as the Europeans cast their attention on a decidedly different African resource—the people themselves.

As the Portuguese in west and east Africa began trading in human lives and the Dutch in South Africa clashed with the native people who, once displaced by the wars, became servants and slaves, other Europeans began calculating the profits that could be made in the slave trade.

While the British were defeated by the American Colonists in 1776, by 1780 they had defeated both the French and the Dutch, and the British Empire remained a powerful force. Soon they established a trade triangle: the British sailed to Africa to capture natives; these captives were transported to the West Indies and the Americas where they were sold as slaves to plantation owners; plantation owners then sold their agricultural products (coffee, sugar, cotton, and tobacco) to the northern states in America and to European interests—all at a substantial profit.

One of many slave ships arriving in America.

When did the **first Africans arrive** in the British colonies of **North America**?

In 1619, when a Dutch ship carrying twenty African Negroes landed at Jamestown, Virginia. They were put to work as indentured servants—not as slaves. Though they had fewer rights than their white counterparts, they were able to gain their freedom and acquire property, which prompted the development of a small class of free Negroes in colonial Virginia. For example, it is documented that Anthony Johnson, who arrived in Virginia in 1621 as a servant, was freed one year later, and about thirty years after that he imported five servants, receiving from Virginia 250 acres of land for so doing.

What prompted widespread **Irish emigration** in the mid-1800s?

In 1845, Ireland's potato crop failed. Though crop failures in Europe were widespread at the time, the blight in Ireland was particularly hard-hitting because of the reliance on a single crop, potatoes, as the primary source of sustenance. The Great Famine that resulted lasted until 1848. The effect was a drastic decline in the Irish population—due to deaths and emigration. It is estimated that between 700,000 and one million people died in Ireland during the Great Famine. And between 1846 and 1854 alone, nearly two million people left the country, in search of a better life elsewhere. Three-quarters of those were headed to the United States.

In the years since the Great Famine, experts have determined that the blight of the late 1840s was caused by a fungus that had probably been introduced to Ireland by a ship from North America, where there had been crop failures in the early 1840s. Sad irony that the very conduit that had likely borne the blight from North America to Ireland also carried immigrating Irish back to North American shores.

IMMIGRATION

When were the **major** waves of **immigration** to the United States?

German immigration reached its peak in 1882. The following year, the United States had the peak year of immigration from Denmark, Norway, Sweden, Switzerland, the Netherlands, and China. But it was just after the turn of the century, in 1902, when U.S. immigration set new records. In this wave, most arrivals were from Italy, Austro-Hungary, and Russia. As a result of the wave, in 1910, 14.7 percent of Americans were foreign-born.

In the late-1990s, immigration was peaking again: The U.S. Census Bureau released a spring-1998 report citing that 9.6 percent of American residents were foreign-born, or roughly one in every ten. This was the highest percentage reported since the 1930s, when 11.6 percent of U.S. residents were natives of another country. However, at the end of the twentieth century, the origin countries had shifted: Latin Americans accounted for about half of all new arrivals, one-fourth were Asian-born, and one-fifth were European.

What measures has the **U.S. government** taken to try to manage immigration?

In 1894, Congress created a Bureau of Immigration. In 1902, the same year that immigration set new records, Congress revised the Chinese Exclusion Act of 1882 to prohibit immigration of Asians from U.S. island territories such as Hawaii and the Philippines. In a February 1908 "gentlemen's agreement," Japan agreed to stop issuing passports to workers for immigration directly to the United States.

After the wave of immigrants in the early twentieth century, Congress stepped in to curb immigration during the 1920s. The Emergency Quota Act, enacted by Congress on May 19, 1921, restricted immigration to 3 percent of U.S. residents of that nationality in 1910. Just three years later, in May 1924, Congress passed the Johnson-Reed Immigration Act, setting the quota at 2 percent of U.S. residents of that nationality as of 1890. The act excluded the Japanese—despite the Japanese ambassador's warning of grave consequences should the United States abandon the "gentlemen's agreement" of 1908. The Johnson-Reed Act did permit close relatives of U.S. citizens to enter as non-quota immigrants and it placed no restrictions on immigration from Canada or Latin America. Consequently, immigration from Canada, Newfoundland, Mexico, and South America peaked.

In 1965, a new U.S. immigration act imposed an overall limit of 120,000 visas per year for Western Hemisphere countries and 170,000 per year for the rest of the world, but immediate relatives of U.S. citizens may enter without regard to these limits.

WARS, OVERTHROWS, & REVOLUTIONS

What was the **Trojan War**?

Homer chronicled the Trojan War in his epic poem the *Iliad* (eighth century B.C.). According to Homer, the Mycenaeans, under their great king Agamemnon, set out to conquer the city of Troy, situated on the Turkish coast at the southwestern part of the Hellespont. The Hellespont (now called the Dardanelles) and the Bosporus are narrow straits that connect the Black Sea with the Aegean Sea. As such, they are the gateway between Europe and Asia, and in Mycenaean times, held the key to control of the profitable Black Sea trade.

In hopes of taking the Black Sea trade, Agamemnon's army attacked the powerful city of Troy around 1200 B.C. After a war that lasted ten years, according to the *Iliad*, the Mycenaeans were victorious. They built a huge wooden horse on wheels and offered it as a gift to the Trojans. Once the horse was inside the city gates of Troy, the Mycenaean soldiers hidden within the wooden horse took the city by storm, ending the decade-long campaign. The mythological war likely reflected a real war that was fought over the Dardanelles about 1200 B.C.

What was the **Peloponnesian War**?

It was the war fought between the Greek city-states of Athens and Sparta between 431 and 404 B.C.; it left Athens ruined. The beginning of the war signaled the end of the Golden Age of Greece.

As the city-states had developed, an intense rivalry grew between Athens and Sparta. The Spartans recruited allies into the Peloponnesian League (the Peloponnese Peninsula forms the southern part of mainland Greece), and together they attacked the Athenian empire, which had been gaining in power.

The war consisted of three stages: The first was the Archidamian War (431–21 B.C.), named for Archidamus, the Spartan king who led the unsuccessful attacks on fortified Athens. In 421, the so-called Peace of Nicias (421–13 B.C.) began, which was negotiated by Athenian politician Nicias. But this truce was broken when an Athenian commander promoted counterattacks on Athens' aggressors in 418 and 415 B.C. The attacks on the Peloponnesian League were unsuccessful, and so the Ionian War broke out (413–404 B.C.). After years of ruinous fighting, the Ionian War finally ended in victory for Sparta, after the Peloponnesian League had not only gained the support of Persia to defeat Athens, but had successfully encouraged Athens' own subjects to revolt. Athens surrendered to Sparta, ending the Peloponnesian War.

What happened to **Athens** after the **Peloponnesian War**?

At the same time that Athens was under attack from Sparta, the city-state also suffered a terrible plague, beginning in 430 B.C., which killed about a third of Athens' citizens. This contributed to Athens' eventual defeat at the hands of its Spartan rivals during the Peloponnesian War: After the plague had claimed so many lives, Athens simply couldn't muster the military leadership and strength that it needed to defeat the increasingly powerful Peloponnesian League. At the end of the fighting, in 404 B.C., Athens was in ruins. Sparta became the dominant city-state in the Greek world. But conflicts—and fighting—continued among the city-states, and Thebes eventually defeated Sparta in 371 B.C. As a result of the ongoing warfare, the Greek economic conditions had declined, and the gap between rich and poor widened. The public spirit that had been the hallmark of the Golden Age of Greece had disappeared. In short, the city-states were no longer the glorious entities they had once been.

While the Greek city-states were in decline, Greece's neighbor to the north, Macedonia, was growing more powerful. In 353 B.C., the Macedonian king, Philip II (382–336 B.C.), launched an attack on Greece.

One of the battles fought in the Trojan War.

The war that resulted did not end until 338 B.C. when Greece was finally conquered. The Macedonian victory was only the first part of Philip's plans: he believed a combined Macedonian-Greek army could defeat the powerful Persians. But he was not to see this happen: Philip was killed by a Macedonian in 336 B.C. and was succeeded by his twenty-year-old son, Alexander, whom history would come to call "the Great." Alexander carried out his father's plan to invade Persia. And two years after Philip's death, Alexander began a ten-year campaign that ultimately conquered the Persian Empire. By the time he was thirty years old, Alexander had conquered much of the known world, expanding his empire from Egypt to India.

How was **Rome** able to **conquer Greece**?

After Alexander the Great died in 323 B.C., his generals divided his empire into successor states, but Greece remained under Macedonian control. Though the Greeks would fight the armies of the Macedonian kings into the 200s B.C., they would not achieve independence, and instead, associations of Greek city-states again fought each other.

Alexander the Great in battle in Egypt.

What were the Punic Wars?

The Punic Wars were three major campaigns that Rome waged to expand its empire. Messina (today a province of Sicily, Italy) was the site of the First Punic War, which began in 264 B.C. when warring factions in the trade and transportation center called for assistance from both Carthage and Rome. The Carthaginians arrived first, and secured the city. But the Romans, who had girded their navy for the battle, arrived and drove the Carthaginians out (241 B.C.), conquering Sicily. Messina became a free city but was allied with Rome.

The rivalry between Rome and Carthage did not end there: The Second Punic War (218–201 B.C.) was largely fought over control of Spain. When the great Carthaginian general Hannibal(247–183 B.C.) captured the Roman-allied city of Sagunto, Spain in 218, he then crossed the Alps and invaded Italy, where he was met by, and defeated, the Roman armies. The deciding battle in the Second Punic War was fought in the North African town of Zama (southwest of Carthage) in 202 B.C. It was there that the Romans, under general Scipio Africanus (236–183 B.C.), crushed the Carthaginians under Hannibal. Rome exacted payments from Carthage, and Carthage was also forced to surrender its claims in Spain. A peace treaty was signed between the two powers in 201 B.C. but it held for five decades.

The Third Punic War erupted in 149 B.C. when the Carthaginians rebelled against Roman rule. By 146 B.C., Carthage, which had been richer and more powerful than Rome when the Punic Wars began, was completely destroyed in this third and final conflict with the Roman army.

Meantime, just to the west, Rome had been conquering lands to become a formidable power in the Mediterranean, and soon began to look eastward to expand its authority. When Rome conquered Macedonia in 197 B.C., Greece was liberated. Fifty years later, in 146 B.C., Greece was conquered by Rome and was divided into provinces. While the city-states still had no military or political power, they nevertheless flourished under Roman rule. And the Romans, who had first started borrowing from Greek thought and culture around 300 B.C., were soon spreading Greek ideas, art, and religion throughout their empire, giving rise to the Greco-Roman culture inherited by modern Western civilization.

Who said "Veni, Vidi, Vici" and what does it mean?

The famous words were written by Roman statesman and general Julius Caesar (100–44 B.C.) as he announced the victory of his army in Asia Minor in early August of 47 B.C. The extraordinarily concise message, which Caesar dispatched to Rome, simply means "I came, I saw, I conquered." The general had defeated Pharnaces II in a fight for control of Pontus, an ancient kingdom in northeast Asia Minor. The brief but decisive battle took place near Zela (in present-day Turkey).

How could an empire so powerful as the Roman Empire have fallen?

One could argue that the Roman Empire collapsed under its own weight: It had become too vast to be effectively controlled by any one ruler.

By the close of the Punic Wars, 146 B.C., Greece, Macedonia, and the Mediterranean coasts of Spain and Africa had been brought under Roman control. Within a century, Rome again began to expand overseas. Under the Roman general Pompey, eastern Asia Minor, Syria, and Judea were conquered. Next, Gaul was conquered by Pompey's rival, Julius Caesar, adding the territory west of Europe's Rhine River to the Roman world. In 31 B.C., in the Battle of Actium, Octavian (Julius Caesar's adopted son and heir) defeated the forces of Antony and Cleopatra, queen of Egypt, and in 30 B.C., Egypt became a Roman province.

In 27 B.C., Octavian became the first Roman emperor and was known as Augustus, meaning "exalted." Though Octavian's rule marked the beginning of the long period of stability called the *Pax Romana,* the Roman Empire had become so large—stretching across Europe and parts of Africa and the Middle East—that only a strong, central authority could govern it. During the two hundred years of the *Pax Romana,* Rome's emperors gradually grew more powerful—to the point that after death, an emperor was worshiped by the people. But soon there were threats to this central control, not the least of which was the spread of Christianity, as well as invasions from the Germanic Goths and the Persians: Theodosius I was the last emperor to rule the entire Roman Empire. When he died in A.D. 395, the empire was split into the West Roman Empire and the East Roman Empire, setting the stage for the decline of the Romans.

The West Roman Empire came under a series of attacks by various Germanic tribes including the Vandals and the Visigoths (the western division of the Goths), who invaded Spain, Gaul (in Western Europe), and northern Africa. These assaults eventually led to the disintegration of the West Roman Empire by A.D. 476.

The East Roman Empire remained more or less intact, but was known as the Byzantine Empire from 476 until 1453 (and was predominately a Greek-oriented culture), when it fell to the Turks.

How was **Rome "sacked"**?

After the split of the empire, the West Roman Empire continued to get weaker and Rome became subject to a series of brutal attacks by Germanic tribes: in A.D. 410, the Visigoths moved into Italy and looted Rome; in 455, the Vandals thoroughly ravaged the city; finally, in 476, the city fell when the Germanic chieftain Odoacer forced Romulus Augustulus, the last ruler of the empire, from the throne. By this time, however, Germanic chiefs had already begun claiming Roman lands and dividing them into several smaller kingdoms. 476 marks the official collapse of the West Roman Empire.

What was the **Hundred Years' War**?

The term refers to a succession of wars between England and France. The fighting began in 1337 and did not end until 1453. However, the period was not one of constant warfare: truces and treaties brought about breaks in the military action between the countries. The reasons for the conflicts were many: England was trying to hang onto its provinces on the European continent; the French threw their support behind the Scots, who had their own battles with the English; the

Why is Joan of Arc known so well as a warrior?

Joan of Arc (1412?–31) led the French into victory over the English in the battle for Orleans in 1429, when she was still a young woman. In 1428, the English forces invaded northern France and took possession of an area that included the city of Reims, where all of France's kings were crowned in the cathedral. Thus, Charles VII, whom France recognized as their king, had never had a proper coronation. It's said that Joan of Arc, an extraordinarily devoted Catholic who was then just a teen, appealed to Charles to allow her to go into battle against the English who were besieging Orleans. Though he was skeptical of her at first (she claimed to have heard the voices of saints), he eventually conceded. In the battlefield, Joan of Arc again overcame the doubts of the French troops and their leaders, who were understandably hesitant to follow the young girl's lead. She eventually proved to them that she was very capable. In April of 1429, in just ten days, Joan of Arc led the French to victory over the English, who fled Orleans.

Still determined to see Charles properly crowned, Joan led a military escort for the king into Reims, where he was at last coronated on July 17, 1429—with Joan of Arc standing beside him. Next, she was determined to have Charles authorize her to try to free Paris from English control. Again, the king acquiesced but this time it turned out badly: She was captured by the French Burgundians (English sympathizers and loyalists), who turned her over to the English. Believing she was a heretic (by all reports Joan of Arc was clairvoyant), the English burned her at the stake in Rouen, France, on May 30, 1431. She is still considered a national hero of France. Recognizing Joan of Arc for her unswerving faith and for having valiantly pursued what she believed her mission to be, the Catholic Church canonized Joan of Arc in 1920. The feast day of St. Joan of Arc is celebrated on May 30.

French wished to control the commercial center of Flanders (present-day Belgium), where the English had set up a profitable wool trade; and finally, the two countries disagreed about who should control the body of water that lies between them—the English Channel. To further complicate matters, marriages between the English and French aristocracy meant that heirs to either throne could find themselves with a foreign relative, allowing them to lay claim to authority over the other country as well. This is what prompted the first war to break out in 1337 when King Edward III of England claimed the French throne on the basis of the fact that his mother was the sister of three French kings. Over the course of the next century, even though England won most of the battles, and for a brief time controlled France (1420–22), it was the French who ultimately won the war in 1453. England lost all its territory on the continent, except Calais, which was also later taken by the French (in 1558).

What was the **impact** of the **Hundred Years' War**?

After waging war with each other for more than a century, in 1453, both England and France emerged as stronger, centralized governments. As the governments had gained strength, the nobility in both countries found themselves with less power and influence than they had enjoyed previously, and the system of feudalism, which before the war had been necessary in the absence of a larger, protective entity, was on the decline. In their strategies against each other, both countries had developed new military tactics. And though England had fewer resources than did France, it still managed to assert itself at sea, marking the beginning of that country's naval prowess.

What were the **Hussite Wars**?

The Hussite Wars were fought in Bohemia (now part of the Czech Republic) between 1420 and 1433. The country was plunged into the thirteen-year war by festering hostilities between peasants (The Hussites) and Christian crusaders. The fighting ended in 1433 with the compromise of the Counsel of Basel and three years later, was officially ended by the Compact of Iglau, in which all parties agreed to accept the Holy Roman Emperor as king of Bavaria. The peasants had succeeded

83

nevertheless in asserting Bohemian nationalism and had severed the country's ties to Germany.

What was the **Peasants' War**?

It was the greatest mass uprising in German history. Fought in 1524–25, the war was in part a religious one that came during the Reformation. In 1517, the German monk Martin Luther (1483–1546) had begun questioning the authority of the Roman Catholic Church. He soon had followers—nobles and peasants alike—and his reform movement spread, giving birth to Protestantism (the Christian beliefs practiced by those who protested against the Catholic Church). While many Protestants were sincere in their faith, some had their own motives for following the movement. German peasants looked to the Reformation to end their oppression at the hands of the noble lords. When the peasants revolted at the end of 1524, they were forcibly suppressed. Some one hundred thousand peasants died. Prior to the uprising, the peasants had aimed to get Martin Luther's endorsement, but he had declined to give it.

What was the **Peace of Augsburg**?

The Peace of Augsburg of 1555 came as a result of the Reformation and effectively carved up Europe between the Roman Catholic Church and the new Lutheran (Protestant) Church. Charles V was Holy Roman Emperor at the time, and though he hated to concede lands to Protestantism, he also wished to end the religious divisions in the empire. Princes, who had themselves converted to the new faith, convinced Charles to allow each to choose the religion for his own land. Thus, the Peace of Augsburg officially recognized the Lutheran church and the right of the people to worship as Protestants.

What was the **Gunpowder Plot**?

In 1605, a group of twelve men who believed the English government to be hostile to Roman Catholics, laid plans to blow up the Houses of Parliament—with King James I and government officials in it. Their scheme was discovered, however, and all of the conspirators were put to death. The event is remembered today in two ways: Every November 5, the day the plot was supposed to be carried out, the English hold a festival in which Guy Fawkes (1570–1606), the fellow who is said to have originated the Gunpowder Plot, is burned in effigy. Further, the vaults beneath the Houses of Parliament are searched before each new session.

What was the **Thirty Years' War**?

The Thirty Years' War (1618–48), like the Hundred Years' War, was actually a series of related conflicts, rather than one long campaign. The conflict in Europe began as a religious one—with hostility between Roman Catholics and Protestants, but eventually turned political before it was ended with the Peace of Westphalia. The war had four periods: The Bohemian (1618–24), the Danish (1625–29), the Swedish (1630–34), and the Swedish-French (1635–48).

In Bohemia (part of the Czech Republic today), the trouble began in the capital of Prague when the archbishop authorized the destruction of a Protestant church. The act angered Bohemian Protestants and those elsewhere in Europe, who believed it was their right—granted by the Peace of Augsburg—to worship as Lutherans. When Holy Roman Emperor Matthias failed to intervene on behalf of the Protestants, Prague became the scene of mayhem in May 1618. Disorder continued in Bohemia even as a new emperor ascended to the throne of the Holy Roman Empire. King Ferdinand II (a Habsburg) wielded an enormous amount of power, and in 1620 he squelched the Bohemian rebellion, which cost the Bohemians their independence. Further, Catholicism was reinstated as the state religion. These events caused other Protestant lands within the Holy Roman Empire to take notice. Soon the kings of Denmark, Sweden, and France entered into their own campaigns—fighting the Holy Roman Empire for control of German lands. But the conflicts weren't strictly about religious freedom: reducing the authority of the powerful Habsburg family became a primary objective.

What was the **Defenestration of Prague**?

The event occurred at the beginning of what came to be known as the Thirty Years' War when Bohemian Protestants, angered at the destruction of their church, appealed to the Holy Roman Emperor Matthias to intervene on their behalf. When the appeal proved unsuccessful, in May 1618, rioting broke out in the Bohemian city of Prague and two of the emperor's officials were thrown out of windows, in other words, they were defenestrated.

What was the **Peace of Westphalia**?

In 1644, Europe, torn by the Thirty Years' War, held a peace conference in Westphalia (in Germany). But the negotiations were four long years in the making. Meanwhile, the fighting continued until 1648, when the Peace of Westphalia was signed. Under this treaty, France and Sweden received some German lands. The agreement also made important provisions for Europe's religions: not only was Lutheranism given the same due as Catholicism, but Calvinism, the religious movement begun by Frenchman John Calvin (1509–64), was also given the official nod.

What was the **Great Northern War**?

It was a war undertaken at the beginning of the eighteenth century that challenged Sweden's absolute monarchy and imperialism. During the seventeenth century, Sweden had become a power in the Baltic region, gradually bringing more and more territory under its control. Even the Peace of Westphalia had granted some German lands to Sweden. But much of Sweden's prosperity and expansion during this period had been under the rule of Charles XI (1655–97). When he was succeeded by his young son, Charles XII (1682–1718) in 1697, the tides were about to turn for Sweden.

In 1700, Denmark, Russia, Poland, and Saxony (part of present-day Germany) attacked Sweden, beginning the Great Northern War. Sweden readily defeated Denmark and the Russians that same year. But Poland and Saxony proved to be more formidable foes, and Charles spent almost seven years fighting—and eventually defeating—them. But the Russian army was to have another chance at the Swedish, and this time they were successful, defeating Charles XII's forces in 1709 at Poltava (Ukraine). Charles fled the country as the war continued, and would not return until 1714. Four years later, the monarch was killed as he observed a battle in what is now Norway. Much of the country's lands in the Baltic had been surrendered and Sweden's period of absolute monarchy came to an end.

How did the **British** come to **control** so much of **North America** during colonial times?

British and French explorers had laid claim to many parts of what is now the United States. During the late 1600s and into the mid-1700s, the two European powers fought a series of four wars in their struggle for control of territory in North America. Three of the wars broke out in Europe before they spread to America where British and French colonists fought King William's War (1689–97), Queen Anne's War (1702–13), and King George's War (1744–48). King William's War saw no gains for either side. After Queen Anne's War, however, both sides signed the Treaty of Utrecht in which France ceded Newfoundland, Acadia, and the Hudson Bay territory to Britain.

The struggle between the two was not settled until a fourth war, the French and Indian War (1754–63), from which Britain emerged the victor and gained control of all of the area east of the Mississippi River as well as French possessions in Canada.

What was the **Seven Years' War**?

It was the war in 1756 between Prussia and Austria—who were fighting over control of Germany. In the conflict, Britain threw its support behind Prussia's king Frederick the Great in his struggle. By 1757, Austria was supported not only by the French (who were fighting the British in North American at the time), but also by Sweden, most of the German states, and, very importantly, by Russia. King Frederick had launched many military initiatives and was in a weakened state by the time his Prussian army faced the Austrians. He was spared certain defeat only by an event in Russia in 1762: with the death of Czarina Elizabeth, who had feared King Frederick, Peter III ascended the Russian throne. Peter, unlike his predecessor, held the Prussian king in high esteem, and not only withdrew Russia's support of Austria, but reached a peace agreement with Austria's enemy, Prussia.

What was the French and Indian War?

The French and Indian War (1754–63) was the last major conflict in North America before the Revolutionary War. Both Britain and France had steadily expanded their territories into the Ohio River Valley. Since the fur trade prospered in this region, both countries wished to control it. Fighting began in 1754 when George Washington and his colonial troops met the French and lost. But the British were not to be put down—even as Washington was being defeated, representatives from seven colonies met in Albany, New York, to plan the initiative against the French, who had built a chain of forts along the Allegheny River in western Pennsylvania.

After early victories for the French, a reinvigorated British force (under the leadership of Britain's secretary of state, William Pitt) took French forts along the Allegheny and met French troops in battle at Quebec. Fighting continued until 1763 with the signing of the Treaty of Paris. The British won the spoils, gaining control of all French lands in Canada as well as French territories east of the Mississippi River, with the exception of New Orleans. (The city was ceded to Spain, along with its holdings west of the Mississippi; Spain had become an ally to France late in the war—in 1762.) In exchange for Havana (Cuba), Spain turned over Florida to the British. France, which had once controlled a vast region of America, retained only two small islands off the coast of Newfoundland (Canada) and two Caribbean islands, Martinique and Guadeloupe.

The Seven Years' War ended on February 15, 1763 with the signing of a peace agreement in Saxony, Germany. The area that Austria had fought to control remained, for the most part, under Prussian rule. There were no other territorial changes in Europe as a result of the war.

AMERICAN REVOLUTION

Who started the **Boston Tea Party**?

Some believe that on December 13, 1773, it was patriot Samuel Adams (1722–1803) who gave the signal to the men, who may have numbered more than one hundred and were dressed as Indians, to board the ships in Boston Harbor and dump the tea overboard. The show of resistance was in response to the recent passage by the British Parliament of the Tea Act, which allowed the British-owned East India Company to "dump" tea on the American colonies at a low price and required that the colonists also pay a duty for the tea. Colonists feared the act would put local merchants out of business and that if they conceded to pay the duty to the British, they would soon be required to pay other taxes as well.

Once the ships carrying the tea had arrived in Boston Harbor, the colonists tried to have them sent back to England. But when Massachusetts Governor Thomas Hutchinson refused to order the return of the ships, patriots organized their show of resistance, which came to be known as the Boston Tea Party.

What were the **Intolerable Acts**?

The so-called Intolerable Acts, also known as the Coercive Acts, were five laws passed by the British Parliament early in 1774. Intended to assert British authority in the colony, the measures were seen as punishment for the Boston Tea Party in December of 1773. In brief, the laws enacted the following: closure of the port of Boston; an English trial for any British officer or soldier who was charged with murder in the colonies; the change of the charter of Massachusetts such that the council had to be appointed by the British and that town meetings could not be held without the (British-appointed) governor's permission; the requirement that the colonists house and feed the British soldiers; and the extension of the province of Quebec southward to the Ohio River.

While the British intention was to bring the Massachusetts colony under control (and actually the fifth act was not intended to have any punitive effect on the colony), the result was instead to unite the colonies in

Why was Bunker Hill
so important in the American Revolution?

The June 1775 battle on the hills outside Boston proved to be the bloodiest battle of the war. After the fighting in April at Lexington and Concord, more British troops arrived in Boston in late May. The Americans fortified Breed's Hill, near Bunker Hill, and on June 17, the British were ordered to attack the Americans there. The patriots, who needed to conserve ammunition, were given the famous direction not to fire until they saw the whites of their enemies' eyes. The American patriots succeeded in driving the British back on their first two charges. But on the third charge, the Americans fled. The Battle of Bunker Hill resulted in more than one thousand injured or dead British soldiers and four hundred American soldiers killed or wounded.

opposition to British rule. In this regard, the acts are seen as a precursor to the American Revolution.

Why is **Paul Revere's** ride so well known?

The April 18, 1775, event was famous in its own right but was memorialized by Henry Wadsworth Longfellow in his poem "Paul Revere's Ride." The verse contains an error about that night that the American Revolution began: The light signal that was to be flashed from Boston's Old North Church (one light if the British were approaching the patriots by land and two if the approach was by sea), was sent not to Revere; it was received by Revere's compatriots in Charlestown (now part of Boston proper). However, Revere did ride that night—on a borrowed horse. He left Boston at about 10 p.m., and arrived in Lexington at midnight to warn Samuel Adams and John Hancock, who were wanted for treason, that the British were coming. The next day, April 19, the battles of Lexington and Concord were fought, starting the Revolutionary War in America.

As an American patriot, Revere (1735–18) was known for his service as a special messenger to the extent that by 1773, he had already been mentioned in London newspapers. Revere also participated in the Boston Tea Party in 1775.

Who were the **minutemen**?

They were volunteer soldiers, ready to take up arms at a minute's notice, who fought for the American Colonies against the British during the Revolutionary War (1775–83). The minutemen, who were trained and organized into the militia before the war began, are most well known for the battles at Lexington and Concord, on April 19, 1775—which marked the beginning of the war. They had been alerted to the approach of the British troops, called redcoats, by the patriot Paul Revere. After the fighting at Lexington and Concord, which left 250 British killed or wounded and about 90 Americans dead, word spread quickly of the fighting, and the Revolutionary War had begun.

Did all of the fighting during the **American Revolution** take place in the Northeast?

No, there was also fighting in the southern colonies. But the struggle between the American colonists and the British was further complicated in the South by the presence of slaves. Land owners feared any fighting in the vicinity would inspire slaves to revolt against them. Knowing this, the British believed they could regain control of the southern colonies more readily than the northern colonies. But in November 1775, the British governor of Virginia offered to free any slaves who would fight for the British. As many as two thousand black slaves accepted the offer and took up arms. But there were also patriots in the South: it was Virginian Patrick Henry (1736–99) who uttered the famous words, "give me liberty or give me death."

In late February 1776, patriot forces confronted and defeated pro-British colonists near Wilmington, North Carolina. The British troops who were sailing from Boston to North Carolina to join the loyal colonists arrived too late to help, and sailed on to Charleston, which that summer was also the scene of fighting.

What was the **Battle of Tippecanoe**?

The battle near present-day Lafayette, Indiana, took place on November 7, 1811, when U.S. troops, under the command of General William Henry Harrison (1773–1841), defeated the Shawnee Indians while their leader, Tecumseh (1768–1813), was away.

The events that led up to the early November confrontation were these: The Shawnee Indians had been steadily pushed back from their ancestral lands along the Cumberland River in Kentucky. Once they settled in the Ohio River Valley, they formed a wall of resistance to further pressure. Resistance fighting began in 1763 and did not end until thirty years later (1793) when the American forces of General Anthony Wayne defeated the Shawnee at Fallen Timbers (in northwest Ohio). Tecumseh was twenty-five years old at the time of this critical defeat of his people. He became determined—despite the counsel of the tribe elders—to halt the westward movement. Tecumseh and his brother, Tenskwatawa, built a settlement on Tippecanoe Creek near the Wabash River. Called Prophet's Town, it became a rallying point for those Indians who resisted displacement by colonists. Soon the Shawnee who had settled at Prophet's Town were joined by bands of Wyandot, Potawatomi, Miami, and Delaware Indians. The British became aware of Tecumseh's defiance and soon supplied Prophet's Town settlers with arms to use against the Americans.

In 1810, the governor of the Indiana Territory, William Henry Harrison, requested a meeting with the Indian chief. But both were suspicious of each other and could not reach an agreement for peace. Westerners who were aware of Tecumseh's armed resistance movement pressured President James Madison to take action, which he did: Under orders from the president, Harrison set out in the fall of 1811 with a force of one thousand men. Arriving at Tippecanoe on November 6, he met with the Indians under a flag of truce and then made camp about a mile away from Prophet's Town. Tecumseh was visiting the Creek in Alabama at the time, trying to rally their support in the white resistance movement. But his brother, Tenskwatawa, rallied the men at Prophet's Town and then, at the break of day, they attacked Harrison's camp. Hand-to-hand fighting ensued in an icy drizzle. The Indian alliance retreated and though Harrison took heavy losses, he had managed to destroy Prophet's Town.

The battle undermined Tecumseh's initiative and launched the career of Harrison, who in 1840, after a successful military career and service in the U.S. Congress, rode the wave of public support all the way to the White House under the slogan, "Tippecanoe and Tyler, Too" (John Tyler was his running mate). Eventually the Shawnee were pushed into Kansas. Tecumseh became an ally of the British in the War of 1812 and was killed in the fighting.

FRENCH REVOLUTION

What was the **Oath of the Tennis Court**?

It was the oath taken in June 1789 by a group of representatives of France's third estate who, having been rejected by King Louis XVI (1754–93) and the first and the second estates, vowed to form a National Assembly and write their own constitution. The pledge set off a string of events that began the French Revolution.

French society had long been divided into three classes, called "estates"—members of the clergy were the first estate, nobles were the second, and everyone else comprised the third. When philosophers such as Jean-Jacques Rousseau (1712–78) came along and challenged the king's supreme authority by promoting the idea that the right to rule came not from God but from the people, it fueled the discontent felt by the long-suffering peasants and the prosperous middle class who paid most of the taxes to run the government but who had no voice.

A government financial crisis brought on by the expense of war forced King Louis XVI to reluctantly call a meeting of the representatives of all three estates, called the Estates General, which had last convened in 1614. During the May 5, 1789, meeting at Versailles, the third estate attempted to seize power from the nobility, the clergy, and the king by insisting that the three estates be combined to form a National Assembly in which each member had one vote; since the third estate had as many representatives as the other two combined, the people would at last have a voice. When the attempt failed, the third estate representatives gathered on a tennis court where they vowed to change the government. Louis XVI began gathering troops to break up the assembly formed by the third estate. Meantime, an armed resistance movement had begun to organize. The situation came to a head on July 14, 1789, with the storming of the Bastille in Paris.

What is **Bastille Day**?

The French national holiday celebrates the July 14, 1789 capture of the Bastille—a fortress dating back to 1370 that was often used by kings to imprison their objectors. As a protest to royal tyranny, Parisians stormed the structure, overpowering the guard. Once the crowd had taken control of the Bastille, which then housed few prisoners but was a storehouse for arms and ammunition, they tore down the symbol of oppression. The event marks the beginning of the French Revolution.

What was the **Reign of Terror**?

It refers to the short but bloody period in French history that began in 1793 and ended July 1794. During this time, Revolutionary leader Maximilien Robespierre (1758–94) led a tribunal that arrested, tried, and put to death more than seventeen thousand people—most of them by guillotine.

In the reforms that followed, the Oath of the Tennis Court and the capturing of the Bastille, France was transformed into a constitutional state, and French subjects became French citizens. An elected legislature was given control of the government. One such elected official was Robespierre who was elected first deputy from Paris and was the leader of the radical popular party. In this new era, those who had been associated with the old regime or those who opposed the revolution became the subjects of persecution. In January 1793, King Louis XVI and his wife, Marie Antoinette, were executed, beginning the Reign of Terror that saw thousands more (mostly those who had made up the powerful first and second estates) suffer a similar fate at the hands of the revolutionaries. To escape certain death, many fled the country—including top-ranking military officials, which made room for the rapid advancement of young military officers such as Napoleon Bonaparte.

The Reign of Terror ended on July 28, 1794, when Robespierre himself was put to death. As he gained power and influence, the revolutionary leader also had become increasingly paranoid, even putting two of his friends to death in 1794. He was overthrown on July 27 by the Revolution of 9th Thermidore, and the next day died by guillotine.

How long did the **French Revolution** last?

The revolution lasted some ten years, and grew increasingly violent as it progressed. It began in mid-1789 when the government found itself nearly bankrupt, and due to festering discontent among the commoners (the prosperous middle class included), that crisis quickly grew into a movement of reform. The revolution ended in 1799 when French general Napoleon Bonaparte seized control of the government. Democracy had not been established in France, but the revolution had important outcomes nevertheless: It had ended the supreme authority of the king, it had strengthened the middle class, and it had sent the message across Europe that the tenets of liberty and equality are not to be ignored.

When did the **Napoleonic wars** begin and end?

The Napoleonic wars began shortly after Napoleon took power and lasted until 1815, when he was finally defeated at the Battle of Waterloo. Ever the general, Napoleon used his power to keep France at war throughout his reign.

After the Coup d'État of 18th Brumaire (November 1799), which had put Napoleon in power, he effected peace, at first: In May of 1800, he marched across the Alps to defeat the Austrians, ending the war with them that had begun eight years earlier. Britain, fearing a growing European power on the continent, had declared war on France in 1793 but, by 1802, had grown tired enough of battle, that it too agreed to peace with Napoleon in the Treaty of Amiens. But the calm in Europe was not to last. By 1803, the diminutive but power-hungry Napoleon had begun to plot an invasion of Britain. Declaring himself emperor in 1804, he initiated a series of campaigns across Europe and by 1806, most of the continent was under his control. He remained, of course, unable to beat the British, whose superior navy gave them supremacy at sea.

95

What was the Coup d'État of 18th Brumaire?

It was the overthrow of the French revolutionary government on November 9, 1799. The coup put Napoleon Bonaparte (1769–1821) in power as one of three counsels intended to head the government.

While Napoleon was in Egypt and Syria waging, what were for the most part, successful military campaigns on behalf of the French government, there was growing discontent back at home with the Directory, the group of five men who had governed since 1795. With his army stranded in the Middle East, Napoleon received word that France might soon be under attack by the Second Coalition (the second in a series of six alliances that formed in Europe in order to stave off French domination). Leaving another man in command of his troops, Napoleon hurried back to France where he was welcomed as a hero. Aided by his brother, Lucien Bonaparte, and the French revolutionary leader Emmanuel-Joseph Sieyes, Napoleon carried out a coup d'état, overthrowing the Directory. A consulate was formed, with the young Napoleon becoming first consul; the other counsels had little influence, acting primarily as advisors to the ambitious Napoleon. The coup marked the end of the French Revolution: After the chaos and violence of the previous decade, the French people looked to Napoleon as a strong leader who could bring order to the country. They did not know that the thirty-year-old possessed a seemingly insatiable hunger for power, which would soon transform the government into a dictatorship. After a brief peace, Napoleon declared himself emperor of France on December 2, 1804, by which time he had already begun to wage a series of wars to gain himself more power in Europe.

But the various alliances (called coalitions) formed by European countries against Napoleon eventually broke him. After he had been defeated in Russia in 1812, the European powers that had long been held in submission by Napoleon formed a sixth and final coalition against

Napoleon Bonaparte.

him: Great Britain, Russia, Sweden, Prussia, and Austria met Napoleon's army at the momentous Battle of the Nations at Leipzig (Poland) on October 16–18, 1813. Napoleon was defeated there in what is sometimes called the War of Liberation, and he retreated to France. The following March, the allies making up the Sixth Coalition took Paris; Napoleon's generals were defeated. He abdicated the throne on April 6. However, that was not the end of the Napoleonic Era: Exiled to the Mediterranean island of Elba, Napoleon returned to Paris on March 20, 1815, believing he could recover power in the unstable atmosphere that followed his abdication. Three months later, he was defeated at the Battle of Waterloo on June 18. It was the last battle of the Napoleonic Wars. He was exiled to St. Helena island where he died in 1821.

What happened at **Trafalgar**?

Cape Trafalgar, on the southwest coast of Spain, was the scene of a decisive victory for Great Britain over Napoleon's navy in 1805. Other than a one-year respite in 1802, France and Britain had not been at war with each other since 1793. Napoleon remained determined to conquer Britain, just as he had most of continental Europe. But when his fleets met those of decorated English General Horatio Nelson (1758–1805) off the coast of Spain, the certain defeat and destruction of Napoleon's navy ended the emperor's hopes of invading England.

The confrontation at Trafalgar was the culmination of a two-year game of cat and mouse between Nelson's fleets and the French under the direction of Admiral Villeneuve (1763–1806), whose sole objective it was to invade Britain. To prevent this from happening, in 1803 Nelson began a two-year blockade of Villeneuve and the French navy at Toulon, France (on the Mediterranean coast). When the French fleets escaped Toulon, attempting to lure the British out to sea, Nelson chased them all the way across the Atlantic—to the West Indies and back—before the showdown off Spain's coast, where the French were joined by Spanish fleets. Meantime, the coast of England remained protected by the British navy, leaving no opportunity for invasion by the French.

On October 21, 1805, seeing the enemy sailing out of Trafalgar, Nelson formed his fleet of twenty-eight ships into two columns, intending to divide and conquer the combined French and Spanish force of thirty-three ships. About noon that day, as they prepared for the confrontation, Admiral Nelson sent out one of the most famous commands of naval history: "England expects that every man will do his duty." While the British prevailed, destroying Napoleon's fleet in less than four hours' time, Nelson was fatally wounded by a sharpshooter, and the English navy hero died just as victory was his. The brave Nelson had seen fate coming: the night before Trafalgar, he had revised his will, and just before the battle had begun, he told Captain Henry Blackwood, "God bless you, Blackwood, I shall never speak to you again." Nevertheless, Nelson died knowing that he had won, uttering the still famous words, "Thank God, I have done my duty."

Why did the **Russians burn Moscow**?

The September 14, 1812 torching of their own city was directed by Tsar Alexander the Great, who wished to prevent Napoleon and his invading armies from reaping the benefits of anything Russian. Through a series of wars, Napoleon had dominated most of Europe by 1805. The authority of Alexander was certainly threatened by the French emperor. In 1805 and 1807, Russia suffered dear losses in battles with Napoleon's armies. In the face of these defeats, what Alexander did next was a stroke of genius, though he had many detractors at the time: Napoleon's forces, though victorious, were weary from fighting and were unable to pursue the Russian armies further. So, Alexander made peace with the emperor in the Treaty of Tilsit. The Russian ruler vowed support of Napoleon, and for his part, Napoleon believed Alexander had extended him a hand of friendship. Instead, the cunning Russian ruler had bought himself and his country the time they needed to gird themselves against powerful Napoleon. By 1812, Russia, its economy dependent on exports, resumed trade with Great Britain, Napoleon's archenemy. This prompted the return of Napoleon's troops to Russia: Later that year, the French emperor marched into Russia with a force of as many as six hundred thousand men, but the Russians still delivered Napoleon a crushing defeat. The Russian army had relied on guerrilla warfare tactics, including burning their own countryside. Napoleon returned to Paris in defeat by the end of the year.

What caused the **War of 1812**?

The war between the young United States and powerful Great Britain largely came about because of France. After the French navy had been crushed by the British under Admiral Nelson at the Battle of Trafalgar, Napoleon turned to economic warfare in his long struggle with the British: He directed all countries under French control not to trade with the British. Its economy dependent on trade, Britain struck back by imposing a naval blockade on France, which soon interfered with United States' shipping. Ever since the struggle between the two European powers had begun in 1793, the United States had tried to remain neutral. But the interruption of shipping to and from the continent and the search and seizure of ships posed significant problems to the American export business: In 1807, Great Britain had issued an Order in Council that required even neutral vessels destined for a continental port to stop first in England; Napoleon countered with the Milan Decree, which stated that any neutral vessel that had submitted to British search be seized.

Back in America, New England, the region most dependent on shipping, nevertheless vehemently opposed entering into war with the British. But the country's economy was depressed as a result of the interruption of exports, and Washington declared war anyway on June 18, 1812—not realizing (in these days before telegraph and radio) that two days before, on June 16, Britain had withdrawn its Orders in Council, lifting its policy of shipping interference, which had been the chief reason for the war declaration. Thus the two countries engaged in fighting for the next two-and-a-half years. On December 24, 1914, the Treaty of Ghent ended the War of 1812. And once again, poor communication led to conflict: troops in New Orleans, unaware of the peace treaty, fought for control over the Mississippi River in the worst battle of the entire war—two weeks after it had officially ended. Though both the United States and Great Britain claimed victory in the War of 1812, neither side had gained anything.

Who were the "War Hawks"?

The War Hawks were a group of Republicans in the United States Congress who advocated war with Great Britain. Elected in 1810, the congressmen took office in 1811, the failure of the Erskine agreement fresh in their memories: That bit of 1809 diplomacy, arranged by British Minister to the United States George Erskine and then U.S. Secretary of State James Madison, would have provided for the suspension of Britain's maritime practices that interfered with U.S. shipping, but the agreement fell apart when Erskine was recalled from office. The relationship between the U.S. and Britain, tenuous since 1807 due to trade embargoes and the impressment of American sailors into British service, deteriorated. The newly elected congressmen were tired of the failure of diplomacy to resolve maritime problems with the British; they further felt that the British were challenging the young United States through their policies, which purportedly included British aid to American Indians in the Northwest. War Hawk leader Henry Clay was named Speaker of the House, and Congress soon passed a series of resolutions to strengthen the army and navy. When Congress was called upon by President James Madison to declare war on the British in June of 1812, it was the War Hawks who swung the close vote. Thus the War of 1812 was declared. Some historians believe the true motive behind the War Hawks was not resolution of the shipping problems, but rather the desire to annex parts of southern Canada to the United States.

Who said, "we have met the enemy and they are ours"?

It was Captain Oliver Hazard Perry (1785–1819) who wrote the famous words in a letter to General William Henry Harrison after defeating the British at the Battle of Lake Erie on September 10, 1813. An improvised U.S. squadron commanded by Captain Perry, twenty-eight years old, achieved the victory in the War of 1812 battle. The message he sent to Harrison (who later went on to become a U.S. president) was: "We have met the enemy and they are ours: two ships, two brigs, one schooner, and one sloop."

What was the **London Protocol**?

It was an 1830 decree that recognized an independent Greek nation after the eight-year Greek War for Independence (1821–29). The London Protocol officially ended Ottoman-Turk rule of Greece, which had begun almost four hundred years earlier.

In 1453, the Ottoman Turks conquered Constantinople (which is today Istanbul, Turkey) and by the end of the decade, they had moved westward to bring the Greek peninsula under their control. The Greeks first tried to overthrow the Turks in 1770 and were aided in this effort by Russian Tsarina Catherine the Great, whose aim it was to replace Muslim rule with Orthodox Christian rule throughout the Near East. But the effort was unsuccessful and it was fifty years before the Greeks would rise again to assert their independence. On March 25, 1821, the Greeks, led by the archbishop of Patras, proclaimed a war of independence against the Turks. Soon, Egypt had thrown its military support behind the Turks, but even the combined force could neither defeat the Greeks nor squelch the revolution. In 1827, Britain, France, and Russia, all sympathetic to the Greek cause, came to their aid. In October of that year, a combined fleet of the three European powers defeated the Turk and Egyptian fleet in the Battle of Navarino, off the Peloponnesus Peninsula. But the deciding moment came when Russia declared war on the Ottoman Empire in

1828, and the Ottoman Turks turned their attention to fighting the Russians. The following year, the Egyptians withdrew from Greece. In March of 1830, the London Protocol was signed by Britain, France, and Russia, recognizing an independent Greece. Weary from the fighting, the Ottoman Turks accepted the terms of the proclamation later that year.

What does "Remember the Alamo" mean?

The saying was a rallying cry for Texans in their war for independence from Mexico. The movement for independence had begun in the winter of 1835–36 when the people of Texas decided to cut off relations with Mexico, and soon turned into a war when the Mexican government sent a force of some four thousand troops, under the command of General Santa Anna, to squelch the rebellion. As the Mexican Army approached, the force of about 150 men who were determined to defend the city of San Antonio, retreated to the Alamo, a Spanish mission built in the previous century. The were joined by another fifty men, but still no match for the Mexicans who kept the Alamo under siege for thirteen days. The Texans, low on ammunition, ceased to return fire and, on the morning of March 6, Santa Anna's troops penetrated the Alamo. The fierce frontiersmen, Davy Crockett among them, are believed to have fought using the butts of their rifles. All the Texans who fought that day at the Alamo died.

Meantime General Sam Houston had assembled his forces and with the rallying cry "remember the Alamo" (and their fellow Texans who had bravely fought and died there), he set out to face the Mexican army and secure independence. This he did, at San Jacinto, Texas, on April 18, 1836, in a quick and decisive battle that had caught Santa Anna's troops by surprise. The following day the Mexican general was captured and made to sign a treaty giving Texas independence.

MEXICAN WAR

Why was the Mexican War fought?

The two-year war (1846–48) was fought over the United States' annexation of Texas. Then-President Andrew Jackson had recognized Texas as independent in 1837, just after Texans had won their war with Mexico. Republic of Texas President Sam Houston felt that protection against a Mexican invasion may be necessary and he eyed annexation to the United States. Meantime, Mexico's president Santa Anna warned that such an action on the part of the United States would be "equivalent to a declaration of war against the Mexican Republic." In June 1844, the Senate rejected a proposed annexation treaty. But later that year Democratic Party nominee James K. Polk, an ardent expansionist, was elected President. Since the annexation of Texas had figured prominently in his campaign platform, interim President John Tyler viewed the victory as a public mandate for annexation, and he recommended that Congress pass a joint resolution to invite Texas into the union. Congress did so in February and President Tyler signed the resolution on March 1, 1845, three days before Polk's inauguration.

Mexico responded by breaking off diplomatic relations with the United States. A border dispute made the situation increasingly tenuous: Texas claimed its southern border was the Rio Grande River while Mexico insisted it was the Nueces River, situated farther north. In June, President Polk ordered Brigadier General Zachary Taylor to move his forces into the disputed area. In November, Washington officials received word that Mexico was prepared to talk. Polk dispatched John Slidell to Mexico to discuss three other outstanding issues: the purchase of California (for $25 million), the purchase of New Mexico (for $5 million), and the payment of damages to American nationals for losses incurred in Mexican revolutions. This last point was critical to the negotiations, as Polk was prepared to have the U.S. assume payment of damages to its own citizens in exchange for Mexico's recognition of the Rio Grande as the southern border of Texas.

But upon arrival in Mexico City, Slidell was refused the meeting—President José Joaquín Herrera had bowed to pressure opposing discussions with the United States. When Polk received news of the scuttled talks, he authorized General Taylor to advance through the disputed territory to the Rio Grande. Meantime, Mexico overthrew Herrera, putting into office the fervent nationalist General Mariano Paredes y Arrillaga, who reaffirmed Mexico's claim to Texas and pledged to defend Mexican territory.

While Polk worked through Slidell to get an audience with the Mexican government, the attempts failed and on May 9, the Cabinet met and approved the President's recommendation to ask Congress to declare war. The next day news arrived in Washington that on April 25 a sizeable

Mexican force had crossed the Rio Grande and surrounded a smaller American reconnaissance party. Eleven Americans were killed and the rest were wounded or captured. On May 11, Polk delivered a message to Congress, concluding, "Mexico has . . . shed American blood upon the American soil. . . . War exists . . . by the act of Mexico herself." By the time the war was officially declared on May 13—just over one year after Polk had been sworn into office, General Taylor had already fought and won key battles against the Mexicans and had occupied the northern Mexico city of Matamoros.

What did the **U.S.** gain from the **Mexican War**?

The Mexican War (1846–48) was officially ended when the U.S. Senate ratified the Treaty of Guadalupe Hidalgo on March 10, 1848. By the treaty, Mexico relinquished roughly half its territory—New Mexico and California—to the United States. Mexico also recognized the Rio Grande as its border with Texas.

Mexico received payments in the millions from the United States, which also assumed the payment of claims of its citizens. Five years later under the terms of the Gadsden Purchase, the United States purchased a small portion of land from Mexico for another $10 million, which was widely regarded as further compensation for the land lost in the war. The territory the United States gained was in present-day Arizona and New Mexico, south of the Gila River.

What is **privateering**?

Privateering is the hiring of privately owned ships and their crews to fight during battle. The practice dates back to the 1400s and it continued well into the 1800s—eventually replaced by the development of strong navies. Privateers were, essentially, gunboats for hire. They played a crucial role in the American Revolution after the Second Continental Congress authorized their use on March 18, 1777, enabling the colonists to capture about six hundred British ships. The Americans would again employ privateers in the War of 1812.

But during times of peace, some privateers turned to pirating, which at least in part prompted European nations to sign the Treaty of Paris of

1856, outlawing privateering. Since the United States had relied on privateers in the past and had yet to develop its own navy, the Americans did not sign the treaty. While there was some privateering during the American Civil War, the need for them soon subsided as navies developed—by enlistment and draft. Privateering has not been used in more than one hundred years.

What was the **War of Reform**?

It was the period in Mexican history from 1858 to 1861 when the federalist government collapsed and civil war ensued. In 1858, President Ignacio Comonfort (1812–63), who had himself become Mexico's leader when he helped overthrow President Santa Anna in 1855, felt political pressure and fled the country. Benito Júarez (1806–72), who was minister of justice and then minister of the interior, assumed the presidency. His position was immediately opposed by centralists who rallied around rebellious army forces. Under this pressure, the federalists, led by Júarez, withdrew from Mexico City and set up the capital at Veracruz, on the Gulf coast. There, they had control over customs receipts, which allowed them to purchase arms and finance their government. Eventually, they defeated the centralists and reentered Mexico City in January of 1861. Júarez was elected president later that year, but his authority was challenged again with the arrival of the French, who quickly put Maximilian in power as emperor of Mexico. Júarez led the country in its successful campaign against the French who were expelled in 1867, when Júarez resumed the presidency. He died in office, in 1872.

AMERICAN CIVIL WAR

Was the **Civil War** all about **abolishing slavery**?

Historians have long debated this question. For years, American school children learned that the question of slavery was the only cause of the Civil War (1861–65): With nineteen free states and fifteen slave states

105

making up the Union, Abraham Lincoln had called the country "a house divided" even before he became president. And while slavery was central to the conflict, the bloody four-year war had other causes as well.

By the mid-1800s, important differences had developed between the South and the North (and many maintain these differences, or vestiges of them, are still with the country today): the economy in the South was agricultural-based while the North was industrialized. The ideals and lifestyles of each reflected these economic realities. Southerners believed their agrarian lifestyle was dependent on the labor of slaves. Long viewed by many Americans to be a necessary evil, by the early 1800s, the view that slavery is morally wrong was beginning to take hold. Northern abolitionists had begun a movement to end slavery in the states. But, except for a small antislavery faction, these views were not shared in the South.

There were other factors that contributed to the declaration of secession and the formation of the Confederacy: disputes between the federal government and the states had limited the power of the states, and this policy was called into question by southerners. Further, the political party system was in disarray in mid-1850s America. The disorder prompted feelings of distrust for the elected politicians who would set national policy. Before the 1860 presidential election, southern leaders urged that the South secede from the Union if Lincoln won.

How did the **South secede** from the nation?

Unhappy with the outcome of the 1860 election and fearing a loss of their agrarian way of life, the southern states began to make good on their promise to secede if Lincoln won the presidency: South Carolina was the first (in December of that year). In January 1861, five more states followed—Mississippi, Florida, Alabama, Georgia, and Louisiana. When representatives from the six states met the next month in Montgomery, Alabama, they established the Confederate States of America and elected Jefferson Davis president. Two days before Lincoln's inauguration, Texas joined the Confederacy. (Virginia, Arkansas, North Carolina, and Tennessee joined in April—shortly after the Civil War had already begun.)

The Civil War, also called the War of Secession and the War Between the States, began on April 12, 1861, when southern troops fired on Fort

A grisly aftermath of the famous Battle of Gettysburg.

Sumter, a U.S. military post in Charleston, South Carolina, and brutal fighting continued for four years. On April 9, 1865, General Robert E. Lee surrendered his ragged Confederate troops to Union General Ulysses S. Grant at Appomattox Court House, Virginia. The war had not only been between the states—it had also been between brothers: the conflict not only divided the nation, it had also divided families. The Civil War took more American lives than any other war in history.

What was the **Sioux Uprising**?

The uprising took place in August and September 1862 in southwestern Minnesota when the Sioux there had been suddenly made to give up half their reservation lands. Their situation was made worse by crop failures. Meantime, while the government debated over whether it would make the payments it owed to Indian nations in gold or in paper currency, the Sioux were also without money. The U.S. agent at the Sioux reservation refused to give out any food to the Indians until their money arrived from Washington. As the Indians grew hungry and angry, white observers could see there was trouble coming and warned the govern-

107

ment. But the situation soon erupted when, in August, four young men who were having a shooting contest suddenly fired into a party of whites, killing five people. The Sioux refused to surrender the four men to the authorities, and, under the leadership of Chief Little Crow, they began to raid white settlements in the Minnesota River valley. A small U.S. military force sent out against the Sioux was annihilated. After-wards, white settlers fled from the region in panic.

On September 23, Minnesota sent out 1,400 men who defeated Little Crow at the Battle of Wood Lake. The raids had already claimed the lives of 490 white civilians. Thirty-three Sioux were killed in the fighting with the military. While most of the Indians, who had taken up arms, fled to the Dakotas, the government began to round up native men who were suspected of participating in the campaign against white settlers. More than three hundred men were tried and sentenced to death—many of them on flimsy evidence. Episcopal Bishop Henry Whipple (1822–1901) interceded on their behalf, making a personal plea to President Lincoln. The Bishop was able to get 265 death sentences reduced to prison terms. But thirty-eight Sioux men, accused of murder or rape, were hung in a public ceremony on December 26, 1862. The Sioux reservation lands were broken up and the remaining Sioux were dispersed. Minnesota, nevertheless, continued to man military posts in that part of the state for years to come.

The events during and after the uprising were brutal for both sides, but many observers had seen that the treatment of the Sioux was going to lead to conflict: One missionary who witnessed the harsh way the policy with the Indians had been carried out, wrote to Bishop Whipple, saying, "if I were an Indian I would never lay down the war club while I lived."

What was **"Custer's Last Stand"**?

The term refers to the defeat of General George A. Custer (1839–76) at the Battle of Little Big Horn on June 25, 1876. Custer had a national reputation as a Civil War general and Indian fighter in the West, and when he and his troops were outnumbered and badly beaten by the Sioux, led by Sitting Bull—just as the country was about to celebrate the hundredth anniversary of the Declaration of Independence—the result was a stunning reversal in the national mood.

What were the Boer Wars?

They were conflicts between the British and the Afrikaners (or Boers, who were Dutch descendants living in South Africa) at the end of the nineteenth century in what is today South Africa. The first war, a Boer rebellion, had broken out in 1880 when the British and the Afrikaners fought over the Kimberley area (Griqualand West) where a diamond field had been discovered. The fighting lasted a year, at which time the South African Republic (established in 1856) was restored. But the stability would not last long: In 1886 gold was discovered in the Transvaal, and though the Afrikaner region was too strong for the British to attempt to annex it, they blocked the Afrikaners' access to the sea. In 1899, the Afrikaner republics of the Orange Free State and the Transvaal joined forces in a war against Britain. The fighting raged until 1902, when the Afrikaners surrendered. For a time after the Boer War, the Transvaal became a British crown colony. In 1910, the British government combined its holdings in southern Africa into the Union of South Africa.

Little Big Horn was part of a series of campaigns known collectively as the Sioux War. Several events led to the conflict that became Custer's Last Stand. The Sioux were nontreaty Indians, which is to say, they had refused to accept the white-dictated limits on their territory. They were outraged at the repeated violation of their lands by the onrush of miners to new gold strikes in the Black Hills of South Dakota. Further, there had been eight attacks by the Sioux on the Crow who were living on reservation land. Finally, Sitting Bull, the chief of the Hunkpapa band of Sioux, refused government demands that he and his people return to reservation lands. Meantime, unbeknownst to the government's military strategists, by the spring of 1876, Sitting Bull had been joined in his cause by other groups of northern Plains tribes, including the Cheyenne led by Crazy Horse. With the government set to use force to return Sitting Bull and his band of Sioux to reservations, the stage was set for a conflict—bigger than any Washington official had imagined.

When Custer rode into Montana territory with his Seventh Cavalry to meet the Sioux, despite orders from his commanding officer, General Alfred Terry, to simply contain the Indians and prevent their escape, he attacked. While historians remain divided on how Custer could have been defeated on that fateful June day, one thing remains certain: Custer and his men were badly outnumbered. Having divided his regiment into three parts, Custer rode with about 225 men against a force of at least 2,000—the largest gathering of Indian warriors in western history. Custer and his soldiers all died. The fighting continued into the next day, with those Indians that remained finally disbanding and returning to their designated territory. Eventually, Sitting Bull and his band had retreated into Canada. Returning to the United States five years later, in 1890, Sitting Bull was killed by authorities.

The battle became the subject of countless movies, books, and songs. It's remembered by some Native Americans as a galvanizing force—proof that brave men who fight for what they believe in can win.

SPANISH–AMERICAN WAR

Why was the **Spanish-American War** fought?

The 1898 war, which lasted only a matter of months (late-April to mid-August) was fought over the liberation of Cuba. During the 1870s, the Cuban people rebelled against Spanish rule. But once that long rebellion had been put down, peace on the Caribbean island did not hold: worsening economic conditions prompted revolution in 1895. American leaders, the bloody American Civil War still in their memories, feared that while the Cuban rebels could not win their battle against the Spanish, suspected the Spanish weren't strong enough to fully put down the insurrection, either. Meanwhile, the American public, fed by a steady stream of newspaper accounts reporting oppressive conditions on the island, increasingly supported U.S. intervention in the Cuban conflict.

In November 1897, President William McKinley did intervene but as a result of political, rather than military, pressure. Consequently, Spain granted Cuba limited self-government within the Spanish empire. However, the move did not satisfy the Cuban rebels, who were determined to achieve independence from Spain. And the fighting continued. Rioting broke out in Havana and in order to protect Americans living there, the U.S. sent the battleship *Maine* to the port on January 25, 1898. On February 15, an explosion blew up the *Maine*, killing more than two hundred people. Blame was promptly—and history would later conclude wrongly—assigned to Spain. While President McKinley again made several attempts to pressure Spain into granting Cuba full independence, it was to no avail. Nevertheless, on April 19, the U.S. Congress passed a joint resolution recognizing an independent Cuba, disclaiming American intention to acquire the island, and authorizing the use of the American army and navy to force Spanish withdrawal. On April 25, the U.S. formally declared that the country was in a state of war with Spain.

In the months that followed, American forces battled the Spanish and Spanish-loyalists in Cuba and the Spanish-controlled Philippines. There was also military activity on Puerto Rico, however, the American forces there met little resistance. Once Santiago, Cuba, was surrendered by the Spanish after the battle at San Juan Hill in July of 1898, it would only be a matter of weeks before a cease-fire was called and an armistice was signed (on August 12), ending the brief war.

What was **San Juan Hill** all about?

On July 1, 1898, during the Spanish-American War, Colonel Theodore Roosevelt led his American troops, known as the Rough Riders, on an attack of the Spanish blockhouse (a small fort) on San Juan Hill, near Santiago, Cuba. Newspaper reports made Roosevelt and the Rough Riders into celebrities, and even after he became U.S. President, Teddy Roosevelt remarked that "San Juan was the greatest day of my life."

San Juan Hill was part of a two-pronged assault on Santiago. While the Rough Riders Regiment attacked the Spanish defenses at San Juan and Kettle hills, another American division, led by General Henry Lawton, captured the Spanish fort at El Caney. The success of the two initiatives on July 1 combined to give the Americans command over the ridges surrounding Santiago. By July 3, the American forces had destroyed Admi-

WARS, OVERTHROWS, & REVOLUTIONS

111

ral Pascual Cervera y Topete's Spanish fleet there. On July 17, the Spanish surrendered the city.

Though the victory was critical to the outcome of the war, the assault on Kettle Hill and San Juan Hill had come at a high price: 1,600 American lives were lost, in a battle that had seen American troops—black and white—fight the Spanish shoulder to shoulder.

What is the **Treaty of Paris**?

There has been more than one Treaty of Paris, but among the most well-known are those of 1783, 1898, and 1951. On September 3, 1783, the Treaty of Paris, which had been under negotiation since 1782, was signed by the British and the Americans, represented by statesmen Benjamin Franklin, John Adams, and John Jay. The agreement officially ended the American Revolution, establishing the United States as an independent country and drawing the boundaries of the new nation—which extended west to the Mississippi River, north to Canada, east to the Atlantic Ocean, and south to Florida, which was given to Spain.

The Treaty of Paris, signed December 10, 1898, settled the conflict that had resulted in the Spanish-American War. This Treaty of Paris, at last, provided for Cuba's full independence from Spain. It also granted control of Guam and Puerto Rico to the United States. The treaty further stipulated that the United States would pay Spain $20 million for the Philippine Islands. However, having done so, the U.S. would soon find the Pacific archipelago embroiled in a conflict similar to the one it had seen on Cuba: Filipinos, determined to achieve independence, promptly revolted in an uprising that lasted from 1899–1901. A civil government was established on the Philippines in 1901, and in November 1935, the Commonwealth of the Philippines was officially established. However, the islands would continue to be the site of conflict in the coming decades, as the United States, again, struggled with a foreign power—this time the Japanese—for control of the Philippines during World War II.

In 1951, in the wake of World War II, Belgium, France, Italy, Luxembourg, the Netherlands, and West Germany signed the Treaty of Paris, which established the European Coal and Steel Community (ECSC). The desire was to bring about economic and political unity among the democratic nations of Europe. This agreement paved the way for the European Union effected by the Maastricht Treaty, an economic agreement signed by representatives of twelve European countries in the Netherlands in 1992.

MEXICAN REVOLUTION

What does **"Viva Zapata!"** mean?

It was the cry that went up in support of the rebel general Emiliano Zapata (1879–1919) whose chief concern during the Mexican Revolution (1910–20) was the distribution of land to the people. An advocate of Mexico's lower classes, Zapata began revolutionary activities against the government of Porfiro Diaz (1830–1915) as early as 1897. Zapata rose to prominence in helping the liberal and idealistic Francisco Madero overthrow Diaz in 1911. With Madero placed in power, Zapata promptly began pressing him for a program to distribute the hacienda (large estate) lands to the peasants. Rebuffed by Madero that same year, Zapata drafted the agrarian Plan of Ayala and renewed the revolution. Madero's government never achieved stability and proved to be ineffective, prompting a second overthrow in 1913: Victoriano Huerta seized power from Madero, the man he had helped put into office, and in the chaos surrounding the coup, Madero was shot and killed.

But Zapata refused to support Huerta and remained a leader of the revolution, continuing his crusade for the people—who supported him with cheers of "Viva Zapata!", meaning "long live Zapata!" The bitter fighting of the revolution continued and soon those who had supported the slain Madero—including Zapata and Pancho Villa—threw their backing behind another revolutionary, Venustiano Carranza. In 1914, Carranza's forces occupied Mexico City and forced Huerta to leave the country. No sooner had Carranza taken office than the revolutionaries began fighting among themselves. Zapata and Pancho Villa demanded dramatic reforms and together they attacked Mexico City in 1914. Five years later, and one year before the end of the revolution, Carranza's army ambushed and assassinated Zapata in his home state of Morelos.

113

Why did the **U.S. government** send troops after **Pancho Villa**?

Villa was sought by the U.S. government because he and his followers had been attacking Americans in 1916—on both sides of the border. In 1915, the United States decided it would back the acting chief of Mexico, Venustiano Carranza, even as he faced attacks from two of his fellow revolutionaries, Emiliano Zapata and Pancho Villa. Four years earlier, Villa (c. 1877–1923) himself had sought to control Mexico after the fall of President Profirio Diaz and was a fierce fighter. When the United States cut off the flow of ammunition to the rebels, Villa earned himself a reputation as a bandit, seeking revenge on Americans in Mexico by stopping trains and shooting the passengers. In 1916, Villa raided the small New Mexican village of Columbus where he killed eighteen people. The attack prompted President Woodrow Wilson to send U.S. soldiers to hunt Villa down and capture him. Though thousands of men were put on the initiative under General John Pershing, they never caught up with the bandit. Wilson withdrew the forces from Mexico after the government there expressed resentment for the U.S. effort—which the Mexican people, President Carranza included, viewed as a meddlesome American interference in the Mexican Revolution. The revolution ended three years later, after ten years of fighting and disorder.

RUSSIAN REVOLUTION

What was **Bloody Sunday**?

The January 22, 1905 event, which is also known as Red Sunday, signaled the beginning of revolutionary activity in Russia that would not end until 1917. On that winter day, the young Russian Orthodox priest, Georgi Gapon, carrying a cross over his shoulder, led what was intended to be a peaceful workers' demonstration in front of the Winter Palace at St. Petersburg. But, as a *London Times* correspondent reported that day, when the crowd was refused entry into the common gathering ground of the Palace Square, "the passions of the mob broke loose like a bursting dam." The Cossack guards and troops, still loyal to the Romanov Tsar Nicholas II (despite Father Gapon's thinking that they too would join the workers in protest), shot into the crowd of demonstrators, killing about one hundred and fifty people— women, children, and young people among them.

Father Gapon, who had intended to deliver to the Tsar a petition on behalf of the workers, was injured during the day's events and later fled in exile. His thinking that the palace guards would come over to the workers' side was not his only miscalculation: Tsar Nicholas was not even at the palace that Sunday, having left days earlier. But Nicholas's reign was threatened by his troops' response to the gathering crowd—so horrific was the bloodshed that the snow-covered streets of St. Petersburg were stained in red: The correspondent for the French newspaper *Le Matin* reported that the Cossacks had opened fire "as if they were playing at bloodshed." The event sent shockwaves through the country, where hostilities had been mounting against Nicholas's ineffective government, and stirred up unrest elsewhere, including in Moscow— where, in a related event, the Tsar's uncle, Grand Duke Serge, was killed in early February. The death was a sure sign that popular anger had centered on the Tsar and his family. In the countryside, the peasants rose up against their landlords, seizing land, crops, and livestock. The events foreshadowed the downfall of tsarist Russia: Though the outbreak in 1905 was unsuccessful in effecting any change and Nicholas remained in power for twelve more years, he was the last tsar to rule Russia.

What did **Rasputin** have to do with the **Russian Revolution**?

Grigory Rasputin (1872–1916) was a Russian mystic and quasi-holy man who rose from peasant farmer to become adviser to Tsar Nicholas II and his wife, Tsarina Alexandra. Sometime in 1905 or shortly thereafter, Alexandra had come into contact with Rasputin, and, showing he was able to effectively treat Nicholas's and Alexandra's severely hemophiliac son Alexis, Rasputin quickly gained favor with the Russian rulers. But the prime minister and members of the legislative assembly, the Duma, could see Rasputin was a disreputable character and they feared his baneful influence on the Tsar. They even tried to exile Rasputin, but to no avail.

By 1913, one year before the outbreak of World War I, the Russian people had become acutely aware of Tsar Nicholas's weakness as a ruler—   115 not only was his government subject to the influence of a pretender like Rasputin, but the events of Bloody Sunday had forever marred the Tsar's reputation. That year, the Romanov Dynasty was marking its three hundredth anniversary: members of the royal family had ruled Russia since 1613. But public celebrations, intended to be jubilant affairs, were instead ominous, as the crowds greeted Nicholas's public appearances with silence.

Russia's entry into World War I proved to be the beginning of the end for Tsar Nicholas, with Rasputin at the front and center of the controversy that swirled around the royal court. During the first year of fighting against Germany, Russia suffered one military catastrophe after another. These losses did further damage to the Tsar and his ministers. In the fall of 1915, urged on by his wife, Nicholas left St. Petersburg and headed to the front, to lead the Russian troops in battle himself. With Alexandra left in charge of government affairs, Rasputin's influence became more dangerous than ever. But in December 1916, a group of aristocrats put an end to it once and for all when, during a palace party, they laced Rasputin's wine with cyanide. Though the posion failed to kill Rasputin, the noblemen shot him and deposited his body in a river later that night. Nevertheless, the damage to Nicholas and Alexandra had already been done: By that time virtually all educated Russians opposed the Tsar, who had removed many capable officials from government office, only to replace them with weak and incompetent executives who had been appointed because they were favored by Rasputin. The stage had been set for revolution.

What was the **Bolshevik Revolution**?

It was the November 1917 revolution in which the Bolsheviks—an extremist faction within the Russian Social Democratic Labor Party (later renamed the Russian Communist Party)—seized control of the government, ushering in the Soviet age. The event is also known as the October Revolution—since by the old Russian calendar (in use until 1918), the government takeover had happened on October 25.

The Bolshevik Revolution was the culmination of a series of events in 1917. In March, Russia, still in the midst of World War I, was in bad shape: shortages of food and fuel made conditions miserable. The people had lost faith in the war effort and were loathe to support it by sending any more young men into battle—only to never return. In the Russian capital of Petrograd (which had been known as St. Petersburg until 1914), workers went on strike and rioting broke out. In the chaos (called the March Revolution), Tsar Nicholas ordered the legislative body, the Duma, to disband, but instead the representatives set up a provisional government. Having lost all political influence, Nicholas abdicated the throne on March 15. He and his family were imprisoned and are believed to have been killed in July of the following year.

Hearing of Nicholas's abdication, longtime political exile Vladimir Lenin (1870–1924) returned from Europe to Petrograd where he led the Bolsheviks in rallying the Russian people with calls for peace, land reform, and worker empowerment (their slogan was "Land, Peace, and Bread"). The Bolsheviks grew in numbers and became increasingly radical, in spite of efforts by the provisional government headed by revolutionary Alexander Kerensky (1881–1970) to curb the Bolsheviks' influence. The only Socialist member of the first provisional government, Kerensky's government proved ineffective and failed to meet the demands of the people. He also failed to end the country's involvement in World War I, which the Bolsheviks viewed as an imperialistic war.

On November 7, the Bolsheviks led workers and disgruntled soldiers and sailors in a takeover of Petrograd's Winter Palace, the scene of Bloody Sunday in 1905 and which had, in 1917, become the headquarters of Kerensky's provisional government. By November 8, the provisional government had fallen.

What was the **Red Terror**?

The Red Terror was the brutal coercion used by the Communists during the tumultuous years of civil unrest that followed the Bolshevik Revolution of November 1917. After the revolution, the Bolsheviks, now called Communists, put their leader Vladimir Lenin into power. Delivering on the Bolshevik promise to end the country's involvement in World War I, Lenin immediately called for peace talks with Germany, ending the fighting on the Eastern Front. (Germany and the other Central Powers would be prevented from victory on the Western Front by the entry of the United States into the war that same year.) But the Brest-Litovsk

Treaty, signed March 3, 1918, dictated harsh—and many believed humiliating—terms to Russia, which was forced to give up vast territories including Finland, Poland, Belarus, Ukraine, Moldavia, and the Baltic States of Estonia, Latvia, and Lithuania.

Meanwhile, Russians had elected officials to a parliamentary assembly. But when the results were unfavorable to Lenin (of the 703 deputies chosen, only 168 were Communists), he ordered his troops to bar the deputies from convening, and so the assembly was permanently disbanded. In its place, Lenin established a dictatorship based on Communist secret police, the Cheka. Further, the radical social reforms he had promised took the form of government takeover of Russia's industries and the seizure of farm products from the peasants. Lenin's hard-handed tactics created opposition to the Communists—colloquially known as the "Reds." The opposition organized their "White" army, and civil war ensued. In September 1918, Lenin was nearly assassinated by a political opponent, prompting Lenin's supporters to organize the retaliative initiative that came to be known as the Red Terror. Though thousands of Communist opponents were killed as a result, the unrest in Russia would not end until 1920. And some believe the ruthless repression of the Red Terror lasted into 1924.

WORLD WAR I

How did **World War I** start?

Though the Great War, as it was called until World War II, was sparked by the June 28, 1914, assassination of Archduke Francis Ferdinand of Austria-Hungary, the war in Europe had been precipitated by several developments. National pride had been growing among Europeans; nations increased their armed forces through drafts; and colonialism was a focus of the European powers, as they competed with each other for control of lands in far off places. Furthermore, weapons and other implements of war had been improved by industry—making them deadlier than ever. So, on that June day in the city of Sarajevo (then the capital of Austria-Hungary's province of Bosnia-Herzegovina), when a gunman named Gavrilo Princip shot down Archduke Ferdinand, it was not surprising that Austria-Hungary responded with force. Since Princip was known to have ties to a Serbian terrorist organization, Austria-Hungary declared war on Serbia. Both sides, however, believed that the battle would be decided quickly. But instead fighting would spread, involving more countries. Four years of fighting—aided by the airplane, the submarine, tanks, and machine guns—would cause greater destruction than any other war to that date.

What **alliances** were forged **during World War I**?

In its declaration of war against Serbia in late July 1914, Austria-Hungary was joined in early August by its ally Germany, which together formed the Central Powers. In October 1914, Bulgaria and the Ottoman Empire joined the Central Powers. (The Allies declared war on the Ottoman Empire in November 1914, after Turkish ships bombarded Russian ports on the Black Sea and Turkish troops invaded Russia.)

When the fighting began, France, Britain, and Russia threw their support behind Serbia, and together were known as the Allies. Eventually, twenty more nations joined the Allies, but not all of them sent troops to the front. Belgium, Montenegro, and Japan joined the Allies in August 1914, with Japan declaring war on Germany and invading several Pacific islands to drive out the Germans. In 1915, Italy and San Marino joined; as fighting wore on, in 1916, Romania and Portugal became Allied nations; and 1917 saw the entry of eight countries, most notably the United States and China, but also Liberia, Greece, Siam, Panama, Cuba, and Brazil. Before the war ended in 1918, Guatemala, Haiti, Honduras, Costa Rica, and Nicaragua all became supporters of the Allies.

What did the *Lusitania* have to do with **World War I**?

World War I was already under way when, in May 7th of 1915, a German U-boat sank the British passenger ship, the S.S. *Lusitania* off the coast of Ireland. The ship had been launched in 1907 by Britain's Cunard Line to become the largest passenger ship afloat. When she was downed in the North Atlantic, 1,200 civilians, including 128 American travelers, were killed. President Woodrow Wilson warned Germany that another

Why did the United States get involved in World War I?

When war broke out in Europe in August 1914, Americans opposed the involvement of U.S. troops, and President Woodrow Wilson declared the country's neutrality. But as the fighting continued and the German tactics threatened civilian lives, Americans began siding with the Allies.

After the sinking of the passenger liner S.S. *Lusitania*, Germany adopted restricted submarine warfare. But early in 1917, Germany again began attacking unarmed ships, this time U.S. cargo boats, goading the United States into the war. Meantime, German U-boats were positioning to cut off shipping to and from Britain, in an effort to force the power to surrender. Tensions between the United States and Germany peaked when the British intercepted, decoded, and turned over to President Wilson a message Germany had sent to its ambassador in Mexico. The so-called "Zimmerman note," which originated in the office of German foreign minister Arthur Zimmerman, urged the German officials in Mexico to persuade the Mexican government into war with the United States. The message was published in the United States in early March. One month later, on April 6, 1917, Congress declared war on Germany after President Wilson had asserted that "the world must be made safe for democracy."

such incident would force the United States into entering the war. They heeded the warning only for a time.

How did **World War I end**?

Though the U.S. had been little prepared to enter the war, the American government mobilized quickly to rally the troops—and the citizens—behind the war effort: In April 1917, the U.S. Regular Army was comprised of just over one hundred thousand men; by the end of the war, the American armed forces stood some five million strong. It was the arrival of the U.S. troops that gave the Allies the manpower they needed to win the war. After continued fighting in the trenches of Europe, which had left almost ten million dead, in November 1918, Germany agreed to an armistice and the Central Powers finally surrendered. In January 1919, Allied representatives gathered in Paris to draw up the peace settlement.

Who were the **Big Four**?

Though the Paris Peace Conference, which began in January 1919, was attended by representatives of all the Allied nations, the decisions were made by four heads of government, called the Big Four—U.S. President Woodrow Wilson, British Prime Minister David Lloyd George, French Premier Georges Clemenceau, and Italian Premier Vittorio Orlando. Other representatives formed committees to work out the details of the treaties that were drawn up with each of the countries that had made up World War I's Central Powers: the Treaty of Versailles was with Germany, the Treaty of St.-Germain was signed with Austria, the Treaty of Neuilly was made with Bulgaria, the Treaty of Trianon was with Hungary, and the Treaty of Sevres with the Ottoman Empire.

How were **Europe's lines** redrawn as a **result of World War I**?

The treaties that came out of the Paris Peace Conference (1919–20) redrew Europe's boundaries—carving new nations out of the defeated powers. The Treaty of Versailles forced Germany to give up territory to Belgium, Czechoslovakia, Denmark, France, and Poland. Germany also forfeited all its overseas colonies and turned over coal fields to France for the next fifteen years. The treaties of St.-Germain and Trianon toppled the former empire of Austria-Hungary (whose archduke had been assassinated in 1914, triggering the war) so that the separate nations of Austria and Hungary were formed, each occupying less than a third of their former area. Their former territory was divided among Italy, Romania, and the countries newly recognized by the treaties—Czechoslovakia, Poland, and the kingdom that later became Yugoslavia. The Treaty of Sevres took Mesopotamia (present-day Iraq), Palestine, and Syria away from the Ottoman Empire, which three years later became the Republic of Turkey. Finally, Bulgaria lost territory to Greece and Romania. However, these new borders would serve to heighten tensions between some countries, as the territorial claims of the newly redrawn nations overlapped with each other.

How did the **Treaty of Versailles** pave the way for **World War II**?

In the aftermath of World War I, Germany was severely punished: One clause in the Treaty of Versailles even stipulated that Germany take responsibility for causing the war. In addition to its territorial losses, Germany was also made to pay for an Allied military force that would occupy the west bank of the Rhine River, intended to keep Germany in check for the next fifteen years. The treaty also limited the size of Germany's military. In 1921, Germany received a bill for reparations: It owed the Allies $33 million.

While the postwar German government had been made to sign the Treaty of Versailles under threat of more fighting from the Allies, the German people nevertheless faulted their leaders for accepting such strident terms. Not only was the German government weakened, but public resentment over the Treaty of Versailles soon developed into a strong nationalist movement—led by one Adolf Hitler.

What was the **Sino-Japanese War**?

There were actually two such wars fought between China and Japan: the first, usually referred to as the Chinese-Japanese War, was in 1894–95 and the second one, referred to as the Sino-Japanese War, began in 1937 but was "absorbed" by World War II.

The war in the late 1800s was fought over control of Korea, which was a vassal state of China. When an uprising broke out in Korea in 1894, China sent in troops to suppress it. Korea's ports had been open to Japan since 1876 and in order to protect its interests there, Japan, too, sent troops to the island nation when trouble broke out. But once the rebellion had been put down, the Japanese troops refused to withdraw. In July 1894, fighting broke out between Japan and China, with Japan emerging as the victor, having crushed China's navy. A peace treaty signed on April 17, 1895, provided for an independent Korea (which only lasted until 1910, when Japan took possession) and for China to turn over to Japan the island of Taiwan and the Liaodong Peninsula (the peninsula was later returned to China for a fee after Russia, Germany, and France forced Japan to return it). The war, though relatively brief, seriously weakened China, and in the imperialist years that followed, the European powers scrambled for land concessions there.

The second war between the Asian powers developed in 1937 when Japan, having already taken Manchuria and the Jehol Province from China, attacked China again. Though China was in the midst of internal conflict—with the nationalist forces of Generalissimo Chiang Kai-shek fighting the Communists under Mao Tse-tung, China nevertheless turned its attention to fighting foreign aggressor. The fighting between the two countries continued into 1941 before war was offically declared by China. In so doing, China was at war not only with the Japanese but their allies as well—Germany and Italy. The conflict then became part of World War II. The second Chinese-Japanese war ended with the surrender of Japan to the Allies in September 1945.

What was the **Boxer Rebellion**?

It was a Chinese uprising in 1900, which was put down through the combined forces of eight foreign countries including Germany, Italy, Japan, Russia, and the United States. The Chinese-Japanese War (1894–95) had seriously weakened China and in 1898, the country agreed to lease its Kiaochow region to Germany. Soon other European countries followed suit and before long, Western influence was being felt in China. This angered many Chinese, including members of a secret society that opposed the Manchu government for having allowed the foreign incursions. Being an athletic group of young men, this group was called "Boxers" by China's Westerners.

Between June 21 and August 14, 1900, Boxers rebelled against anything foreign and began a raid of the country that was intended to drive out all foreign influence. The uprising was aimed at not only Westerners and foreign diplomats, but also missionaries, Chinese Christians, and any Chinese who were thought to support Western ideas. Houses, schools, and churches were burned. Much of the destruction was in Beijing and when foreign diplomats there called for help, it arrived from eight countries. The Manchu government did not welcome this interference in its affairs and promptly declared war on the eight nations.

On September 7, 1901, the Manchu government signed a peace settlement with the foreign countries. The Boxer Protocol called for China to punish officials who had been involved in the rebellion and pay damages in the hundreds of millions of dollars. The United States, Britain, and Japan later returned part of the money to China, specifying that it be used for educational purposes.

WORLD WAR II

How did **World War II start**?

The war began on September 1, 1939, when Germany invaded Poland, which was soon crushed by Adolf Hitler's war machine. But while the Nazis moved in from the west, Poland was under attack by the Soviets from the north and east. The events in the eastern European country had set the stage for a major conflict.

After Poland, the Germans moved into Denmark, Luxembourg, the Netherlands, Belgium, Norway, and France, taking control as they went. By June 1940, only Great Britain stood against Hitler, who was joined by Axis power Italy. Before long, fighting had spread into Greece and northern Africa.

In June 1941, Germany invaded the Soviet Union, enlarging the scope of the conflict again. The world's focus on war-torn Europe, Japan executed a surprise attack on the U.S. military bases at Pearl Harbor, Hawaii, in December 1941, which involved Americans in the war.

How **many countries** were part of the **Axis powers**?

The Axis, which was forged in 1936, included an alliance of three nations—Germany, Italy, and Japan. These major powers were joined by six smaller countries, the Axis "satellites"—Albania, Bulgaria, Finland, Hungary, Romania, and Thailand. But together these countries never comprised the unified front and strength that the Allied powers did.

Adolf Hitler looks on at a rally in Nuremberg.

Germany started the war on September 1, 1939, and was joined in June of 1940 by Italy and Albania. In the middle of 1941, Bulgaria, Hungary, Romania, and Finland joined the Axis effort. Japan entered the war on December 7, 1941 with its attack on the U.S. Navy Base at Pearl Harbor, Hawaii. Thailand was the last Axis country to enter the war, on January 25, 1942.

Which **countries** comprised the **Allies in World War II**?

The three major Allied powers were Great Britain, the United States, and Soviet Union. Their leaders, Winston Churchill, Franklin Roosevelt, and   **125**

Joseph Stalin, were referred to as the Big Three. These leaders and their military advisors developed the strategy to defeat the Axis countries—though Stalin, for the most part, acted alone on the Soviet front. China also joined the Allies, as a major power. Forty-six other countries became part of the Allied front before the war was over.

Poland, invaded by powerful Germany, entered the war on September 1, 1939, and within days, Great Britain entered into fighting against Germany. Australia, New Zealand, India, France, South Africa, and Canada also allied with Great Britain, as did Norway, Denmark, Belgium, the Netherlands, and Luxembourg in 1940—all of them under siege by Nazi Germany. Greece entered the war later that year, as did Yugoslavia in the spring of 1941. It was June 22, 1941 that the Soviet Union entered the war. And in the days after the Japanese bombing of the U.S. naval base at Pearl Harbor, Hawaii, on December 7, 1941, twelve more Allied countries became involved in the war, chief among them, the United States and China. (The others, with the exception of Czechoslovakia, were all Latin American countries—Panama, Costa Rica, the Dominican Republic, Haiti, Nicaragua, El Salvador, Honduras, Cuba, and Guatemala.) The year 1942 saw three more countries join the Allies—Mexico in May, Brazil in August, and Ethiopia in December. In 1943 and 1944—in what were perhaps the darkest days of the war—Iraq, Bolivia, Iran, and Columbia joined the effort, followed by the tiny country of San Marino (significant since it is situated wholly within the boundaries of Italy), Colombia, and Liberia. February and March of 1945 saw another wave of nations siding with the Allies—the South American countries of Ecuador, Paraguay, Peru, Chile, Venezuela, Uruguay, and Argentina; along with the Middle Eastern countries of Egypt, Syria, Lebanon, and Saudi Arabia. Mongolia (the Mongolian People's Republic), in Central Asia, was the last to join the Allies, on August 9, 1945.

What is **D-day**?

The military uses the term D-day to designate when an initiative is set to begin, counting all events out from that date for planning. For example, "D-day minus two" would be a plan for what needs to happen two days before the beginning of the military operation. While the military planned and executed many D-days during World War II, most of them

What was the Battle of the Bulge?

The term refers to the December 16, 1944, German confrontation with the American forces in the Ardennes Mountains, a forested plateau range that extends from northern France into Belgium and Luxembourg. Even though Germany appeared to be beaten at this late point in the war, Hitler rallied his remaining forces together and launched a surprise assault on the American soldiers in Belgium and Luxembourg. But Germany could not sustain the front, and within two weeks, the Americans had halted the German advance near Belgium's Meuse River. The offensive became known as the Battle of the Bulge because of the shape of the battleground on a map.

The Ardennes Mountains were also the site of conflict earlier in World War II (in 1940) as well as in World War I (in 1914 and 1918).

landings on enemy-held coasts, it was the June 6, 1944, invasion of Normandy that went down in history as *the* D-Day.

Why is **Normandy** so famous?

Normandy, a region in northwestern France that lies along the English Channel, is known for the June 6, 1944 arrival of Allied troops, which proved to be a turning point in World War II. Officially called Operation Overlord and headed by General Dwight D. Eisenhower, the initiative had been in the planning since 1943 and it constituted the largest seaborne invasion in history. After several delays due to poor weather, the Allied troops crossed the English Channel and arrived on the beaches of Normandy on the morning of June 6. At the end of the day, they had taken hold of the beaches—a firm foothold that would allow Allied troops to march inland against the Nazis, pushing them back to Germany. Eleven months of bloody conflict followed before the May 7, 1945 German surrender.

Why did the **Japanese** attack **Pearl Harbor**?

There is still disagreement among historians, military scholars, and investigators about why the island nation of Japan issued this surprise attack on the U.S. military at Pearl Harbor. Some believe that Japan had been baited into making the attack in order to marshal public opinion behind U.S. entry into World War II; others maintain that the United States was unprepared for such an assault, or at least, the Japanese believed Americans to be in a state of unreadiness; and still others theorize that Pearl Harbor was an all-or-nothing gamble on the part of Japan to knock America's navy out of the war before it had even entered into the fray.

The facts are these: In 1941, Japanese troops had moved into the southern part of Indochina, prompting the United States to cut off its exports to Japan. In fall of that year, as General Hideki Tojo became prime minister of Japan, the country's military leaders were laying plans to wage war on the United States. On December 7, Pearl Harbor, the hub of U.S. naval power in the Pacific, became the target of Japanese attacks, as did the American military bases at Guam, Wake Island, and the Philippines. But it was the bombing of Pearl Harbor that became the rallying cry for Americans during the long days of World War II—since it was at this strategic naval station, which had been occupied under treaty by the U.S. military since 1908, that Americans had felt the impact of the conflict.

What happened at **Pearl Harbor**?

On the night before the attack, the Japanese moved a fleet of thirty-three ships to within two hundred miles of the Hawaiian island of Oahu, where Pearl Harbor is situated. More than three hundred planes took off from the Japanese carriers, dropping the first bombs on Pearl Harbor just before eight o'clock in the morning on December 7, 1941. There were eight American battleships and more than ninety naval vessels in the harbor at the time. Twenty-one of these were destroyed or damaged, as were three hundred planes. The biggest single loss of the day was the sinking of the battleship U.S.S. *Arizona*, which went down in less than nine minutes. More than half the fatalities at Pearl Harbor that infamous December day were lost on the *Arizona*. By the end of the raid, more than 2,300 people had been killed and about the same number were wounded.

Pearl Harbor forever changed the United States and its role in the world. When President Franklin Roosevelt addressed Congress the next day, he called December 7 "a date which will live in infamy." The United States declared war against Japan, and three days later, on December 11, Germany and Italy—Japan's Axis allies—declared war on the United States. The events of December 7 had brought America into the war, a conflict from which it would emerge as the leader of the Free World.

Why did **General MacArthur** vow to return?

Two weeks after the Japanese bombing of the U.S. military bases at Pearl Harbor and the Philippines, Japan invaded the Philippine Islands. General Douglas MacArthur (1880–1964), the commander of the Army forces in the Far East, led the U.S. defense of the archipelago. He had begun to organize his troops around Manila Bay when in March 1942, he received orders from the President to leave the islands. When he reached Australia, MacArthur said, "I shall return," in reference to the Philippines. Under new commands, MacArthur directed the Allied forces' offensive against Japan throughout the Southwest Pacific Islands. After a string of successes, on October 20, 1944, MacArthur made good on his promise, landing on the Philippine island of Leyte, accompanied by a great invasion force. By July of the following year, the general had established practical control of the Philippines. When Japan surrendered in August, MacArthur was made the supreme commander of the Allies, and as such, he presided over the Japanese surrender aboard the U.S.S. *Missouri* on September 2. He received the Medal of Honor for his defense of the Philippines, but he wasn't the only hero in the MacArthur family: his father had received the nation's highest military award during the Civil War.

Who was **"Rosie the Riveter"**?

The term referred to the American women who worked factory jobs as part of the war effort on the home front, where auto plants and other industrial facilities were converted into defense plants to manufacture airplanes, ships, and weapons. As World War II wore on, more and more men went overseas to fight, resulting in a shortage of civilian men. And so, women pitched in. However, at the end of the war, many of these women were displaced as the men returned to their jobs and civilian life. Nevertheless, the contribution of Rosie the Riveter was instrumental to the war effort.

Who was "Tokyo Rose"?

Wartime radio broadcasts by a woman calling herself Tokyo Rose were a propaganda effort intended to weaken the resolve of the American and Allied troops. Axis nations hired one Iva d'Aquino, a traitor, to broadcast what were supposed to be demoralizing messages from Japan. Heard by soldiers and sailors in the Pacific, they either disregarded the messages or found them mildly amusing. The Axis powers did the same from Germany where "Axis Sally" aired messages that were heard in Europe. The Allied powers also engaged in some psychological warfare: American planes dropped pamphlets over Germany, telling of Nazi defeats.

How did World War II end?

In 1944, three years after the United States entered the war, the Allied forces commandeered full frontal assaults on the two major Axis forces: Germany and Japan. On June 6, 1944, the Allied forces invaded Normandy, causing the Nazi troops to retreat within their own borders. With an onslaught of bombings in major German cities, including Hamburg, the Nazis were irreversibly weakened. After successfully liberating Russia, thousands of Allied troops, made up of American, British, Canadian, and Russian soldiers, invaded Germany on March 4, 1945. The following month, sensing imminent defeat, Adolf Hitler commited suicide. On May 6, 1945, Germany surrendered, which ended the war in Europe.

However, the battle with Japanese forces would seem quite the challenge for the Allied troops. Even though the Japanese troops endured many upsets, a hope for a surrender seemed distant as Japan adopted a "fight to the death" philosophy with its use of two thousand kamikaze suicide planes.

Sensing that further conflict with Japan would result in more casualties for the Allied troops, President Truman sought for an immediate and effective end to the war. With Japan ignoring pleas for a surrender, on August 6, 1945, the B-29 *Enola Gay* dropped an atomic bomb on the

What are V-E Day and V-J Day?

V-E Day stands for Victory in Europe Day, and V-J Day stands for Victory over Japan Day. After the German surrender was signed in Reims, France (the headquarters of General Dwight D. Eisenhower), in the wee hours of May 7, 1945, U.S. President Harry S Truman declared May 8 V-E Day—the end of the World War II fighting in Europe.

But it was not until the Japanese agreed to surrender on August 15, 1945, that World War II ended. September 2, 1945, was declared the official V-J Day since it was then that Japan signed the terms of surrender on the U.S.S. *Missouri* anchored in Tokyo Bay.

Japanese city of Hiroshima, killing sixty thousand people. Three days later, another bomb was dropped on the city of Nagasaki, killing an additional thirty thousand soldiers and citizens. On August 15, 1945, Japan finally surrendered, ending a war that is estimated to have killed over fourteen million people (soldiers and citizens) worldwide.

Were any countries besides **Switzerland** neutral during **World War II**?

Yes, in its official stance of neutrality, Switzerland was joined by Spain, Portugal, Sweden, Turkey, and Argentina. However, findings during the late-1990s indicated the neutrality of these countries—with the exception of Argentina—was not an absolute policy. A 1998 report released by U.S. Undersecretary of State Stuart Eizenstat indicated that the Swiss had converted Nazi gold to Swiss francs and that Germany had used that exchange to buy minerals from Spain, Portugal, Sweden, and Turkey. The report further pointed out that Sweden had allowed a quarter of a million Nazi troops to cross its country in order to reach neighboring Finland, where the Germans fought Soviet forces.

Eizenstat, who headed a U.S. government effort to determine where Nazi gold ended up, was assisted in his research by State Department histori-

Nagasaki after the atomic bomb was dropped in 1945, causing a swift end to World War II.

ans. Although the investigation's reports were critical of these neutral countries, Eizenstat also pointed out that all of the countries were in difficult positions during the conflict—Switzerland was completely surrounded by German-occupied countries. Nevertheless, Jewish groups brought law suits against the Swiss government and three Swiss banks for their role in converting looted Nazi gold into currency during World War II.

How was it that **Anne Frank's diary** survived World War II?

The young German-Jewish girl's diaries, which chronicle twenty-six months of hiding from the German authorities in Amsterdam during World War II, were given to her father, Otto Frank, when he returned to Holland from Auschwitz after the war. The notebooks and papers had been left behind by the secret police, and were found in the Frank family's hiding place by two Dutch women who had helped the fugitives survive. Otto Frank published his daughter's diaries in 1947. Twenty years later, Doubleday released the English-language edition, *The Diary of a Young Girl*. It was subsequently made into a play and a film, both called *The Diary of Anne Frank*.

The diary is an astonishingly poignant account of the suffering—and heroism—during the Nazi occupation of the Netherlands. Anne Frank, born in 1929, had known religious persecution her entire life. She was only four years old when her family escaped Nazi Germany in 1933 and fled to the Netherlands. During the Nazi occupation of that country (beginning in 1942), the Frank family hid in a secret annex behind her father's office at 263 Prinsengracht in Amsterdam. It was there that Anne lived with seven others for just over two years, recording her thoughts in three notebooks. But the family was finally found by the Nazis, who arrested them and put them in German concentration camps. In March 1945, two months before the German surrender, Anne Frank died of typhoid fever in the Bergen-Belsen concentration camp. Of the eight who had hidden in the secret annex, Anne's father, Otto, was the only survivor.

Who is **Che Guevara**?

Ernesto "Che" Guevara (1928–67) was an idealist who became involved in revolutionary movements in at least three countries. The Argentinian, who had earned his degree in medicine in Buenos Aires in 1953, believed that social change and the elimination of poverty could only come about through armed conflict. Guevara met Fidel Castro in Mexico in 1954, and served his guerrilla forces as a physician and military commander during the Cuban Revolution (1956–59). Once in power, Castro appointed Guevara as president of the National Bank of Cuba. Between 1965 and 1967, Guevara became active in leftists movements in Congo and in Latin America. He was leading a force against the Bolivian government when he was killed in 1967.

How old is **guerrilla warfare**?

Guerrilla warfare dates back to ancient times but got its name during the Peninsular War of 1809–14 when Napoleon fought for control of the Iberian Peninsula (Spain and Portugal). In Spanish, *guerilla* means "small war." The resistance to Napoleon's troops employed tactics that are typical of what we know as guerrilla warfare—fighting in small bands, ambushes, sudden raids, and sabotage.

It is Chinese Communist leader Mao Tse Tung who, in his twenty-two-year fight against the Chinese Nationalists (1927–1949), is believed to have developed the techniques of modern guerrilla warfare. Chairman Mao slowly but surely gained the support and sympathy of the common people—in particular those living in rural areas. Eventually, he had control of the masses who believed the reforms he would make once in office would be favorable to them. The people would provide the manpower and supplies that would sustain the fight. If any followers faulted in their loyalty to the cause, they would be punished.

Today, guerrillas rely on terrorist attacks against governments, goading the military into action, which, in turn, rallies the public in its outrage against government. In this way, guerrilla movements can gain popular support over time. Such movements are by no means limited to the countryside: urban attacks, including kidnaping and assassination. Such guerrilla measures have led to the outbreak of civil wars.

Why did the **United States** get involved in the **Korean War**?

Americans became involved in the Korean conflict when the United Nations, only five years old, called upon member countries to give military support to South Korea, which had been invaded by troops from Communist-ruled North Korea on June 25, 1950. The UN considered the invasion to be a violation of international peace and called on the Communists to withdraw. When they did not, sixteen countries sent troops, and some forty countries sent supplies and military equipment to the aid of the South Korean armies. About 90 percent of the UN aid had come from the United States. But North Korea received aid too—the Chinese sent troops and the Soviet Union provided equipment for them to sustain the war, which lasted until July 27, 1953. After three years of fighting, an armistice was called, but a formal peace treaty was never drawn up between the neighboring countries, prompting the U.S. to maintain military forces in South Korea in an effort to discourage any acts of aggression from the north.

What was the **Vietnam War** all about?

In the simplest terms, the long conflict in Southeast Asia was fought over the unification of Communist North Vietnam and non-Communist

South Vietnam. The two countries had been set up in 1954. Prior to that, all of Vietnam was part of the French colony of Indochina. But in 1946, the Vietnamese fought the French for control of their own country. The United States provided financial support to France, but the French were ultimately defeated in 1954. Once France had withdrawn its troops, an international conference was convened in Geneva to decide what should be done with Vietnam. The country was divided along the 17th parallel into two partitions, which were not intended to be permanent. But the elections that were supposed to unify the partitions were never held. Ho Chi Minh took power in the north while Emperor Bao Dai, for a while, ruled the south.

But the Communist government in the north opposed the non-Communist government of South Vietnam and believed the country should still be united. The North Vietnamese supported anti-government groups in the south and over time, stepped up aid to those groups. These Communist-trained South Vietnamese were known as the Viet Cong. Between 1957 and 1965, the Viet Cong struggled against the South Vietnamese government. But in the mid-1960s, North Vietnam initiated a large-scale troop infiltration into South Vietnam and the fighting became a full-fledged war.

China and the Soviet Union provided the North Vietnamese with military equipment, but not manpower. The United States provided both equipment and troops to non-Communist South Vietnam in its struggle with the Viet Cong and North Vietnam. By 1969, there were more than half a million American troops in South Vietnam. This policy was controversial back in America, where protests to involvement in the Vietnam War continued until the last of the American troops were brought home in 1973. In January of that year, the two sides had agreed to a cease-fire, but the fighting broke out again after the American ground troops left. On April 30, 1975, South Vietnam surrendered to North Vietnam and the war, which had lasted nearly two decades, ended. North Vietnam unified the countries as the Socialist Republic of Vietnam.

For its part, the North Vietnamese called the conflict a "war of national liberation": They viewed the long struggle as an extension of the earlier struggle with France. They also perceived the war to be another attempt by a foreign power (this time the United States) to rule Vietnam.

A soldier fighting in Vietnam.

Why did the **United States** get **involved in Vietnam**?

The policy of involvement in the Vietnam conflict began when President Harry S Truman provided U.S. support to the French in their struggle to retain control of Vietnam (then part of French Indochina) in the mid-1950s. Washington believed that in the Cold War era, the United States must come to the assistance of any country threatened by Communism. Truman's successors in the White House, Dwight D. Eisenhower, John F. Kennedy, and Lyndon B. Johnson, also believed in this school of thought, fearing a domino-effect among neighboring nations—if one fell, they'd all fall.

Why did so **many Americans protest** U.S. involvement in the **Vietnam War**?

The Vietnam War divided the American public: The antiwar movement maintained that the conflict in Southeast Asia did not pose a risk to U.S. security (contrary to the domino effect that Washington foresaw), and in the absence of a threat to national security, protesters wondered "what are we fighting for?" Meantime, President Lyndon Johnson slowly stepped up the number of troops sent to Vietnam. Many never came home and those who did, came home changed. Mass protests were held, including the hallmark of the era, the sit-in. Protesters accused the American government of not only involving Americans in a conflict where the country had no part, but of supporting a corrupt, unpopular—and undemocratic—government in South Vietnam.

Even those Americans who supported the nation's fight against Communism became frustrated by the United States' inability to achieve a decisive victory in Vietnam. Even for the so-called hawks, the mounting costs of the war hit home when President Johnson requested new taxes. As the casualty count soared, public approval of U.S. participation in Vietnam dropped. By the end of the decade, under increasing public pressure, the government began to withdraw Americans from Vietnam. The evacuation of the ground troops was not complete until 1973. But even then soldiers who were missing in action (MIAs) and prisoners of war (POWs) were left behind.

What happened in **Grenada**?

On October 25, 1983, about three thousand U.S. Marines and Army Rangers landed on the Caribbean island. The number included about three hundred military personnel from neighboring Antigua, Barbados, Dominica, Jamaica, St. Kitts-Nevis, St. Lucia, and St. Vincent. The arrival followed the October 12–19 coup in which Prime Minister Maurice Bishop was overthrown and killed by a hardline Marxist military council headed by General Hudson Austin.

While the United Nations and friends of the U.S. condemned President Ronald Reagan for the action, American troops detained General Austin and restored order on the island. Governor-general Sir Paul Scoon formed an interim government to prepare for elections. Most of the U.S. military presence was withdrawn by December 1983, with nominal forces remaining on the island through most of 1985.

President Reagan justified the tactic by citing that the coup had put in danger American students on the island, but prevailing political conditions on tiny Grenada were more likely to have inspired the show of force: Increasingly stronger ties between Grenada and Cuba had made many American officials nervous—they feared the island would be used as a way-station for shipping Soviet and Cuban arms to Central America.

What did **President Bush** mean when he said the U.S. had to **"draw a line in the sand"**?

The President was reacting to Iraqi leader Saddam Hussein's act of aggression when on August 2, 1990, his troops invaded neighboring Kuwait. The "line in the sand" that Hussein crossed was soon defended: On January 16, 1991, Operation Desert Storm was launched to defend the Arab nation of Kuwait against Iraq, whose military dictator had not only invaded Kuwait but proclaimed it a new Iraqi province. Bush averred that "this will not stand," and in order to protect U.S. oil supplies in the country, the President mobilized U.S. forces, which were joined by a coalition of thirty-nine nations, to soundly and quickly defeat Iraq.

Why was the **Persian Gulf War** important?

The six-week war, telecast around the world from start to finish, was significant because it was the first major international crisis to take place in the post-Cold War era. The United Nations proved to be effective in organizing the coalition against aggressor Iraq. Leading members of the coalition included Egypt, France, Great Britain, Saudi Arabia, Syria, and the United States. The conflict also tested the ability of the United States and the Soviet Union to cooperate in world affairs.

GOVERNMENT, LAW, & POLITICS

EGYPTIAN CIVILIZATION

What was the **first national government**?

It is believed to have been that of the first Egyptian king, Menes, who united Upper and Lower Egypt in 3110 B.C. and founded a central government at Memphis (near present-day Cairo). Ruling for sixty-two years, Menes established the first of what would eventually number thirty dynasties that ruled ancient Egypt for nearly three thousand years—until 332 B.C.

By the time the 3rd Dynasty began around 2700 B.C., the central government was well established and strong—kings and queens were believed to be half-human and half-god. They lived in magnificent luxury: Palaces and temples were built for them and filled with exotic goods from other lands. These treasures were even buried with the pharaohs—to be enjoyed in the afterworld. It was during the 3rd Dynasty that the five-hundred-year period known as the Old Kingdom or the Pyramid Age began, a period that saw the building of gigantic pyramids for Egypt's kings.

Was **King Tut** the greatest ruler of **ancient Egypt**?

No, in fact, King Tut's reign was relatively unimportant in the vast history of ancient Egypt. A ruler of the 18th Dynasty, Tutankhamen

(1370–52) was in power from age nine (1361 B.C.) until his death at the age of eighteen—a nine-year period that would be of little significance were it not for the November 1922 discovery of his tomb in the Valley of the Kings near ancient Thebes (modern Luxor). Of the twenty-seven pharaohs buried near Thebes, only the tomb of the minor king, Tutankhamen, was spared looting through the ages. Having not been opened since ancient times, the tomb still contained its treasures.

In the antechamber of the tomb, English archeologist Howard Carter (1873–1939) found more than six hundred artifacts including funerary bouquets, sandals, royal robes, cups and jars, a painted wooden casket, life-size wooden statues of Tutankhamen, animal-sided couches, disassembled chariots, and a golden throne. In the burial chambers, a team of archeologists discovered four golden shrines and the golden coffin containing the royal mummy of Tutankhamen—complete with a golden mask covering his head and shoulders.

Earlier in his career, Carter had discovered the tombs of King Tut's predecessors, Queen Hatshepsut (c. 1520–c. 1468 B.C.) and King Thutmose IV (d. 1417 B.C.), both of whom were also rulers during Egypt's 18th Dynasty.

EMPIRES

THE ROMAN EMPIRE

Who were the most **well-known rulers** of the **Roman Empire**?

The five hundred years of the Roman Empire (27 B.C.–A.D. 476) gave history some of its most noteworthy—and most diabolical—leaders. The "major" emperors are names that most every student of Western civilization is familiar with: Augustus, Tiberius, Caligula, Claudius, Nero, Trajan, Marcus Aurelius, Diocletian, and Constantine I (called "the Great").

Augustus, Tiberius, Caligula, Claudius, and Nero were the first five emperors, a succession covering seventy-five years of Roman rule. Octavian (first century B.C.), later known as Augustus, became Roman Emperor when, after the assassination of his uncle, Julius Caesar, a power struggle ensued and he defeated Mark Antony and Cleopatra. Under Augustus's rule (27 B.C.–A.D. 14) began the two hundred years of the *Pax Romana*, a period of relative peace (no power emerged that was strong enough to sustain conflict with the Roman army). During the *Pax Romana*, Rome turned its attention to the arts, literature, education, and trade. As second emperor of Rome, Tiberius (42 B.C.–A.D. 37) eventually allowed the influence of the Roman politician and conspirator Sejanus to affect him. Tiberius was the adopted son of Emperor Augustus, and though he had been carefully schooled and groomed to take on the role, ultimately he became a tyrannical ruler—the final years of his reign were marked by viciousness and cruelty. Upon Tiberius's death, he was succeeded (in A.D. 37) by his nephew, Caligula, meaning "Little Boots," since at an early age he had been dressed as a soldier. For a short time, Caligula ruled with moderation. But not long after he came to power, he fell ill and thereafter, he exhibited the erratic behavior for which he is known. Most scholars agree that Caligula must have been mentally unstable. He was murdered in 41, and Claudius, also nephew to Tiberius, was proclaimed emperor. Claudius (10 B.C.–A.D. 54) renewed the expansion of Rome, waging battle with Germany, Syria, and Mauretania (present-day Algeria and Morocco), and conquering half of Britain. Though his administration was reportedly well run, he had his enemies—among them his niece Agrippina the Younger who is believed to have murdered him in 54, after securing her son, Nero, as successor to the throne. In Nero (37–68), the early Roman Empire had perhaps its most despotic ruler: though his early years in power were marked by the efficient conduct of public affairs, in 59 he had his mother assassinated (she reportedly had tried to rule through her son), and Nero's legacy from that point is one of ruthless behavior. He was involved in murder plots, ordered the deaths of many Romans, instituted the persecution of Christians, and led an extravagant lifestyle that emptied the public coffers. He was declared a public enemy by the Roman Senate and in 68, took his own life.

While the first century A.D. was marked—with the exception of Augustus—by extreme rulers, the second century A.D. was marked by the leadership of soldiers and statesmen. Trajan (53–117), who ruled from the year 98 until his death nineteen years later, is best known for his military campaigns, which expanded Rome's territory. He was also a

141

builder—constructing bridges, roads, and buildings. When Marcus Aurelius (121–80) ascended to emperor in 161, he had already been in public office for more than twenty years. A man of great experience, he was reportedly both learned and of gentle character. His generals put down revolting tribes, and, in addition to winning victories along the Danube, his troops also fought barbarians in the north. Diocletian (245 or 248–313 or 316) had served as an army commander before becoming emperor in 284. In an effort to effectively rule the expansive territory, he divided it into four regions, each with its own ruler (though Diocletian was the acknowledged chief). Two years before he abdicated the throne (305), he began the persecution of Christians—a surprising move since he had long been friendly toward them. Unlike many of his predecessors who died in office, Diocletian had a retirement, which he reportedly spent gardening.

Constantine the Great (ruled 306–37) is notable for reuniting the regions that Diocletian had created, bringing them all under his rule by 324. He was also the first Roman emperor to convert to Christianity. Finally, Theodisius I (also called "the Great") is known to many since he was the last to rule the united Roman Empire (375–95).

Why was **Julius Caesar** murdered?

The Roman general and statesman Julius Caesar (100 B.C.–44 B.C.) was stabbed to death in the senate house by a group of men, including some of his former friends, who viewed him as an ambitious tyrant and a threat to the Roman Republic. The date of the assassination, March 15, fell into relatively common usage thanks to William Shakespeare's tragedy, *Julius Caesar* (late 1590s), which has a soothsayer warning the Roman general to "Beware the ides of March." After Caesar's death in 44 B.C., a triumvirate was formed to rule Rome—with Lepidus, Octavian (who would in 27 B.C. become Augustus, the Roman Empire's first ruler), and Marc Antony sharing power. It was Mark Antony (c. 83–30 B.C.), of "Antony and Cleopatra" fame, who aroused the mobs against Caesar's conspirators, driving them out of Rome.

The events illustrate the controversy about Julius Caesar: While some clearly viewed him as a demagogue who forced his way into power, others considered the patrician-born Caesar a man of noble character

Military and political leader Julius Caesar leading his Roman troops into battle.

who defended the rights of the people in an oligarchic state—where the government was controlled by a few people who had only their own interests in mind. This divided opinion has followed Caesar throughout history.

While opinion is still divided on what kind of a ruler Caesar really was, there can be no denying his contributions—both to Rome (which would soon emerge as the Roman empire) and to modern civilization. In his battles, Caesar brought the provinces of Italy under control and defeated his former co-ruler, General Pompey (who had, along with Caesar and Crasius, formed the First Triumvirate)—effectively ending the

143

oligarchy that had ruled Rome. In so doing, he had succeeded in ending the disorder that had plagued Rome for decades and laid the groundwork for the formation of the empire under his grandnephew Augustus in 27 B.C. While Caesar was in office, he planned and carried out several reforms—not the least of which was the Julian calendar, which he introduced in 46 B.C. The Gregorian calendar we use today evolved from it.

Caesar also left a legacy of literature: He penned a total of ten books on his battles in Gaul (58–50 B.C.) and on the civil war, which he had more or less started in 49 B.C. These clear commentaries are still considered masterpieces of military history.

Was **Attila the Hun** really a savage?

While Attila (c. 400–453) may have possessed some of the worthwhile qualities of a military leader, the King of the Huns was no doubt a ruthless and fierce figure. He is believed to have ascended through the ranks of the Hun army, coming to power as the leader of the nomadic group in 434. By this time, the Huns (who originated in central Asia) had occupied the Volga River valley in the area of present-day western Russia. At first, like his predecessors, he was wholly occupied with fighting other barbarian tribes for control of lands. But under Attila's leadership, the Huns began to extend their power into central Europe. He waged battles with the Eastern Roman armies, and, after murdering his older brother and co-ruler Bleda in 445, went on to trample the countries of the Balkan peninsula and northern Greece—causing terrible destruction along the way. As Attila continued westward with his bloody campaigns, which each Hun fought using his own weapons and his own savage technique, he nearly destroyed the foundations of Christianity. But the combined armies of the Romans and the Visigoths defeated Attila and the Huns at Châlons (in northeastern France) in June of 451, which went down in history as one of the most decisive battles of all time. From there, Attila and his men moved into Italy, devastating the countryside before Pope Leo I (c. 400–61) succeeded in persuading the brutal leader to spare Rome. (For this and other reasons, Leo was later canonized, becoming Saint Leo.) Attila died suddenly—and of natural causes—in 453, just as he was again preparing to cross the Alps and invade Italy anew.

Why was Constantine I called "the Great"?

Roman emperor Constantine the Great (c. 275–337) is credited with no less than beginning a new era in history. His father, Constantius, was ruler of the Roman Empire until his death in 306. Though Constantine was named emperor by Roman soldiers, a power struggle ensued. During a battle near Rome in 312, Constantine, who had always been sympathetic toward Christians, reportedly saw a vision of a flaming cross. He emerged from the conflict both converted and victorious. For the next twelve years, Constantine ruled the West Roman Empire while Licinius (also tolerant to Christians) ruled the East. But a struggle between the two emperors ended in death for Licinius and beginning in 325, Constantine ruled as sole emperor.

During his reign, Christians regained freedom of worship and the Christian church became legal. In 325, he convened the Council of Nicaea (from whence Christians got the Nicene Creed). In moving the capital of the Roman Empire to Byzantium (in 330), Constantine shifted the Empire's focus from west to east and laid the foundation for the Byzantine Empire. The Eastern Orthodox Church regards Constantine as a saint.

How was the **Byzantine Empire** formed?

The Byzantine Empire was a continuation of the Roman Empire—its citizens even called themselves Romans. Two dates are given for the formation of the Byzantine Empire, which, though boundaries shifted constantly, were centered in Asia Minor and the Balkan Peninsula: In A.D. 395, upon the death of emperor Theodosius the Great, the Roman Empire was divided into two—East and West. In the years that followed, the West Roman Empire was subject to repeated attacks from nomadic barbarian groups, and Rome finally fell in 476. The East Roman Empire survived as the Byzantine Empire, which, after the fall of Rome, laid claim to much of the lands in the west.

145

However, many historians date the beginning of the Byzantine Empire earlier—at A.D. 330, when Roman emperor Constantine the Great moved the capital of the then-united Roman Empire from Rome to Byzantium (present-day Istanbul, Turkey—it was subsequently known as Constantinople). By this definition of the empire, Constantine the Great was its first ruler. He was succeeded by nearly one hundred rulers, over the course of more than a thousand years of Byzantine rule. At its height, during the sixth century reign of Justinian I (483–565), the empire included parts of southern and eastern Europe, northern Africa, and the Middle East. The Byzantine Empire ended when the Ottoman Turks conquered Constantinople in 1453.

What is the **Byzantine Empire's role** in history?

The Byzantine Empire (330 or 395–1453) is considered a link between ancient and modern civilizations. Though the empire was constantly fighting off invaders, it was plagued by religious controversies, and marred by political strife, but as the heir of the Roman world, it allowed for the customs of Greco-Roman civilization to mix with those of the East and with Christianity. The fall of the Byzantine Empire in 1453 typically marks the beginning of the modern era.

What was the **Ottoman Empire**?

It was a vast Turkish state founded in the thirteenth century by the Osmani Turks—Turks who were led by descendants of Osman I (1258–c. 1326). By the middle of the next century, the Ottoman Empire consisted roughly of modern-day Turkey (the terms "Turkey" and "Ottoman Empire" are used interchangeably). But conquests during the 1400s included the Byzantine Empire (in 1453) and at its height, the Ottoman Empire extended over an area that included the Balkan Peninsula, Syria, Egypt, Iraq, the northern coast of Africa, Palestine, and parts of Arabia, Russia, and Hungary. The capital was placed at Constantinople (present-day Istanbul). Thus the Turks established a Muslim empire that would remain a formidable force and influence in the region and in Europe for the next three centuries.

During the 1500s and 1600s, the Ottoman Empire was the most powerful in the world. It reached its most glorious heights during the reign of

Süleyman the Magnificent (ruled 1520–66): It was he who added parts of Hungary to the Ottoman territory. He also tried to take Vienna, but failed. He did succeed in strengthening the Ottoman navy, which dominated the Mediterranean Sea. Süleyman was not only an expansionist, but also a patron of the arts and a builder: he ordered the construction of mosques (to spread the Islamic religion throughout the empire), bridges, and other public works.

But by the time World War I began in 1914, the empire had been in decline for some three hundred years and only consisted of Asia Minor, parts of southwestern Asia, and part of the Balkan Peninsula. As one of the losing Central Powers, the Ottoman Empire was dissolved in 1922 by the peace treaties that ended the first world war.

THE DYNASTIES

What was the **Tang Dynasty**?

The Tang (617–907) was the sixth-to-last Chinese dynasty. It's well known since the period saw great achievements not only in government and business, but in letters and the arts—principally lyrical poetry, formal prose, painting, sculpture, and porcelain pottery. The first published book, *The Diamond Sutra*, was produced during this time (in 868). Considered a golden age of Chinese civilization, the Tang was also an age of great expansion: At its height, the empire stretched from Turkmenistan in the west to Korea (which was a vassal state) in the east, and from Manchuria to northern India. As a result, trade prospered, with Chinese jade, porcelain, silk, rice, spices, and teas exported to India, the Middle East, and Europe. One historian called the Tang "the consummate Chinese dynasty . . . formidable, influential, and innovative."

One of the Tang's innovations was the balance of administrative power: government was separated into three main branches—the Imperial Secretariat (which organized the emperor's directives into policies); the Imperial Chancellery (which reviewed the policies and monitored bureaucracy); and the Department of States Affairs (which carried out the policies through the administration of six ministries). Add to this triumvirate a "Board of Censors," which ensured that corruption was kept to a minimum. This form of government outlasted the Tang Dynasty: Subsequent monarchies perpetuated the system into the twentieth century.

Yet another example of the forward thinking of the Tang Dynasty was in civil service. Candidates for public service were trained in the Confucian principles before they took an exam that would qualify them for official duty.

How vast was **Genghis Khan's** dynasty?

It is said that Genghis Khan's (A.D. 1167–1227) empire was larger than that of Alexander the Great's. Khan's ability to obtain such a huge dynasty sprang from a strong fierceness that resulted in a harsh imprisonment as a child.

Mongol ruler Genghis Khan was born Temujin in A.D. 1167, by his Mongol chieftain father, Yesukai. Yesukai chose the name Temujin for his newly born son after defeating an enemy tribesman of the same name. At age thirteen, Yesukai was murdered, and young Temujin was appointed leader of the Mongols. But because of his age, a chief from another tribe proclaimed himself leader of the Mongols. Since Temujin was just a young boy, he was viewed as weak, but still a threat, and the new ruler had Temujin imprisoned.

The capture of Temujin was meant to break both his mind and body. Ironically, it gave him the boldness that would later on enable him to amass such a great empire. His imprisoners had him in a yank, a wooden yoke that shackled his shoulders to his wrists. At night, young Temujin escaped from his shackles and killed a guard. His bold escape won him followers, and as an adult, Temujin overthrew the Tartars and soon began increasing his tribe. In 1206, after conquering several more tribes, his followers named Temujin Genghis Khan, meaning "greatest of rulers, emperor of all men." Khan gained much respect and loyalty from his huge army made up of various tribes. He uniformed his men by enforcing strict punishment for disobedience and rewards for allegiance. Before his death, in 1227 (from a fall off a horse), Genghis Khan's rule extended from Hungary across Asia to Korea, and from Siberia to Tibet. This massive empire was handed down to his grandson, Kublai Khan.

Great Mongol leader and warrior Genghis Khan.

Besides being known as a fierce warrior and ruler, Genghis Khan has been credited to advancing his Mongolian tribes with the establishment of a comprehensive legal system and an efficient horse and rider communication system, comparable to the pony express.

What were the **highlights** of the **Ming Dynasty**?

The focus on Chinese culture that was the hallmark of the Ming Dynasty (1368–1644) was both its strength and its weakness. After the foreign Mongols (who dynasty had been established by Genghis and Kublai

Why is Charlemagne so well known?

Charlemagne's notoriety with history students is due not only to the ruler's great accomplishments during his lifetime, but also to the fact that these accomplishments were documented: His biography, titled *Vita Caroli Magni (The Life of Charlemagne)* was written by a fellow named Einhard (770?–840), who was his adviser.

Charlemagne (742–814), or Charles the Great, became king of the western Franks when his father (Pepin the Short) died in 768. Upon the death of his brother, Carloman, in 771, Charles became king of all the Franks. (The Franks were the descendants of Germanic tribes who settled in the Rhine River region.) He then went on to conquer much of western Europe, including Saxony, Lombardy, northeastern Spain, and Bavaria. He sometimes employed brutal tactics in bringing people and regions under control: During the last two decades of the eighth century, he used mass executions to subdue Saxon rebellions. Nevertheless, Charlemagne succeeded in uniting all of these areas under one empire, and on Christmas day 800, he had Pope Leo III crown him Emperor of the West. As a patron of the arts, literature, and science, Charlemagne revived western Europe, which had been in decline since the fall of the West Roman Empire (in 476). He is credited with laying the foundation for the Holy Roman Empire and the European civilization that developed later in the Middle Ages. He ruled until his death in 814.

Khan in the early 1200s–1260) were overthrown as rulers of China in 1368, the Ming emperors returned their—and their subjects'—attention to those things that are distinctively Chinese. The focus on Chinese culture produced a flowering in the arts, evidenced by the name "Ming" itself—meaning "bright" or "brilliant." It was architects working during this period who produced the splendor of Beijing's Forbidden City. Ming porcelain, bronze, and lacquerware are coveted collector items today. Additionally, the novel and drama flourished.

And though the Ming rulers promoted this artistic renaissance and reinstated Confucianism and the program of civil service suspended by the Mongols, the rulers' myopia prevented them from seeing the threat of the nomadic Manchu people on the horizon. In 1644, the Manchus invaded from the north and conquered China, setting up the last dynastic period in Chinese history (it lasted until 1912). Nevertheless, it was the Ming, and not the Manchu, who formed the last great and truly Chinese dynasty.

FERDINAND AND ISABELLA

Why were **Spain's King Ferdinand** and **Queen Isabella** so powerful?

The 1469 marriage of Ferdinand (1452–1516) and Isabella (1451–1504) brought previously separate Spanish kingdoms (Aragon and Castile) under their joint control. Together the monarchs went on to rule Spain and expand their realm of influence until Isabella's death in 1504. (Ferdinand ruled without his wife thereafter.) Theirs was a reign that seemed to have religion on its side: In 1496, Pope Alexander VI conferred upon each of them the title "Catholic," as in, "Ferdinand the Catholic" and "Isabella the Catholic." And for good reason since the king's and queen's most well-known acts seemed to have been motivated by their beliefs.

It was Ferdinand and Isabella who in 1478 established the infamous Spanish Inquisition, a court that imprisoned or killed Catholics who were suspected of not following religious teachings. While the Inquisition was aimed at discovering and punishing Muslims and Jews who had converted to Catholicism but who were thought to be insincere, soon all Spaniards came to fear its power. In 1482, the monarchs undertook a war with the (Muslim) Moors, conquering the last Moorish stronghold at Granada in 1492, and forcing them back to Africa after four centuries of occupation—and influence—in the Iberian Peninsula (Spain and Portugal). The recovery of Iberia had been motivated by religion; when the king and queen expelled the Moors, they also believed they were expelling Islam from their kingdom.

151

That year, 1492, was a fateful one for the Spanish: Not only were the Moors driven out, but Ferdinand and Isabella also turned their attention to the Jewish "threat," expelling them, too. (Those who remained, went underground with their faith; those Iberian Jews who migrated spread their division of Judaism, called Sephardim, to North Africa and the Middle East.)

Most students of history know 1492 best as the year that explorer Christopher Columbus sailed to the New World. It was Ferdinand and Isabella who sponsored his voyage—believing that the conquered lands would not only add to their authority but would provide new territory for the spread of Catholicism. The Spaniards soon emerged as a formidable sea power in the Atlantic.

For all their fervor, Isabella and Ferdinand were also interested in education and the arts, and sponsored advances in both areas during their reign. Their legacy included their grandson Charles V, who, through marriage, became Holy Roman Emperor (ruled 1519–58) as one of the all-powerful Habsburgs.

ROYALTY

Who were the **Habsburgs**?

The Habsburgs were Europe's most powerful royal family. Even if one chose to argue the point of power, there can be no arguing the longevity of the house of Habsburg: They supplied Europe with a nearly uninterrupted stream of rulers for more than six hundred years.

Also spelled Hapsburg (which is closer to the pronunciation, HAPS-berg), the name came from the castle of Habichtsburg (meaning "Hawk's Castle"), built during the early eleventh century in Switzerland. The first member of the family to bear the name was Count Werner I (who died in 1096). It was Werner's descendant, Rudolf I (1218–91), who was elected king of Germany and the Holy Roman Empire in 1273. When Rudolf conquered Austria three years later, he established that country as the family's new home. Austria, Bohemia, Germany, Hungary, and Spain were among the European states ruled by the house of

Habsburg. With only one exception, the Habsburg family also ruled the Holy Roman Empire from 1438 (when Albert II was elected) until 1806.

It was the reign of Emperor Charles V during the sixteenth century that the Habsburg influence reached its high-water mark. When Philip I married Joan of Castile in 1496, it assured that their son Charles V (1500–58) would inherit the crown of Spain, which he did in 1516. (Charles was grandson to Spain's Ferdinand and Isabella.) He also inherited the rest of what, by then, was a vast empire, and he ruled as Holy Roman Emperor from 1519 until 1556. He is considered the greatest of all the Habsburgs, though he did face problems. Chief among these were the Protestant Reformation; opposition from his lifelong rival, Francis I (1494–1547), king of France; and the Ottoman Turks, who were at the height of their power during his reign. Nevertheless, he was a successful ruler and his accomplishments included Spain's conquest of lands in the New World—Mexico (at the hands of Cortés) and Peru (by Pizarro).

In 1867, the Habsburg empire was reorganized as the Austro-Hungarian Monarchy. That monarchy was dissolved in 1918, after World War I, with the Treaty of Versailles establishing new boundaries for the successor states.

Who were the **Romanovs**?

The Romanov family ruled Russia from 1613 until 1917, when Nicholas II—the last Russian tsar—was overthrown by the Russian Revolution. Established by Michael Romanov, grandnephew to Ivan the Terrible (ruled 1533–84), there were eighteen Romanov rulers including Peter the Great (ruled 1682–1725) and Catherine the Great (ruled 1762–96).

While these two tsars are among the best-known of the Romanov dynasty, the epithet "the Great" can be misleading: There were accomplishments on both their parts, but both Peter and Catherine increased their power at the expense of others. Peter is recognized for introducing Western European civilization to Russia and for elevating Russia to the status of a great European power. But he also relied on the serfs (the peasants who were little more than indentured servants to the lords) not only to provide the bulk of the funding he needed to fight almost continuous wars, but for the manpower as well: most soldiers were serfs. The man responsible for establishing schools (including the Academy of Sciences), reforming the calendar, and simplifying the alphabet also carried out ruthless reforms. Peter's most vain-glorious act was, perhaps, to move the capital from Moscow to the city he had built for himself on the swampy lands ceded by Sweden—St. Petersburg (it was known as Petrograd from 1914 to 1924 and as Leningrad between 1924 and 1991). As his "window on Europe," Peter was succeeded in making the city into a brilliant cultural center.

For her part, Catherine the Great may well be acknowledged as a patron of the arts and literature (one who corresponded with the likes of French thinker Voltaire), but she, too, increased the privileges of the nobility while making the lives of the serfs even more miserable. Her true colors were shown by how she ascended to power in the first place: In 1744, she married Peter (III), who became tsar of Russia in 1762. That same year, Catherine conspired with her husband's enemies to depose him. He was later killed. And so Catherine came to power, proclaiming herself tsarina. She began her reign by attempting reforms, but a peasant uprising (1773–74) and the French Revolution (which began in 1789) prompted her only to strengthen and protect her absolute authority. Like Peter the Great, she, too, extended the frontiers of the empire through a series of conquests. By the end of her reign (in 1796), Catherine had reduced even the free peasants to the level of serfdom.

As the last tsar of Russia, Nicholas II (ruled 1894–1917) likely suffered not only the recrimination that was due him, but the public hostility that had accumulated over centuries of ruthless Romanov leadership. Nicholas's difficulties came to a head when he got Russia involved in World War I (1914–18)—which produced serious hardships for the Russian people and for which there was little public support. Once Tsar Nicholas was overthrown (and later killed) in the Russian Revolution, Bolshevik leader Vladimir Lenin set about extracting Russia from the conflict by agreeing to severe concessions to Germany. Oddly enough, the Romanov family had, in the fourteenth century, originated with a German nobleman, Andrew Kobyla, who had emigrated to Russia.

What is the **House of Tudor**?

It was the Royal family that ruled England for well over a century—from 1485 to 1603. The name Tudor came from a Welshman, Owen Tudor, who sometime after 1422 married Henry V's widow, Catherine of Valois. The family did not come to power until Henry VII ascended the throne in 1485, ending the bitter, thirty-year War of the Roses—during which two noble families, the houses of Lancaster and York, struggled against each other for control of the throne. (The conflict earned its name since the badge of each house depicted a rose, one red and the other white.) In taking power, Henry VII became the head of the House of Lancaster, and in 1486 married into the House of York, thus uniting the two former enemies and founding his own Tudor dynasty.

The Tudors' rule included the monarchies of Henry VIII, whose second wife was the infamous Anne Boleyn, and who broke England's ties with the Roman Catholic Church to set up the Church of England; Mary I, Henry VIII's daughter from his first marriage (to Katharine of Aragón), who in 1554 married Spain's Philip (II) to form a temporary alliance and realigned England with the Catholic Church, undertaking the persecution of Protestants in England and earning herself the name "Bloody Mary"; and Elizabeth I, who defeated the Spanish Armada in 1588 and presided over the Elizabethan Age, one of England's high-water marks. During the Elizabethan Age (1558–1603), England dominated the seas to become a European power; culture flourished (with the likes of William Shakespeare and Sir Edmund Spenser producing works that would long outlive the era); colonization began (with Sir Walter Raleigh and others establishing British settlements in North America); and industry and commerce flourished.

The Tudors are credited with strengthening the monarchy in England. They were succeeded by the House of Stuart in 1603, when James I ascended the throne. It is that James who gave the world the King James Version of the Bible. He is also notable for having been the son of Mary Queen of Scots—whom his predecessor, Elizabeth I, had reluctantly put to death.

Who was **Mary Queen of Scots**?

Mary Stuart was born in 1542 to James V of Scotland and his wife Mary of Guise. When she was but six days old, James died, making her queen. Her mother ruled the country as a regent until 1561, when, still a teenager, Mary officially took on her duties. She was, by all reports, a beautiful and charming young woman whose courage and mettle would be tested by time. When she ascended the throne, she inherited her mother's struggle with the Protestants, led by John Knox, a former Catholic priest who had become involved in the Reformation. As a Roman Catholic, Mary Queen of Scots became subject to harsh verbal attacks issued by Knox, who denounced the pope's authority and the practices of the Church. But this was not the worst of her troubles: In 1565, Mary wed her English cousin, Lord Darnley, in an attempt to secure her claim to the English throne as successor to Elizabeth I, also her cousin. But Mary's ambitions would be her undoing. She quickly grew to dislike her husband, who soon became aligned with her Protestant opponents and successfully carried out a plot to murder—in her presence—Mary's adviser, David Rizzio. Surprisingly, the two became reconciled shortly thereafter (a politically savvy move on Mary's part) and Mary conceived a child, James, who was born in 1566. One year later, Darnley, who had enemies of his own, was murdered. Mary promptly married the Earl of Bothwell, whom she had fallen in love with well before becoming a widow. Bothwell had been accused of Darnley's murder, and though he was acquitted, his marriage to their queen shocked Scotland. The people took up arms, forcing Mary to abdicate the throne in 1567. She was twenty-five years old.

Fleeing to England, Mary Queen of Scots was given refuge by Elizabeth I and though she was technically a prisoner, Mary nevertheless was able to conspire with Elizabeth's enemies—including English Catholics and the Spanish—in attempts to kill her. When one such plot was discovered in 1586, Mary was charged as an accomplice and put on trial. Found guilty, she was put to death in 1587, though Elizabeth hesitated to take such action.

Meantime, Mary's son, James VI of Scotland, had taken on his responsibilities in 1583—after Scotland had been ruled on his behalf by regents since Mary's abdication some sixteen years earlier. He had promptly formed an alliance with Elizabeth I and, in 1587, accepted with resignation his mother's execution. In 1603, James succeeded Elizabeth, becoming James I, King of England, uniting Scotland and England under one throne. The union was made official about a century later (in 1707) when Parliament passed the Act of Union.

Who are the **Windsors**?

Windsor is the family name of the royal house of Great Britain. The name has interesting origins, which can be traced back to the 1840 marriage of Queen Victoria to her first cousin Albert, the son of the Duke of Saxe-Coburg-Gotha (in present-day Germany). As a foreigner, Prince Albert had to overcome the distrust of the British public, which he did not only by proving himself to be a devoted husband to Queen Victoria, but by demonstrating his genuine concern in Britain's national affairs. Victoria and Albert had nine children. Their oldest son became King Edward VII upon Victoria's death in 1901. But Edward's reign lasted only until 1910, when he died and his son, George V, ascended the throne. George was king during World War I (1914–18), and in 1917, with Britain and Germany bitter enemies, he denounced his ties and claims to Germany, superseding his grandfather's (Prince Albert's) family name of Wettin and establishing the House of Windsor.

Thus, George V was the first ruling member of the House of Windsor. The others were Edward VIII, who abdicated the throne in 1936 so that he could marry American heiress Wallis Simpson; George VI, who became king upon his brother Edward's abdication and who would work tirelessly during World War II to keep up the morale of the British people; and Elizabeth II, George VI's elder daughter, who still reigns as Queen of England today. Elizabeth, who ascended the throne in 1952, proclaimed that she and all her descendants who bear the title prince or princess are to be known as Windsor.

SEMINAL DOCUMENTS AND BASIC TENETS

Why is the **Magna Carta** so important?

The Magna Carta, arguably the most famous document in British history, has had many interpreters since it was signed by King John (who was under pressure to do so) on June 15, 1215, "in the meadow which is called Runnymede, between Windsor and Staines," in Surrey, England. Drawn

What is habeas corpus?

The writ of habeas corpus (which is roughly translated from the Latin as "you should have the body") is considered a cornerstone of due process of law. It means that a person cannot be detained unless he or she is brought before the court so that the court can determine whether or not the person is being lawfully held. The notion dates back to medieval England and it was the English who introduced the concept in the American colonies. Many historians believe that habeas corpus was implied by the Magna Carta (1215). The U.S. Constitution (1788) guarantees that the writ of habeas corpus is upheld—except in times of rebellion or invasion, when it may be suspended.

up by English barons who were angered by the king's encroachment on their rights, the charter has been credited with no less than insuring personal liberty and putting forth the rights of the individual, which include the guarantee of a trial by jury: "No freeman shall be arrested and imprisoned, or dispossessed, or outlawed, or banished, or in any way molested; nor will be set forth against him, nor send against him, unless by the lawful judgment of his peers, and by the law of the land."

King John, also called John Lackland, had a long history of abuse of power: While his brother Richard I was still king, John tried to wrest the throne from him. Though he failed in his effort, when Richard died in 1199, John did ascend to king, inheriting four French duchies (which he soon lost). Upon his refusal to recognize the new archbishop of Canterbury, John was excommunicated. In order to regain favor with the pope, he was forced to give up his kingdom (1213) and receive it back as a papal fief. He was further required to pay an annual tribute to the pope. It was in raising funds that John ran into trouble with England's powerful barons, who were outraged at and tired of his interference in their affairs. The barons drafted the sixty-three chapters of the Magna Carta, writing it in the king's voice, and met John along the banks of the Thames River as he returned from an unsuccessful invasion of France.

The document, which John was forced to put his seal to, asserted the rights of the barons, churchmen, and townspeople, and provided for the king's assurance that he would not encroach on their privileges. In short, the Magna Carta stipulated that the king, too, was subject to the laws of the land.

In that the Magna Carta made a provision for a Great Council, to be comprised of nobles and clergy who would approve the actions of the king vis-à-vis his subjects and ensure the tenets set forth in the charter were upheld, it is credited with laying the foundation for a parliamentary government in England.

After signing it, John immediately appealed to Pope Innocent III, who issued an annulment of the charter. Nevertheless, John died before he could fight it and the Magna Carta was later upheld as the basis of English feudal justice. It is still considered by many to be the cornerstone of constitutional government.

Why was **Oliver Cromwell** important to **British history**?

English soldier and statesman Oliver Cromwell (1599–1658) was a key player in a chain of events that shaped modern British government. The events began when Charles I (1600–49) ascended the throne in 1625 and shortly thereafter married a Catholic French princess, immediately raising the ire of his Protestant subjects. This was not the end of England's problems with King Charles: After repeated struggles with the primarily Puritan Parliament, Charles dismissed the legislative body in 1629 and went on to rule without it for eleven years. During this period, religious and civil liberties were seriously diminished, and political and religious strife prevailed. Fearing the king's growing power, Parliament moved to raise an army, and soon civil war broke out (1642–48). Like the French Revolution, fought one hundred and fifty years later, the struggle in England was largely one between a king who claimed to rule by "divine right" and a government body (in this case Parliament) that claimed the right to govern the nation on behalf of the people.

Enter military leader Oliver Cromwell: After two years of indecisive battles in the English Civil War, Cromwell led his Parliamentary army troops to victories at Marston Moor (1644) and Naseby (1645), which resulted in Charles's surrender. But when Charles escaped his captors in

159

1647, the fighting was briefly renewed. It was ended once and for all in 1648. When the king was tried the following year, Cromwell was among those leading the charge to have Charles executed. The king's opponents had their way and, having abolished the monarchy, soon established the Commonwealth of England, installing Oliver Cromwell as "Lord Protector." Though he endeavored to bring religious tolerance to England and was somewhat successful in setting up a quasi-democratic government (he declined to take the title of king in 1657), his leadership was constantly challenged by those who wished to restore the Stuart monarchy. When Cromwell died in 1658, he was succeeded by his son, Richard (1626–1712), whose talents were not up to the challenges put to the Lord Protector. The movement to restore the monarchy—particularly the Stuart line—gained impetus, and Richard Cromwell was soon dismissed and went to live outside of England for the next twenty years.

Charles II, the son of Charles I, ascended the throne in 1660, beginning the eight-year period known as the Restoration. As Charles and his successor, James II, tried to reassert the absolutism of the Stuart monarchy, they butted heads with Parliament—particularly when it came to financial matters. Finally in 1688, James II was deposed in the so-called "Glorious Revolution." William III (grandson of Charles I) and his wife, Queen Mary II (daughter of James II), were placed on the throne. Though the House of Stuart remained in power, there was an important hitch: Parliament compelled William and Mary to accept the Bill of Rights (of 1689), which asserted that the crown no longer had absolute power in England and that it must rule responsibly through the nation's representatives sitting in Parliament. Thus, the English Civil War (also called the Protestant Revolution) and the influence of Oliver Cromwell and other parliamentarians laid the foundation for England's constitutional monarchy.

What was the **Bill of Rights of 1689**?

The English bill, accepted by King William III (1650–1702), who ruled jointly with his Protestant wife Queen Mary II (1662–94), seriously limited royal power. After a struggle between the Stuart kings and Parliament and the subsequent ousting of King James II, Parliament presented the Bill of Rights to King William and Queen Mary as a condition of their ascension: The document not only described certain civil and political rights and liberties as "true, ancient, and indubitable," but it also ironed out how the throne would be succeeded. This point was of critical importance to the future of England—the article stipulated that no Roman Catholic would rule the country. Since the Bill of Rights served to assert the role of Parliament in the government of England, it is considered one of the seminal documents of British constitutional law.

What was the **Act of Settlement**?

The 1701 decree reiterated the Bill of Rights of 1689 by stating that the king or queen of England must not be a Roman Catholic and must also not be married to a Roman Catholic. The Act of Settlement further stipulated that the sovereign must be a member of the Protestant Church of England. The measure was passed by Parliament, in part due to fear of the Jacobites—supporters of the Stuart king, James II, who had been exiled in 1688 by William II in the "Glorious Revolution." The Jacobites (not to be confused with the French Jacobins, the political party that came to power during the French Revolution), sought to keep the House of Stuart in power. Due to the line of succession, however, the Act did not take effect until 1714, when Queen Anne (1665–1714) died and left no successors to the throne. She was the last Stuart ruler of England.

What did the **Declaration of Independence** say?

The Declaration, adopted July 4, 1776, has long been regarded as history's most eloquent statement of the rights of the people. In it, not only did the thirteen American colonies declare their freedom from Britain, they also addressed the reasons for the proclamation (naming the "causes which impel them to the separation") and cited the British government's violations of individual rights, saying "the history of the present King of Great Britain is a history of repeated injuries and usurpations," which aimed to establish "an absolute Tyranny over these States."

The opening paragraphs go on to state the American ideal of government—an ideal that is based on the theory of natural rights. The Declaration puts forth the fundamental principles that a government exists for the benefit of the people and that "all men are created equal." As the chairman of the Second Continental Congress committee that prepared the Declaration of Independence, it was Thomas Jefferson who wrote and presented the first draft to the Continental Congress on July 2, 1776.

The passage that is most frequently quoted is this: "We hold these truths to be self-evident, that all men are created equal, that they are endowed by their Creator with certain unalienable Rights, that among these are Life, Liberty and the pursuit of Happiness. That to secure these rights, Governments are instituted among Men, deriving their just powers from the consent of the governed, That whenever any Form of Government becomes destructive of these ends, it is the Right of the People to alter or to abolish it, and to institute new Government, laying its foundation on such principles and organizing its powers in such form, as to them shall seem most likely to effect their Safety and Happiness."

Why did **John Hancock** go down in history as *the* notable signer of the **Declaration of Independence**?

Most Americans know that when they're putting their "John Hancock" on something, it means they're signing a document. It's because of the fifty-six men who signed their names to the historic document, it was Hancock (1737–93) who, as president of the Second Continental Congress, signed the declaration first.

The events were as follows: On July 2, 1776, Thomas Jefferson presented the draft of the declaration to the Second Continental Congress, which had convened in Philadelphia more than a year earlier (on May 10, 1775). The congressional delegates of the thirteen colonies then deliberated and debated the draft, making some changes: A section was deleted that condemned England's King George III (1738–1820) for encouraging slave trade. Other changes were cosmetic in nature. On July 4, the final draft of the Declaration was adopted by Congress and it was then that it was signed by Hancock. The document was then printed. A few days later, on July 8, the Declaration was read to a crowd who assembled in the yard of the State House. On July 19, the Congress ordered that the Declaration be written in script on parchment. It is that copy that in early August was signed by all fifty-six members of the Second Continental Congress. The Declaration is housed, along with the U.S. Constitution and the Bill of Rights, in the National Archives Building in Wash-

What were the Articles of Confederation?

This American document was the forerunner to the U.S. Constitution. Drafted by the Continental Congress at York, Pennsylvania, on November 15, 1777, and ratified in 1781, it had shortcomings that were later corrected by the Constitution: The Articles provided the states with more power than the central government, stipulating that Congress rely on the states for the collection of taxes and to carry out the acts of Congress.

It is largely thanks to Alexander Hamilton that the Articles were thrown out: realizing they made for a weak national government, Hamilton led the charge to strengthen the central government—even at the expense of the states. Eventually, he won the backing of George Washington, James Madison, John Jay, and others, which led to the convening of the Philadelphia Constitutional Convention—where the ineffectual Articles of Confederation were overthrown.

One lasting provision of the Articles of Confederation was the Ordinance of 1787: signed in an era of westward expansion, the ordinance set the guidelines for how a territory could become a state (a legislature would be elected as soon as the population had reached five thousand voting citizens—which were men only, and the territory would be eligible for statehood once its population had reached sixty thousand).

ington, D.C., where it is on display to the public. John Hancock went on to become governor of Massachusetts (1780–85 and 1787–93).

What was the **Virginia Plan**?

It was the famous plan, drafted by James Madison, put forth by the Virginia delegates to the Constitutional Convention, which convened on May 25, 1787. After taking a few days to set the ground rules and elect officers, on May 29, the delegation from Virginia, led by Edmund Jennings Randolph (1753–1813), proposed a plan to write an all-new constitution rather than attempting to revise and correct the weak Articles of Confederation. There was opposition (sometimes called the New Jersey Plan) and the issue was debated for weeks. Eventually, a majority vote approved the Virginia Plan and the delegates began work drafting a document that would provide a strong national government for the United States.

Who wrote the **U.S. Constitution**?

In spirit, the U.S. Constitution was created by all of the fifty-five delegates to the meeting that convened on May 25, 1787, in Philadelphia's Independence Hall. Thomas Jefferson called the Constitutional Convention "an assembly of demi-gods," and with good cause: The delegates were the young nation's brightest and best. When the states had been called upon to send representatives to the meeting, twelve states answered by sending their most experienced, most talented, and smartest men—Rhode Island, which feared the interference of a strengthened national government in state affairs, sent no one to Philadelphia.

Even in such stellar company, the document did have to be written. While many had a hand in this process, it was New York lawyer and future American politician and diplomat Gouverneur Morris (1752–1816) who actually took on the task of penning the Constitution, putting into prose the resolutions reached by the convention. Morris had the considerable help of the records that James Madison (1751–1836) of Virginia had kept as he managed the debates among the delegates and suggested compromises. In that capacity and in that he designed the system of checks and balances among Congress, the President, and the Supreme Court, Madison had considerable influence on the document's language, quite rightfully earning him the designation "Father of the Constitution."

The original document, drafted by Morris, is preserved in the National Archives Building in Washington, D.C. While the Constitution has been amended by Congress, the tenets set forth therein have remained with Americans for more than two centuries, and have provided proof to the countries of the world that a constitution outlining the principles and purposes of its government is necessary to good government.

What are the rights **specified** in the **U.S. Bill of Rights**?

The Bill of Rights, which became law on December 15, 1791, comprise the first ten amendments to the U.S. Constitution (1787) and is meant to guarantee individual liberties.

The First Amendment, which is perhaps most often cited by Americans, guarantees freedom of religion, of speech, and of the press, as well as the right to assembly peaceably and the right to petition the government for a redress of grievances. The Second Amendment guarantees the right to keep and bear arms (explaining, "a well regulated militia being necessary to the security of a free State"). The Third Amendment forbids peacetime quartering of soldiers in private dwellings without consent of the owner. The Fourth Amendment forbids unreasonable searches and seizures.

The fifth through the seventh amendments establish basic standards of jurisprudence. The Fifth (which long ago fell into common usage with the phrase, "s/he's pleading the Fifth") guarantees that a person will not be compelled to testify against himself. The amendment also ensures that a criminal indictment can only be handed down by a grand jury (twelve to twenty-three people who determine if a trial is necessary), and prohibits double jeopardy (being prosecuted twice for the same criminal offense). The Sixth Amendment protects the rights of accused persons in criminal cases by guaranteeing a speedy and fair trial, an impartial jury, and the right to counsel. The Seventh Amendment guarantees trial by jury. The Eighth Amendment prohibits excessive bail, excessive fines, and cruel and unusual punishment.

The Ninth Amendment, which is one that many Americans are probably unable to cite, is an important one nevertheless: It states that simply because a right is not enumerated in the Constitution, it does not mean that the people do not retain that right.

The Tenth Amendment relinquishes to the state governments those powers the Constitution did not expressly grant the federal government or deny the states. In other words, it limits the power of the federal government to that which is granted in the Constitution.

Why was the **Bill of Rights added** to the **U.S. Constitution**?

The United States Constitution, adopted in 1788, contained few personal guarantees. In fact, there was some initial opposition to the new Constitution—much of it based on the lack of specific guarantees of individual rights. It was Father of the Constitution and future President James Madison, then a member of the U.S. House of Representatives, who in December 1791, led Congress to adopt the ten constitutional amendments that became known as the Bill of Rights. Most of the rights focus on individual liberties that had been cited in the Declaration of Independence as having been violated by the British. Most of these specific grievances had not been addressed by the Constitution; therefore, the Bill of Rights was added to cover this ground.

Who **determines** whether a law **violates the liberties** guaranteed by the **Bill of Rights**?

It is the job of the U.S. Supreme Court to decide whether or not a law impinges upon the liberties listed in—or implied by—the Bill of Rights. The difficult task before the Supreme Court justices is in determining what rights are implied. Such questions prompt months of hearings and deliberations before a decision can be reached as to the constitutionality of a contested law. The judicial body makes its determinations based on a majority vote of the nine justices (one chief justice and eight associates). Established as the highest court in the country by Article 3 of the Constitution, the Court has ultimate authority in all legal questions that arise pertaining to the Constitution. Called the "court of last resorts," the Supreme Court both interprets the acts of Congress (including laws and treaties) and determines the constitutionality of federal and state laws (under the 14th Amendment, the Court has upheld that most of the Bill of Rights also applies to state governments).

What are **blue laws**?

The term "blue laws" refers to laws that are intended to enforce moral conduct. They originated in colonial times in Puritan New England, and got the name because they were printed on blue paper. Some blue laws prescribed proper conduct for the Sabbath, which included no working, no sports, and no drinking. The early blue laws of New Haven, Connecticut, were widely publicized a 1781 book, *A General History of Connecticut*. The author, Samuel Peters (1735–1826), took some freedoms with the text, however, and even invented a few laws of his own. Since blue laws violate individual freedoms, most of them have been repealed through the years. If a community still has blue laws on its books today, they are not likely to be enforced.

Who are considered the **Founding Fathers of the United States**?

The term is used to refer to a number of American statesmen who were influential during the revolutionary period of the late 1700s. Though definitions vary, most include the authors of the Declaration of Independence and the signers of the U.S. Constitution among the nation's Founding Fathers.

Of the fifty-six members of the Continental Congress who signed the Declaration of Independence (July 4, 1776), the most well-known are John Adams and Samuel Adams of Massachusetts, Benjamin Franklin of Pennsylvania, John Hancock of Massachusetts, and Thomas Jefferson of Virginia.

The thirty-nine signers of the Constitution (September 17, 1787) includes notable figures such as George Washington (who would go on, of course, to become the first President of the United States), Alexander Hamilton (who, as a former military aid to George Washington, went on to become the first U.S. Secretary of the Treasury), and James Madison (who is called the "Father of the Constitution" for his role as negotiator and recorder of debates between the delegates). At eighty-one years of age, Benjamin Franklin was the oldest signer of the Constitution and was among the six statesmen who could claim the distinction of signing both it and the Declaration of Independence (the others were George Clymer, Robert Morris, George Read, Roger Sherman, and James Wilson).

Patriots and politicians conspicuous by their absence from the Constitutional Convention of 1787 were John Adams and Thomas Jefferson, who were performing other government duties at the time, and would each go on to become U.S. Presidents; Samuel Adams and John Jay, who were not appointed as state delegates but who continued in public life, holding various federal and state government offices (including governor of their states); and Patrick Henry of Virginia, who saw no need to go beyond the Articles of Confederation (1777) to grant more power to the central government. Henry's view on this issue foreshadows the discon-

King Louis XVI taking his oath as wife
Marie Antoinette looks on.

tent that crested nearly one hundred years later when twelve southern
states (including Patrick Henry's home state of Virginia) seceded from
the Union, causing the Civil War to break out.

Adams, Franklin, Hancock, Jefferson, Washington, Hamilton, Madison,
Jay, and Henry. These are the names that come to mind when the words
"Founding Fathers" are uttered. Each of them had a profound impact in
the political life of the United States—even beyond their starring roles
as patriots and leaders during the American revolutionary era. However,
it's important to note that in many texts and to many Americans, the
term Founding Fathers refers only to the men who drafted the U.S. Con-

stitution since it is that document that continues—more than two hundred years after its signing—to provide the solid foundation for American democratic government.

Did **Marie Antoinette** really say **"let them eat cake"**?

No, the widely quoted phrase was incorrectly attributed to her, and the entire story was probably made up. Nevertheless, the legend is not far from fact: The daughter of a Holy Roman Emperor (Francis I), the beautiful Marie Antoinette (1755–93) was accustomed to a life of luxury. Unhappy in her marriage to Louis XVI, King of France, she pursued her own pleasurable interests with abandon. Despite the economic problems that plagued France at the time, she lived an extravagant lifestyle, which included grand balls, a "small" palace at Versailles, theater, gambling, and other frivolities. She was completely disinterested in the affairs of the nation. Many French people blamed her for corruption in the court. In short, she did much to earn herself the terrible reputation that has followed her through history.

Unpopular in her own day, one of the stories that circulated about her had Marie Antoinette asking an official why the Parisians were angry. When he explained to the queen that it was because the people had no bread, she replied with, "Then let them eat cake." The French Revolution, which began in 1789, soon put an end to Marie Antoinette's excesses. Along with her husband, she was put to death by guillotine in 1793.

What were the **Rights of Man**?

In 1789, the French assembly made the Declaration of the Rights of Man and of the Citizen, meant to flesh out the revolutionary cry of "Liberty, Equality, and Fraternity." Influenced by the U.S. Declaration of Independence, as well as, the ideas of the Enlightenment, the document guaranteed religious freedom, the freedom of speech and of the press, and personal security. It proclaimed that man has natural and inalienable rights, which include "liberty, property, personal security, and resistance to oppression. . . . " The declaration further stipulated that "No one may be accused, imprisoned, or held under arrest except in such cases and in such a way as is prescribed by law" and that "Every man is presumed innocent until he is proved guilty. . . . " The declaration was subsequently written into the preamble of the French constitution (1791). However, the Code Napoleon superceded many of the ideas it set forth.

What was the **Code Napoleon**?

In 1800, just after Napoleon Bonaparte had come to power in France, he appointed a commission of legal experts to consolidate all French civil law (as opposed to criminal law) into one code. The process took four years, and when the so-called Code Civil went into effect on March 21, 1804, it was in the year that Napoleon named himself emperor of France (which he did in December), and so, took on the alternate name of the Code Napoleon (or Napoleonic Code). The code went into force throughout France, Belgium, Luxembourg, and in other French territories and duchies in Europe.

The code represented a compromise between Roman law and customary law. Further, it accommodated some of the radical reforms of the French Revolution (1789–99). The Code Civil set forth laws regarding individual liberty, tenure of property, order of inheritance, mortgages, and contracts. The code had broad influence—in Europe, as well as, in Latin America, where civil law is prevalent. As opposed to the common law of most English-speaking countries, civil law judgments are based on codified principles, rather than on legal precedent. Therefore, for example, under the Code Civil, an accused person is guilty until proven innocent (as opposed to common law, which holds that a person is innocent until proven guilty).

What were **Napoleon's Hundred Days**?

The term refers to Napoleon Bonaparte's last one hundred days as ruler of France. Having been defeated by his enemies—a coalition of European powers Britain, Sweden, Austria, and Prussia, who aligned themselves against Napoleon's domination, the emperor abdicated the throne in spring of 1814, and was exiled to the island of Elba in the Mediterranean Sea. There he heard of the confusion and discontent that ensued upon his descent from the throne. He left Elba, and with over a thousand men, arrived on the French coast at Cannes and marched inland to

Paris. Hearing of his arrival, the new Bourbon king, Louis XVIII, fled. On March 20, Napoleon began a new reign, but it was only to last until the European allies defeated him again, at the Battle of Waterloo, June 12–18, after which he was permanently exiled to the British island of St. Helena, where he remained until his death in 1821.

What was the **Kitchen Cabinet**?

It was the name given to President Andrew Jackson's unofficial group of advisers—who reportedly met with him in the White House kitchen. The Kitchen Cabinet was influential in formulating policy during Jackson's first term (1829–33) in office—many believe because the president's real cabinet, which he convened infrequently, had proved ineffective. But Jackson drew harsh criticism for relying on his cronies in this way. When Jackson reorganized the cabinet in 1831, the Kitchen Cabinet disbanded. It had included then Secretary of State Martin Van Buren, who went on to become president; F. P. Blair, editor of *The Washington Post* who was active in American politics and later helped get Lincoln elected to office (1860); and Amos Kendall, another journalist who was a speech writer for Jackson and who went on to become U.S. postmaster general.

But Jackson's favoritism to his circle of friends did not end with the Kitchen Cabinet: During his presidency, the spoils system was in full force: Jackson gave public offices as rewards to many of his loyal supporters. Though the term "spoils system" was popularized during Jackson's terms in office (it was his friend, Senator William Marcy who coined the phrase, when he stated, "to the victor belong the spoils of the enemy"), Jackson was not the first president to grant political powers to his party's members. And the practice continued through the nineteenth century. However, beginning in 1883, laws were passed that gradually put an end to—or at least limited—the spoils system.

What was the **Know-Nothing movement**?

It was a U.S. political movement during the mid-1800s: Americans who feared the foreign influence of immigrants (there was an influx of new arrivals in the 1840s) banded together, sometimes in secret societies, in order to uphold what they believed to be the American view. When people who were thought to be members of these groups were asked about their views and activities, the typical response was "I don't know," which gave the movement its name.

The Know-Nothings worked to elect only "native" Americans (i.e. United States–born citizens) to political office and they advocated the requirement for citizenship be twenty-five years of residence in the United States. Since many immigrants came from European countries and were Roman Catholics, the Know-Nothings also opposed the Catholic Church.

In 1843, Know-Nothings formed the American Republican party. By 1854, they had allied themselves with factions within the Whig party and in the state elections held that year, Know-Nothings swept the vote in Massachusetts and Delaware, nearly carried New York and Pennsylvania, and polled substantial votes in the South. The following year, the Know-Nothings dropped much of their secrecy and became known simply as the American party. It was the issue of slavery that finally split the party in the national election of 1856 and the group dissolved after that. Anti-slavery members of the American party joined the newly formed Republican party.

Who were the **Whigs**?

Whigs were members of political parties in Scotland, England, and the United States. The name is derived from *whiggamor* (meaning "cattle driver"), which was a derogatory term used in the seventeenth century to refer to Scottish Presbyterians who opposed King Charles I of England. (Charles was deposed in a civil war and was subsequently tried in court, convicted of treason, and beheaded). The Whigs, who were mostly merchants and landed gentry, supported a strong Parliament. They were opposed by the aristocratic Tories who upheld the power of the king. For a short period during the eighteenth century, the Whigs dominated political life in England. After 1832, they became part of the Liberal party.

At about the same time, the Whig party in the United States emerged as one of the two major American political parties. The other was the Democratic party Americans still know today, which supported President Andrew Jackson (1767–1845) for re-election in 1832. Though

Who started the Underground Railroad?

American abolitionist, lecturer, and nurse Harriet Tubman (1826–1913) set up the network to emancipate slaves. Tubman was motivated to do so after she had made her way to freedom, and desired to bring her family north as well: "I had crossed the line of which I had so long been dreaming. I was free; but there was no one to welcome me to the land of freedom."

For the next ten years, Tubman acted as a "conductor" on the Underground Railroad, making at least fifteen trips into southern slave states, and guiding not only her parents and siblings, but more than two hundred slaves to freedom in the North. She was called "Moses" for her efforts to emancipate slaves. These journeys to freedom were demanding and often dangerous missions and though Tubman was small in stature, she possessed extraordinary leadership qualities. Author and reformer Thomas Wentworth Higginson called her "the greatest heroine of the age."

Jackson's first term of office had proved to be somewhat controversial, the Whigs were unable to elect their candidate, and Jackson (called "Old Hickory") went on to a second term. In the election of 1840, the Whigs, whose leadership had united the two factions within the party, were finally successful in putting their candidate in the White House. But William Henry Harrison (1773–1841) died after only a month in office, and his successor, John Tyler (1790–1862), alienated the Whig leaders in Congress and they ousted him from the party. The Whigs went on to put Zachary Taylor (in 1848) in the White House, but two years later he, too, died in office. His successor, Millard Fillmore (1800–74), remained loyal to the Whigs, but there were problems within the party. The last Whig presidential candidate was General Winfield Scott in 1852, but he was defeated. Shortly thereafter, the Whig party broke up over the slavery issue. Most of the Northern Whigs joined the Republican party, while most of the Southern "Cotton" Whigs joined the Democratic party.

Why did **President Lincoln** make the **Emancipation Proclamation** while the Civil War was still being fought?

As the war raged between the Confederacy and the Union, it looked like victory would be a long time in the coming: In the summer of 1862, things seemed grim for the federal troops when they were defeated at the Second Battle of Bull Run. But in September, with the Battle of Antietam, the Union finally forced the Confederates to withdraw across the Potomac into Virginia. Lincoln decided that this withdrawal was success enough for him to make his proclamation, and on September 22, he called a Cabinet meeting. That day he presented to his Cabinet the Preliminary Emancipation Proclamation.

The official Emancipation Proclamation was issued later, on January 1, 1863. This final version differed from the preliminary one in that it specified emancipation was to be effected only in those states that had been in rebellion (i.e., the southern states). This key change had been made because the President's proclamation was based on Congressional acts giving him authority to confiscate rebel property and forbidding the military from returning slaves of rebels to their owners.

Abolitionists in the North criticized the President for limiting the scope of the edict to those states in rebellion, for it left open the question of how slaves and slave-owners in the loyal states should be dealt with. Nevertheless, Lincoln had made a stand, which served to change the scope of the Civil War to a war against slavery.

On January 31, 1865, just over two years after the Emancipation Proclamation, Congress passed the Thirteenth Amendment, banning slavery throughout the United States. Lincoln, who had lobbied hard for this amendment, was pleased with its passage. The Confederate states did not free their four million slaves until after the Union was victorious on April 9, 1865.

Did the **Emancipation Proclamation outlaw slavery** in Europe?

Actually, the slave trade ended first in Britain, in 1807, when authorities agreed with the growing number of abolitionists (who argued that slavery is immoral and violates Christian beliefs) and outlawed the trade. In

1833, slavery was abolished throughout the British colonies as the culmination of the great antislavery movement in Great Britain.

In the United States, the slave trade was prohibited in 1808, but slavery was still legal—and profitable. Consequently, trade on the black market continued until Britain stepped up its enforcement of its antislavery law by conducting naval blockades and surprise raids off the African coast, effectively closing the trade.

Slavery finally came to an end after 1870, when slavery was outlawed throughout the Americas.

What was the **suffragist movement**?

During the mid- to late 1800s, American women began organizing and, in increasing numbers, demanding the right to vote. The movement was begun by women who sought social reforms, including outlawing slavery, instituting a national policy of temperance, and securing better work opportunities and better pay. These reformers soon realized that in order to make change, they needed the power of the vote.

Among the leaders of the suffragist movement was feminist and reformer Elizabeth Cady Stanton (1815–1902). She joined with antislavery activist Lucretia Mott (1793–1880) to organize the first women's-rights convention in 1848 in Seneca Falls, New York, launching the woman suffragist movement. In 1869, Stanton teamed with Susan B. Anthony (1820–1906) to organize the National Woman Suffrage Association. That same year, another group was formed—the American Woman Suffrage Association, led by women's rights and antislavery activist Lucy Stone (1818–93) and her husband Henry Brown Blackwell (1825–1909). In 1870, the common cause of the two groups was strengthened by the passage of the 15th Amendment, which gave all men—regardless of race—the right to vote. When the two organizations joined forces in 1890, they formed the National American Woman Suffrage Association (NAWSA).

The founders of the American women's movement were later joined—and replaced—by a new generation of leaders, which included Stanton's daughter Harriot Eaton Blatch (1856–1940). The suffragists appealed to middle-class and working-class women alike, as well as to students and

Feminist Susan B. Anthony.

radicals. They also became activists: Not only did they wage campaigns at the state level, distribute literature, organize meetings, make speeches, and march in parades, they also picketed, lobbied in Washington, and even chained themselves to the White House fence. If jailed, many resorted to hunger strikes. Their efforts eventually created the groundswell of support needed for Congress to pass legislation granting American women the right to vote. However, the movement's early leaders—Stanton, Mott, Anthony, Stone, and Blackwell—did not live to see the culmination of their efforts: It was not until 1920 that the 19th Amendment was added to the U.S. Constitution, guaranteeing women the right to vote in all state and federal elections.

British women had also been engaged in securing the right to vote. There, the movement was led by Emmeline Pankhurst (1858–1928). As a barrister, she authored Great Britain's first woman-suffrage bill in the late 1860s and the Married Women's Property acts of 1870 and 1882. Founding the Women's Franchise League in 1889, five years later, the group secured *married* women the right to vote in local elections. Pankhurst went on to found the Women's Social and Political Union in 1906. By 1912, that group was employing militant tactics to further its goals. Unlike her counterparts in the United States, Pankhurst did live to see full suffrage given to women.

Did **all** countries of the world **grant women the right to vote**?

In granting women the right to vote, both Great Britain and the United States were preceded by New Zealand and Australia. New Zealand gave all women full voting rights in 1893, and in 1902, Australia extended women the right to vote in national elections. The early 1900s saw full voting rights for American and British women, but for Canadian, Finnish, German, and Swedish women as well. France, Italy, India, China, and Japan followed in the mid-1900s. By the 1990s, the only country in the world that extended voting rights to men but not to women was Kuwait.

What was **Teapot Dome**?

Teapot Dome was a notorious scandal—on a level with Watergate and Whitewater. While the early-1920s abuses of power affected then President Warren G. Harding (1865–1923), it was not Harding who was implicated in the crimes. Albert Bacon Fall (1861–1944), Harding's Secretary of the Interior, secretly transferred government oil lands at Elk Hills, California, and Teapot Dome, Wyoming, to private use. Without a formal bidding process, Fall leased the Elk Hills naval oil reserves to American businessman Edward L. Doheny in exchange for an interest-free "loan" of $100,000. Fall made a similar arrangement with another businessman, Harry F. Sinclair of Sinclair Oil Corporation—leasing the Teapot Dome reserves in exchange for $300,000 in cash, bonds, and livestock.

The scandal was revealed in 1922 and committees of the U.S. Senate and a special commission spent the next six years sorting it all out. By the time the hearings and investigations were concluded in 1928, Harding had died (in 1923); Fall had resigned from office and taken a job working for Sinclair; all three players—Doheny, Sinclair, and Fall—had faced charges; and the government had successfully sued the oil companies for the return of the lands. The punishments were light, considering the serious nature of the charges: Fall was convicted of accepting a bribe, fined $100,000, and sentenced to a year in prison, while Doheny and Sinclair were both indicted but later acquitted of the charges against them, which included conspiracy and bribery.

How were **Theodore and Franklin Roosevelt** related?

The two men—who remain among the country's most well-known presidents—were distant cousins. Theodore Roosevelt was born in New York City in 1858, and following a career in public service that included organizing the first volunteer cavalry regiment that was known as the Rough Riders, the ardent outdoors enthusiast became vice president in 1901. When President McKinley died in office later that year (on September 14), "Teddy" Roosevelt succeeded him as president. He was elected in his own right in 1904, and went on to serve until 1909—spending nearly two full terms in the White House.

Teddy Roosevelt was president of the United States when he walked his niece, Eleanor Roosevelt (1884–1962), down the aisle on March 17, 1905. The young woman was marrying her distant cousin Franklin Roosevelt, who had been courting her since he entered college at Harvard in 1900.

Franklin Delano Roosevelt was born in Hyde Park, New York, in 1882. Like his fifth cousin Theodore, Franklin went on to a life of public service, which bore some remarkable similarities to that of his cousin: Both Theodore and Franklin served as assistant secretary of the U.S. Navy (1897–98 and 1913–20, respectively) and both were governors of New York (1899–1900 and 1929–33, respectively). As presidents, both served the nation for more than one term—but Franklin Roosevelt goes down in history for being the only president to be elected for third and fourth terms. (Though he governed responsibly, the U.S. Congress in 1951 did vote for passage of the 22nd Amendment, limiting presidential tenure to just two terms.) Both served the country in times of conflict: For

Theodore, it was the Russo-Japanese War—which he was instrumental in ending with the Treaty of Portsmouth (N.H.) on September 5, 1905, and for which he was awarded the Nobel prize for peace the following year. Franklin Roosevelt was one of the so-called Big Three leaders—along with Britain's Winston Churchill and the Soviet Union's Joseph Stalin, he coordinated the Allied Nations' effort against Nazi Germany and Japan. He, too, was a champion of peace, having been central in laying plans for the United Nations.

It's an interesting note, however, that when Teddy Roosevelt ran for office in 1912, he was opposed by his young Democratic cousin Franklin, then a state senator in New York, who supported Woodrow Wilson (1856–1924) in the presidential race. After Wilson was elected, he appointed Franklin Roosevelt as assistant secretary of the Navy—a post that delighted him for combining his vocation (politics) with his avocation (ships), and one that certainly furthered his political career. By the end of World War I (1914–18), Franklin Roosevelt was a well-known national figure.

Theodore and Franklin also shared an interest in outdoor activities. But Franklin's participation in sport was curtailed when he was stricken with polio in August 1921. The thirty-nine-year-old Roosevelt was paralyzed for a time, and though he regained movement and was able to walk with braces, he never fully recovered. Through fierce determination he continued his life of public service, becoming president in 1933. He saw the country through two of its most trying periods—the Great Depression (1929–40) and World War II (1939–45). He died suddenly of a brain hemorrhage in April 1945.

What did the **U.S. government** do to try to end the **Great Depression**?

The Great Depression had begun with the stock market crash on "Black Thursday," October 29, 1929. But many factors had contributed to the financial crisis including overproduction, limited foreign markets (due to war debts which prevented trading), overexpansion of credit—as well as stock market speculation. Soon the country was in the grips of a severe economic downturn that affected most every American. Some were hit harder than others: many lost their jobs (sixteen million people

179

were unemployed at the depth of the crisis, accounting for about a third of the workforce); families were unable to make their mortgage payments and lost their homes; hunger was widespread—since there was no money to buy food. The sight of people waiting in bread lines was a common one.

It was amidst this crisis, which was soon felt overseas, that Franklin Roosevelt took office as president in 1933. In his inaugural address, he called for faith in America's future, saying "The only thing we have to fear is fear itself." Roosevelt soon rolled out a program of domestic reforms called the New Deal. For the first time in American history, the federal government took a central role in organizing business and agriculture. Roosevelt initiated aid programs and directed relief in the way of public works programs that would put people back to work. The new government agencies that were set up included the Public Works Administration, Federal Deposit Insurance Corporation, Security and Exchange Commission, National Labor Relations Board, Tennessee Valley Association, the National Recovery Administration, and the Civilian Conservation Corps. These government organizations soon become known by their initials (PWA, FDIC, SEC, NLRB, TVA, NRA, CCC). Roosevelt's critics charged him with giving the federal government too much power and began calling his New Deal "alphabet soup." The president even became widely known as FDR.

Though these measures alleviated the situation and did put some Americans back to work, the country did not pull out of the Depression until industry was called upon to step up its production in order to provide arms, aircraft, vehicles, and supplies for the war effort. It was during the early days of World War II (1939–45) that the nation recovered. Many of the agencies of the New Deal are still part of the federal government today.

Was the **holocaust** really directed by **the German government**?

Yes. When fervent nationalist Adolf Hitler (1889–1945) rose to power in Germany in 1933 he quickly established a reign of terror based on his philosophy that the German (Aryan) race is superior to all others. He established a violent policy against Jews: Those who did not flee the country were rounded up and sent to concentration camps, where they were kept without cause. This was even prior to Hitler's acts of military

Men taking advantage of the many rescue missions established during the Great Depression.

aggression in Europe. But after German troops invaded Poland and World War II began, the Führer's anti-Semitic campaign was accelerated. Jews in Germany and in Nazi-occupied countries of Europe were severely persecuted. Those who were put into concentration camps—the most notorious of which were Auschwitz, Treblinka, Buchenwald, and Dachau—were exterminated, many of them in gas chambers. By the end of the war, in 1945, Hitler's "final solution to the Jewish question" had been under way for some twelve years, and six million Jews had been systematically murdered by the Nazis. As his defeat was imminent, the despotic ruler took his own life in 1945. He had destroyed the Jewish community in Europe. Many of Hitler's leaders were later tried by an international court at Nuremberg.

What was the **Long March**?

The Long March began in October 1934 when Mao Tse-tung led Chinese Communist forces (the Red Army of China), numbering one hundred thousand men and women, on an epic walk across China. The Nationalist Army in pursuit, the Communist marchers crossed eighteen mountain

181

chains and twenty-four rivers to cover six thousand miles. Almost all women and children died along the way. In 1935, twenty to thirty thousand people finally reached Shaanxi (Shensi) Province in the north, where the Red Army established a stronghold. It was there that Mao, one of the earliest members of the Chinese Communist party, formulated his own philosophy that came to be known as Maoism. He had adapted Marxism to the Chinese conditions—replacing Karl Marx's urban working class with the peasant farmers as the force behind revolution. The Red Army went on to defeat the Nationalists in 1949; Mao was named chairman of the People's Republic of China, a Communist state, that same year.

UNITED NATIONS

What was the **League of Nations**?

The League of Nations was the forerunner to the United Nations. It was an international organization established by the Treaty of Versailles at the end of World War I (1914–18). Since the United States never ratified that treaty, it was not a member.

The league was set up to handle disputes among countries and avoid another major conflict such as the Great War (which is how World War I was referred to until the outbreak of World War II). But the organization proved to be ineffective—it was unable to intervene in such acts of aggression as Japan's invasion of Manchuria (1931), Italy's conquest of Ethiopia (1935–36) and occupation of Albania (1939) by Fascist leader Benito Mussolini, and Germany's takeover of Austria (1938) by Adolf Hitler.

The organization dissolved itself during World War II (1939–45). Though unsuccessful, the League of Nations did establish a basic model for a permanent international organization.

How was the **United Nations formed**?

Officially the UN was not formed until October 1945. However, events during World War II had paved the way for the founding of the international peacekeeping organization that is so familiar to people around the globe.

The fighting of World War II began in 1939 and Nazi Germany soon conquered much of Europe. Leaders of nine nations—Belgium, Czechoslovakia, France, Greece, Luxembourg, the Netherlands, Norway, Poland, and Yugoslavia—met with Britain and its Commonwealth states in London. There, on June 12, 1941, the countries signed the Inter-Allied Declaration, vowing to work together for a free world. Two months later, on August 14, U.S. President Franklin Delano Roosevelt (1882–1945) and British Prime Minister Winston Churchill (1874–1965) signed the Atlantic Charter. In it the two leaders outlined their aims for peace.

On January 1, 1942, the "Declaration by the United Nations" was signed by twenty-six countries who pledged to work together to fight the Axis powers and they agreed not to make peace separately. The term United Nations is said to have originated with Roosevelt.

In late November and early December 1943, the Big Three—Roosevelt, Churchill, and Soviet Premier Joseph Stalin (1879–1953)—met in Teheran, Iran, for the first time during the war. There these Allied Nations leaders cited the responsibility of a United Nations organization in keeping the peace once the war was over. Though ending the war was first and foremost in the minds of these leaders, all had seen two world wars fought in close succession and were determined that the nations of the world could work together to prevent such a thing from happening again. In August 1944, at the Dumbarton Oaks Conference in Washington, D.C., representatives of Britain, the United States, the Soviet Union, and China met to make plans for the peacekeeping organization that had been envisioned by the world's leaders. The outcome of that meeting, which lasted into October, was the basic concept for the UN Security Council as we know it—with the world's (five) major powers having permanent seats on the council and a limited and rotating membership beyond that.

When the Big Three met again at the Yalta Conference (in the Soviet Union) in February 1945, again they discussed matters that were central to ending the fighting with Germany and with Japan. But Roosevelt, Churchill, and Stalin also announced that a conference of the United Nations would open in San Francisco on April 25 of that year.

Having directed the United States' massive war effort, Roosevelt did not live to see the end of World War II or the creation of the international peacekeeping body. Roosevelt died suddenly on April 12, 1945. (The war in Europe ended May 7.) Nevertheless, during the closing days of World War II, the UN was chartered—the representative of the Allied Nations met as promised in San Francisco. On June 26, 1945, the governing treaty was signed by the delegates. On October 24, 1945, shortly after the war ended, the United Nations officially came into existence when the required number of nations approved the Charter. Fifty nations were members of the UN.

When did the **United Nations begin its work**?

Very soon after it was chartered: The first meeting of the UN was held January 10, 1946, when the inaugural session of the General Assembly opened in London. Weeks later, on February 14, the UN voted to make its headquarters in the United States—which it did, completing a complex in Manhattan, overlooking New York's East River, in 1950.

Since it was founded, more than one hundred nations have joined the UN, bringing total membership to more than 150—accounting for almost all of the world's independent countries. Representatives of member countries work to keep peace and ensure security for people around the globe. When fighting does arise, the UN endeavors to work with the warring nations to resolve the conflict. Though not always successful in its role as peacekeeper or peace-negotiator, the organization has provided a forum for debate, which has prevented some disputes from developing into major wars. And through its various agencies, the UN provides assistance to developing nations, promotes humanitarian causes, and sends relief to war-torn areas.

However, some critics have also charged the international organization with arbitrarily defining borders between countries, saying these drawn boundaries divided ethnic groups and resulted in conflicts (such as in the Middle East and in Africa).

Why was **Mohandas Gandhi** called "Mahatma"?

Mohandas Gandhi was called Mahatma (meaning "great-souled") by the common people who viewed him as India's national and spiritual leader. He is considered the father of his country. Born in India on October 2, 1869, Gandhi studied law in Britain as a young man. Practicing briefly

What are the bodies and agencies of the United Nations?

The United Nations' charter establishes six main bodies and explains their duties and operating methods: the General Assembly is the major forum—all member nations are represented there and the Assembly can discuss any issue that is deemed to be relevant and important to the UN; the Security Council has the major responsibility for preserving peace; the Economic and Social Council investigates economic questions and works to improve living standards; the Secretariat is the UN's administrative body, helping all organs do their work; the Trusteeship Council assists non-self-governing territories; and the International Court of Justice hears disputes between member nations. Except for the last one, all bodies convene in the UN headquarters in New York City. (The International Court of Justice meets in The Hague.)

Since the charter was written, the United Nations has established numerous agencies, committees, and commissions to help carry out its work around the world. Among those that are most well known to the public are UNESCO (the United Nations Educational, Scientific, and Cultural Organization), which encourages the exchange of ideas among nations; UNICEF (the United Nations International Children's Emergency Fund), which assists children and adolescents worldwide, particularly those in devastated areas or developing countries; the World Health Organization (WHO), which promotes high health standards around the globe; the International Labor Organization (ILO), which works to improve labor conditions and protect workers; and the IMF (International Monetary Fund), which addresses currency and trade issues.

in India, he then traveled to British-controlled South Africa on business. Observing oppressive treatment of Indian immigrants there, he held his first campaign of passive resistance. Gandhi would later become very well known for this method of protest, called *satyagraha* (meaning "firmness in truth").

A very young Gandhi.

Back in India as of 1915, Gandhi organized a movement of the people against the British government there: Britain had taken control of India during the 1700s and remained in power. After World War I (1914–18), Indian nationalists fought what would be a long and sometimes bitter struggle for political independence. While Gandhi's protests took the form of nonviolent campaigns of civil disobedience, such as boycotts and fasts (hunger strikes), he was more than once arrested by the authorities for causing disorder as his actions inspired more extreme measures on the part of his followers, whose protests took the form of rioting.

As a member and, later, the president of India's chief political party, the Indian National Congress, Gandhi led a fight to rid the country of its rigid caste system, which organizes Indian society into distinct classes and groups. In Gandhi's time, not only were there four varna, or social classes, but there was a fifth group of "untouchables" who ranked even below the lowest class of peasants and laborers. Improving the lot of the untouchables was of tantamount importance to the leader, who by this time had abandoned Western ways in favor of a life of simplicity.

Beginning in 1937, Gandhi became less active in government, giving up his official roles, but continued to be regarded as a leader of the independence movement. During World War II, he was arrested for demanding British withdrawal. Released from prison in 1944, Gandhi was central to the postwar negotiations that resulted in an independent India in 1947. A believer in the unity of mankind under one God, he remained tolerant to Christian and Muslim beliefs. Amidst an outbreak of violence between Hindus and Muslims, Gandhi was on a prayer vigil in New Delhi when a Hindu fanatic fatally shot him in 1948.

Was **Indira Gandhi related** to **Mohandas Gandhi**?

No, the two were in no way related—except by events. After India achieved independence in 1947, the country's first prime minister was Jawaharlal Nehru (1889–1964) who had been a follower of Mohandas Gandhi, the great leader of India's long struggle for autonomy from Great Britain. During his entire tenure (1947–64) as leader of India, Nehru was assisted by his only child, Indira (1917–84), who in 1942 married a man named Feroze Gandhi—of no relation to Mohandas Gandhi. Indira Gandhi took an active role in India's national affairs.

After her father died, she went on to become prime minister in 1966. However, hers was a troubled tenure. Found guilty of employing illegal election practices, Indira Gandhi was ousted by her political opponents in 1977. Determined to return to power, she was re-elected to parliament in 1980 and again served as prime minister until her death in 1984. She was assassinated by two of her own security guards—Sikhs who were motivated by religious reasons. Her son and successor Rajiv Gandhi (born 1944) was also assassinated—in 1991.

MIDDLE EAST POLITICS

When was **Israel formed**?

As a modern state, Israel was formed by decree in 1948. In the wake of World War II, the United Nations formed a special committee to address the British control of Palestine—the region in the Middle East (southwest Asia) that borders the Mediterranean Sea to the west, Lebanon to the north, Syria and Jordan to the east, and Egypt (the Sinai Peninsula) to the southwest; the narrow piece of land comes to a point in the south, where it fronts the Gulf of Aqaba. In November 1947, the United Nations carved Israel out of the Palestine region; areas of Palestine that were not designated as Israel were divided between neighboring Arab countries. Modern Israel's first leader, David Ben-Gurion (1886–1973), proclaimed an independent Israel on May 14, 1948. Born in Poland, Ben-Gurion had arrived in Palestine as a young man of about twenty years and became extremely active in efforts to assert Jewish autonomy in the region. He served as prime minister from 1949 to 1953 and again between 1955 and 1963. But Israel's history goes back much farther than these twentieth-century events. And, having such a long history, it is also a complicated one.

Israel was an ancient kingdom in Palestine, formed under King Saul in 1020 B.C. Israel included the lands in Canaan—the Promised Land of the Hebrew tribes who descended from the people the prophet Moses led out of Egypt. But the kingdom was subsequently divided and by the eighth century B.C., it had ceased to exist. Nevertheless, the area remained home—and Holy Land—to the Hebrews (Israelites) who had settled there.

The entire region of Palestine, including the former kingdom of Israel, subsequently came under the control of various empires. Palestine saw the rule of the Assyrians, the Chaldeans, the Persians, the Macedonians under Alexander the Great, and the Romans (the area was the Roman province of Syria in the time of Jesus). After Roman rule, Palestine was, with only one exception, ruled by various Muslim (Islamic) dynasties, including the Ottoman Empire (1516–1917). It was in 1917 that Palestine came under control of the British, who proclaimed in the Declaration of Balfour to support the establishment of a national home for the Jews living there. However, Britain reversed this policy in 1939 at the same time the area was seeing an influx of Jewish people who were escaping persecution in Europe. Jews in Palestine opposed British control, and at the same time fighting intensified between Jews and Arabs.

The 1947 decision of the United Nations to establish a Jewish homeland resulted in nearly two years of fighting between Israelis and Arabs in the region. And though boundaries among the various states were determined anew in 1949, fighting in the region continued with the Arab-Israeli Wars of 1956, 1967, 1973–74, and 1982. Unrest prevailed throughout the 1980s and into the 1990s when the two sides began discussions to resolve the long conflict.

What is the **Palestinian Liberation Organization**?

In 1964, Arabs in Palestine formed the PLO (Palestinian Liberation Organization), which sought to establish an area of autonomy (self-rule). Dominated by then-guerrilla leader Yasir Arafat (b. 1929), the PLO regarded Israel as an illegitimate state and became determined to establish a Palestinian state in the region. In 1974, the PLO was recognized by the United Nations and by Arab countries as the governing body of the Palestinian people; however the Palestinians remained without a homeland and continued to fight for one, often resorting to terrorist tactics.

But under Arafat's leadership in 1993, the PLO and Israel officially recognized each other, signing agreements that led to the withdrawal of Israeli troops from the Gaza Strip and most cities and towns of the West Bank by early 1996.

In 1994, Arafat and Israeli leaders Yitzhak Rabin (1922–95) and Shimon Peres (b. 1923) were awarded the Nobel Peace Prize for their peace

189

What were the Camp David Accords?

Camp David Accords is the popular name for a 1979 peace treaty between Israel and Egypt. The name stuck since President Jimmy Carter (b. 1924) met with Israel's Menachem Begin (1913–92) and Egypt's Anwar Sadat (1918–81) at the Presidential retreat at Camp David, Maryland. The treaty was actually signed on March 26, 1979, in Washington, D.C., with Carter as a witness to the agreement between the warring Middle Eastern nations.

The pact, which was denounced by Arab countries, provided for the return of the Sinai Peninsula to Egypt. The mountainous area, adjacent to Israel and at the north end of the Red Sea, had been the site of a major campaign during the Arab-Israeli War of 1967 and had been occupied by Israel since. The transfer of the Peninsula back to Egypt was completed in 1982. The Camp David Accords had also outlined that the two sides would negotiate Palestinian autonomy in the occupied West Bank and Gaza Strip. However, Sadat was assassinated in 1981 and this initiative saw no progress as a result of the Camp David Accords.

efforts. In January 1996, Palestinians in the Gaza Strip and the Palestinian-controlled parts of the West Bank elected a legislature and a president (Arafat) to govern these areas.

What was the **basis** of the **conflict** over the **Gaza Strip and the West Bank**?

The conflict is rooted in Jewish and Arab claims to the same lands in the Palestine region, which was under British control between 1917 and 1947. The Gaza Strip is a tiny piece of territory along the eastern Mediterranean Sea and adjacent to Egypt. After the nation of Israel was established and boundaries were determined in 1948, the Gaza Strip—bounded on two sides by the new Israel—came under Egyptian control. The Arab-Israeli war of 1967 resulted in Israeli control and occupation of the Gaza. But unrest continued and in 1987–88, the region was the site of Arab uprisings known as the Intifada. An historic accord between the Palestinian Liberation Organization (PLO) and Israel, signed in May 1994, provided for Palestinian self-rule in the Gaza Strip. This has been in effect since.

The West Bank—which does *not* neighbor the Gaza Strip—is an area on the east of Israel, along the Jordan River and Dead Sea. The West Bank includes the towns of Jericho, Bethlehem, and Hebron. The holy city of Jerusalem is situated on the shared border between Israel and the West Bank. By the United Nations mandate (1947) that established the independent Jewish state of Israel, the West Bank area was supposed to become Palestinian. But Arabs who were unhappy with the UN agreement in the first place attacked Israel, and Israel responded by occupying the West Bank. A 1950 truce brought the West Bank under the control of neighboring Jordan; this situation lasted until 1967, when Israeli forces again occupied the region. Israelis soon began establishing settlements there, which provoked the resentment of the Arabs. The Intifada uprisings that began in the Gaza Strip in 1987 soon spread to the West Bank. In 1988, Jordan relinquished its claim to the area, but fighting between the PLO and Israeli troops continued. Peace talks began in 1991 and the agreements that provided for Palestinian self-rule in the Gaza Strip also provided for the gradual return of West Bank lands to Palestinians. The city of Jericho was the first of these lands.

Though both Israel and the PLO officially recognized each other, and the Palestinians in 1996 began setting up their own government for the Gaza Strip and Palestinian areas of the West Bank, tensions between the two groups remain.

Who coined the term **Iron Curtain**?

It was British Prime Minister Winston Churchill (1874–1965) who, in a March 1946 speech in Fulton, Missouri, remarked that "an iron curtain has descended across the Continent." The statesman, who had been instrumental in coordinating the Allied victory in World War II, was commenting on Soviet leader Joseph Stalin's tactics in Eastern Europe, which indicated the Soviets were putting up barriers against the West— and building up Soviet domination behind those barriers.

Just as he had issued (unheeded) warnings of the threat posed by Nazi Germany prior to World War II, Churchill astutely observed the rapidly emerging situation in Eastern Europe: In 1946, the Soviets installed Communist governments in neighboring Romania and in nearby Bulgaria; in 1947 Hungary and Poland came under Communist control as well; and the following year, Communists took control of Czechoslovakia. These countries, along with Albania, Yugoslavia, and Eastern Germany, soon formed a coalition of Communist allies and the Eastern bloc was formed. The United States and its democratic allies formed the Western bloc. The stage was set for the Cold War.

What was the **Berlin airlift**?

It was the response in 1948–49 to the Soviet blockade of West Berlin. After World War II, the German city had been divided into four occupation zones—American, British, French, and Soviet. But from that June 1945 event, it did not take long for the Cold War between the Western powers and the Soviet Union to heat up. When the Americans, British, and French agreed to combine their three areas of Berlin into one economic entity, the Soviets responded by cutting the area off from all supply routes. In June 1948, all arteries—road, rail, and water—into West Berlin were blocked by Soviet troops. Since Berlin was completely surrounded by the Soviet-occupation zone, the Soviets clearly believed it would be an effective move that would prompt the Western countries to pull out. But the move failed: the Americans, British, and French set up the Berlin airlift. For the next eleven months, West Berlin was supplied with food and fuel entirely by airplanes. The Soviets lifted the blockade in May 1949, and the airlift had ended by September.

How did the **Soviet Union form**?

The Soviet Union was officially created in 1922 when Russia joined with Ukraine, Belorussia, and the Transcaucasian Federation (which became Armenia, Azerbaijan, and Georgia) to form the Union of Soviet Socialist Republics (U.S.S.R.). These republics were later joined by nine others and territories were redrawn so that by 1940, the union consisted of fifteen Soviet Socialist republics—Armenia, Azerbaijan, Belorussia (now Belarus), Estonia, Georgia, Kazakhstan, Kirghiz (now Kyrgyzstan),

Latvia, Lithuania, Moldavia (now Moldova), Russia, Tadzhikistan (also spelled Tajikistan), Turkmenistan, Ukraine, and Uzbekistan.

How many leaders did the Soviet Union have?

From its formation in 1922 (just five years after tsarist Russia had fallen in the revolution of 1917), the U.S.S.R. had ten leaders. But only five of these had meaningful tenure (either due to length of time served or true authority): Lenin, Stalin, Khrushchev, Brezhnev, and Gorbachev.

After tsarist Russia ended with the revolution of 1917, Bolshevik leader Vladimir Lenin (1870–1924) became head of the Soviet Russian government as chairman of the Council of People's Commissars (the Communists), dissolving the elected assembly, and establishing a dictatorship. This lasted for six years: When Lenin died of a stroke in 1924, Joseph Stalin (1879–1953)—who had been an associate of Lenin—eliminated his opposition, and in 1929 established himself as a virtual dictator. Stalin ruled the U.S.S.R. through World War II, and though he was aligned with the United States, Britain, and the other Allied Nations during that conflict, soon after the war, he began a build-up of power in Eastern Europe—leading to the Cold War. Even though Stalin's domestic policies were extremely repressive and he ruled largely by terror, he remained in power until his death in 1953.

After Stalin died in 1953, the Soviet Union entered a brief period of struggle among its top leaders: Deputy Premier Georgy Malenkov (1902–88), a longtime Stalin aide, came to power. In 1955, Malenkov was forced to resign and he was succeeded by his (and Stalin's) former defense secretary, Nikolai Bulganin (1895–1975). However, Bulganin was a premier in name only; the true power rested with Communist party Secretary Nikita Khrushchev (1894–1971) who expelled Bulganin and officially took power as premier in 1958.

Khrushchev denounced the oppression of the long Stalin years—which had ended only five years earlier—and worked to improve living standards. On the international front, he pursued a policy of "peaceful coexistence" with the West and even toured the United States in 1959, meeting with President Dwight D. Eisenhower (1890–1969). In 1960, a U.S. reconnaissance plane was shot down over the U.S.S.R., raising doubts among the Soviets about Khrushchev's policy toward the West. Further

193

troubles at home resulted from widespread hunger due to crop failures. Meantime, Khrushchev advanced the cause of space exploration by the Soviets—beginning the so-called Space Race. Eventually, his stance on international issues, which included a rift with Communist China, led to his downfall. He was removed from power in October 1964.

Khrushchev's ouster (which was a forced retirement) had been engineered by his former ally and political adviser Leonid Brezhnev (1906–82). With Khrushchev out of the way, technically Brezhnev was to lead the country with premier Alexei Kosygin (1904–81). But as head of the Communist Party, it was Brezhnev who truly held the power. By the early 1970s, Brezhnev emerged as the Soviet chief—even though Kosygin remained in office until 1980. During his administration, Brezhnev kept tight control over the Eastern Bloc (Communist countries), built up the Soviet Union's military (in what became an arms race with the United States), and did nothing to try to reverse the downward trend of the Soviet Union's economy.

When Brezhnev died in 1982, he was succeeded by Yuri V. Andropov (1914–84). However, Andropov died two years later and Konstantin Chernenko (1911–85) replaced him as premier. When Chernenko, too, died an untimely death in March 1985, Mikhail S. Gorbachev (b. 1931) became head of the Communist Party and leader of the Soviet Union. With Gorbachev, the reign of the old guard of Stalin-trained leaders had come to an end. Gorbachev's policies of openness to the West and economic development led to the disintegration of the Soviet Union, with Communist rule ending in 1991 and each Soviet republic setting up its own government.

What were the **Five-Year Plans**?

These were the plans initiated by Soviet premier Joseph Stalin (1879–1953) in order to speed industrialization of the U.S.S.R. and organize agriculture under the collective control of the Communist government. The first five-year plan began in 1928 and subsequent plans were carried out until 1958, at which time the new Soviet leadership developed a seven-year plan (1959–65) aimed at matching—and surpassing—American industry. Under Soviet Premier Leonid Brezhnev (1906–82), the five-year plans were reinstated in 1966 and continued until the dissolution of the Soviet Union in 1990–91. Other Communist countries

What was the détente?

A détente is a relaxation of strained relations—particularly between nations. The détente of the Cold War era began after Nikita Khrushchev (1894–1971) rose to power in the Soviet Union in 1958 and initiated a plan of peaceful coexistence with the West. During the 1960s, the United States and the U.S.S.R. entered a phase of improved relations, which saw the signing of the Nuclear Nonproliferation Treaty (1968), the Strategic Arms Limitation Treaty (known better as the SALT-1 treaty; 1972), and the Helsinki accords (1975)—which pledged increased cooperation between the nations of Eastern and Western Europe.

Some historians refer to the détente as the end of the Cold War, while others view it more as an intermission: When the Soviet Union under Leonid Brezhnev (1906–82) invaded neighboring Afghanistan in 1979 to put down an anti-Communist movement there, tensions between the two super-powers (the U.S. and the U.S.S.R.) heightened dramatically. Further, Brezhnev had been steadily building up Soviet arms during his tenure. These events brought an end to the détente.

also instituted five-year plans—all with the goal of bringing industry, agriculture, and the distribution of goods and services under government control.

What were the **Jim Crow laws**?

The term "Jim Crow laws" refers to any law or practice that segregated blacks from whites. Jim Crow was a stereotype of a black man described in a nineteenth-century song-and-dance act. The first written appearance of the term is dated 1838, and by the 1880s, it had fallen into common use in the United States. Even though Congress passed the Fourteenth Amendment in 1868 prohibiting states from violating equal protection of all citizens, southern states passed many laws segregating

195

blacks from whites in public places. These "Jim Crow laws" were finally found to be unconstitutional during the mid-1900s.

What was the **Supreme Court's** role in **racial segregation**?

Though most segregation laws (or "Jim Crow laws") were overturned by decisions of the Supreme Court during the 1950s and 1960s, the Court was righting its own wrong: In the late-1800s, in the years following the Civil War and the abolition of slavery, the Supreme Court made rulings that actually supported segregation laws at the state level. The most famous of these was the 1896 case of *Plessy v. Ferguson*, in which the highest court in the land had upheld the constitutionality of Louisiana's law requiring separate but equal facilities for whites and blacks in railroad cars. (One strong dissenting opinion came from Associate Justice John Marshall Harlan, who declared ("the Constitution is color blind.") Following the *Plessy v. Ferguson* decision, states went on to use the "separate but equal" principle for fifty years, passing Jim Crow laws that stipulated racial segregation in public schools, transportation, and in recreation, sleeping, and eating facilities. This meant there were drinking fountains, benches, restrooms, bus seats, hospital beds, and theater sections designated as "Whites Only" or "Colored." One Arkansas law even provided that witnesses being sworn in to testify in a courtroom be given different Bibles depending on the color of their skin.

Two landmark Supreme Court decisions came in 1954 and 1960 in the cases of *Brown v. Board of Education* and *Boynton v. Virginia*. In the first case, parents of black children in the Topeka, Kansas, elementary schools charged that the segregation of white and black students in the public schools denied black children the equal protection cited in the Fourteenth Amendment (1868). The parents were supported in their fight by the NAACP, whose legal counsel included Thurgood Marshall (1908–93). On May 17, 1954, the Supreme Court ruled that segregated schools do violate the equal protection clause, overturning the "separate but equal" doctrine of *Plessy v. Ferguson*. The federal government again made a stand against state segregation laws when in December 1960, chief appellant lawyer Thurgood Marshall argued the case of Howard University law student Bruce Boynton before the Supreme Court. Again ruling in favor of the plaintiff, who had charged that the segregation

laws at the Richmond, Virginia, bus station violated the federal anti-seg-
regation laws, Washington had sent a clear message to the states that
public facilities were for the use of all citizens, regardless of color. These
decisions, combined with the activism of the Civil Rights movement,
outlawed racial segregation.

Were **activists** the only ones who were vocal about opposing **segregation**?

No: Segregation was opposed at every level of black society, as well as by
many whites. The voices of the Civil Rights movement included wage
laborers, farmers, educators, athletes, entertainers, soldiers, religious
leaders, politicians, and statesmen—all of whom had experienced the
oppression of Jim Crow laws and policies in the United States.

Before W. E. B. Du Bois (1868–1963) rose to prominence as an educator and writer, he chose to leave the security of his home in Great Bar-
rington, Massachusetts, to attend college at Nashville's Fisk University.
There, in 1885, he encountered Tennessee's Jim Crow laws, which
strictly divided blacks and whites. He was so intimidated by the
"southern system" that he rarely left the campus, and he ultimately
returned to New England to complete his studies at Harvard University. He did, however, go back to the South, becoming a professor of economics and history at Atlanta University (1897–1910, 1932–44). As one
of the first exponents of full and equal racial equality, in 1909, Du Bois
helped found the NAACP (National Association for the Advancement of
Colored People), which provided leadership during the Civil Rights
movement.

In 1942, a young Georgia man named John Roosevelt Robinson
(1919–72) was drafted into the military. Robinson applied for Officer's
Candidate School at Fort Riley, Kansas, and although he was admitted
to the program, he and the other black candidates received no training
until pressure from Washington forced the local commander to admit
blacks to the base's training school. Later Robinson became a second
lieutenant, and continued to challenge the Jim Crow policies on military bases: Robinson quit the base football team in protest when the
army decided to keep him out of a game with the nearby University of
Missouri, because that school refused to play against a team with black

members; at Fort Hood, Texas, Robinson protested segregation on an army bus. His protests led to a court-martial. Acquitted in November 1944, Robinson was honorably discharged—before the end of World War II (1939–45): The army had no desire to keep this black agitator among the ranks, and, as Robinson later put it, he was "pretty much fed up with the service." In 1947, "Jackie" Robinson became the first black baseball player in the major leagues, when he joined the Brooklyn Dodgers.

In the post-war years, American diplomat Ralph Bunche (1904–71) attracted public attention when he rejected an offer from President Harry S. Truman to become an assistant secretary of state. The Howard University professor, who had worked for the Office of Strategic Services during the war, explained that he declined the position because he did not want to subject his family to the Jim Crow laws of Washington, D.C. Bunche spoke out frequently against racism and in 1944, he co-authored the book, *An American Dilemma: The Negro Problem and Modern Democracy*, which examined the plight of American blacks.

How did the Civil Rights movement begin?

It began on Thursday, December 1, 1955, as Rosa Parks (b. 1913), a seamstress who worked for a downtown department store in Montgomery, Alabama, made her way home on the Cleveland Avenue bus. Parks was seated in the first row that was designated for blacks. But the white rows in the front of the bus soon filled up. When Parks was asked to give up her seat so that a white man could sit, she refused. She was arrested and sent to jail.

Montgomery's black leaders had already been discussing a protest against the racial segregation on the city buses. They soon organized, with Baptist minister Martin Luther King Jr. (1929–68) as their leader. Beginning on December 5, 1955, thousands of black people refused to ride the city buses: the Montgomery Bus Boycott had begun. It lasted more than a year—382 days—ending only when the U.S. Supreme Court ruled that segregation on city buses was unconstitutional. The protesters and civil rights activists had emerged the victors in this—their first and momentous—effort to end segregation and discrimination in the United States.

Rosa Parks.

Parks, who lost her job as a result of the arrest, acted on her own beliefs that she was being unfairly treated, but in so doing, she had taken a stand and given rise to a movement.

What is a **Poll Tax**?

It is a tax that is levied on every adult in a society as a prerequisite for voting. In other words, if a poll tax is in effect and a person wishes to vote in an election, he or she would first need to pay the tax in order to vote; if the tax were not paid, then the person would not be eligible to vote in the

199

election. The poll tax system has a long history, but since 1964 it has been illegal in U.S. federal elections and since 1966, in all government elections held in the United States. The reason is that a poll tax hits low-income people most severely and serves to disenfranchise them from the government process. It's no coincidence that poll taxes were outlawed in the United States during the Civil Rights movement: Some southern states had tried to use poll taxes as a way of excluding blacks from voting.

JOHN F. KENNEDY

What was the **Bay of Pigs**?

Bay of Pigs is the name of an unsuccessful 1961 invasion of Cuba, which was backed by the U.S. government. About 1,500 Cuban expatriates living in the United States had been supplied with arms and trained by the U.S. Central Intelligence Agency (CIA). On April 17, 1961, the group of men who opposed the regime of Cuba's Fidel Castro (b. 1926) landed at the Bahia de Cochinos (Bay of Pigs) in west-central Cuba. Most of the rebels were captured by the Cuban forces; others were killed. In order to secure the release of the over 1,100 men who had been captured during the invasion, private donors in the U.S. accumulated $53 million in food and medicine, which was given to Castro's government in exchange for the rebels' release. The failed invasion came as a terrible embarrassment to the Kennedy administration and many believe the Bay of Pigs incident directly led to the Cuban Missile Crisis.

What was the **Cuban Missile Crisis**?

The 1962 events, which happened very quickly, nevertheless constituted a major confrontation of the Cold War (1947–89). After the disastrous Bay of Pigs invasion—when the U.S. backed Cuban expatriates in an attempt to oust Fidel Castro, the Soviet Union quietly began building missile sites in Cuba. Since the island nation is situated just south of Florida, when U.S. reconnaissance flights detected the Soviet military

An end to Camelot: Jacqueline Kennedy, with her two children, attending husband John F. Kennedy's funeral.

construction projects there, it was an alarming discovery. On October 22, 1962, President John F. Kennedy (1917–63) demanded that the Soviet Union withdraw its missiles from Cuba. Kennedy also ordered a naval blockade of the island. Six days later, the Soviets agreed to dismantle the sites, ending the crisis.

Why is **Kennedy's presidency** called **"Camelot"**?

The term was actually assigned by Jacqueline Bouvier Kennedy (1929–94). Shortly after the assassination (November 22, 1963), the former First Lady was talking with a journalist when she described her husband's presidency as an American "Camelot," and asked that his memory be preserved. Camelot refers, of course, to the time of King Arthur and the Knights of the Round Table, and has come to refer to a place or time of idyllic happiness. John Fitzgerald Kennedy's widow, who had with such fortitude and grace, guided her family and the country through the sorrow and anguish of the president's funeral, quite naturally held sway over the American public. So when she suggested that the shining moments of her husband's presidency were reminiscent of the legends of Camelot, journalists quickly picked up on it. Despite subsequent revelations that there were difficulties in the Kennedy marriage, public opinion polls indicate that the image of Camelot—albeit somewhat tarnished—has prevailed.

What were the **"killing fields"**?

Once Communist leader Pol Pot, head of the Khmer Rouge guerrillas, took over the Cambodian government in 1975, he ordered a collectivization drive, rounding up anyone who was believed to have been in collusion with or otherwise supported the former regime of Lon Nol during the five-year civil war. The government-instituted executions, forced labor (in so-called re-education camps), and famine combined to kill an estimated three million people during Pol Pot's reign.

What happened at **Watergate**?

Watergate is a complex of upscale apartment and office buildings in Washington, D.C. and was the setting for one of Washington's most infa-

Who were the Khmer Rouge?

The Khmer Rouge (or "Red Khmer") were a group of Cambodian Communists led by radical leader Pol Pot. Between 1970 and 1975, the Khmer Rouge guerrilla force, supported by Communists from neighboring Vietnam, waged a war to topple the government of Lon Nol. On April 16, 1975, Lon Nol's regime fell and the next day, the Khmer Rouge seized the Cambodian capital, Phnom Penh. The ruthless revolutionary leader Pol Pot became prime minister of a Communist Cambodia and instituted a reign of terror.

A Vietnamese invasion (1978–79) ousted the Khmer Rouge and installed a regime they supported. Civil wars were fought throughout the 1980s. The warring factions, who had made various alliances among themselves, finally signed a peace treaty in 1991, and under the watchful eye of the United Nations, elections were held in 1993. The resulting constitution provided for a democratic government with a limited monarchy. At this point, the Cambodian leadership seemed to come full circle—with Norodom Sihanouk being crowned king in 1993: In 1970, Sihanouk had been deposed by Lon Nol, whose regime became the target of the Khmer Rouge. Pol Pot, the former head of the Khmer Rouge, continues to lead a revolutionary force in Cambodia.

mous political scandals. In July 1972, five men were caught breaking into the Democratic party's national headquarters located there. Among these men was James McCord Jr.—the security coordinator of the Committee for the Re-election of the President (CRP). McCord was among those working to get Republican President Richard Nixon (1913–94) elected to a second term in office.

All five men who were caught in the break-in were indicted on charges of burglary and wire-tapping, as were CRP aide G. Gordon Liddy and White House consultant E. Howard Hunt Jr. Five of the men pleaded guilty to the charges. McCord and Liddy were tried and found guilty.

In February 1972—five months before the break-in at Watergate, President Nixon had traveled to China, becoming the first U.S. President to visit that country. In May, he traveled to Moscow where he signed the Strategic Arms Limitation Treaty (SALT-1)—the first such treaty between the United States and the U.S.S.R. When the election was held in November, Nixon won in a landslide victory over the Democratic candidate George McGovern (b. 1922–98).

But early in his second term, which began in 1973, the Watergate affair became a full-blown political scandal when convicted Burglar James McCord wrote a letter to District Court Judge John Sirica charging a massive cover-up in the Watergate break-in. A special senate committee began televised investigations into the affair and before it was all over, about forty people, including high-level government officials, had been charged with crimes including burglary, wiretapping of citizens, violating campaign finance laws by accepting contributions in exchange for political favors, the use of government agencies to harm political opponents, and sabotage.

Among those prosecuted were former White House Counsel John Dean and Attorney General John Mitchell. It was revealed that members of the Nixon administration had known about the Watergate burglary. It was also discovered that the president had taped conversations in the Oval Office. When Dean and Mitchell were convicted, public confidence in President Nixon plummeted. In July 1974, the Judiciary Committee of the House of Representatives was preparing articles of impeachment (including one that charged the president with obstruction of justice) against the president. But Nixon felt the pressure and chose to resign on August 9, 1974. He was the first and so far only U.S. president to resign from office.

Shortly after taking office, Nixon's successor, Gerald R. Ford (b. 1913) pardoned Nixon. But Watergate remains a dark chapter in the nation's history.

What was the **Iran-Contra affair**?

It was a series of actions on the part of U.S. federal government officials, which came to light in November 1986. The discoveries had the immediate affect of hurting President Ronald Reagan (b. 1911), whose policy of anti-terrorism had been undermined by activities initiated from his own executive office. Following in-depth hearings and investigations into "who knew what, when," special prosecutor Lawrence Walsh submitted his report on January 18, 1994, stating that the dealings with Iran and with the contra rebels in Nicaragua had "violated United States policy and law."

The tangled string of events involved Reagan's National Security advisers Robert McFarlane and Admiral John Poindexter, Lieutenant Colonel Oliver North (Poindexter's military aide), the Iranian government, and Nicaraguan rebels. The U.S. officials had evidently begun their dealings with the goal of freeing seven Americans who were being held hostage by Iranian-backed rebels in Lebanon. President Reagan had met with the families of the captives and was naturally concerned about the hostage situation. Under pressure to work to free the hostages, McFarlane, Poindexter, and North arranged to sell an estimated $30 million in spare parts and anti-aircraft missiles to Iran (then at war with neighboring Iraq). In return, the Iranian government would put pressure on the terrorist groups to release the Americans.

Profits from the arms sale to Iran were then diverted by Lieutenant North to the contras in Central America who were fighting the dictatorial Nicaraguan government. Congress had already passed laws that prohibited U.S. government aid to the Nicaraguan rebels; the diversion of funds certainly appeared to violate those laws. The Iran-Contra affair led to North's dismissal and to Poindexter's resignation. Both men were prosecuted. Though the hostages were freed, Reagan's public image was seriously damaged by how the release had been effected.

During the Iran-Contra hearings in 1987, National Security Commission officials revealed that they had been willing to take the risk of providing arms to Iran in exchange for the safe release of the hostages because they all remembered the failed rescue attempt in 1980 when the U.S. government had worked to free hostages being held at the U.S. Embassy in Tehran, Iran.

Nevertheless, the deal with Iran had supplied a hostile country with American arms that could then be used against the United States. In 1987, when Iran attacked Kuwaiti oil tankers that were registered as American and laid mines in the Persian Gulf, the United States sent in the Navy, which attacked Iranian patrol boats—and accidentally shot down a civilian passenger jet, killing all the people on board.

205

What is **apartheid**?

Apartheid is a system of racial segregation in South Africa. (The word *apartheid* means "separateness" in the South African language of Afrikaans.) Under apartheid, which was formalized in 1948 by the Afrikaner Nationalist party, the minority whites were given supremacy over nonwhites. The system separated nonwhite groups from each other so that mulattoes/mixed race, Asians (mostly Indians), and native Africans were all segregated. The policy was so rigid that it even separated native Bantu groups from each other. Blacks were not allowed to vote—even though they were (and are) the majority population. Apartheid was destructive to the society as a whole and drew international protest. But the South African government adhered to the system, claiming it was the only way to keep the peace among the groups. In 1961, the country even went so far as to withdraw from the British Commonwealth in a dispute over the issue.

Protesters against apartheid staged demonstrations and strikes—which became violent. South Africa grew increasingly isolated as countries opposing the system refused to trade with the apartheid government. During the 1980s, an economic boycott put pressure on the white minority South African government to repeal apartheid laws. It finally did so and in 1991, apartheid was officially abolished.

White South African leader F. W. de Klerk (b. 1936), who was elected in 1989, had been instrumental in ending the apartheid system. In April 1994, South Africa held the first elections in which blacks were eligible to vote. Not surprisingly, black South Africans won control of parliament, which in turn elected black leader Nelson Mandela (b. 1918) as president; de Klerk was retained as deputy president. The two men won the Nobel prize for peace in 1993 for their efforts to end apartheid and give all of South Africa's peoples full participation in government. De Klerk resigned as deputy president in 1996.

What is the **"Irish Question"**?

The Irish Question is an ages-old and very complicated problem that encompasses land ownership, religious, and political issues between Ireland and Britain. The chronology of events is as follows:

12th century: A feudal landowning system is imposed on Ireland by the British, creating an absentee landlord class and an impoverished Irish peasantry.

1700s: The English try to impose Protestantism on a largely Catholic Ireland; Irish rebellions flair.

1800: The Act of Union unites England and Ireland, forming the United Kingdom. Though Ireland has representation in Parliament, it is divided.

1800s: The British crown begins to populate the six counties of Ulster (in northeastern Ireland) with Scottish and British settlers, giving the area a Protestant character. The division deepens between the twenty-six counties of southern Ireland and Ulster Ireland: The north becomes increasingly industrialized and Protestant while the south remains agricultural and Catholic.

1840s: Irish discontent with British rule heightens when a great famine strikes Ireland, resulting in widespread hunger, illness, and death. Many who survive emigrate to seek a better life elsewhere.

1858: A secret revolutionary society forms in Ireland and among Irish emigres in the United States. Called the Fenian movement, the group's objective is to achieve Irish independence from England by force. Fenians stage rebellions, which are suppressed by the British.

1868: The head of the Liberal party, William Gladstone (1809–98), becomes British prime minister. He will become prime minister three more times during the last four decades of the century. Gladstone becomes an advocate for the peaceful settlement of the Irish question.

1870: Parliament passes the First Land Act, encouraging British landlords to sell land and providing reduced-rate loans to Irish tenants wishing to buy land.

1875: Irish nationalist leader C. S. Parnell (1846–91) enters British Parliament. He uses filibusters to prevent Parliament from discussing anything but the Irish Question.

1886: C. S. Parnell forms an alliance with Prime Minister William Gladstone. The First Home Rule Bill (providing for Irish self-government) is introduced in Parliament but fails to pass.

1893: The Second Home Rule Bill is introduced in Parliament. It is passed by the House of Commons but fails to be passed by the Lords.

1905: An Irish nationalistic movement called Sinn Fein (meaning "we ourselves") forms under the leadership of Arthur Griffith (1872–1922). The group seeks to establish an economically and politically independent Ireland.

1912: The Third Home Rule Bill is introduced in Parliament. Again, the House of Commons passes the legislation providing for Irish self-government. Fearing domination by Catholic southern Ireland in the event of Irish Home Rule, there is agitation—including threat of civil war—in Ulster (northern) Ireland. To prevent the outbreak of violence, the Lords, therefore, exclude Ulster Ireland from the provisions of the Home Rule Bill. It does not take effect due to continued unrest.

1916: Refusing to accept the divided Ireland proscribed by the British Parliament, revolutionary Sinn Fein member Michael Collins (1890–1922) organizes a guerrilla movement led by the Irish Republican Army (IRA). The nationalist organization becomes dedicated to the unification of Ireland.

1920: Parliament passes the Government of Ireland Act, establishing separate domestic legislatures for the north and south, as well as continued representation in the UK Parliament. The six northern counties of Ireland accept the act and become Northern Ireland. The twenty-six southern counties refuse to accept the legislation.

1921: The Anglo-Irish Treaty is signed, providing for the twenty-six counties of southern Ireland to become the Irish Free State (now the Irish Republic).

1922: The Irish Free State, headed by Sinn Fein leader Arthur Griffith, is officially declared. It gradually severs its ties to Britain.

1927: Sinn Fein ends as a movement but some intransigent members join the IRA, and Sinn Fein becomes the political arm of the Irish Revolutionary Army.

1939–45: IRA violence and its pro-German stance cause both Irish governments to outlaw the organization, which goes underground.

1969: The IRA splits into an "official" majority, which disclaims violence, and a "provisional" wing, which stages attacks on British troops in

Northern Ireland via random bombings and other terrorist acts. Still determined to forge a unified and independent Ireland, the IRA continues to stage acts of violence into the 1990s. At times, bombings become part of everyday life in Belfast, Northern Ireland. London is also the target of random IRA bomb attacks.

1996: June 6, Britain and Ireland agree on an agenda for multi-party peace negotiations on Northern Ireland, but finding ways to disarm Northern Ireland's rival guerrilla groups remains an obstacle to political settlement.

1998: On May 22, 71 percent of voters in Northern Ireland vote for an agreement on a power-sharing government, which is also backed by 94 percent of the voters in the Republic of Ireland. The peace agreement is designed to heal the divisions between Catholics and Protestants that have left 3,400 dead, 40,000 injured, and millions of dollars of property damage. Irish Prime Minister Bertie Ahern has a simple message for those who still aim to promote violence: "Forget it. The people on whose behalf you claim to act have spoken. Your ways are the ways of the past."

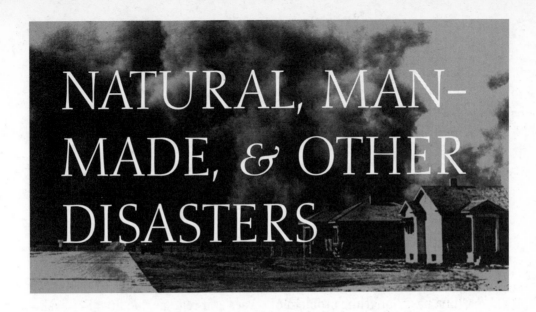

NATURAL, MAN-MADE, & OTHER DISASTERS

When was the **Johnstown Flood**?

The disastrous flood most often referred to by that name is the one that occurred on May 31, 1889, when a dam on the Conemaugh River gave way fourteen miles into the mountains, releasing a torrent of water that rushed into the Pennsylvania town at a rate of fifty miles per hour, killing more than two thousand people (some sources place the estimate as high as five thousand lives lost). At the time of the flood, the town had a population of about thirty thousand, meaning the flood killed between 6 and 16 percent of the people who lived there. The rush of water hit with a force strong enough to have tossed a forty-eight-ton locomotive one mile.

In 1977, Johnstown was again the site of a disastrous flood—though advance warning systems helped minimize the loss of life to seventy-seven.

How does the **Great Flood of 1993** compare with other floods?

The flood, which occurred in the summer of 1993, was immense: So much of Iowa was under water that a satellite image (monitoring moisture on the earth) made the flooded area look like it was the size of Lake Michigan or Lake Superior. The area that was under water was roughly equivalent to twice the size of Massachusetts. Even so, the Great Flood resulted in a smaller water-covered area than did floods earlier in the century (in 1926 and 1973).

211

Due to heavy rainfall during the spring and summer of 1993, the Mississippi River widened to as much as seven miles at some points, and the Missouri River also overflowed its banks—despite the levee system that had been put in place by the federal government earlier in the century. The flood took 50 lives, displaced 85,000 people from their homes, destroyed 8,000 homes, damaged the contents of another 20,000 homes, stranded 2,000 loaded barges, and resulted in just over 400 counties being declared disaster areas. The property and crop losses totaled $15 billion. Forty-eight people perished.

Which **country** has the **worst floods**?

China has a longtime problem of severe and regular flooding. For example, the Huanghe (Yellow) River typically floods two out of every three years. And because river valleys are densely populated, the human toll is often great. One of the worst floods in history took place in China in 1887, when more than nine hundred thousand people lost their lives. In 1954, rising waters claimed more than thirty thousand Chinese.

Pakistan, India, and Bangladesh have also been the sites of disastrous floods in the twentieth century, with hundreds of thousands of lives lost.

What have been the **deadliest tropical storms** in the world?

The deadliest tropical storms are not hurricanes but rather cyclones—those that sweep out of the Bay of Bengal (in the Indian Ocean), striking the Indian subcontinent, which is densely populated. These storms have been known to kill a 100,000 people or more. The fatalities numbered over five hundred thousand when a 1970 cyclone struck East Pakistan (Bangladesh). A May 1991 storm packing 145-mile-per-hour winds and 20-foot waves, swept over Bangladesh's low-lying coastal plain, where at least ten million people live. There was no place for them to seek shelter from the advancing sea. The exact death toll is unknown, however it is estimated that hundreds of thousands of people perished.

Which **hurricanes** have caused the **most damage in the U.S.**?

Florida has seen some of the country's most damaging hurricanes, including Andrew, which hit south Florida in 1992. On September 8,

What was the worst hurricane in U.S. history?

It depends on how "worst" is defined—in human toll, damage, or intensity. The most severe loss to American lives from a hurricane occurred in Galveston, Texas, in 1900, when a September 8 storm claimed between 6,000 and 8,000 lives. In its death toll, it was the worst recorded natural disaster in North American history. In intensity, the category–4 storm remains one of the most intense hurricanes to strike the United States. (Hurricane strength is measured on the Saffir-Simpson scale, where category–1 is the weakest and category–5 is the strongest.)

The most damage caused by a hurricane to date was when Hurricane Andrew slammed into the south Florida coast in 1992. A category–4 storm, Andrew walloped the Bahamas on August 22, killing four people, before moving west where it hit near Miami two days later, killing fifteen people and leaving a quarter of a million people homeless, many of them in the city of Homestead. Andrew continued across the state, and into Louisiana, causing as much as $25 billion in damage before it lost strength.

The most intense storm to hit the United States (between 1900 and 1994) is one that struck the Florida Keys in 1935; the unnamed hurricane was a category–5 storm.

1965, hurricane Betsy roared across that state, packing winds of up to 145 miles per hour and then moved into Louisiana and Mississippi, killing twenty-three people over the course of fifteen days. Betsy racked up nearly $6.5 billion in damages. More recently, the Florida panhandle was hit by Hurricane Opal in 1995, causing $2-3 billion in damages and claiming at least eighteen lives.

Other states have also been hit hard by hurricanes: On August 17, 1969, Hurricane Camille hit the Mississippi Gulf Coast with 190-mile-per-hour winds. The category-5 storm remains the second-most intense hurricane to hit the United States (second to the Florida hurricane of 1935). As Camille continued on her path of destruction, she struck Virginia and

West Virginia even harder, leaving 248 people dead, 200,000 homeless, and totaling property damage of $5.2 billion. In mid-September 1989, Hurricane Hugo slammed into the Virgin Islands, Puerto Rico, and the Carolinas, killing more than seventy and leaving hundreds of thousands homeless. The total damage cost over $7.1 billion.

On September 21, 1938, Long Island and much of New England were hit by a tropical hurricane that struck without warning. Within a few hours, the storm had wrought more damage than the Great Chicago Fire of 1871 or the San Francisco earthquake and fire of 1906. The storm claimed 680 lives, destroyed 2 billion trees, and caused about $3.6 billion in property damage. The hurricane also caused lasting environmental damage. In August 1955, Hurricane Diane swept through New England, causing widespread flooding and wind damage. At least 186 lives were lost. Damages were almost $4.2 billion. The Northeast was battered again in 1972 when Hurricane Agnes claimed 122 lives and caused $6.4 billion in damage.

(Note that all damage figures are given in 1990 U.S. dollars, with the exception of Hurricane Andrew.)

How long have hurricanes been given names?

Officially, since 1951 when storms in the Atlantic were named according to the military alphabet (Able, Bake, Charley, etc.). In 1953, forecasters began using women's names, with a new list of names provided for each hurricane season. Storms in some areas of the Pacific began being named in 1959, and by 1964, all regions of the Pacific were using the naming convention—which helps meteorologists track more than one storm at any given time, makes clear the communication of warnings, and facilitates study since the names of major hurricanes are retired to avoid confusion later. In 1979, equality was brought to the naming process, introducing men's names as well as multicultural names to each season's list.

The practice of naming tropical storms, however, predates the convention that was developed by forecasters in 1950: Puerto Ricans were known to christen storms, giving them the name of the saint whose liturgical day it was when the storm struck. The U.S. military also— informally—named storms during World War II.

Since each season's storms are named in alphabetical order, there is a preponderance of storms beginning with the letters A, B, and C. However, in 1995, Hurricane Opal slammed into the Florida Panhandle on October 4, and was part of the worst storm season since 1933: Not since forecasters began naming hurricanes, had they reached the letter O.

How **frequently** have **tidal waves** occurred throughout the world?

Tidal waves, or *tsunamis* (the Japanese term for "harbor waves"), typically occur about every six years in the Pacific Ocean, and most often during March, August, and November. The waves are created not by tides but by seismic movements (earthquakes), which cause chains of waves that move across the water at more than five hundred miles per hour. Upon reaching shallow water, the waves grow in height, sometimes to a hundred feet or more, as was the case in 1883, when tsunamis reaching up to 130 feet hit an Indonesian island, destroying more than 150 villages and claiming some 36,000 lives.

In ancient times, it is believed that a tidal wave destroyed the Minoan Greek culture—a people who lived on the island of Crete (in the Mediterranean Sea). In about 1450 B.C., Crete was struck by a two-hundred-foot tidal wave, which either demolished the island or weakened it such that it could be taken over by the Myceneans, who were Greek mainlanders.

While tsunamis (tidal waves) continue to strike along the Pacific Rim, damage is often minimized by sophisticated instruments that help meteorologists monitor and predict disastrous weather, alerting the public to evacuate from areas of possible danger.

Has a **tidal wave** ever **hit the United States**?

Yes, in fact the largest tidal wave ever recorded hit Alaska in 1964; it was 220 feet high. The March 28 event was brought on by an earthquake measuring 9.2 on the Richter scale. The seismic wave (tsunami) hit the southwest part of the state.

Hawaii also sees an occasional tidal wave, or tsunami, though the most remarkable one hit the islands before they became a state. On April 1,

1946, all of the water drained from the three-mile-wide harbor at Hilo, which was immediately followed by a tidal wave that rushed onshore, destroying the waterfront. The process repeated itself twice, and resulted in the death of more than 150 people in Hawaii.

DROUGHTS

What is the **history** of **drought in the United States**?

The United States has suffered many a drought; among the most severe are:

1749: A drought in New England resulted in fires, as powder-dry pastures caught fire.

1853: The Southwest was parched by a drought that continued into 1854.

1874: Cattle ranchers in the West experienced the first year of a drought that lasted for a decade.

1881: In addition to severe drought in the Southwest, the eastern United States also became parched. The water supply in New York City was depleted, resulting in deaths there and elsewhere.

1883: Drought gripped the northern plains states.

1886: A decade of intermittent drought began on the Great Plains. The damage included the loss of livestock, crops, as well as the failure and foreclosure of many farms.

1917: Drought once again took hold in the western plains.

1930: Just as the country was gripped by the Depression, unprecedented drought parched the South and Midwest. The government responded with $45 million in relief money.

1934: Drought and high winds created the Dust Bowl in the plains.

What is the Dust Bowl?

The Dust Bowl refers not so much to a geographic area, but rather to an event: In the spring of 1934, the country in the grips of the Great Depression, farmers across the Great Plains of the United States witnessed two great dust storms. First, in mid–April, after days of hot, dry weather and cloudless skies, forty- to fifty-mile-per-hour winds picked up and took with them the dry soil, resulting in thick, heavy clouds. In Texas and Oklahoma, these dirt clouds engulfed the landscape. The next month was extremely hot and on May 10, a second storm came up as the gales returned, this time creating a light brown fog.

The Dust Bowl covered three hundred thousand square miles across New Mexico, eastern Colorado, Texas, western Oklahoma, and Kansas. The damage was great: Crops, principally wheat, were cut off at ground level or torn from their roots; cattle that had eaten dust-laden grass eventually died from "mud balls"; dust drifted, creating banks against barns and houses, while families tried to keep it from penetrating the cracks and crevices of their homes by using wet blankets, oiled cloths, and tape, only to still have everything covered in grit. Vehicles and machinery were clogged with dirt. And in addition to the farmers who died in the fields, suffocated by the storm, hundreds of people suffered from "dust pneumonia."

The following day, May 11, experts estimated that twelve million tons of soil fell on Chicago as a dust storm blew in off the Great Plains, and the same storm darkened the skies over Cleveland. Two days later, on May 12, the dust clouds had reached the eastern seaboard. Between the two storms, 650 million tons of topsoil had blown off the plains.

1936: Hot, dry, cloudless weather prevailed into 1937, at a dear cost to crops and livestock. This, combined with the effects of the Depression, caused great hardships for many Americans.

1952: Drought reduced grain harvests and impacted ranchers whose cattle were unable to graze. Areas in thirteen Midwestern states were declared disaster areas in 1953. The drought lasted five years and was more severe than that in the 1930s, but a Dust Bowl was prevented from recurring due to government conservation and planting efforts.

1965: A major drought in the northeastern United States prompted water-conservation measures in New York City—including turning off the air conditioning in sealed skyscrapers.

1976: California was gripped by a drought that lasted a year and forced compulsory water rationing.

1980: Western Iowa, most of Illinois, all of Indiana, and much of Ohio were hit by drought rivaling those of 1934, 1936, and 1952–53. Dry, hot weather also prevailed in the Southeast, Southwest, and plains states.

1983: U.S. corn farmers experienced the worst drought since 1936.

1987: California experienced the first of five straight years of drought, which was controversial as well: Farmers, who were growing crops not indigenous to the area, controlled more than 80 percent of the water supply—a fact that angered residents in the state's growing urban areas.

1988: Drought reduced North American crops, compelling the U.S. to import—for the first time in history—grain for domestic needs.

1993: The Southeast experienced a withering drought even as the waters of the Mississippi and Missouri rivers were on the rise, flooding vast areas of eight Midwestern states.

What were the **effects** of the Dust Bowl?

In the spring of 1934, after the dust had settled, the reaction among many Great Plains farm families was to flee: More than 350,000 people packed up their belongings and headed west—their lives forever changed by the disaster of the Dust Bowl. In his 1939 novel *The Grapes of Wrath*, American writer and Nobel–prize laureate John Steinbeck (1902–68) chronicled the harrowing and sorrowful westward journey of one Oklahoma family who were among the so-called "Okies" who deserted their farmlands in the devastated area of the Great Plains and sought a better life elsewhere.

However, nature alone was not to blame for the Dust Bowl: By the end of the nineteenth century, farmers, aided by the advent of large tractors and combines that could both harvest and thresh grain, settled across the Great Plains, uprooting the buffalo grass, which had held moisture in the soil and so, had kept it from blowing away. Even strong winds and extended droughts had not disturbed the land when it was covered by the undisturbed grassland. But as a result of World War I (1914–18), the demand for wheat increased. And farmers responded by planting more than twenty-seven million new acres of wheat. By 1930, there were almost three times as many acres in wheat production as ten years earlier, which meant that the grass that had kept the earth from blowing had been torn up. When the next dry period came and the wind picked up, the Dust Bowl resulted.

After the Dust Bowl, the government stepped in to remedy the problem: soil conservation became the focus of federal agencies, and the U.S. Forest Service undertook a project to plant a "shelter belt" of trees, within a one-hundred-mile-wide zone, from Canada to the Texas Panhandle. Recovery was aided by these measures as well as by the return of the rains. Soon the buffalo grass had grown back, helping to ensure that the Dust Bowl would not recur.

When was **the Great Famine**?

Typically the term is used to refer to the Great Irish Famine, which began in 1845. That year saw crop failures across Europe, resulting in widespread hunger and disease, claiming 2.5 million lives. The famine was especially severe in Ireland where many peasants exported their grain and millet, and therefore depended on potatoes for sustenance. The failure of the crop in 1845 was the twentieth in Ireland since 1727, and it marked the beginning of the Great Famine—which lasted into 1848 due to successively more disastrous failures each year. The crops had failed due to blight (previously unknown to Ireland), which had been caused by a mircoscopic organism (fungus)—believed to have been introduced by a ship from North America. British charity and government relief, unfortunately, did little to alleviate the suffering. The resulting famine was responsible for a drastic decline in the Irish population—due both to deaths and to emigration. Between seven hundred thousand and one million people died in Ireland and nearly two million people left the country, in search of a better life elsewhere.

Ilustration of the Irish Famine.

Another famine that is sometimes referred to as such was the Great Famine of Bengal, which occurred about a century before the famine in Ireland: In 1769, ten million Indians died, wiping out one-third of the population.

And still more severe famines have not been distinguished as "great": In 1878, just after the famine in Ireland, up to twenty million Chinese died as a two-year drought held Asia in its grips, causing widespread crop failures. It is still considered the worst famine in history.

What were the **harshest blizzards** to hit the **United States**?

Regions of the United States—particularly the Great Plains, Midwest, and New England—are no strangers to extreme winter weather, but some storms do stand out. In March 1888, the northeastern United States were hit by a blizzard dubbed the "Great White Hurricane." After a warm spell that had caused the buds to open on trees in New York's Central Park, on March 12 the temperature in the city plummeted to 10.7 degrees Fahrenheit and winds off the Atlantic built up to forty-eight miles per hour, bringing unpredicted snow that continued intermittently until the early morning of March 14. The three-day accumulation totaled 20.9 inches, and snowdrifts fifteen to twenty feet high halted traffic. The snowfall was even higher elsewhere, averaging forty inches or more in areas of southeastern New York and southern New England. The storm extended down into Chesapeake Bay, isolating the nation's capital from the world for more than a day. Two hundred ships were lost or grounded, and at least one hundred seamen died. A total of at least four hundred people died, half of them in New York City alone. Just two months before this Nor'Easter, another blizzard had swept through the High Plains, moving eastward into Minnesota. There, high winds, blowing snow, and sudden drops in temperature combined to make it a dangerous storm, killing many people and thousands of cattle.

The Great Blizzard of 1993 caused loss of life and extensive damage all along the eastern seaboard—from Florida to Maine. More than three hundred people died, almost fifty of them at sea, and economic losses totaled $3–6 billion. While several so-called "100-year storms" have bombarded the East Coast in the 1990s alone (there had been another just a few months earlier, in December 1992), the statistics of the March '93 storm are impressive indeed, probably qualifying it as the Storm of the Century. Wind gusts exceeded seventy-five miles per hour all along the East Coast, with winds exceeding one hundred miles per hour measured at various points, including Flattop, North Carolina. Tennessee saw the highest snowfall of the storm, with fifty-six inches at Mount LeConte. Snowfall amounts were also heavy in the northeast, but snow accumulated as far south as the Florida Panhandle. Experts estimated that the amount of water that fell (in the form of snow) was equivalent to forty days' flow of the mighty Mississippi River past New Orleans. According to record-low barometer readings, this storm surpassed hurricanes Hugo (1989) and Hazel (1954).

However, Midwesterners and residents of the northern Great Plains will likely argue that storms such as the Great Blizzard of 1993 are relatively common in their regions. To wit: Another storm that could easily vie for the title Storm of the Century occurred January 10–11, 1975, in the upper Midwest. The blizzard was accompanied by winds of ninety miles per hour and wind chills as low as minus 80 degrees Fahrenheit. Trains were stranded in snowdrifts, and at least eighty people perished. Ranchers and farmers were hard hit, losing some fifty-five thousand head of livestock.

What are the **largest** known **volcanic eruptions** in history?

Scientists measure volcanic eruptions by the amount of material that a volcano ejects into the atmosphere. Based on this measurement system, the largest eruptions include (in descending order of strength) one at Yellowstone Park in the United States, some six hundred thousand years B.C.; another at Toba, Indonesia, about 74,000 B.C.; a Tambora, Indonesia, eruption in A.D. 1815; Santorini, Greece, in 1470 B.C.; Laki, Iceland, in A.D. 1783 (which also produced the largest known lava flow in recorded history); and another in Indonesia, at Krakatau, in A.D. 1883.

The eruption in Yellowstone is hard to fathom: The volcano (which would have been located in present-day Wyoming) left a crater that measures 30 by 45 miles and released 10,000 cubic kilometers of material into the atmosphere. To put this into perspective, consider that the next largest eruption, that at Toba released one-tenth that amount, or 1,000 cubic kilometers. The one at Tambora released one-tenth of the Toba amount, or 100 cubic kilometers. All of the others released about 10 cubic kilometers of earth debris into the atmosphere.

While the 1980 eruption of Mount St. Helens in southwestern Washington state is also considered among the largest known eruptions in history and is the largest eruption in the modern history of the forty-eight contiguous Unites States, it released a comparatively small amount of material—one cubic kilometer. Nevertheless, the damage was great after the volcano, which had been quiet for 123 years, erupted, claiming more than 60 lives.

What were the **deadliest volcanic eruptions** in history?

The April 5, 1815, eruption of Mount Tambora in Indonesia was the deadliest yet, killing some 92,000 people. Another Indonesian eruption later in the nineteenth century—this time at Karkatoa—claimed 36,417 lives in late–August 1883.

On the French island of Martinique in the West Indies, Mount Pelee erupted on August 30, 1902, and more than 29,000 people perished. A relatively recent and deadly eruption was that on November 13, 1985, at Nevada del Ruiz, Columbia: it took 23,000 lives.

Iceland's Skaptar volcano erupted in 1783. While the number of lives lost may not qualify it among this short list of "deadliest" volcanoes, the human toll was great indeed: 20 percent of the country's population died.

These statistics can be misleading, since it would appear that volcanic eruptions are becoming less deadly. On the contrary, because of population growth, more people are living closer to volcanoes—both active and inactive. The result is that since the beginning of the twentieth century, an average of 845 people die every year because of volcanic eruptions. Compare this figure with the estimated average death toll of 315 people per year between 1600 and 1900.

EARTHQUAKES

How did **ancient** societies interpret **catastrophic weather events**?

Different cultures developed wholly unscientific explanations for dramatic weather events or other natural phenomena—explanations typically rooted in the existing mythology or folklore of its people. For example, the ancient Maya (in the Yucatan Peninsula) believed earthquakes were the gods' way of thinning out an over-crowded population. The Indians in central Mexico are believed to have worshiped the grasshopper—or locust—after swarms destroyed their crops. One Japanese myth maintained that the entire island string rested on the back of a giant catfish who would grow restless and flop around when the gods were displeased, resulting in an earthquake. According to Hawaiian myth, the volcano goddess Pele causes Mount Kilauea to erupt whenever she has a temper tantrum.

What is the **strongest earthquake** ever measured?

It was one measuring 9.6 on the Richter scale: It shook Chile on May 22, 1960. Thousands died there. The quake also spawned tsunamis (tidal waves), which claimed 61 lives in Hawaii, 120 in Japan, and 20 in the Philippines.

What was the **worst earthquake** in modern history?

It was a July 28, 1976, quake that rocked the Chinese city of Tangshan at four o'clock in the morning. In less than a minute, 89 percent of the homes and 78 percent of the industrial buildings were destroyed, killing 250,000 people, according to the official reports. However, international observers believe the death toll was even higher—about 750,000, which meant that the quake claimed three-fourths of the area's total population.

A quake had not occurred in that region in six centuries and the area was considered to be at low risk for earthquakes. Consequently, the building codes in the region were not stringent enough for the structures to withstand the force of the quake.

China was also the site of the worst earthquake recorded: On January 24, 1556, a quake rocked the Shanxi province, killing more than 830,000 people.

How disastrous was the **San Francisco Earthquake**?

The quake of 1906 struck at 5:12 a.m. on April 18, and registered 8.3 on the Richter scale. Twenty seconds of trembling were followed by forty-five to sixty seconds of shocks. The quake cracked water and gas mains, which resulted in a fire that lasted three days and destroyed two-thirds of the city. The destruction and loss of lives were great: As many as 3,000 (of San Francisco's 400,000 people) were killed; the entire business district was demolished; 3 out of 5 homes had either crumbled or burned; 250,000 to 300,000 people were left homeless; and 490 city blocks were destroyed.

The quake proved to be something of a milestone for American journalism: The offices of the city's newspapers, the *Examiner* (owned by William Randolph Hearst), the *Call*, and the *Chronicle*, had all burned. But the first day after the disaster, the three papers joined forces across the bay in Oakland to print a combined edition, the *California Chronicle-Examiner*. Across the country, Will Irwin of the *New York Sun*, who had been a reporter and editor at the *San Francisco Chronicle* from 1900 to 1904, wrote a story titled "The City That Was," which he had completed from memory alone. It was picked up by papers around the country and became a classic of journalism. The San Francisco tragedy demonstrated the newfound ability of the American press to create an instant national story out of a local event.

The Bay Area was hit again by a sizeable quake in 1989. As millions tuned in to watch the World Series at Candlestick Park outside San Francisco, the cameras began to shake. Because of television coverage of

What is the strongest earthquake recorded in an urban area?

It is believed to be a November 1, 1755, earthquake that struck Lisbon, Portugal. The quake may have registered at least 9.0 on the Richter Scale and lasted six or seven minutes. The port city was demolished and more than sixty thousand people perished. It was felt as far away as Sweden and generated a tidal wave (tsunami) that struck the West Indies with twelve-foot waves.

The catastrophe in Lisbon generated an intense debate among European philosophers who tried to explain why God destroyed that particular city, then the seat of the Holy Inquisition, during High Mass on All Saints' Day.

the baseball game, the earthquake had literally been broadcast live around the world. Once again, fires resulted from broken gas mains and the damage was extensive. The so-called Loma Pietra quake registered 7.1 on the Richter scale, claimed 67 lives, and damaged $15 billion worth of property. San Francisco's Marina district was particularly hard hit—at least in part due to the fact that the area was built largely on landfill, including debris from the 1906 quake.

The San Francisco Earthquake of 1906 remains the worst to ever hit an American city.

FIRES

How much **damage** was done by the **Great Fire of London**?

The fire, which began early in the morning on Sunday, September 2, 1666, and burned for four days and nights, consumed four-fifths of the city (which was then walled), plus sixty-three acres lying just outside the city walls. The blaze began in Pudding Lane near London Bridge and quickly spread through crowded wooden houses to the Thames wharf warehouses. The destruction included London's Guildhall, the Custom House, the Royal Exchange, and St. Paul's Cathedral. Additionally, forty-four livery company halls, eighty-six churches, and more than thirteen thousand houses were destroyed.

Though the fire was unquestionably disastrous, London soon rebuilt and became one of Europe's most modern cities. The fire had also destroyed thousands of old buildings where lice-infested rats had lived and which were responsible for spreading the plague through the English city.

Was the **Chicago Fire** really started by a cow?

It's alleged that the fire, which burned from October 8 to 9, 1871, was started by a cow (usually described as belonging to a Mrs. O'Leary) kicking over a kerosene lantern on Dekoven Street. The blaze destroyed three and a half square miles of the city and took 250 lives.

The following entry, dated October 17, from the diary (published in 1933 by W. W. Norton) of Chicago resident Julia Newberry, who was in Paris at the time of the fire, describes the damage:

"The fire began at twelveth street on Sunday night Oct. It swept the two magnificent avenues, & every building on the South side from twelveth street to the river. The Court House, with the original copy of Father's will & no one knows how many invaluable papers, legal documents, records, the beautiful Crosbie Opera house, a perfect bijoux of a theatre, all the banks, insurance offices, railway depots, churches, & block after block of stores, unequalled any where. And then oh misery, the fire, the red, angry, unrelenting fire, leapt across the river, & burnt & burnt, till Mr Mahlon Ogden's house was the only one left standing up to Lincoln Park. Yes the whole North Side is in ashes. . . . "

But the damage was not limited to the city of Chicago alone: Sparks lit forest fires that destroyed more than a million acres of Michigan and Wisconsin timberland, burning from October 8 to October 14. These fires were responsible for the loss of more than one thousand lives in the logging town of Peshtigo, Wisconsin, and in sixteen surrounding communities.

Though the United States has suffered other disastrous fires, including an 1835 blaze in New York City, which destroyed some five hundred buildings, the Chicago Fire is the worst fire tragedy in the recorded history of North America.

Like the Great Fire of London two hundred years earlier, a flurry of building activity followed in the city, making Chicago one of the United States' most architecturally impressive urban centers. In fact, the fire was the impetus for the development of the Chicago School of architecture, also called the Commercial style (since most of it was devoted to office buildings, warehouses, and department stores). The Chicago School was instrumental in establishing the modern movement of architecture in the United States.

What was the public reaction to the **Triangle Shirtwaist Factory** fire?

The March 25, 1911, blaze, which killed 146 people (most of them women), prompted public outrage and led to the immediate passage of fire safety legislation and reforms. The Triangle Shirtwaist Factory occupied the top three floors of an office building. It was one of the most successful garment factories in New York City, employing some one thousand workers, mostly immigrant women. But the conditions were hazardous: the space was cramped, accessible only via stairwells and hallways so narrow that people had to pass single-file, only one of the four elevators was regularly in service, the cutting machines in the workroom were gas-powered, scraps of fabric littered the work areas, the water barrels (for use in case of fire) were not kept full, and the no-smoking rule was not strictly enforced. In short, it was an accident waiting to happen.

When the fire broke out on a weekend (the cause is unknown since the building was charred so badly), about half of the employees were there. Smoke and fire, however, were not the only causes of death: In the panicked escape, people were trampled, fell in elevator shafts, jumped some seven stories to the pavement below, and were killed when a fire escape melted from the heat of the fire and collapsed.

The fire happened during a time of labor reform, but clearly reforms, including those improving worker safety, had not come soon enough. The disaster became a rallying cry for the movement: tens of thousands of people marched in New York City, in tribute to those who had died and called attention to the grave social problems of the day, when laborers were subject to extremely poor—and dangerous—work conditions.

In New York State, the fire safety reforms for factories came right away: the legislature appointed investigative commissions to examine factories statewide, and thirty ordinances in New York City were enacted to enforce fire prevention measures. One of the earliest was the Sullivan-Hoey Fire Prevention Law of October, 1911, which combined six agencies to form an efficient fire commission. Soon factories were required to install sprinkler systems.

The Triangle Shirtwaist Factory fire became an object lesson for the entire nation, prompting the consolidation of reform efforts. The much-needed labor reforms, which addressed the miserable working conditions, did not come until years later.

What was the **impact** of the fire at the **MGM Grand in Las Vegas**?

The November 21, 1980, blaze, which killed eighty-five people and injured more than six hundred, led to a nationwide revision of local fire codes, giving the tragic event large-scale political significance. The MGM Grand Hotel had, in fact, passed fire inspections, but the building, which was then the world's largest gambling casino, had been eight years in the making. Between the time it was designed (fire protection systems included) and the time it was built, the building no longer complied with the always-improving safety standard for high-rises. A short-circuit started the blaze, which sent thick black smoke through the air ducts and escape stairwells in the twenty-one floors of guest rooms. Since more people were harmed or killed by smoke inhalation than by the fire itself, the American public became aware of the danger of smoke—over and above that of fire.

The event was a catalyst for change: Prior to the November fire, most communities had not required existing buildings to be retrofitted every time fire safety code changed and improved. After the fire, many communities chose to require building owners to comply with current protection capabilities.

What happened to the **Tacoma-Narrows suspension bridge**?

In 1940, the new 853-meter (about 2,800-foot) bridge carrying traffic across Washington's Puget Sound was hit by high winds, causing it to buckle and undulate. In the simplest of terms, an engineering error allowed one of the suspensions to give way in the wind, and the bridge became ribbon-like, moving in waves. It was ten years before a second span was opened over the body of water. The 1940 accident prompted engineers and bridge designers to be more cautious in the design of suspension bridges. The first wire suspension bridge in the U.S. had been built in 1842: The 358-foot-long and 25-foot-wide bridge spanned the Schuylkill River, near Philadelphia, Pennsylvania. It was supported by five wire cables on either side, and was built by U.S. civil engineer Charles Ellet Jr. The first chain suspension bridge in the U.S. was built in 1800.

Why was the *Titanic* thought to be **unsinkable**?

The R.M.S. *Titanic* was state of the art—a huge and luxurious ocean-liner equipped with the latest and best. The ship's size afforded it great stability; its structure included more steel than had been used in previous ships; it was built with a double bottom—both skins were heavier and thicker than those of other ships. The hull was divided by fifteen bulkheads (upright partitions) that rose five decks forward and aft, and four decks midship. These transverse bulkheads divided the ship into sixteen compartments—"watertight" chambers—any two of which could take on water without sinking the ship. This marvel of modern technology, which was to be the jewel in the crown of the White Star Line, was given a fitting name: "titanic" is a Greek word meaning "having great force or power." And it was described as "practically unsinkable."

However, the ship designer did not—and could not—prepare the ship for what happened on the night of April 14, 1912. Just before midnight, the *Titanic* was speeding—at twenty-one knots—through the North Atlantic, even though the crew had been warned by other ships that the unusually

What are the facts about the *Titanic?*

As the brainchild of Lord Pirie and J. Bruce Ismay, *Titanic* was a marriage of British technology and American money: Pirie was head of Harland & Wolff, a firm known for building the sturdiest and best ships in the British Isles, and Ismay was chairman of the White Star Line, owned by American financier J. Pierpont Morgan's International Mercantile Marine.

In 1907, Pirie and Ismay came up with a plan to compete with the topnotch Cunard liners by surpassing them both in size and luxury. The ship they planned, *Titanic*, was built in Belfast along with her sister ship, *Olympic*, which Titanic exceeded in gross tonnage but not in length. *Titanic* was eight hundred and eighty-two feet long, ninety-two feet wide, and weighed 46,328 gross tons; nine steel decks rose as high as an eleven-story building. Registered as a British ship and manned by British officers, *Titanic* was launched on May 31, 1911.

The ship was everything Pirie and Ismay had planned. *Titanic's* size not only allowed more room to accommodate the increasing number of steerage and low-fare passengers who were immigrating to the United States at the time, but also featured lavish elegance for first- and second-class travelers. Creature comforts included the first shipboard swimming pool, a Turkish bath, a gymnasium, and a squash court. First-class cabins were nothing

calm waters were full of ice. When the *Titanic's* two watchmen, who were not using binoculars, sighted an iceberg in the ship's path, it was only a quarter mile away. The ship was turned to the port (left), but it was too late. The underwater shelf of the ice tore through the plating on the starboard (right) side of the ship—creating six thin slits that eventually opened into a twelve-foot square hole. The effect was similar to filling an ice tray with water: Once one "watertight" chamber had filled, the rushing water spilled over the top and into the next. The boat sank within two and a half hours, taking more than 1,500 people with her.

short of opulent—including coal-burning fireplaces in the sitting rooms and full-size, four-poster beds in the bedrooms. Additionally, there were a loading crane and a compartment for automobiles. The ship's hospital even featured a modern operating room.

With her steerage full and some of society's most prominent individuals on board, the R.M.S. *Titanic* left the docks at Southampton, England, on April 10, 1912; New York Harbor was her final destination. On April 14, the fifth day of her maiden voyage, the ship was traveling in the exceptionally calm and icy waters of the North Atlantic, near Newfoundland. At 11:40 p.m., *Titanic* scraped an iceberg, sustaining a three-hundred-foot gash along the starboard (right) side—from the bow to about midship. The *Titanic*, which immediately began taking on water, sank in two hours and forty minutes, on the night of April 15.

Only 711 of the 2,224 aboard survived, and the 1,513 lost included John Jacob Astor IV; R. H. Macy's Isidor Straus; copper heir Benjamin Guggenheim; and traction heir Harry Elkins Widener. Survivors—mostly women and children who had been traveling as first class passengers—were picked up by the *Carpathia*, which was fifty-eight miles away when it received *Titanic*'s distress signals. It took three and a half hours for *Carpathia* to reach the site of the disaster, by which time the *Titanic* was gone.

Titanic came to symbolize human arrogance: The ship owners and operators believed the Titanic was impervious to nature. Consequently, the ocean-liner had not been equipped with the lifeboats it would need in order to rescue everyone on board. In fact, *Titanic*'s lifeboats had room for about half the passengers. Since there had been no safety drills on board, many lifeboats were launched only half-full. The enormous loss of life—which included society's most prominent individuals as well as ordinary families who were immigrating to America—stands out as one of the great tragedies in the history of transportation.

The *Titanic* ship as it sinks.

What **effect** did the sinking of the *Titanic* have on sea travel?

The sinking of the *Titanic* brought about new regulations to increase the safety of sea travel. First, and perhaps most simply, all ships are required to carry enough lifeboats such that there is one spot for each person on board. (When *Titanic* sailed, the number of required lifeboats was based on the ship's tonnage—not on the number of passengers and crew.) Also, new rules required lifeboat drills to be held soon after a ship sails.

Shipping lanes were moved farther south, away from the ice fields, and are monitored by a patrol. Ships approaching ice fields are required to slow down or alter their course.

Additionally, ship radios must be monitored around-the-clock, have access to an auxiliary power source should the engine fail, and have a range of at least one hundred miles. Until 1912, most ships employed only one wireless operator. Such was the case on the *California*, which was less than twenty miles from *Titanic* when wireless operator Jack Phillips sent out the distress signal. However, the operator on the *California* was not on duty at that hour. Phillips stayed at his station, desperately trying to reach a nearby ship, and eventually went down with *Titanic*.

In the aftermath of the disaster, the U.S. Congress moved quickly to pass the Radio Act of 1912, which required that radios be manned day and night, that they have an alternate energy source (besides the ship's engine), and that they have a range of at least one hundred miles. Further, operators must be licensed, adhere to certain band widths, and observe a strict protocol for receiving distress signals. (This was the beginning of the Federal Communications Commission, or FCC.) These measures were meant to rid the airwaves of those amateur operators who had confused official operators the night of April 15, 1912. One erroneous wireless message transmitted by amateurs that night had the *Titanic* moving safely toward Halifax.

AIRSHIP/AIRPLANE ACCIDENTS

What happened to the *Hindenburg*?

The image of the large airship bursting into flames is familiar to many: *Hindenburg*, a German vessel and the largest airship ever built, exploded while it was trying to land at Lakehurst, New Jersey, at about 7:25 p.m. on May 6, 1937. *Hindenburg* had just completed a trans-Atlantic flight and had dropped its mooring lines to the ground crew when the hydrogen gas that kept the airship afloat caught fire. Within thirty-two seconds, *Hindenburg* was nothing but smoldering rubble on the ground. Sixty-two of the ninety-seven people on board survived the crash. In addition to the thirty-five passengers and crew who lost their lives, one member of the American ground crew also perished. Though the cause of the fire and subsequent explosion has never been conclusively determined, it is believed that an atmospheric electrical spark—not sabotage—ignited hydrogen gas that was flowing from a leak. The fact that the outer cover of the tail section had been observed to flutter just seconds before the explosion lends credence to the explanation that there had been a gas leak.

The crash was thoroughly documented. Though travel by airship had been going on for more than twenty-five years and some fifty thousand passengers had been transported without a single fatality, the airship's landing in New Jersey was still an event for which many spectators turned out. Airships were still a marvel of technology, and the *Hindenburg* in particular was worth seeing since it was the largest airship afloat. Even though *Hindenburg* was more than twelve hours behind schedule (due to weather over the Atlantic), the arrival was eagerly anticipated. The entire event was caught on film, and that documentary was later widely shown in movie newsreels. Newspaper and radio coverage also helped link the *Hindenburg* and airship travel on the whole—with terrifying technological disaster.

The highly publicized crash effectively ended airship travel. A sister ship, the *Graf Zeppelin*, was en route from Rio de Janeiro back home to Germany when news of the Hindenburg disaster came in. Upon arrival, the *Graf Zeppelin* was grounded until the cause of the *Hindenburg*'s crash was known. No passenger airships took flight again. Two years later, an airplane carried its first paying passenger across the Atlantic.

Today, airships—"blimps"—are used by major corporations such as Goodyear during national events, primarily sporting events. Some airships are also used for reconnaissance and patrol.

Why did the *Hindenburg* use hydrogen to keep afloat?

The fact that *Hindenburg* used hydrogen might have been the airship's only flaw; and it had been made necessary by the political climate of the time.

Hindenburg was the fulfillment of German airship designer Hugo Eckener, whose Zeppelin Company had enjoyed years of experience and success, even as other airship companies folded. But by 1934, Eckener felt that his very successful *Graf Zeppelin*, which had made several tran-Atlantic trips was not well suited to such long-distance flights. Eckener envisioned a larger and speedier airship. In the *Hindenburg*, which took her maiden flight on March 4, 1936, Eckener's vision had been made real. Named for the German war hero and president, Field Marshal Paul von Hindenburg, the immense airship measured 803 feet in length and had a diameter of 135 feet, allowing it to hold nearly twice as much gas as other airships. The vessel was equipped with the latest technology, including four Daimler-Benz diesel engines that allowed the ship to travel as fast as eighty-five miles per hour.

The *Hindenburg* before its tragedy.

Hindenburg was also a luxury-liner: it featured private cabins, showers, dining room, promenade decks, picture windows, and even a pressurized and sealed smoking room! (Cigarettes, pipes, and cigars had to be lit using an electric lighter; matches were strictly forbidden on board.)

But there was one problem: *Hindenburg* had been designed to be lifted by helium. But helium was scarce at the time and the United States refused to sell any to Germany, which had been taken over by Adolf Hitler. The American government suspected the Germans might soon have military plans for their airships. Thus, the *Hindenburg* was forced to use hydrogen— seven million cubic feet of this flammable gas.

Had there been any other **airship disasters** before *Hindenberg*?

Yes, in fact, as Eckener and the Zeppelin Company laid plans in 1934 to build the large and luxurious *Hindenberg*, most other nations with airship programs had either abandoned them or were about to since all had experienced disastrous and fatal crashes. One of these was when the British dirigible *R-101* burned on October 5, 1930, northwest of Paris while on her maiden voyage to Australia. That disaster claimed fifty-four lives.

235

What is the worst airplane crash in history?

The worst mid-air collision was on September 10, 1976, when a British Airways Trident collided with a Yugoslav DC-9 in the skies near Zagreb, Yugoslavia. 176 people were killed. The worst single-plane accident happened on August 12, 1985, when a Japan Air Lines Boeing 747 crashed into a mountain on a domestic flight, killing 520 people.

Since it was the result of a deliberate act, some might argue that the worst airplane disaster in history was when a Pan Am 747 exploded in midair over Lockerbie, Scotland, on December 21, 1988, killing all 259 on board, plus 11 on the ground. Though other airplane disasters have resulted in more lost lives, the Lockerbie incident is believed to have been carried out by a Mideastern terrorist, making it perhaps more catastrophic than an air accident.

Another particularly tragic air accident took place on July 3, 1988, when the skipper of the U.S. warship Vincennes in the Persian Gulf mistook an Iran Air A300 Airbus for an attacking plane and shot it down. 290 people died. The following year, U.S. government officials offered reparations to survivors of the dead.

BOMBINGS

Was the **World Trade Center bombing** really part of a larger plan of terrorism?

Yes, during the FBI investigation that followed the February 26, 1993 tragedy, it was learned that the World Trade Center was only one of several intended targets of an Islamic extremist group. The bomb explosion in lower Manahattan killed six people, and started a fire that sent black smoke through the 110-story twin towers, injuring hundreds and forcing one hundred thousand people to evacuate the premises.

Days later, on March 4, twenty-five-year-old Mohammed A. Salameh, an illegal Jordanian immigrant, was arrested in Jersey City, New Jersey. Salameh was later found to be a follower of self-exiled Islamic fundamentalist leader Sheik Omar Abdel Rahman, who was wanted by Egypt for having incited anti-government riots in 1989. In June, after further arrests, investigators seized Arab terrorists they accused of plotting to blow up several landmarks of New York City, including the United Nations headquarters and the Holland and Lincoln tunnels. U.S. authorities then arrested Rahman and imprisoned him seventy-two miles northwest of New York on suspicion of complicity in the World Trade Center bombing. On October 1, 1995, a federal jury found Rhaman and nine other militant Muslims guilty of conspiring to carry out a campaign of terrorist bombings and assassinations aimed at forcing Washington to abandon its support of Israel and Egypt.

Was the **Oklahoma City bombing** the worst act of terrorism on U.S. soil?

Yes, the most destructive act of terrorism in American history took place at 9:02 a.m. on April 19, 1995, when a truck bomb exploded outside the Alfred P. Murrah Federal Building in Oklahoma City, Oklahoma. Of the 168 people who were killed, 19 were children. Another 500 people were injured. The blast, which investigators later learned had been caused by a bomb made of more than two tons of ammonium nitrate and fuel oil, sheered off the front half of the nine-story building and left a crater eight feet deep and thirty feet wide. Nearby buildings were damaged or destroyed, including a YMCA daycare center, where many children were seriously injured. The force of the explosion shattered windows blocks away. Survivors of the blast and others in the vicinity began rescue efforts right away. Eventually more than 3,600 people from around the country participated in rescue operations, including police, firefighters, and members of the Federal Emergency Management Agency.

Police and FBI agents arrested members of a U.S. right-wing militant group who were suspected of wanting to avenge the April 19, 1993, FBI/ATF raid on the Branch Davidian religious compound in Waco, Texas. Former Army buddies Timothy J. McVeigh, 27, and Terry L. Nichols, 40, were indicted on August 10, 1995, on eleven charges each. The two were tried separately and convicted in federal court. McVeigh

237

What happened on Apollo 13?

On April 13, 1970, a damaged coil caused an explosion in one of the oxygen tanks on the moon-bound U.S. spacecraft, leaving astronauts Jim Lovell, Jack Swigert, and Fred Haise in a disastrous situation. While NASA had experienced a previous disaster—in 1967 when three astronauts died in a fire on the launchpad—Mission Control had not faced anything like this before.

After hearing a loud bang and seeing their oxygen tank empty, the Apollo 13 astronauts reported to Mission Control at the Johnson Space Center, "OK, Houston, we've had a problem." The ensuing real-life drama proved that to be an understatement. The crew moved into the craft's tiny Lunar Module, designed to keep two men alive for just two days. The astronauts four days from home, NASA engineers had their work cut out for them. Among other measures, the temperature in the module was lowered to 38 degrees Fahrenheit to conserve oxygen and electricity. The world was waiting and watching as the module splashed down in the South Pacific—just barely ahead of the failure of oxygen. All three astronauts survived the disaster, which came to be known as the "successful failure," since Apollo 13 never reached its destination but, despite circumstances, made it back to Earth safely.

was found guilty of murder and conspiracy in June 1997, and a federal jury sentenced him to death. Nichols was later found guilty of conspiracy and involuntary manslaughter, but in January 1998, the jury deadlocked on the sentence, which was then to be decided by the judge.

Officials believe the Murrah building was targeted in the anti-government attack since it housed fifteen federal agencies, including offices of the Social Security Administration, Housing and Urban Development, the Drug Enforcement Administration, and the Bureau of Alcohol, Tobacco, and Firearms, as well as several defense department offices and a government-run day care center.

Is the **bombing** of buildings a **late-twentieth-century** phenomenon?

Though the bombing of the World Trade Center in New York and of the Murrah Federal Building in Oklahoma City happened only two years apart, this kind of violence is not new to American turf. In 1920, a bomb explosion on September 16 ripped through the J. P. Morgan Bank Building in New York, killing thirty people, injuring two hundred more, and causing $2 million in property damage.

Further, the many bombings carried out by white supremacists during the Civil Rights movement in the 1960s are also testimony to the fact that, sadly, this is not a new phenomenon. Between 1962 and 1965, as the Council of Federated Organizations worked to register voters in Mississippi, racial extremists turned to violence. Among the tactics used—in addition to shootings, beatings, and lynchings—were bombings. During Freedom Summer (the summer of 1964) alone, more than sixty-five homes, churches, and other buildings were bombed in Mississippi.

Most Americans remember the bombing of the Sixteenth Street Baptist Church in Birmingham, Alabama, on September 15, 1963. Two hundred people were attending Sunday services at the time. Four young African American girls were killed in the incident. But the sorrow of that day did not stop there: The bombing provoked racial riots, and police used dogs to control the crowds. Two black schoolboys were killed in the fracas.

What happened to the *Challenger*?

On January 28, 1986, at Cape Canaveral, Florida, NASA launched the twenty-fifth mission of its space shuttle program. The *Challenger* carried a crew of seven, including thirty-seven-year-old Christa McAuliffe, who was to be the first official teacher in space. She was slated to broadcast a series of lessons to schoolchildren throughout America. The crew's commander was Francis Scobee, who had piloted a 1984 shuttle mission; the pilot was Michael Smith, who was making his first flight in space; mission specialists Ellison Onizuka, Ronald McNair, and Judith Resnick were all experienced space travelers; and payload specialist Gregory Jarvis was making his first space flight.

That cold and clear January morning, the *Challenger*'s takeoff was delayed by two hours. Freezing temperatures overnight had produced

239

ice on the shuttle and launchpad, which prompted NASA to conduct inspections to assess the condition of the craft prior to takeoff. Finally, at 11:38 a.m., *Challenger* was launched into space. Just seventy-three seconds later and at an altitude of forty-eight thousand feet—the craft still in view of the spectators on the ground—*Challenger* burst into flames. While NASA controllers were aware of what had happened (they had, among other things, heard pilot Michael Smith utter "Uh oh" just one second prior to the explosion), it took a moment for the spectators to understand. But as the fireball grew bigger and debris scattered, the spectators, including family and friends of the crew, fell silent.

The crew, inside a module that detached from the shuttle during the blow-up, evidently survived the explosion but died upon impact after a nine-mile free-fall into the Atlantic Ocean. Six weeks after the disaster, the crew module was recovered from the ocean floor; all seven were buried with full honors.

Investigations into the crash revealed that the O-rings on the shuttle's solid rocket boosters had failed to work; due to the low temperatures, the O-rings had stiffened and thereby lost their ability to act as a seal. A government commission recommended a complete redesign of the solid rocket booster joints, along with a review of the astronaut escape systems to work toward achieving greater safety margins, regulation of the rate of shuttle flights to maximize safety, and a sweeping reform of the shuttle program's management structure. The space agency retrenched. It was almost three years later—on September 29, 1988—before another American shuttle flew in space.

Is it **true** that the engineers of the *Challenger*'s **O-rings** warned NASA that the devices might fail?

Yes, unfortunately the advice of the engineers went unheeded, with the manufacturer, Morton Thiokol, ultimately giving NASA the go-ahead in the hours before *Challenger*'s takeoff. On January 27, 1986, the night before the planned takeoff, the temperature at Cape Canaveral, Florida, dropped to well below freezing. Since no shuttle had been launched in temperatures below 53 degrees Fahrenheit, NASA undertook a late-night review to determine launch readiness. As a contractor, Morton Thiokol participated in this process, with their engineers expressing concerns about the O-rings on the shuttle's solid rocket boosters. They feared the rings would stiffen in the cold temperatures and lose their ability to act as a seal. Since the space agency was under pressure to launch the shuttle on schedule, NASA managers pushed the manufacturer for a go or no-go decision. The managers of Thiokol, who were aware that the O-rings had never been tested at such low temperatures, signed a waiver stating that the solid rocket boosters were safe for launch at the colder temperatures.

Challenger was launched the next morning, at 11:38 a.m. At about one minute into the flight, a flame became evident, and seconds later, the spacecraft exploded. All seven crew members died. Investigators later concluded that it was indeed the O-rings, which had failed to act as a seal (just as the engineers had predicted), that had caused the accident.

INDUSTRIAL ACCIDENTS

What was **Love Canal**?

When Love Canal, a community east of Niagara Falls, New York, made international headlines in August of 1978, it was only after the neighborhood had already been the subject of local newspaper stories since 1976. And sadly, more headlines followed—into 1980. What had become clear during these years was that Love Canal was toxic. Community residents had experienced unusually high incidences of cancer, miscarriages, birth defects, and other illnesses. There were also reports that foul odors, oozing sludge, and multicolored pools of substances were emerging from the ground; and children and animals returned from outdoor play with rashes and burns on their skin.

Unbeknownst to the residents, all of these problems were attributable to the history of the site upon which their community had been built. Beginning in 1947, the Hooker Electrochemical Company had used Love Canal, with its clay walls, to dump 21,800 tons (43 million pounds) of chemical waste. In 1953, the company sold the canal to the Niagara School Board for the sum of one dollar. The deed acknowledged the buried chemicals, although it did not disclose their type or toxicity. A disclaimer protected the firm from future liability. The canal pit was subsequently sealed with a clay cap designed to prevent rainwater from disturbing the chemicals. Grass was planted. Soon Love Canal had become a fifteen-acre field. The following year, a school was under construction on the site. In 1955, four hundred elementary school children began attending classes there and playing on the surrounding fields. Development happened fast: roads, sewers, and utility lines crisscrossed the site, disrupting the soil.

While residents began to discern problems as early as 1958, when they complained of nauseating smells and incidences of skin problems, it was not until the mid-1970s that the extent of the hazard became evident. It was then that unusually heavy rainfalls caused chemicals to surface. A portion of the schoolyard collapsed, strange substances seeped into basements, and trees and gardens died. In October 1976, the *Niagara Gazette* began investigating these problems, but an official investigation did not begin until the following April. By this time, the site was a disaster: toxins were found in storm sewers and basements, exposed chemical drums leaked substances, and air tests detected dangerously high chemical levels in homes. Further testing identified more than two hundred different compounds at the site, including twelve carcinogens and fourteen compounds that can affect the brain and central nervous system.

The residents of Love Canal organized, forming citizen groups including the Love Canal Homeowners Association. These groups succeeded in getting media coverage and in pressuring public officials to act. Finally on August 2, 1978, the New York State Health Commissioner declared Love Canal unsafe. Six days later, President Jimmy Carter approved emergency assistance and New York Governor Hugh Carey announced that funds would be used to purchase homes nearest to the canal.

While more than two hundred families perceived to be in danger were moved, in 1980 problems resurfaced when researchers found that blood tests of residents showed abnormally high chromosome damage, and the state recommended that pregnant women and infants be removed from homes—even those that had been certified as safe. In May 1980, conflict ensued between three hundred Love Canal homeowners and officials from the Environmental Protection Agency. On May 21, President Carter declared a second emergency at Love Canal. This time the actions were more comprehensive: Almost eight hundred families were evacuated, and their homes were either destroyed or declared unsafe until further clean-up could be done. Four years later, a new clay cap was installed over the canal. It was also in 1984 that Occidental Petroleum, parent company of the firm that had dumped chemicals in Love Canal, reached a $20-million settlement with residents.

What **impact** did **Love Canal have**?

The effect of the crisis was felt on many levels—by area residents whose lives were forever changed by the hazards, by residents nearby Love Canal who feared for their own safety, by Americans across the country who lived near other chemical waste sites, as well as by every American adult for whom Love Canal had become synonymous with hazardous-waste problems.

At the government level, the tragic events at Love Canal helped to speed the passage of the Comprehensive Environmental Response, Compensation, and Liability Act of 1980. Also known as the "Superfund," the legislation set up a multibillion-dollar fund to clean up the nation's worst toxic disasters. The Environmental Protection Agency (EPA) assigned clean-up priority to some twelve hundred abandoned and potentially contaminated waste sites.

Along with the chemical plant explosion at Bhopal, India, in 1984, Love Canal also contributed to a "community-right-to-know" provision, which was part of the 1985 Superfund Amendments and Reauthorization Act. The new legislation gave all citizens the right to know what chemicals were produced, stored, or buried in their neighborhoods.

What happened at **Three Mile Island**?

The March 1979 accident, which might be called a near melt-down, at the nuclear power station near Harrisburg, Pennsylvania, was eventually contained. Had it not been, the damage would have been on a level with that of the Chernobyl (Ukraine) disaster, which happened some seven years later. Instead, Three Mile Island served as a wake-up call, reminding the American public and its utility companies of the potential risks involved in nuclear energy.

What was the impact
of the accident at Three Mile Island?

Prior to the March 1979 events at Three Mile Island, it was thought that the danger of a nuclear meltdown was almost negligible. Though there were safety systems in place, none of them would have prevented a complete catastrophe. Since the accident, the American Nuclear Regulatory Commission (NRC) and utility companies have worked together to resolve the problems that were revealed. Among the efforts and requirements put into place were: more stringent licensing procedures for operators; better training of plant operators in the event of an emergency; wider sharing of information on emergency management systems; effort to locate new plants outside of densely populated areas; more rigid quality assurance standards at all plants; strict implementation of the standards, which are subject to review by the NRC; and emergency evacuation plans that must be approved by the Federal Emergency Management Agency (FEMA). Even with these improvements to safety programs, the accident at Chernobyl in 1986 again produced worldwide concern over the hazards of nuclear power.

The sequence of events at Three Mile Island was as follows: At 4 a.m. on Wednesday, March 28, an overheated reactor in Unit II of the power plant shut down automatically (as it should have); Metropolitan Edison Company operators, guided by indicators that led them to believe water pressure was building (and an explosion was therefore imminent), shut down those pumps that were still operating; the shut-down of all the pumps caused the reactor to heat further; then, tons of water poured out through a valve that was stuck open; this water overflowed into an auxiliary building through another valve that was mistakenly left open. This final procedure, which took place at 4:38 a.m., released radioactivity.

Since there was no cooling system in operation, the reactor in Unit II was damaged. But this was not the end of it: The radiation within the buildings was released into the atmosphere and at 6:50 a.m., a general emergency was declared. Early that afternoon, the hydrogen being created by the uncovered reactor core accumulated in a containment building and exploded. Since hydrogen continued to be emitted, officials feared another—catastrophic—explosion. Worse yet, they feared the reactor would become so hot that it would melt down. The effect of a meltdown would be that the superheated material would eat its way through the bottom of the plant and bore through the ground until it hit water, turning the water into high-pressure steam, which would erupt, spewing radioactivity into the air.

As technicians worked to manage the crisis, radiation leaked into the atmosphere off and on through Wednesday and Thursday. On Friday the governor of Pennsylvania ordered an evacuation: some 144,000 people were moved from the Middletown area. The situation inside the plant remained tenuous as a hydrogen bubble developed and increased in size, again raising fear of explosion. Meantime, public alarm was mounting as the media attempted to monitor the ongoing crisis. Finally, on Sunday, April 1, the plant was visited by President Jimmy Carter. At about the same time, the hydrogen bubble began to decrease in size, ending the crisis.

What was the **worst industrial accident** in world history?

It was the gas leak at a Union Carbide chemical plant in Bhopal, India, on December 3, 1984. At about 12:30 a.m., methyl isocyanate (MIC), a deadly gas, began escaping from the pesticide plant, and it spread southward, eventually covering forty square kilometers. Within a few hours, thousands of Bhopal residents were affected by the asphyxiating gas. General symptoms included severe chest congestion, vomiting, paralysis, sore throat, chills, coma, fever, swelling of legs, impaired vision, and palpitations. Estimates of the total death toll range from the official government estimate of three thousand up to ten thousand victims, a figure based on what medical professionals described. In total, two hundred thousand people were directly or indirectly affected by the poisonous gas.

Bhopal police had moved into action within hours of the accident, closing the plant and arresting its manager and four of his assistants. The five men were charged with "culpable homicide through negligence."

245

Union Carbide dispatched a team of technical experts from its Danbury, Connecticut, headquarters, but upon arrival at the plant, they were turned away by local authorities. Meanwhile, the Indian Central Bureau of Investigation seized the plant's records and log books and ordered an inquiry into the accident. Union Carbide Chief Executive Officer Warren M. Anderson flew to Bhopal, but he was promptly arrested, along with two officials of the company's Indian subsidiary. The corporate executives were charged with seven offenses including criminal conspiracy, culpable homicide not amounting to murder, making the atmosphere noxious to health, and causing death by negligence. Anderson was later released on bond.

Upon learning of this horrific event, U.S. President Ronald Reagan sent a message conveying the grief shared by him and the American people. Multinational corporations, including Union Carbide, were vilified in the press; the Soviet news agency accused such companies of marketing "low-quality products and outdated technology to developing countries." Indian Prime Minister Rajiv Gandhi, who had visited the disaster site and announced immediate creation of a $4-million relief fund for victims, vowed that he would prevent multinational corporations from setting up "dangerous factories" in India.

The implications of the industrial accident were many. It prompted public scrutiny of safety systems at chemical plants around the globe. Given the number of plants where poisonous chemicals are produced and stored, some observers believe chemical accidents could happen as often as once in every ten years. Union Carbide, of course, suffered financially; the stock dropped more than twelve points, wiping out 27 percent, or almost $1 billion, of its market value, in about one week. Damage claims were filed on behalf of the victims, with noted American criminal attorney Melvin Belli filing one of them in the amount of $15 billion.

In addition to the thousands who died in Bhopal, others suffered from long-term effects including chronic lesions of the eyes, permanent scarring of the lungs, and injuries to the liver, brain, heart, kidneys, and the immune system. In the years after the accident, studies showed that the rate of spontaneous abortions and infant deaths in Bhopal were three to four times the regional rate.

An aerial view of the Chernobyl Nuclear Power Plant.

What caused the **nuclear accident** at **Chernobyl**?

The April 1986 accident—the world's worst nuclear power plant disaster—was caused by explosions at the Soviet power plant, sending radioactive clouds across much of northern Europe. The trouble began at 1:24 a.m. on Saturday, April 26, when Unit 4 of the Chernobyl Nuclear Power Plant, about seventy miles outside of the Ukrainian capital of Kiev, was rocked by two enormous explosions. The roof was blown off the plant and radioactive gasses and materials were sent more than a half mile into the atmosphere. Though two workers were killed instantly, there was no official announcement about the hazardous blast. It was the Swedes who detected a dramatic increase in wind-borne radiation, and on April 28—two full days after the accident—news of the event was briefly reported by the Soviet news agency, Tass.

Two weeks later, on May 14, First Secretary Mikhail Gorbachev appeared on national television to explain what officials knew about the accident. Over the following months, more details were revealed. The explosions had been caused by an unauthorized test carried out by plant operators, who were trying to determine what would happen in the event of a power outage. However, there were six critical errors made by workers

247

during the testing, which combined to spell disaster. Perhaps the most significant of these mistakes was turning off the emergency coolant system: Once the test was under way, further mistakes caused the core to heat to more than 5000 degrees Celsius, producing molten metal that reacted with what cooling water was left to produce hydrogen gas and steam, resulting in a powerful explosion. What caused the second explosion is not as clear and experts disagree on what might have happened. Some theorize that it was a pure nuclear reaction.

What was the **impact** of the **disaster at Chernobyl**?

As the worst nuclear power plant disaster to date, the Chernobyl accident had far-reaching effects. More than thirty firefighters and plant workers died just after the accident, but the long-term effects are far more grave: experts estimate that between 6,500 and 45,000 people could die as a result of cancer caused by exposure to radiation. Total fallout from the accident eventually reached a level ten times that of the atomic bomb dropped on Hiroshima, Japan, during World War II.

No one was more severely effected than the Ukrainian people who had made their homes nearby. All plants and animals in the immediate area and downwind of the plant were heavily contaminated with radioactive fallout. More than ten years after the accident, food still could not be planted in the region, and some experts predict the surrounding farmland will not be arable again for tens or maybe even hundreds of years. Since the soil is still contaminated, residents continue to face serious health risks posed by their environment. The death toll is high, and mounting, as those exposed to the radiation suffer long-term effects that turn fatal.

Still other parts of the European continent were also effected: some Italian vegetables were found to be contaminated; reindeer meat in Lapland was declared unfit for human consumption, also due to radioactive contamination; and for a time, fresh meat from Eastern Europe was banned by the EC (European Community).

There are continued worries that Unit 4, where the accident took place, is still emitting dangerous levels of radioactivity. In an attempt to seal it, a steel-and-concrete structure was built over the ruins, but by 1992, it had leaked, prompting officials to lay plans to build a second enclosure—on top of the original.

Since the type of nuclear power plant (called RMBK) in use in the former Soviet Union is no longer in use elsewhere in the world, non-Soviet scientists had few lessons to learn from the event. One American nuclear expert remarked that "most of the lessons from Chernobyl have been learned already and applied in the United States." However, opinion remains divided over the relative safety of nuclear power in general.

PHILOSOPHY, SCIENCE, & INVENTION

PHILOSOPHERS

How old is **Taoism**?

It dates back to the sixth century B.C. when it was founded by Lao-tzu (604 B.C.–?), who believed in inaction and simplicity—which he combined with religious practices to form the mystical philosophy of the Tao (Dao), the path of virtuous conduct.

Lao-tzu reasoned that since humans face a "cloud of unknowability," they ought not to react to things at all. He viewed the world as a pendulum with the Tao as its hinge. Anyone who struggles against the current of life is like an insect caught at the end of a pendulum—swinging back and forth, and suffering with each movement. But by crawling along the hinge (Tao) to reach the top, a place of complete stillness is found. Lao-tzu advised that people do away with their desires, avoiding that which is extreme, extravagant, or excessive, and steering clear of any competition.

Taoism is still relevant to many today. When it was developed some twenty-six centuries ago, the philosophy filled a spiritual void that was not addressed by the practical doctrines of traditional Confucianism. (One legend had it that Lao-tzu rebuked a young Confucius for his pride.) The Tao also contributed greatly to Buddhism, especially in its emphasis on meditation and sudden enlightenment.

One of the great thinkers of the Chinese Taoist School was Chuang-tzu (c. 365–c. 290 B.C.), who constructed an apolitical, transcendental philosophy, that promoted an individual's spiritual freedom.

Who was **Confucius** and why do people still quote him?

Confucius (551–479 B.C.) was a Chinese philosopher whose real name was K'ung Ch'iu; Confucius is the Latinized version. Born into a class of lesser nobility, his father died before Confucius had turned three and he was raised in humble circumstances by his mother. He lived in the middle of China's feudal period, during which there were enormous problems, including famine and poverty, that had been brought on by weak emperors and, consequently, chronic warfare among rival feudal states. Because of his upbringing, Confucius possessed a profound sympathy for the common people. In his view, the feudal princes, only interested in their own personal gain, were responsible for the suffering of the people. Confucius set out on a reform mission: Through teaching, he would endeavor to train a new generation of leaders.

He assembled a group of intelligent disciples whom he trained in literature, music, human relations, and most importantly, ethics. Confucius believed that government leaders did not have to be experts in administration. Instead, they must be humane, honest, and above corruption and personal gain. Along with his disciples, he taught his students that it is the role and obligation of rulers to secure the happiness of their subjects. Confucius had considerable success in placing his former pupils in positions of government power. When the men who had been trained by him were sent into service, even corrupt rulers valued their honesty.

Confucius's philosophy held that good government could only be achieved by ethical leaders. He also believed that the family provides the model for all human relations. In time, he became the most revered person in Chinese history, but his teachings are familiar to other cultures as well.

Why was **Socrates** condemned to death?

Socrates (470–399 B.C.), the Greek philosopher who is credited, along with Plato and Aristotle, for laying the foundations of Western thought, had many followers in his own time but his ideas and methods were

Chinese philosopher Confucius.

controversial, too, which led him to be tried before judges and sentenced to death. His charge: not worshiping the Athenian gods and for corrupting the young.

Except for military service, Socrates spent his entire life in Athens where he was known for his slovenly appearance as well as for his moral integrity, self-control, and his quest for wisdom. He lived during a time when attention was turning away from the physical world (of the heavens) and toward the human world (of the self, the community, the law). He participated in this turning point by walking the streets of Athens, engaging people—including rulers who were supposed to be wiser then he—in conversation. In these conversations, he employed what came to be known as the Socratic method—a series of seemingly simple questions designed to elicit a rational response. Through this series of questions, which usually centered around a moral concept such as courage, the person being questioned was intended to realize that he did not know what he thought he knew. Thus divested of false notions, the person could then participate in the quest for knowledge.

Though he left no writings, Socrates's student, Plato, documented his recollections of dialogues with his teacher. A staunch believer in self-examination and self-knowledge, Socrates is credited with saying that "the unexamined life is not worth living." He also believed that the *psyche* (or "inner self") is what should give direction to one's life—not appetite or passions.

What was **Plato's** relationship to **Socrates** and **Aristotle**?

Plato (c. 428–348 B.C.) was a disciple of Socrates and a teacher of Aristotle. The philosophies of the three combined to lay the foundations of Western thought.

With the death sentence of his master and spiritual father, Socrates, in 399 B.C., Plato's dissatisfaction with the Athenian government reached its peak. Traveling throughout the Mediterranean after the death of Socrates, Plato returned to Athens in 387 B.C., and one mile outside of the city, he established the Academy, a school of philosophy, which was supported entirely by philanthropists; students paid no fees. One of the pupils there was young Aristotle, who remained at the Academy for twenty years before venturing out on his own.

What is Plato's "Theory of Ideas"?

The theory, or doctrine, of ideas (also called the "Theory of Forms") is Greek philosopher Plato's expression of his belief that there are "forms" that exist outside the material realm, and therefore are unchanging—they do not come into existence, change, or pass out of existence. It is these ideas that, according to Plato, are the objects of knowledge. Further, he posited that the body, the seat of appetite and passion, which communes with the physical world (rather than the world of ideas), is inferior to the intellect. He believed the physical aspect of human beings to be irrational while the intellect, or reason, was deemed to be rational.

The origins of Plato's theory can be traced to Socrates who believed that the psyche (inner spirit) has intuitive access to divinely known principles or truths, which he attempted to formulate through his conversations with others. Indeed, the Socratic dialogues, written by Plato, reveal that Socrates was striving to define the exact nature of the traditional Greek moral virtues of piety, temperance, and courage.

Plato wrote a series of dialogues in which Socrates figures prominently. The most highly regarded of these is the *Republic*, in which Plato discusses justice and the construction of an ideal state. It was his belief that people would not be able to eliminate injustice from society until rulers became philosophers: "Until all philosophers are kings, or the kings and princes of this world have the spirit and power of philosophy, and political greatness and wisdom meet in one, and those commoner natures who pursue either to the exclusion of the other are compelled to stand aside, cities [states] will never have rest from their evils—no, nor the human race." Also on the subject of the ideal state, Plato wrote but did not finish *Laws*. His other works include *Symposium*, which considers ideal love; *Phaedrus*, which attacks the prevailing notions about rhetoric; *Apology*, which is a rendering of the speech Socrates delivered at his own trial in 399 B.C.; and *Phaedo*, which discusses the immortality of the soul and is supposed to be a record of Socrates's last conversation before he drank hemlock and died.

Why is **Aristotle** considered one of the **greatest minds in Western history**?

The system of philosophy that Aristotle (384–22 B.C.) developed became the foundation for European philosophy, theology, science, and literature. The Aristotelian system may be so much a part of the fabric of Western culture that the only effective way to describe his philosophy is through example.

Among his writings on logic is *Organon*, meaning "tool" or "instrument." Here, he defines the fundamental rules for making an argument. While other thinkers may well have formulated the argument before Aristotle, no one had made a systematic study of it. In *Organon*, Aristotle puts forth a method for coming to a conclusion based on circumstantial evidence and prior conclusions, rather than on the basis of direct observation. This deductive scheme, called a syllogism, is made up of a major premise, a minor premise, and a conclusion. For example: every virtue is laudable [major premise]; courage is a virtue [minor premise]; therefore courage is laudable [conclusion]. (It is worth noting, however, that the belief in deductive logic was later rejected by English philosopher Sir Francis Bacon in 1620, in favor of an inductive system, or one that is based on observation.)

In *Poetics*, Aristotle expounded upon his literary views. He maintained that epic and tragedy portray human beings as nobler than they truly are, while comedy portrays them as less noble than they really are. In order to explain how tragedy speaks to the emotions of the spectator, Aristotle introduced the idea of catharsis. He separated tragedy from epic with the distinction that tragedy maintains unity of plot (later translated as unity of plot, time, and place), while the epic does not. Because of the keen understanding evident in *Poetics*, the work has illuminated literary criticism since antiquity.

In addition to logic and rhetoric, Aristotle wrote on natural science (*Physics, Metaphysics, On the Heavens, Parts of Animals, On the Soul,* and *On Plants,* for example) and on ethics and politics (*Politics*). Most of these writings are compilations of notes for and from lectures delivered to his students at the Lyceum. Among his students were Ptolemy and Alexander the Great.

Did **Aristotle** develop his own **philosophy** or did he only further **Plato's**?

A student of Plato's for twenty years, Aristotle's ideas were unquestionably influenced by his teacher. However, Aristotle developed his own doctrine, which he applied to many subjects.

Aristotle rejected Plato's theory of Ideas (or theory of Forms). While Aristotle, too, believed in material and form (which is to say the physical being and the unchanging, non-material truths), unlike his teacher, he believed that it is the concrete (material) that has substantial being. Aristotle viewed the basic task of philosophy as explaining why and how things are, or how they become what they are.

What does **"epicurean"** really mean?

While "epicurean" has come to refer to anything relating to the pleasure of eating and drinking, it is an oversimplification of the beliefs of the Greek philosopher Epicurus (341–270 B.C.), from whose name the word was derived. While Epicurus did believe that pleasure is the only good, and that it alone should be humankind's pursuit, later scholars misinterpreted the philosophy as a license for sensory excess. In actuality, Epicurus defined pleasure not as unbridled sensuality but as freedom from pain and peace of mind, which can only be obtained through simple living.

In about 306 B.C., Epicurus established a school in Athens, which came to be known as the Garden School since residents provided for their own food by gardening. There he and his students could live a life of simplicity, prudence, honor, and justice. In this way, they could achieve tranquility, which is the ultimate goal in life. He further believed that intellectual pleasures are superior to sensual pleasures, which are fleeting. In fact he held that one of the greatest and most enduring pleasures is friendship. These ideas were put forth by the Greek poet Lucretius (94 B.C.–55 B.C.).

While the Epicurean school endured for several centuries, ultimately Christian leaders deemed the philosophy a pagan creed. However, some critics have posited that the writer of Ecclesiastes in the Old Testament of the Bible was likely a member of the Garden School and that the Epistles of Saint Paul in the New Testament were strongly influenced by Epicurean thought. In more recent times, U.S. President Thomas Jefferson was a self-proclaimed Epicurean.

What were **Sir Francis Bacon's** beliefs?

The English philosopher and author was one of the great minds of the Scientific Revolution. Bacon (1561–1626) believed that humankind's accepted notions about nature should be aggressively challenged. As a young man studying at Trinity College, he had concluded that the Aristotelian system was without merit. He argued that the understanding of nature was being held back by the blind acceptance of the beliefs of the ancient philosophers. A religious person, Bacon nevertheless maintained that theology should *not* be questioned: he believed that rational inquiry can unlock the secrets of nature—but not of the human soul. Bacon, therefore, insisted on the separation of philosophy and theology—an idea that ran counter to the academic traditions of the time. Consequently, he was also a staunch proponent of educational and scientific reform.

Trained in law, during his lifetime Bacon served as a royal diplomat in France, was admitted to the bar, and was elected to Parliament. He penned several seminal works including *Essayes* (1597), which consists of practical wisdom and shrewd observations; *Advancement of Learning* (1605), a survey of the state of knowledge (Bacon was attempting to enlist the support of the King in the total reform of education and science in England); and *Novum Organum* (1620), in which he put forth a new method for understanding nature.

What is the **"doctrine of idols"**?

This was a phrase used by Sir Francis Bacon in his written attack on the widespread acceptance of the thinking of ancient philosophers such as Aristotle, Plato, and even Copernicus. In his 1620 work *Novum Organum*, Bacon vehemently argues that the progress of the human is held back by adhering to certain concepts, which it does not question.

Why is Descartes considered the father of modern philosophy?

French mathematician and philosopher René Descartes (1596–1650) was living in Holland when he published his first major work, *Discourse on Method,* in 1637. In this treatise, he extended mathematical methods to science and philosophy, asserting that knowledge is the product of clear reasoning based on self-evident premises. This idea provided the foundation for modern philosophy, which dates from the 1600s to the present. (Modern philosophy was preceded by Medieval philosophy—400s–1600s, which was preceded by that of ancient times—dating from the seventh century B.C.)

Among Descartes's most significant contributions is his invention of analytical geometry, but he may be most well-known for the familiar phrase, "I think, therefore I am" (*Cogito ergo sum*, in Latin). This assertion is based on Descartes's theory that only one thing cannot be doubted, and that is doubt itself. The next logical conclusion is therefore that the doubter must exist.

The philosopher's other major works are *Meditations* (1641) and *Principles of Philosophy* (1644). His philosophy became known as Cartesianism (from *Cartesius*, the Latin form of his name).

By hanging on to these concepts, or "idols," humankind proceeds in error in its thinking. The double edge is that in holding to notions accepted as true, we run the danger of dismissing any new notion. To overcome the twin problems of arrogance and skepticism, Bacon advocated a method of persistent inquiry. He believed that humans can understand nature only by carefully observing it with the help of instruments. He went on to describe scientific experimentation as organized, involving many scientists, and requiring the support of leaders. Thus, Bacon is credited with no less than formulating modern scientific thought.

What is **natural law**?

Natural law is the theory that some laws are fundamental to human nature, and as such they can only be known through human reason—without reference to manmade law. Roman orator and philosopher Cicero (106–43 B.C.) insisted that natural law is universal, meaning it is binding to governments and people everywhere.

What is **international law**?

As interpreted by Dutch jurist and humanist Hugo Grotius (1583–1645), natural law prescribes the rules of conduct among nations, resulting in international laws. It was Grotius who, in his 1625 work *Concerning the Law of War and Peace*, wrote what has been considered the definitive text on international law, asserting the sovereignty and legal equality of all states of the world. But the notion also had its detractors, English philosopher Thomas Hobbes (1588–1679) among them. Hobbes insisted that since international law is not enforced by any legal body above the nations themselves, it is not legitimate.

Since the seventeenth century, however, international law has evolved to become more than just theory. During the 1800s and early 1900s, the Geneva Convention (1864) and the Hague Conferences (1899, 1907) set forth the rules of war. Today, treaties (between two or among many countries), customary laws, legal writings, and conventions all influence international law, which is also referred to as "the law of nations." Further, it is enforced by the International Court of Justice (a UN body) as well as by world opinion, international sanctions, and the intervention of the United Nations (apart from the International Court of Justice).

What is the **social contract**?

The social contract is the concept that human beings have made a deal with their government, and within the context of that agreement, both the government and the people have their roles. The theory is based on the idea that humans abandoned a natural (free and ungoverned) state in favor of a society that provides them with order, structure, and, very importantly, protection.

Through the ages, many philosophers have considered the role of both the government and its citizens within the context of the social contract. In the theories of English philosopher John Locke (1632–1704), the social contract was inextricably tied to natural law. Locke argued that people first lived in a state of nature, where they had no restrictions on their freedom. Realizing that conflict arose as each individual defended his or her own rights, the people agreed to live under a common government, which offers them protection. But in doing so they had *not* abandoned their natural rights. On the contrary, argued Locke, the government should protect the rights of the people—particularly those of life, liberty, and property. Locke put these ideas into print, publishing his two most influential works in 1690: *Essay Concerning Human Understanding* and *Two Treatises of Government*. These works firmly established him as the leading "philosopher of freedom." His writings profoundly influenced Thomas Jefferson, as is evident in the Declaration of Independence, which asserts that there are "self-evident truths" (the idea of natural law), that people are "endowed by their Creator with certain unalienable rights" (the concept of natural rights), and that among these are "Life, Liberty, and the pursuit of happiness."

Philosopher Jean Jacques Rousseau (1712–78), one of the great figures of the French Enlightenment, later published a book on the subject: In his *Social Contract* (1762), he outlined that people enter into a contract among themselves and it's incumbent upon them to establish their government and its systems. People "have a duty to obey only legitimate powers," said Rousseau, meaning that only the people can determine their government. Rousseau's ideas helped promote the cause of both the French (1789–99) and the American (1775–83) revolutions. The concept of the social contract as defined by Rousseau also materialized in the Declaration of Independence, which proclaims that "Governments are instituted among Men, deriving their just powers from the consent of the governed," and "whenever any Form of Government becomes destructive of these ends, it is the Right of the People to alter or to abolish it." The 1917 "American's Creed," written by William Tyler Page of Maryland, also asserts these same principles: "I believe in the United States of America as a government of the people, by the people, for the people; whose just powers are derived from the consent of the governed. . . . "

What is **empiricism**?

Empiricism is the philosophical concept that experience, which is based on observation and experimentation, is the source of knowledge. According to empiricism, the information that a person gathers with his or her senses is the information that should be used to make decisions, without regard to reason or to either religious or political authority. The philosophy gained credibility with the rise of experimental science in the eighteenth and nineteenth centuries, and it continues to be the outlook of many scientists today. Empiricists have included John Locke (1632–1704), who asserted that there is no such thing as innate ideas—that the mind is born blank and all knowledge is derived from human experience; clergyman George Berkeley (1685–1753), who believed that nothing exists except through the perception of the individual, and that it is the mind of God that makes possible the apparent existence of material objects; and David Hume (1711–76), who evolved the doctrine to the extreme of radical skepticism, repudiating the possibility of certain knowledge.

What did **Thomas Paine** believe?

American political philosopher and author Thomas Paine (1737–1809) believed that a democracy is the only form of government that can guarantee natural rights. The British-born Paine arrived in the American colonies in 1774. Two years later he wrote *Common Sense*, a pamphlet that galvanized public support for the Revolutionary War (1775–83), which was already under way. During the struggle for independence, Paine wrote and distributed a series of sixteen papers, called *Crisis*, upholding the rebels' cause in their fight. Paine penned his words in the language of common speech, which helped his message reach a mass audience in America and elsewhere. He soon became known as an advocate of individual freedom. And the fight for freedom was one that he waged in letters: In 1791–92, Paine, now back in England, released *The Rights of Man*, a work in which he defended the cause of the French Revolution (1789–99) and appealed to the English to overthrow their monarchy. For this he was tried and convicted of treason in his homeland. Escaping to Paris, the philosopher became a member of the revolutionary National Convention. But during the Reign of Terror (1793–94) of revolutionary leader Robespierre, Paine was imprisoned for being English. An American minister interceded on Paine's behalf, insisting that Paine was actually an American. Paine was released on this technicality. He remained in Paris until 1802, and then returned to the United States. Though he played an important role in the American Revolutionary War by boosting the morale of the colonists, he nevertheless lived his final years in poverty as an outcast.

Why are **Kant's philosophies** still relevant?

Immanuel Kant (1724–1804) remains one of the great modern thinkers because he developed a whole new philosophy, one that completely reinterpreted human knowledge. A professor at Germany's Königsberg University beginning in 1755, Kant lectured widely and was a prolific writer. His most important work came somewhat late in life—after 1775. It was in that year that he undertook "a project of critical philosophy," in which he aimed to answer the three questions that, in his opinion, have occupied every philosopher in Western history: "What can I know? What ought I do? For what may I hope?"

Kant's answer to the first question (What can I know?) was based on one important conclusion: what a person can know or make claims about is only his or her experience of things, *not* the things in themselves. The philosopher arrived at this conclusion by observing the certainty of math and science: He determined that the fundamental nature of human reality (metaphysics) does not rely on or yield the genuine knowledge of science and math. For example, Newton's law of inertia—a body at rest tends to remain at rest, and a body in motion tends to remain in motion—does not change based on human experience. The law of inertia is universally recognized as correct and as such it is a "pure" truth, which can be relied on. But human reality, argued Kant, does not rest on any such certainties. That which a person has no sensory experience of cannot be known absolutely. Kant therefore reasoned that free will cannot be proved or disproved—nor can the existence of God.

Even though what humans can know is extremely limited, Kant did not become skeptical. On the contrary, he asserted that "unknowable things" require a leap of faith. He further concluded that since no one can disprove the existence of God, objections to religion carry no weight. In this way, Kant answered the third question posed by philosophers (For what may I hope?).

After arriving at the conclusion that each person experiences the world according to their own internal laws, Kant began writing on the problem of ethics, answering the second question (What ought I do?). In 1788, he published the *Critique of Practical Reason*, asserting that there is a moral law, which he called the "categorical imperative." Kant argued that a person could test the morality of his or her actions by asking if their motivation should become a universal law—applicable to all people: "Act as if the maxim from which you act were to become through your will a universal law." Kant concluded that when a person's actions conformed with this "categorical imperative," then he or she was doing their duty, which would result in goodwill.

Kant's theories have remained relevant to the world of philosophy: modern thinkers have either furthered the school of thought that Kant initiated, or they have rejected it. Either way, the philosopher's influence is still felt. It's interesting to note that among his writings is an essay on political theory (*Perpetual Peace*), which first appeared in 1795: In it, Kant described a federation that would work to prevent international conflict; the League of Nations and the United Nations, created more than a century after Kant, are the embodiments of this idea.

What is **existentialism**?

Existentialism is not a single school of thought but rather a label applied to several systems that are influenced by the theories of Danish philosopher Sören Kierkegaard (1813–55). Existentialist thinkers consider one problem: human existence in an unfathomable universe. However, in considering this "plight," philosophers have arrived at different conclusions.

The founder of existentialism, Kierkegaard rejected the principles put forth by traditional philosophers such as Georg Hegel, who had considered philosophy as a science, asserting that it is both objective and certain. Kierkegaard overturned this assertion, citing that truth is not objective but rather subjective—that there is no such thing as universal truths. Kierkegaard maintained that human beings must make their own choices, based on their own knowledge and within limited time. When he wrote on the subject, Kierkegaard frequently used pseudo-

What is the Hegelian dialectic?

It is the system of reasoning put forth by German philosopher Georg Hegel (1770–1831) who theorized that at the center of the universe there is an absolute spirit that guides all reality. According to Hegel, all historical developments follow three basic laws: each event follows a necessary course (in other words, it could not have happened in any other way); each historical event represents not only change but progress; and that one historical event, or phase, tends to be replaced by its opposite, which is later replaced by a resolution of the two extremes. This third law of Hegel's dialectic is the "pendulum theory" discussed by scholars and students of history—that events swing from one extreme to the other before the pendulum comes to rest at middle. The extreme phases are called the thesis and the antithesis; the resolution is called the synthesis. Based on this system, Hegel asserted that human beings can comprehend the unfolding of history. In this way, he viewed the human experience as absolute and knowable.

nyms, a practice he defended by intimating that he was putting the onus on his readers to determine what is true—that they shouldn't rely on the "authority" of his philosophies.

In the twentieth century, heirs to Kierkegaard's school of thought included German philosopher Martin Heidegger (1889–1976), who rejected the label "existentialist," and the French writer Jean-Paul Sartre (1905–80), the only self-proclaimed existentialist. They grappled with the dilemma that human beings must use their free will to make decisions—and assume responsibility for those decisions—without knowing conclusively what is true or false, right or wrong, good or bad. In other words, there is no way of knowing absolutely what the correct choices are, and yet individuals must make choices all the time, and be held accountable for them. Sartre described this as a "terrifying freedom." However, theologians such as Karl Barth (1886–1968) and Paul Tillich (1886–1965) reconsidered the human condition in light of Christianity, arriving at far

Karl Marx.

less pessimistic conclusions than did Sartre. For example, Tillich asserted that "divine answers" exist. Similarly, Jewish philosopher Martin Buber (1878–1965), who was also influenced by Kierkegaard, posited a personal and direct dialogue between the individual and God.

What is **Marxism**?

Marxism is an economic and political philosophy named for its origina-tor, Karl Marx (1818–83). Marx was a German social philosopher and revolutionary who, in 1844, met in Paris another German philosopher,

Friedrich Engels (1820–95), beginning a long collaboration. Four years later, they wrote the *Communist Manifesto*, laying the foundation for socialism and communism. Marx is most well known for *Das Kapital* (*The Capital*), which took him thirty years to complete and was published in three volumes—the first in 1867, and the second and third after his death in 1885 and 1894.

The cornerstone of Marxism, to which Engels greatly contributed, is the belief that history is determined by economics. Based on this premise, Marx asserted that economic crises will result in increased poverty, which in turn will inspire the working class (proletariat) to revolt, ousting the capitalists (bourgeoisie). According to Marx, once the working class has seized control, it will institute a system of economic cooperation and a classless society. Marx predicted the failure of the capitalist system, based on his belief that the history of society is "the history of class struggle." He and Engels viewed an international revolution as inevitable.

While Marxism still has its followers in the late twentieth century, most scholars have discredited Marx's predictions, citing improved conditions for workers in industrialized nations, which has been brought about by the evolution of capitalism.

What is the **difference** between **socialism** and **communism**?

In practice, there is little distinction between the two systems—which both rely on the elimination of private property and the collective ownership of goods. But in theory, there are distinctions between the two. According to Marxism, socialism is a transition state between capitalism and communism: In socialism, the state (or government) still exists, and is in control of property and the programs for collectivization. Marxist theory holds that communism is the final stage of society—after the state has dissolved. In a communist society, economic goods and property are distributed equally among the people.

What was **Nietzsche's** philosophy about the **"will to power"**?

The German philosopher Friedrich Nietzsche (1844–1900) developed many theories of human behavior, and the will to power was one of these. While other philosophers (including the ancient Greek Epicurus) argued

267

that humans are motivated by a desire to experience pleasure, Nietzsche asserted that it was neither pleasure nor the avoidance of pain that inspires humankind, but rather the desire for strength and power. He further averred that in order to gain power, humans would even be willing to embrace pain. However, it's critical to note that he did not view this will to power strictly as a will to dominate others: Nietzsche glorified a superman (*Ubermensch*), an individual who could assert power over him- or herself. He viewed artists as one example of an *Ubermensch*—since that person had successfully harnessed his or her instincts through creativity and in so doing had actually achieved a higher form of power than would the person who only wished to dominate others. A notable exception to Nietzsche's esteem for artists was the composer Richard Wagner (1813–83), whom the philosopher opposed. Since Wagner led an immoral lifestyle, unlike the *Ubermensch*, he had not gained power over his own instincts.

Nietzsche was a professor of classics at the University of Basel in Switzerland from 1868 to 1878. Retiring due to poor health, he turned to his writing, which included poetry. In 1889, he suffered a mental breakdown and died the next year. After his death, his sister, Elisabeth Förster-Nietzcshe (1846–1935), altered her brother's works in editing, and thus, changed their meaning. In 1895, she had married an anti-Semitic agitator, Bernhard Förster (1843–89) who, with his wife, attempted to establish a pure Aryan colony in Paraguay. The effort failed, and Förster took his own life. These events and more importantly, the changes to the philosopher's own words, gave rise to the popular misconception that Nietzsche's philosophies had given rise to Nazism.

What is **Nazism**?

Short for National Socialism, "Nazi" was a derisive abbreviation that nevertheless held. The Nazi doctrine rests on three philosophies—extreme nationalism, anti-Semitism, and anti-Communism. The German defeat in World War I (1914–18) resulted in severe punishment of that country and its seriously diminished role in Europe. Consequently, the doctrines of Nazism took hold, as they appealed to the masses with promises of a rebuilt Germany.

The "bible" of Nazism was Adolf Hitler's *Mein Kampf* (*My Struggle*; 1923), which asserted the superiority of a "pure" Aryan race led by an infallible ruler (the Führer), the reestablishment of a German empire (the Third Reich), and the systematic annihilation (holocaust) of what Nazis perceived to be Germany's worst enemies—the Jews and the Communists.

Nazis ruled Germany from 1933, when Hitler rose to power as head of the National Socialist German Workers' Party. In their own country, they enforced their policies through a secret police (the Gestapo), storm troops (called the SS), and Hitler's bodyguard (called the SA). Elsewhere in Europe, the Nazis used sheer force in imposing their system. Their aggression and ruthlessness resulted in World War II. Nazism ended in 1945, when Hitler killed himself and Germany lost the war. The doctrine was outlawed thereafter.

MAJOR SCIENTIFIC ADVANCES

Who was **Pythagoras**?

Known by students today for the Pythagorean theorem (the square of the length of the hypotenuse is equal to the sum of the squares of the lengths of the other two sides), Pythagoras was a Greek philosopher and mathematician who lived in the sixth century B.C. and whose followers kept "Pythagoreanism" alive into the middle of the fourth century B.C. Religious in nature (some have referred to the society as a "cult"), the group believed in the functional and even mystical significance of numbers and made considerable advances in mathematics and astronomy. Pythagoras left no writings, which has prompted some scholars to believe that no such person ever existed, but rather that any doctrines ascribed to Pythagoras are actually attributable to a group of people. Whatever the case, the Pythagorean legacy is real. It includes the following: the word *calculus* (Pythagoreans used lines, triangles, and squares made of pebbles to represent numbers—and the Latin word for pebble is calculus); they reduced astronomy and music to numerical patterns and studied them as mathematical subjects; and they were the first to suggest (as early as the sixth century B.C.) that the Earth is spherical (not flat) and that the Earth, Moon and planets revolve around the Sun.

269

What was the Ptolemaic System?

It was a scheme devised by the ancient Greek astronomer Ptolemy, born about 170 B.C. (he died 100 B.C.). He proposed a system that placed the Earth directly at the center of the universe—with the Sun, Moon, and planets all orbiting around the Earth. However, Ptolemy observed that the movement of the planets did not match his scheme and so he added small orbits (epicycles) to it to try to make it work.

Even though it was erroneous—and complicated—the Ptolemaic System was functional enough to make predictions of planetary positions. The system took hold, influencing thinking for 1,400 years. The Roman Catholic Church adopted the system as part of its doctrine, which the church hierarchy held to even when Polish astronomer Nicholas Copernicus refuted it in 1543, arguing that the Sun, not the Earth, was the center of the universe. In the 1570s, accurate measurements of planet positions that had been taken by Danish astronomer Tycho Brahe proved that the Ptolemaic system was inaccurate. But it was not until 1609, when German astronomer Johannes Kepler devised a better explanation of planetary orbits, that the Ptolemaic system was put to rest.

Why is **Euclid** considered so important to math?

The Greek mathematician Euclid (330?–270? B.C.) is considered the father of geometry. He used axioms (accepted mathematical truths) to develop a deductive system of proof, which he wrote in his textbook *Elements*. This book proved to be a great contribution to scientific thinking and includes Euclid's proof of the Pythagorean Theorem.

Euclid's first three postulates, with which he begins his *Elements*, are familiar to anyone who has taken geometry: 1) it is possible to draw a straight line between any two points, 2) it is possible to produce a finite straight line continuously in a straight line, and 3) a circle may be described with any center and radius.

What is the **Copernican view** of the universe?

The Copernican view of the universe, proposed in 1507, argued that the Earth was only one of several galactic bodies that orbited the Sun. This theory, put forth by the Polish astronomer Nicholas Copernicus (1473–1543), was controversial in its day for it ran counter to the astronomical beliefs that had held sway for some 1,300 years—those of the Ptolemaic System, which maintained that the Earth was the center of the universe and that the Sun and planets all revolve around it.

Copernicus devised his scheme out of necessity really: He had found that using the Ptolemaic system to predict the positions of the planets over long periods of time yielded haphazard results. Once he made the assumption that the Sun, rather than the Earth, was the center of the solar system and that all the planets orbited the Sun, Copernicus realized that tables of planetary positions could be calculated much more easily—and accurately.

However, Copernicus was not the first to put forth such a radical idea: the Greek astronomer Aristarchus of Samos (c. 270 B.C.) was the first to maintain that the Earth rotates on an axis and revolves around the Sun. But it was Ptolemy's ideas that took hold; not Aristarchus's. Copernicus did, however, take the argument a step further, averring that the Earth itself is small and unimportant compared with the rest of the universe.

But the Copernican view had its problems, too: he assumed that the planetary orbits were perfectly circular. Because of this error, he found it necessary to use some of Ptolemy's cumbersome epicycles (smaller orbits centered on the larger ones) to reduce the discrepancy between his predicted orbits and those that he observed. It was not until Johannes Kepler that the elliptical orbit of the planets was put forth.

What were **Galileo's** contributions to **science** and **mathematics**?

Galileo Galilei (Italian; 1564–1642) is credited with no less than establishing the modern method of experimentation. He was the first scientist and thinker to try to prove or disprove theory by conducting tests and observing the results. Prior to Galileo, scientific theory was purely based on hypothesis and conjecture. It was in the interest of conducting accurate tests and in making precise observations that Galileo developed a number of inventions including the hydrostatic balance (a device designed to measure the density of objects) in about 1586, and the thermometer (one of the first measuring devices to be used in science) in 1593.

The invention most widely credited to Galileo is the telescope, however he did not originate the instrument, but rather improved it (in 1609). He was also the first to use a telescope to study the skies, which led him to a series of discoveries, all in 1610: the Moon shines with reflected light; the surface of the Moon is mountainous; the Milky Way is made up of countless stars; and Jupiter has four large satellites—he was even able to correctly estimate the period of rotation of each of these moons, which he named "Medicean stars" (for his benefactor, Cosimo de Medici). Galileo was also the first to observe the phases of Venus, which are similar to the Moon's and to discover sunspots.

Prior to these astronomical discoveries, Galileo had already made significant contributions to science. In 1589, when he was only twenty-five years old, he had published a treatise on the center of gravity in solids. From 1602 to 1609, he had studied the motion of pendulums and other objects along arcs and inclines. From these observations, he concluded that falling objects accelerate at a constant rate. This law of uniform acceleration later helped Isaac Newton (1642–1727) derive the law of gravity. Galileo also demonstrated that the path of a projectile is a parabola.

Galileo was a professor of mathematics at Pisa (1589–91) and at Padua (1592–1610). In 1610, he was appointed philosopher and mathematician extraordinary to the grand duke of Tuscany, Cosimo de Medici.

Why was **Galileo** tried for heresy by the **Inquisition**?

The trouble began for Galileo in 1613 when he published *Letters on the Solar Spots*, in which he advocated the Copernican system of the universe, which proposed that the Earth (along with other galactic bodies) revolved around the Sun. This view ran contrary to the Roman Catholic Church, whose long-held astronomical beliefs were based on Ptolemy's theory that the Earth was the center of the universe. Thus, in 1616, the Pope issued a decree declaring the Copernican system to be "false and erroneous," and Galileo was ordered not to support it.

Astronomer Galileo.

When a new pope, Urban VIII, was put in place in 1624, Galileo traveled to Rome to make an appeal that the edict against the Copernican theory be revoked. The pope declined to do so, but he did give Galileo permission to write about the Copernican system, under the condition that he not give it preference over the church-sanctioned Ptolemaic model. So, in 1632, Galileo published again: *Dialogue Concerning the Two Chief World Systems*, however, contained unconvincing objections to the Copernican view. The church saw through it and summoned the author to Rome to stand before the Inquisition. Galileo was accused of violating the original edict of 1616, was put on trial for heresy, and was found guilty. Though he was ordered to recant, at some point he uttered the famous statement: "And yet it moves," a reference to the Copernican theory that the Earth rotates on its axis.

Galileo was supposed to be imprisoned, but the pope commuted this sentence to house arrest at Galileo's home near Florence, where he died blind at the age of seventy-eight.

Why is **Johannes Kepler** considered important to modern **astronomy**?

It was German astronomer Kepler (1571–1630) who put forth the theory that planets, including the Earth, rotate around the Sun in elliptical orbits. But he had the work of Tycho Brahe to thank for this.

In 1600, Kepler moved to Prague (Czech Republic), where he began working as an assistant to the flamboyant Brahe, a Danish aristocrat who years earlier (in 1576) had set up the first real astronomical observatory in history. Brahe's benefactor in this work was none other than King Frederick II, who was a patron of science. In the observatory, Brahe had made and recorded extraordinarily accurate observations of planetary positions. Even though he rejected the Copernican (Sun-centered) view of the universe because it violated scripture, he also realized that his observations of the planets could not be explained by the Ptolemaic System. He soon put forth his own theory of planetary orbit. The Tychonic Theory was something of a compromise between the two models that had been put forth: it followed Copernicus's theory in that it, too, had the planets orbiting around the Sun; but it kept to the Ptolemaic belief that the Sun orbited around the Earth (to account for a year). The theory was ignored.

Halley's Comet spotted in 1910.

But when Brahe hired Kepler in 1600, he turned over his observations to him and charged him with the task of devising a theory of planetary motion. As a mathematician, Kepler was the right man for the job and he devoted himself to the effort for the next twenty years. At one point, Kepler had devised a scheme that almost matched Brahe's observations, but not quite. Believing Brahe's observations were perfectly accurate, Kepler threw out the scheme and started again. Finally, he gave up on using circles and epicycles and began working with an ellipse. The results matched Brahe's data. In 1609, Kepler published his first two laws of planetary motion: a planet orbits the Sun in an ellipse, not a circle (as Copernicus had believed); and a planet moves faster when near the Sun, and slower when farther away.

We also have Kepler to thank for a word that is in everyday use: satellite. After Galileo discovered the moons of Jupiter, Kepler used a telescope to view them for himself. He dubbed them satellites, a name that stuck.

When did **Halley's Comet** first appear?

Its first noted appearance was in 239 B.C., but it was British astronomer Edmund Halley (1636–1742) who noted that the bright comet he   275 observed in 1682 followed roughly the same path as those that had been observed in 1531 and 1607. He suggested that they were all the same comet and that it would reappear in 1758. It did reappear, and it was therefore named for Halley, who was England's second Astronomer Royal. It's also worth noting that it was Halley who encouraged his friend and fellow scientist Sir Isaac Newton to write his theory of gravity, which he did: *Principia Mathematica*, which Halley used his own money to publish, appeared in 1687, and is considered a seminal work for modern science.

Halley's Comet has been observed by astronomers every time it has appeared since 239 B.C. Most recently seen in 1985–86, the comet will make another appearance in 2061, and roughly every seventy-six years thereafter.

Did **Sir Isaac Newton** really formulate the **laws of motion** after observing an apple falling from a tree?

While it may sound more like legend than fact, Newton held that it was true. In 1666, Isaac Newton (1642–1727), who was newly graduated from Cambridge University, escaped Bubonic-plagued London, and was visiting the family farm. There he saw an apple fall to the ground, and he began considering the force that was responsible for the action. He theorized that the apple had fallen because all matter attracts other matter, that the rate of the apple's fall was directly proportional to the attractive force that the Earth exerted upon it, and that the force that pulled the apple was also responsible for keeping the moon in orbit around the Earth.

But he then set aside these theories, and turned his attention to experimenting with light. Finally, in the 1680s, Newton revisited the matter of the apple, taking into consideration Galileo's studies of motion (1602–09), from which the Italian scientist had concluded that falling objects accelerate at a constant rate. In 1687, Newton, with the considerable support of his friend Edmund Halley (of Halley's Comet fame), published *Mathematical Principles of Natural Philosophy (Principia Mathematica)*, which outlined the laws of gravity and planetary motion. Newton had arranged Galileo's findings into three basic laws of motion: a body at rest tends to remain at rest, and a body in motion tends to remain in motion (this is the law of inertia); the force to move a body is equal to its mass times acceleration; and for every action, there is an equal and opposite reaction. These three laws allowed Newton to calculate the gravitational force between the Earth and the moon.

Did **Newton** invent **calculus**?

Yes, Newton did invent calculus. But so did German mathematician Gottfried Leibniz (1646–1716)—independently of Newton. Both men had developed calculus in the context of trying to explain the laws of physics. Newton's development of calculus predated that of Leibniz, but he had failed to publish it. Leibniz published his results in 1684; Newton followed suit in 1693. Each used different symbols and notations, but Leibniz's were considered superior and were more widely adopted, causing friction between the men. Their conflict became a matter of national pride, with English scientists refusing to accept Leibniz's version. Nevertheless, since Newton's system predated that of Leibniz, he is credited as the originator.

Is **Thomas Edison** the greatest inventor to date?

Some believe that he is, and for good reason: Thomas Alva Edison (1847–1931), the so-called "Wizard of Menlo Park," registered 1,300 patents in his name during his lifetime, more than any other individual in American history. His best-known inventions include an automatic telegraphy machine, a stock-ticker machine, the incandescent light bulb (1878), the phonograph (1877), and the motion picture machine (kinetoscope; 1891). Edison also made one major scientific find during his research, when he observed that electrons are emitted from a heated cathode—the phenomenon is known as the "Edison effect."

When Edison was still in his twenties, he set up a laboratory where fifty consulting engineers worked with him on various inventions. By his own description, the Newark, New Jersey, plant was an "invention factory." It operated for six years, during which Edison was granted about two hundred new patents for work completed there. The laboratory is regarded by most as the first formally organized non-academic research center in the United States. By 1876, Edison had outgrown his Newark facilities and arranged for the construction of a new plant at Menlo Park,

Inventor Thomas Alva Edison.

New Jersey. His most productive work was accomplished at this location over the next decade.

Is it true that **Edison** had no formal education?

It's almost true: Thomas Edison (1847–1931) had no formal education to speak of. Born in Milan, Ohio, Edison's father moved the family to Port Huron, Michigan, in 1854. There young Thomas attended school for the first time—in a one-room schoolhouse where he was taught by the Reverend and Mrs. G. B. Engle. But this arrangement lasted just a few months: The boy grew impatient with his schooling—behavior his teachers interpreted as a sign of mental inferiority. When Edison overheard Mrs. Engle refer to him as "addled," he reported it to his mother, Nancy, who promptly withdrew him from the school. From then on, his mother schooled him at home, introducing young Edison to natural philosophy—a mixture of physics, chemistry, and other sciences. He showed a natural inclination for science and by the age of ten, he was conducting original experiments in their home.

Edison furthered his education through voracious reading. He sought, and was granted, permission to sell periodicals, snacks, and tobacco to passengers on the train between Port Huron and Detroit, some sixty miles away. During the layover in downtown Detroit, Edison spent his time at the public library, where, according to his own recollection, he read not a few books, but the library. Even though he lacked a formal education, Edison possessed a keen mind and a natural curiosity. Further, he had the benefit of the schooling provided by his mother as well as access to a library of books, of which he took full advantage.

Then something happened that changed Edison's life: While still a young man, he lost his hearing. Biographer Matthew Josephson explains that the deafness had two effects on Edison: not only did he become "more solitary and shy," but Edison turned with an even greater intensity toward his studies and he began to "put forth tremendous efforts at self-education, for he had absolutely to learn everything for himself."

How extensive were **George Washington Carver's** agricultural discoveries?

The American botanist and agricultural chemist George Washington Carver (c. 1864–1943) won international fame for his research, which included finding more than three hundred uses for peanuts and more than one hundred uses for sweet potatoes. The son of slave parents, Carver was born near Diamond, Missouri, and through his own efforts obtained an education, earning a bachelor's of science degree in 1894 and his master's of science in agriculture in 1896. That year he joined the faculty of Alabama's Tuskeegee Institute (now Tuskeegee University), where he served as director of agricultural research until his death in 1943. His first research projects centered on soil conservation and agricultural practices. Carver gave lectures and made demonstrations to southern farmers—particularly black farmers—to help them increase crop production. He then turned his attention to finding new uses for two southern crops—peanuts and sweet potatoes. Carver found that peanuts could be used to make a milk substitute, printer's ink, and soap, among other things. He also found new uses for soybeans and devised products that could be made from cotton waste. His efforts were all intended to improve the economy in the South and better the way of life of southern black farmers.

Carver was lauded for his accomplishments: he was named a fellow of the Royal Society of Arts of London (1916); he was awarded the Spingarn Medal for distinguished service in agricultural chemistry (1923); and he was bestowed with the Theodore Roosevelt Medal for his valuable contributions to science (1939).

What did **Alfred Nobel** do?

The Swedish chemist whose name is known around the world because of the Nobel prize, invented dynamite. Even though dynamite improved the safety of explosives, like others who have invented materials of destruction, Alfred Nobel (1833–96) became concerned with how his invention would be used. So in his will, he set up a fund to award people who make strides in the sciences, literature, and very importantly, in promoting international peace. It's interesting to note that Alfred Nobel was a pacifist; he was involved in the explosives industry since it was his family's business. The Nobel Prize has been awarded annually, except for 1940–42, since 1901. Recipients in any of five categories (peace, chemistry, physics, physiology or medicine, and literature) are presented with a gold medal and a substantial monetary award (in the hundreds of thousands of dollars today). A sixth, related prize is the Nobel Memorial Prize in Economic Science, which was established in 1968 by the Swedish national bank, and first awarded in 1969.

Why is the **equation $E = mc^2$** historically significant?

The famous equation was put forth in 1905 by German-born physicist Albert Einstein (1879–1955) and became important to history largely because it laid the foundation for nuclear energy.

In the formula, E stands for energy, m stands for mass, and c-squared is a constant factor equal to the speed of light squared. The equation illustrates the relationship between, and exchangeability of, energy and matter. In the 1930s, when scientists discovered a way to split atoms (the minute particles of which elements are made), they learned that the subatomic particles that were created have a total mass less than the mass of the original atom: In other words, when the atom was split, part of the mass of the atom had been changed into subatomic particles but some of it had been converted into energy. Using Einstein's formula $E = m(c^2)$, the scientists calculated how much energy was produced by splitting an atom. This atom-splitting method for creating energy is the basis for nuclear energy. The term "nuclear" refers to the atomic process—which uses the nucleus or central portion of an atom to release energy. Today, we live in the nuclear age—where power and weapons are produced using the atomic process for creating energy.

Why did **Einstein** write to **President Roosevelt** urging U.S. development of the **atom bomb**?

Albert Einstein, who was born in Germany in 1879, and subsequently educated in Switzerland (where he also became a naturalized citizen), was an ardent pacifist. But, being a brilliant observer, he quickly perceived the threat posed by Nazi Germany. Einstein was visiting England in 1933 when the Nazis confiscated his property in Berlin and deprived him of his German citizenship. Some might call it lucky that the Nobel prize–winning (1921) scientist was out of the country when this happened—in the coming years, other Jews certainly suffered worse fates at the hands of Adolf Hitler's anti-Semitic programs.

Einstein moved to the United States, where he took a position at the Institute for Advanced Study in Princeton, New Jersey. There he settled and later became an American citizen (1940). In August 1939, just before Adolf Hitler's German troops invaded Poland and began World War II (1939–45), Einstein wrote a letter to President Franklin Roosevelt (1882–1945), urging him to launch a government program to study nuclear energy. He further advocated the United States build an atomic bomb, cautioning that such an effort might already be underway in Germany.

The United States did in fact begin development of the atomic bomb, which releases nuclear energy by splitting heavy atomic particles. The program was called the Manhattan Project, and was centered at Oak

Ridge, Tennessee, and Hanford, Washington, where scientists worked to obtain sufficient amounts of plutonium and uranium to make the bombs. The bombs themselves were developed in a laboratory in Los Alamos, New Mexico. The project was funded by the government to the tune of $2 billion. The first atomic device (made of plutonium) was tested in Alamogordo, New Mexico, on July 16, 1945. And less than a month later the United States dropped atomic bombs on Hiroshima (August 6) and Nagasaki (August 9), Japan, forcing the Japanese to surrender.

After the war, Einstein, who was always interested in world and human affairs, advocated a system of world law that he believed could prevent war in the Atomic (or Nuclear) Age. As a Zionist Jew, in 1952, he was offered the presidency of the relatively new state of Israel (founded 1947), but he declined the honor. He died in New Jersey in 1955.

Why is **Enrico Fermi's** name so closely associated with **nuclear energy**?

The Italian-born physicist Enrico Fermi (1901–54) carried out experiments and led projects that have led him to be referred to as one of the chief architects of the nuclear age. In 1934, Fermi announced that he had discovered elements beyond uranium; but what he had really done, and which was later proved, was split the atom. In 1938, just before World War II, this process was named nuclear fission. And one year later, Albert Einstein would write a letter to President Roosevelt, urging the American government to study this process, which releases energy. Also in 1938, Fermi was awarded the Nobel prize for physics and he escaped Italy, where the Fascist regime of Benito Mussolini (1883–1945) had taken hold. Fermi became a professor of physics at Columbia University in 1939, where he taught for three years. In 1942, he got involved in the Manhattan Project, which was developing the atomic bomb. In that capacity, he directed the first controlled nuclear chain reaction.

After World War II, Fermi, who had become an American citizen in 1944, taught at the University of Chicago and continued his research on the basic properties of nuclear particles. In 1953, he had an element named after him, *fermium*, an artificially created radioactive element. The Atomic Energy Commission honors accomplishments in physics with the Enrico Fermi Award.

What is the Doomsday clock?

The clock represents the threat of nuclear annihilation. It was created by the board of directors of *Bulletin of the Atomic Scientists* and the clock first appeared on the cover of that magazine in 1947—two years after the United States had used two nuclear weapons against Japan (at Hiroshima and Nagasaki) to end World War II. The atomic scientists developed the idea in order to illustrate the threat of total destruction posed by nuclear weapons. On the clock, midnight is the time of destruction. When the clock first appeared, the scientists had put the time at seven minutes before midnight. In the decades since, the clock had been adjusted based on either the proliferation of or agreements to control nuclear weapons.

The closest it ever came to "doomsday" was two minutes until midnight. This was in 1953, shortly after the United States and the Soviet Union each tested hydrogen bombs. The farthest the minute hand has ever been from striking the hour of midnight was in 1991 when the United States and the Soviet Union signed the Strategic Arms Reduction Treaty (START) and announced cuts in nuclear weapons. The scientists moved the clock to read seventeen minutes until midnight.

In the late 1990s, the clock read at fourteen minutes to midnight, but the 1998 testing of nuclear weapons in Pakistan and India, neighboring countries long at odds with each other, resulted in the clock being forwarded by five minutes—to just nine minutes before midnight.

Why was **Oppenheimer** investigated for disloyalty to the United States?

American physicist J. Robert Oppenheimer (1904–67), who had directed the Los Alamos laboratory where the first atomic bomb was developed and built, was investigated by the government in 1953–54 because of his opposition to the United States' development of a hydrogen bomb. He was also suspected of having ties with the Communist party, and therefore was viewed as a security risk.

Following World War II, Oppenheimer, seeing the devastating and awesome power of the atomic bomb his laboratory had created, became a vocal advocate of international control of atomic energy. When the United States began developing the hydrogen bomb (also called a "thermonuclear bomb" because of the high temperatures that it requires in order to create a reaction), Oppenheimer objected on both moral and technical grounds: The hydrogen bomb is a far more destructive weapon than the atomic bomb.

In 1953, Oppenheimer was suspended from the U.S. Atomic Energy Commission (AEC) because he was believed to pose a threat to national security. Hearings were held, but the New York-born and Harvard-educated scientist was cleared of charges of disloyalty. A decade later, in 1963, the organization gave Oppenheimer its highest honor, the Enrico Fermi Award, for his contributions to theoretical physics. Indeed, Oppenheimer had done much to further the science during his lifetime: As a member of the faculty of the University of California Berkeley, he established a center for research in theoretical physics; he also taught at the California Institute of Technology; and he served as director of the Institute for Advanced Study in Princeton, New Jersey, from 1947 to 1966. There he knew Alfred Einstein—who accepted a position at the institute in 1933 and remained there until his death in 1955.

How did **Charles Darwin** come to develop his **theory of evolution**?

The English naturalist (1809–82) was attending Cambridge when, through a friend, he gained appointment as naturalist aboard the H.M.S. *Beagle*. The around-the-world voyage began in 1831, and Darwin was able to gather data on flora, fauna, and geology in the world's southern lands—the South American coasts, the Galapagos, the Andes Mountains, Australia, and Asia. The trip lasted into 1836, and in the years that followed Darwin published and edited many works on natural history—though none of them put forth his theory of evolution. (It's interesting to note that Darwin's paternal grandfather, Erasmus Darwin, 1731–1802, was a physician, botanist, and poet, who in 1803 wrote the verse titled "The Temple of Nature or the Origin of Society"—which anticipated the theory of evolution that his grandson would one day put forth.)

Revolutionary thinker and naturalist Charles Darwin.

Encouraged by Sir Charles Lyell (1797–1875), who is considered the father of modern geology, Charles Darwin wrote out his theory. Coincidentally, he received the abstract of an identical theory of natural selection, formulated by English naturalist Alfred Russell Wallace (1823–1913)—who had arrived at his conclusions independently of Darwin. Wallace had made his formulation of evolution based on his study of comparative biology in Brazil and the East Indies. In 1858, Darwin published both his work as well as the abstract written by Wallace. The following year, Darwin backed up his theory in *Origin of Species*, which was found to be scientifically credible. He added to this work with *The Descent of Man* in 1871.

What Darwin put forth was that all life originated with a simple, primordial protoplasm (the fundamental material of which all living things are composed). In his theory of natural selection, Darwin posited that those species that are best adapted to the environment are the species that survive and reproduce.

While organic evolution and natural selection had a profound impact on the world of science (which further studied and supported the concepts), they jarred much of the religious community and created a controversy. Creationists, who believe the origin story put forth in the bible—the story of Adam and Eve in the Garden of Eden, objected to Darwin's theories. Debate between evolution and creationism ensued, most notably in the so-called Scopes "monkey trial" of July 1925: Dayton, Tennessee public school teacher John T. Scopes was charged with violating a state law that prohibited the teaching of evolution. Though he was defended by one of the most acclaimed attorneys of all time, Clarence Darrow (1857–1938), faced with the prosecution of another prominent lawyer, William Jennings Bryan (1860–1925), Scopes lost the case. But Scopes was later released on a technicality. The law was eventually repealed (in 1967).

Though scientific research has largely substantiated the theory of evolution described by Charles Darwin, the theory of creation still has its followers, mostly religious fundamentalists.

Who are the **Leakeys** and what did they discover?

The prominent British family has included four scientists who have made significant anthropological findings in East Africa. Family patriarch Louis S. B. Leakey (1903–72) was born near Nairobi, Kenya, the oldest child of British missionaries. There he grew up, learning the tribal language of the Kikuyu people before he learned English, and wandering the countryside where he discovered primitive stone arrowheads and tools. While attending Cambridge University, Leakey determined that he would pursue a career in archeology, and he went on to earn his doctorate degree.

Louis Leakey married archeologist and artist Mary Douglas (1913–96) in 1936. Returning to Leakey's boyhood home to conduct their work, the husband-and-wife team made their first discovery of note in 1948. Near Lake Victoria, Kenya, they found more than thirty fragments of the skull of an ape-like creature. Scientists concluded that the animal was a common ancestor of humankind and apes—and had lived between twenty-five and forty million years ago.

The Leakeys made their most well-known discoveries in neighboring Tanzania during the late 1950s and into the 1960s, proving that human evolution was centered in Africa. At the Olduvai Gorge, a thirty-five-mile-long ravine, the archeologists discovered layers of the earth's history—including almost one hundred forms of extinct animal life. They also unearthed the fossils of a near-man, *Zinjanthropus*, who possessed a brain about half the size of modern human's and who walked upright at a height of about five feet—roughly 1.75 million years ago. Because he lived on a diet of nuts and meat, the discovery came to be called "Nutcracker Man." Subsequent findings at the gorge included that of *Homo habilis*, called "Able Man" since it is believed that he made use of the stone tools found nearby. Louis Leakey later decided the two humanlike creatures, Able Man and Nutcracker Man, had actually lived in the same place at the same time—meaning that the evolution of humankind was not along the linear path as had been thought.

While Leakey's controversial conclusion challenged the scientific community, so would the finds of their scientist son Richard (b. 1944): In the decades that followed his parents' discoveries at Olduvai Gorge, Richard pursued his own projects at Lake Turkana in north-central Kenya. There Richard discovered more than two hundred early-man fossils. Like his father, Richard Leakey is part of a husband-and-wife team of scientists. In 1971, he married British-born Meave Epps (b. 1942), a zoologist and paleontologist who had been hired by Louis Leakey in 1965 to work on his African digs. Together Richard and Meave Leakey, along with American anthropologist Alan Walker, have discovered and identified some of the oldest-known human-like fossils. In 1994 and 1995, near Lake Turkana, the team found prehistoric fossils, identified as *Australopithecus anamensis*, humanlike creatures that lived about four million years ago.

What is the **big bang theory**?

It is a theory of the origin of the universe. According to the big bang theory, the universe began as the result of an explosion that occurred between fifteen and twenty billion years ago. Over time, the matter created in the big bang broke apart—forming galaxies, stars, and a group of planets we know as our solar system. The theory was first put forth by Edwin Hubble (1889–1953) who observed that the universe is expanding uniformly and objects that are at greater distances are receding at greater velocities. In the 1960s, Bell Telephone Laboratories scientists discovered weak radio waves that are believed to be all that remains of the radiation from the original fireball. The discovery further supported Hubble's theory, which puts the age of the universe between fifteen and twenty billion years.

Astronomers have observed that the galaxies are still moving away from each other and that they'll probably continue to do so forever—or at least for about the next seventy billion years. If the galaxies did come together again, scientists believe that all of the matter in the universe would explode again (in other words, there would be another big bang), and the result would be consistent with that of the first—it would produce a universe much like the one we live in.

Another supporter of the big bang theory is British theoretical scientist Stephen Hawking (b. 1942). In 1988, Hawking, who is known for his theories on black holes (gravitational forces in space, made by what were once stars), published his ideas in the best-selling book *A Brief History of Time: From the Big Bang to Black Holes*.

How did **Carl Sagan** popularize science?

Carl Sagan (1934–96), a Cornell University astronomy and space science professor, became known to many Americans via his thirteen-part television program, *Cosmos*, which aired on PBS (Public Broadcasting Service) affiliates in the fall of 1980. The show covered a variety of science topics—including the origin and evolution of life on Earth, the evolution of the human brain, black holes, time travel, space exploration, and the ultimate fate of the universe. The program did so well—for a time ranking as the highest-rated regular series in public television history— that it also spun off a book by the same name. *Cosmos*, the book, became a bestseller and is still in print.

INVENTION

How old is the **compass**?

The first compass dates back to the first century B.C., when the Chinese observed that pieces of lodestone, an iron mineral, always pointed north when they were placed on a surface. There is evidence that Arab sailors were using compasses as early as A.D. 600, and as Arab influence spread north into Europe, so did the compass. By the fourteenth century, European ships carried maps that were charted with compass readings to reach different destinations. Prince Henry of Portugal (1394–1460) advanced the use of compasses in navigation by encouraging sailors and map-makers to coordinate their information to make more accurate maps of the seas. Also in the fifteenth century, an important discovery was made by none other than Christopher Columbus (1451–1506), who noticed that as he sailed to the New World, his compass did not align directly with the North Star. The difference between magnetic north and true north is called declination. In the sixteenth and seventeenth centuries, came better understanding of the earth's magnetic fields as well as the development of super magnets.

American Elmer Sperry (1860–1930) built the first gyrocompass, a device that works day or night, anywhere on Earth, even at the poles where lines of force are too close together for magnetic uses to function properly. When the gyrocompass is pointed north, it holds that position. Before the compass, which simply indicates north by a means of a magnetic needle or needles that pivot, sailors used the Sun, the Moon, and the stars to determine direction and navigate.

When did sailors begin using **latitude** and **longitude** to navigate?

It was after Englishman John Harrison (1693–1776) presented his ship's chronometer to London's Board of Longitude in 1736. The instrument was accurate to within one-tenth of a second per day (1.3 miles of longitude). Since it was set to the time of O° longitude (Greenwich time), it enabled navigators to fix longitudinal position by determining local time. Even though Harrison's award-winning invention was heavy (weighing sixty-six pounds), complicated, and delicate, it was improved upon so that it could be used on any sea-faring vessel under any weather conditions.

How long have **sundials** been in use?

Sundials, which indicate the time of day by the shadow cast by a stick, pin, or other object, usually on a horizontal plate, have been in use since before the sixth century B.C., when both the ancient Chinese and Egyptians used the device to tell time. Sundials proved to be a fairly accurate indicator of the passage of time. But it has its problems: a sundial can be difficult to read, the markings have to be adjusted according to latitude, and the readings differ with the seasons.

When was **January 1** made the first day of the **new year**?

In 45 B.C., when Julius Caesar reorganized the Roman calendar and made it solar-based rather than lunar-based. It was then that he moved the beginning of the new year to January 1. But until 1752, in England and in the American colonies, March 25, which represented the spring equinox, was the beginning of the new year. For example, March 24, 1700, was followed by March 25, 1701. In 1752, the British government changed the system to comply with a January 1 new year.

How old is the **oldest clock**?

The first mechanical timekeeping device was a water clock called a clepsydra, which was used from about 1500 B.C. through the Middle Ages. One very elaborate clepsydra was constructed for Emperor Charlemagne

How old is Greenwich Mean Time?

It dates back to 1884. Once the clock came on the scene (about 1275 A.D.) and allowed humans to keep accurate time, they realized that the sun did not rise at the same time all over the world. The problem of the varying times of sunrise and sunset by region was addressed by the adoption of Greenwich Mean Time, which gave us time zones. Greenwich Mean Time is measured according to when the sun crosses the Greenwich Meridian, which is at zero degrees longitude and passes through the Greenwich Observatory, England.

in A.D. 800: Upon the hour, it dropped a metal ball into a bowl. Because of problems with water (it evaporated, froze, and eroded the surfaces of its container), a more accurate device was needed. It's believed that the first completely mechanical clock was developed by a monk around A.D. 1275: The clock was driven by the slow pull of a falling weight that had to be reset to its starting position after several hours. The clocks in monasteries were also among the first to be fitted as alarm clocks: striking mechanisms were added to the timekeeping devices so that the monks would know when to ring the monastery bell.

Who invented the **thermometer**?

While the Greeks made simple thermometers as early as the first century B.C., it wasn't until Galileo (1564–1642) that a real thermometer was invented. It was an air thermometer, in which a colored liquid was driven *down* by the expansion of air, so that as the air got warmer (and expanded), the liquid dropped. This is unlike ordinary thermometers in use today—which rely on the colored liquid of mercury to rise as it gets warmer.

In 1612, Santorio Santorio (1561–1636), a friend of Galileo, adapted the device to measure the body's change in temperature due to illness. (The

291

clinical thermometer wasn't Santorio's only invention: As the first physician to use precision instruments in the practice of medicine, Santorio had also developed the pulse clock.)

Nonetheless, it was a full century before thermometers had a fixed scale. This was provided in 1713 by German physicist Daniel Fahrenheit (1686–1736).

TRANSPORTATION

Who invented the **steam engine**?

Like many other modern inventions, the steam engine had a long evolution. It was first conceived of by Hero of Alexandria in the first century B.C. The mathematician invented many "contrivances" that were operated by water, steam, or compressed air. These included not only a fountain and a fire engine, but, of course, the steam engine. Englishman Thomas Newcomen (1663–1729) developed an early steam engine (about 1711) that was used to pump water. (He was improving on a previous design, which had been patented by another inventor in 1698.)

But it was Scottish inventor James Watt (1736–1819) who substantially improved Newcomen's machine, patenting his own steam-powered engine in 1769. It was the first practical steam engine, and Watt's many improvements to the earlier technology paved the way for the use of the engine in manufacturing and transportation during the Industrial Revolution (c. 1750–c. 1850; Britain was just on the cusp of this new age when Watt patented his engine). The steam engine was eventually replaced by more efficient devices such as the turbine (developed in the 1800s), the electric motor (also developed in the 1800s), the internal-combustion engine (first practical engine built in 1860), and the diesel engine (patented 1892). Nevertheless, James Watt's steam engine played a critical role in moving society from an agricultural-based to an industrial-based economy. Watt's legacy also includes "horsepower" and "watts" as units of measure.

How old are **trains**?

Trains date as far back as the sixteenth century when primitive railroads operated in the underground coal and iron ore mines of Europe. These systems consisted of two wooden rails that extended into the mines and across the mine floors. Wheeled wagons were pulled along the rails by men or by horses. Early in the eighteenth century, mining companies expanded on this rail system, bringing it above ground to transport the coal and iron ore. Workers found that they could cover the wooden rails with iron so they wouldn't wear out as quickly. Before long, rails were made entirely of iron.

Meantime, the steam engine had been developed. An engineer in the mines of Cornwall, England, Richard Trevithick (1771–1833), constructed a working model of a locomotive engine in 1797. Three years later, he built the first high-pressure steam engine. He made quick progress from there, building a road carriage, which on Christmas Eve 1801, became the first vehicle to convey passengers by steam. Two years later, the inventor had built the world's first steam railway locomotive.

In 1825, progress in rail transportation was made by another English inventor, George Stephenson (1781–1848), who, after patenting his own locomotive engine (1815), finished construction on the world's first public railroad. The train ran a distance of about twenty miles, conveying passengers from Stockton to Darlington, England. Five years later, Stephenson completed a line between Liverpool and Manchester. Rail travel caught on quickly—and remains an efficient means of transport today, with commuters around the world relying on trains to get them to work each day. While Stephenson went on to build more railways, and build a family business in the process, Trevithick did not fare nearly as well: Though he later found other uses for the high-pressure steam engine (including rock boring, dredging, and agriculture), he died penniless.

Did **Henry Ford** invent the **automobile**?

While Henry Ford (1863–1947) transformed American industry, changed the way we travel, and the way we live and work, he did not invent the automobile. Just before the turn of the century, there were several inventors who were tinkering with gas-powered vehicles, and by the time Ford had finished his first working car, the Duryea brothers

Henry Ford sitting in one of his first automobiles, the Quadricycle.

(Charles, 1861–1938; Frank, 1869–1967) had demonstrated the first successful gas-powered car in the United States and Ransom Olds already had a car in production. Even prior to the work of these American inventors and entrepreneurs, Europeans had made strides in developing the automobile.

The automobile is the result of a series of inventions, which began in 1769 when French military engineer Nicolas-Joseph Cugnot (1725–1804) built a steam-powered road vehicle. In the early 1800s, other inventors also experimented with this idea. And the steam-powered vehicle was put into production—both in Europe and the United States. In 1899, William McKinley (1843–1901) became the first U.S. president to ride in a car—a Stanley Steamer, built by the Stanley brothers, twins Francis (1849–1918) and Freelan (1849–1940).

A breakthrough in developing gas-powered automobiles came in 1860, when an internal combustion engine was patented by Frenchman Jean-Joseph Etienne Lenoir (1822–1900). But the car, as we know it, was born when, in 1885, Germans Gottlieb Daimler (1834–1900) and Carl Benz (1844–1929), working independently of each other, developed the forerunners of the gas engines used today. In 1891–92, French company

Panhard et Levassor designed a front-engine, rear-wheel drive automobile. This concept remained relatively unchanged for nearly one hundred years. Until 1900, Europeans led the world in the development and production of automobiles. In 1896, the Duryea Motor Wagon Company turned out the United States' first production motor vehicle. The gas-powered cars were available for purchase that same year.

The development of the car was helped by advances in rubber and in the development of tires during the nineteenth century, with names like Charles Goodyear (1800–60), John Boyd Dunlap (1840–1921), and the Michelin brothers (Andre, 1853–1931; Edouard, 1859–1940) figuring prominently.

It's worth noting that even after the gas engine was invented, which was ultimately more efficient than the steam-engine, the car's development continued along parallel tracks: About 1891, American William Morrison successfully developed an electric car. Electric cars were soon put into production and by the turn of the century, they accounted for just under 40 percent of all American car sales.

Who invented the **assembly line**?

The founder of the Ford Motor Company, Henry Ford (1863–1947) is credited with the creation of the assembly line, an industrial innovation that allowed cars to be produced quickly and efficiently. In 1913, ten years after founding Ford Motor Company, Henry Ford installed the first moving assembly line in one of his manufacturing plants.

The innovation proved to be the beginning of the consumer age: The assembly line allowed greater efficiencies in auto production, which, in turn, reduced the price of a quality car, putting it in reach of the ordinary person. Soon, manufactured goods of every variety would be mass produced.

Who invented the **airship**?

The airship, a lighter-than-air aircraft that has both propulsion (power) and steering systems, had a long evolution. The first successful power-driven airship was built by French engineer Henri Giffard, who in September

Who invented the hot-air balloon?

It was Frenchmen Joseph-Michel (1740–1810) and Jacques-Etienne (1745–99) Montgolfier, who were brothers involved in papermaking. They built the first practical balloon, which was filled with hot air. On June 5, 1783, the Montgolfiers launched a large balloon at a public gathering in Annonay, France. It ascended for ten minutes. Three months later, they sent a duck, a sheep, and a rooster up in a balloon—and the animals were landed safely. This success prompted the Montgolfiers to attempt to launch a balloon carrying a human. In October 1783, French scientist Jean-François Pilâtre de Rozier (1756–85) became the first person to make a balloon ascent—but the balloon was held captive (for safety). However, Pilâtre de Rozier was also one of two men who made the first free flight in a hot-air balloon: He and another man ascended to a height of about three hundred feet over Paris on November 21, 1783, and drifted over the city for about twenty-five minutes. Hot-air ballooning, which proved to be better than the rival hydrogen-filled balloon developed in France at about the same time, became very popular in Europe. In January 1785, hot-air balloonists successfully crossed the English Channel, from Dover, England, to Calais, France. Across the Atlantic, hot-air balloons made their debut in Philadelphia in 1793—before a crowd that included George Washington (1732–99), who was then president of the United States.

1852, flew his craft a distance of seventeen miles from Paris to Trappes at an average speed of five miles per hour. The airship was cigar-shaped with a gondola that supported a three-horsepower steam engine. Though it included a rudder, the craft proved difficult to steer. Austrian David Schwarz is credited with designing the first truly rigid airship, a craft that he piloted—unsuccessfully—in November 1897; the airship crashed.

The inventor whose name is most often associated with airships (also called dirigibles after 1885) is Ferdinand von Zeppelin (1838–1917), who designed, built, and flew the first successful rigid airship in 1900. The

Zeppelin (as the aircraft came to be known), flew at a top speed of about seventeen miles per hour. The German aeronaut steadily improved his craft in the years that followed and in 1906 set up a manufacturing plant where the *Zeppelins* were built. In 1909, Zeppelin helped establish the world's first commercial airline; the transport was wholly via airship. The crafts saw military use during World War I, but after the *Hindenburg* crashed on landing in New Jersey in 1937, the airships began to decline in use—both military and commercial. Their decline largely paralleled advances in the development of airplanes.

Did the **Wright brothers** really invent the **airplane**?

The Wright brothers were the first to successfully build *and* fly an airplane; and both events went virtually unnoticed at the time. The owners of a bicycle shop in their hometown of Dayton, Ohio, Wilbur (1867–1912) and Orville (1871–1948) Wright were interested in mechanics from early ages. After attending high school, the brothers went into business together and, in their spare time, began tinkering with gliders. They consulted U.S. weather reports to determine the most advantageous spot to conduct flying experiments. They concluded it was Kitty Hawk, North Carolina. There in 1900 and 1901, on a narrow strip of sand called Kill Devil Hills, they tested their first gliders that could carry a person. Back at their bicycle shop in Ohio, they constructed a small wind tunnel (about six feet in length) where they ran experiments using wing models to determine air pressure. As a result of this research, the Wright brothers were the first to write accurate tables of air pressures on curved surfaces.

Based on their successful glider flights and armed with their new knowledge of air pressure, Orville and Wilbur Wright designed and built an airplane. They returned to Kitty Hawk, on the shores of North Carolina in September 1903, to try the craft out. But weather prevented them from doing so until December. It was days before Christmas when, on December 17, 1903, the Wright brothers made the world's first flight in a power-driven, heavier-than-air machine. Orville piloted the craft a distance of 120 feet and stayed in the air twelve seconds. They made a total of four flights that day, and Wilbur could claim the longest—fifty-nine seconds of flight time that covered just over 850 feet.

It was not a news event: The brothers had witnesses (a few spectators on the beach in North Carolina) and there were a handful of newspaper accounts of the Wrights' marvelous feat, but they were inaccurate. After they made a public announcement in January 1904, *Popular Science Monthly* published a report (in March) as did another magazine. Other than these scant notices, the Wrights received no attention for their accomplishments. Many were trying to do what the Wrights had done, however, the public was skeptical that any man-made machine heavier than the air could take flight. The doubt played a role in the lack of acclaim. Meantime, the brothers continued their experiments at a field near Dayton: In 1904 and 1905 they made 105 flights, but totaled only forty-five minutes in the air.

Nevertheless, the Wright brothers persisted, and in spite of the skepticism, which initially included that of the U.S. government, in 1908, Orville and Wilbur Wright signed a contract with the Department of War to build the first military airplane. Only then did they receive the media attention they deserved. A year later, they set up the Wright Company to manufacture airplanes. In spring 1912, Wilbur became sick and died; three years later Orville sold his share in the Wright Company and retired. The plane piloted by the two brothers in December 1903 near Kitty Hawk is on display at the National Air and Space Museum in Washington, D.C.

COMMUNICATIONS

Who invented the **telegraph**?

Though the invention came as the result of several decades of research by many people, Samuel F. B. Morse (1791–1872) is credited with making the first practical telegraph in 1837. Morse was a portrait painter in Boston when he became interested in magnetic telegraph in about 1832. With technical assistance from chemistry professor Leonard Gale (1800–83) and financial support from Alfred Vail (1807–59), Morse conducted further experiments. He also developed Morse code, a system of variously arranged dots and dashes, which could be used to transmit

Alexander Graham Bell testing the first phone line.

messages. (For example, the most frequently used letter of the alphabet is *e*, which is rendered in Morse code by using one dot; the less frequently used *z* is rendered by two dashes followed by two dots.) By 1837, Morse had demonstrated the telegraph to the public in New York, Philadelphia, and Washington. He received a patent for his telegraph in the United States in 1840. In 1843, his invention got a boost when the U.S. Congress approved an experimental line, to be built between Washington, D.C., and Baltimore, Maryland. The following year, on May 24, 1844, Morse sent his first message across that line—"What hath God wrought!" Vail was on the receiving end of the wire.

Who invented the **telephone**?

The invention credit goes to Alexander Graham Bell, but Thomas Edison improved its quality with a carbon transmitter that he developed after Bell had already patented the telephone.

Alexander Graham Bell (1847–1922), a Scottish-American who came to the United States in 1871 as a teacher of speech to the deaf, pioneered the electric telephone in 1875. Bell believed that sound-wave vibrations

299

could be converted into electric current at one end of a circuit, and that at the other end of the circuit, the current could be reconverted into identical sound waves. He had described this idea to his father as early as 1874, and might have conceived of it as early as 1865.

On June 2, 1875, while trying to perfect a method for carrying more than two messages simultaneously over a single telegraph line, Bell heard the sound of a plucked spring along sixty feet of wire. In 1876, the first voice communication was made by means of impulses transmitted through wires when Bell, who had a laboratory accident and called out to his assistant, "Watson, please come here. I want you." Thomas Watson (1854–1934) was on another floor of the building with the receiving apparatus, and distinctly heard Bell's message. That same year, the Bell telephone was patented in the United States and exhibited at the Philadelphia Centennial Exposition.

When was the **radio** invented and what was its first use?

The radio, or "wireless" as it was once called, was born in 1895 when Italian physicist and inventor Guglielmo Marconi (1874–1937) carried out experiments with wireless telegraphy near Bologna, Italy. He followed up on this success the following year by transmitting telegraph signals—through the air—from Italy to England. By 1897, he had founded his own company in London, Marconi's Wireless Telegraph Company, Ltd., and set about establishing communication lines across the English Channel to France (this he achieved in 1898). In 1900, still a young man in his mid-twenties, Marconi set up the American Marconi Company. He made steady improvements from there, including sending out signals on different wavelengths, so that multiple messages could be transmitted at one time, without interfering with each other. The first trans-Atlantic message—from Cornwall, England, to Newfoundland, Canada, was sent and received in 1901.

At first the technology was regarded as a novelty, and few understood how it could possibly work. But in January 1901, a Marconi wireless station at South Wellfleet, Massachusetts (on Cape Cod), received Morse code messages as well as faint music and voices from Europe. That event was to change the public's perception of the new technology: Before long, Americans had become accustomed to receiving "radiograms"—

messages transmitted via the wireless.

In 1906, the first radio broadcast of voice and music was made: The event originated at Brant Rock, Massachusetts, on Christmas Eve—and the program was picked up by ships within a radius of several hundred miles. That accomplishment resulted from the invention of another radio pioneer, American engineer Reginald Aubrey Fessenden (1866–1932), who patented a high-frequency alternator (1901) that was capable of generating continuous waves rather than intermittent impulses.

American inventor Lee De Forest (1873–1961) has been called "the father of radio," and for good reason: In 1910, he broadcast opera singer Enrico Caruso's (1873–1921) tenor voice over the airwaves. De Forest followed that up in 1916 by transmitting the first radio news broadcast. Both he and Fessenden patented some three hundred inventions each. For his part, in developing wireless communication, Marconi was awarded the Nobel Prize for physics in 1909.

When was **photography** invented?

The concept of still photography dates back to the tenth century when Islamic scientists developed the camera obscura (Latin for "dark chamber")—a darkened enclosure with a small aperture (opening) to admit light. The light rays would cast an inverted image of external objects onto a flat surface opposite the aperture. This image could be studied and traced by someone working inside the camera obscura, or the image could be viewed from the outside of the camera, through a peep-hole.

In the sixteenth century, the Italian scientist Giambattista della Porta (1538–1615) published his studies on fitting the aperture of the camera obscura with a lens to strengthen or enlarge the image projected. Made increasingly versatile through additional improvements, the camera obscura become popular among seventeenth and eighteenth-century European artists.

But the camera obscura could only project images onto a screen or a piece of paper. During the 1800s, scientists experimented with ways of making the images permanent. Among those who made advances in the photographic process were French physicist Joseph Nicéphore Niépce, who produced the first negative image in 1826; Niépce later formed a partnership with Louis Jacques Daguerre, who in 1839, succeeded in making a direct positive image on a silver plate, known as the

301

daguerreotype; English scientist William Henry Fox Talbot developed a paper negative (c. 1841), which could be used to print any number of paper positives; and early in the century, English astronomer Sir John Herschel was the first to produce a practical photographic fixing agent. All of these milestones made photography a practical way of permanently recording real-life images.

The breakthrough in still photography was the Kodak, introduced in 1888 by American George Eastman (1854–1932). The Kodak camera used film that was wound on rollers, eliminating the glass photographic plates that had been in use. The box-shaped camera made photography accessible to everyone—including amateurs. By the early 1900s, the Eastman Kodak Company had become the largest photographic film and camera producer in the world. George Eastman has been credited with mass-producing the moment: Before the Kodak (a word he made up because he was fond of the letter *k)*, photography had largely been the domain of professionals who were commissioned to take portraits of the well-to-do and prominent members of society. Once the Kodak became widely available, photographs preserved the faces of ordinary people and the events of everyday life.

Who invented the **television**?

The television, which may seem to many to be a decidedly American invention, was actually the outcome of a series of inventions by a cast of international characters. As early as 1872, British engineer Willoughby Smith, inspired by an experiment on selenium rods, imagined a system of "visual telegraphy." Five years later, the tube technology that would make television possible was developed in Strasbourg, Germany, by physicist Ferdinand Braun (1815–1918). He invented a cathode-ray tube (also known as the Braun tube), which improved the Marconi wireless (radio) technology by increasing the energy of sending stations and arranging antennas to control the direction of radiation.

In 1907, Russian physicist Boris Rosing proposed using Braun's tube to receive images—something he called "electric vision." One year later, Alan Campbell Swinton suggested using the cathode-ray tube to both receive and transmit images. That same year, the idea of using cathode-ray tubes to scan images for the purpose of television was published, and by 1912, it was being worked on by Rosing and his former pupil, Vladimir Zworykin, in Russia.

In 1923, a competing technology, which was entirely mechanical, reached an early milestone when British inventor John Logie Baird demonstrated an electrified hatbox with disks, which constituted the world's first working television set. But the race was still on and in that same year, Zworykin advanced the tube-based technology when he patented the iconoscope (which would become the television camera). In 1924, Zworykin patented the kinoscope (television tube).

It was an American, Philo Farnsworth, an Idaho farm boy, who in 1927, transmitted the first electronic picture via a cathode-ray dissector tube. Farnsworth had been inspired by accounts of Rosing's work in the Soviet Union to transmit moving pictures by electricity. As early as 1922, the then-teenaged Farnsworth had come up with the basic design of the television apparatus. And five years later, he built the first operating, all-electronic television system, passing up the Soviet inventors, Rosing and Zworykin.

Regularly scheduled U.S. television began on April 30, 1939, when President Franklin D. Roosevelt opened the New York World's Fair (billed as "The World of Tomorrow") with a speech that was the first presidential talk to be televised. The National Broadcasting Company (NBC) coverage of the fair's opening initiated its weekly television scheduling, a victory for parent company RCA, whose president, David Sarnoff, founded NBC and is considered one of broadcasting's pioneers.

When was **color television** invented?

In 1940, Hungarian-American engineer Peter Carl Goldmark (1906–77), the head of the Columbia Broadcasting System's research and development laboratory, came up with a technology that broke down the television image into three primary colors through a set of spinning filters in front of black and white, caused the video to be viewed in color. His system gave way in the 1950s to an RCA system whose signals were compatible with conventional black-and-white TV signals.

In September 1962, the ABC network began color telecasts, for three and a half hours a week. By this time, competitor NBC was broadcasting

303

68 percent of its prime time programming in color, while CBS had opted to confine itself to black and white after having transmitted in color earlier. By 1967, all three networks were broadcasting entirely in color.

It was not until 1967 that color television was broadcast in England: On July 1, the BBC-2 transmitted seven hours of programming, most of it coverage of lawn tennis from Wimbledon.

When was the first **fax machine** developed?

The fax may seem like a recent invention, but it was invented long ago—it took more than one hundred years for the machines to become part of everyday life. In 1842, Scottish philosopher and psychologist Alexander Bain (1818–1903) invented the first, albeit crude, fax machine. The scanning technology was improved enough by 1924 that newspapers began using the device to transmit photographs. By the 1930s, Wirephotos were an important component of newspaper reports. It was not until the 1980s that faxes came into widespread use—as manufacturers produced the more compact and affordable machines that are visible in most every place of business today.

COMPUTERS

Who invented the **computer**?

English mathematician Charles Babbage (1792–1871) is recognized as the first to conceptualize the computer. He worked to develop a mechanical computing machine called the "analytical engine," which is considered the prototype of the digital computer.

While attending Cambridge University in 1812, Babbage conceived of the idea of a machine that could calculate data faster than humans could—and without human error. These were the early years of the Industrial Revolution and the world Babbage lived in was growing increasingly complex. Human errors in mathematical tables posed serious problems for many burgeoning industries. It was after graduating from Cambridge that Babbage returned to the idea of a computational aid. He spent the rest of his life and much of his fortune trying to build such a machine, but he was not to finish. Nevertheless, the never-completed "analytical engine" (on which he began work in 1834) was the forerunner to the modern digital computer. It used punch cards to store data, and was intended to print answers.

It was more than one hundred years later that the first fully automatic calculator was invented—development began in 1939 at Harvard University. Under the direction of mathematician Howard Aiken (1900–73), the first electronic digital computer, called Mark I, was invented in 1944. (The Mark II followed in 1947.) The first computer to handle both numeric and alphabetical data with equal facility was the UNIVAC (Universal Automatic Computer), developed between 1946 and 1951 at the University of Pennsylvania.

Who wrote the **first computer program**?

The first functional computer program was written by Grace Murray Hopper (1906–92), an admiral of the United States Navy. She wrote a program for the Mark I computer (developed in 1944), the first fully automatic calculator. During the 1950s, Hopper directed the work that developed one of the most widely used computer programming languages, COBOL (Common Business Oriented Language). She is also credited with coining the slang term *bug* to refer to computer program errors. The story goes that her machine had broken down, and when she looked into the problem, she discovered a dead moth in the computer. As she removed it, she reportedly announced that she was "debugging the machine." Hopper served the U.S. navy for forty-three years—from 1943 to 1986, and retired as its most senior officer. She was also a professor at Vassar College and a programmer for the Sperry Rand Corporation from 1959 to 1971. She is one of the pioneers of computer science.

The very first computer program written, though never used, was also by a woman: the English baroness Augusta Ada Byron (the poet Lord Byron's daughter, born 1815) wrote it for Charles Babbage's "analytical engine," which was never completed, and so the program was not tested.

Microsoft founder Bill Gates.

Who invented the **first personal computer**?

The credit goes to Stephen G. Wozniak and Steven Jobs—college dropouts who founded Apple Computer in 1976. They spent six months developing the crude prototype for Apple I, which was bought by some six hundred hobbyists—who had to know how to wire, program, and set up the computer. Its successor, Apple II, was introduced in 1977, as the first fully assembled, programmable microcomputer, but still required customers to use their televisions as screens and to use audio cassettes for data storage. It retailed for just under $1,300.

When did **IBM** enter the personal computer business?

IBM (International Business Machine, organized in 1924) had long been an industry leader in developing and producing computers for business and science, but in August 1981, the company jumped into the consumer business, competing with upstart Apple for a share in the personal computer (PC) business. The PC introduced by IBM used a Microsoft disk-operating system (MS-DOS) and soon captured 75 percent of the market. Observing the company's enormous success, other firms began producing IBM "clones," which could use the same software as the IBM PC.

When was computer giant **Microsoft** founded?

It wasn't all that long ago—1975, that computer whiz Bill Gates founded what is now the dominant manufacturer of computer software (so dominant that the company has faced anti-trust allegations from the federal government). Gates was only nineteen years old when he founded the business with his friend Paul Gardner Allen, and he had dropped out of Harvard to do so. It paid off: Gates was a billionaire by age thirty. Though he's undoubtedly a math ace (he scored a perfect 800 in math on his SATs and began writing programs when he was all of thirteen), Gates has more than once credited the success of Microsoft to not his own programming skills—but to hiring the best programming talent for the Redmond, Washington-based company.

Why was the **Internet** invented?

It was invented in the late 1960s so that U.S. Department of Defense researchers could share information with each other and with other researchers. The Advanced Research Projects Agency developed the Internet and its users, who were mostly scientists and academics, soon saw the power of the new technology: Wires linking computer terminals together in a "web" of networks allow people anywhere in the world to communicate with each other over the computer.

The technology caught on, and by spring 1998, it was estimated that Internet usage had surpassed fifty million individual users, and Internet connections could be found in businesses, libraries, classrooms, and homes. At the same time, the Internet was growing so fast that traffic was doubling every one hundred days.

Even though it was developed by the government, the Internet is not government-run. The Internet Society, which is made up of volunteers, addresses usage and standards issues.

How old is the **World Wide Web**?

The Web, the part of the Internet that provides users with graphics, audio, and video, is not very old—it was first developed in 1990 by English computer scientist Tim Berners-Lee, who wrote the Web software at the CERN physics laboratory near Geneva, Switzerland. The Web became part of the Internet in 1991, and has played a major role in the growing popularity of the international computer network, making information more accessible to the user via multimedia interfaces.

When was **email** invented?

Short for "electronic mail," email was in use by the end of the 1970s. The use of modems, which connected computers via phone lines, allowed for the transmission of electronic messages. Within a decade of its introduction, email had become widely used as a communications mode.

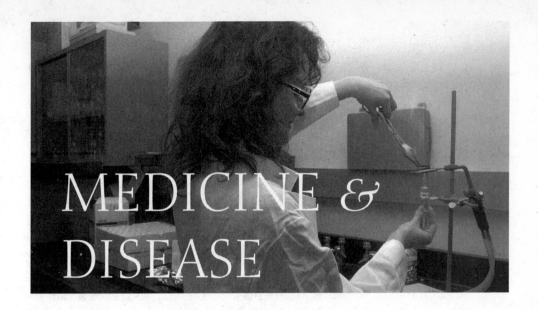

MEDICINE & DISEASE

ANCIENT MEDICINE

How **long** have people been **getting sick**?

Humankind has suffered from illnesses since we first appeared on the earth about three million years ago. But in the absence of medical knowledge—which only began about five thousand years ago, ailments and sickness were assumed to have been brought on by angered gods or evil spirits. Some traditional religions still survive today, in which practitioners believe they must appease the gods and spirits through offerings and sacrifices in order to stave off, or rid themselves of, illness. These are practices carried out by witch doctors or healers. In prehistoric times, such superstitious beliefs resulted in the first "medical" procedure, in which a hole was drilled into the patient's skull—this practice was believed to allow evil spirits to escape the body and thereby rid the body of sickness. Fossil findings showing this method of treatment dates back about ten thousand years. One vestige of ancient treatments of illness that still has relevance today is the use of plants and plant substances as drugs.

Who was the **first physician** in history?

The first physician known by name was Imhotep, an Egyptian who lived in 2600 B.C. Also considered a sage, Imhotep lived in a time when the Egyptians were making progress in medicine. The advances (c. 2500

B.C.) included a textbook on the treatment of wounds, broken bones, and even tumors. Imhotep was later worshiped as a god by the Egyptians.

What is the **Hippocratic Oath**?

The Hippocratic Oath is the pledge taken by many medical students upon graduation or upon entering into practice. While the text of the oath varies by translation, one important line reads, "I will prescribe regiment for the good of my patients according to my ability and my judgement and never to harm anyone." The vows are attributed to the Greek physician and teacher Hippocrates (c. 460–377 B.C.), who practiced on the island of Cos. Unlike his predecessors, who relied on superstitious practices in order to treat patients, Hippocrates believed that diseases were brought on not by supernatural causes, but by natural ones. He further believed that disease could be studied and cured; this assertion forms the basis of modern medicine, which is why Hippocrates is called the father of medicine.

It is largely owing to another prominent Greek physician that the oath was handed down through history: Galen (A.D. 129–c. 199) was physician to Roman emperors Marcus Aurelius and Commodus. He demonstrated that arteries carry blood, not air (as had been thought), and like Hippocrates, Galen believed in the four humors of the body. He left medical texts that for centuries were considered the authoritative works on medical practice. Galen's writings reveal that he regarded Hippocrates, who had lived and worked many centuries earlier, as the model physician. Thus the Hippocratic Oath is sworn today to avow the ethical practice of medicine.

What are the **"four humors"**?

The four humors are the bodily fluids—blood, phlegm, yellow bile, and black bile, originating in the heart, brain, liver, and spleen, respectively. One work assigned to Greek physician Hippocrates (c. 460–377 B.C.), *Nature of Man*, asserts that illness is caused by an imbalance of the four humors (fluids) in the body. The presence of these humors was thought to determine the health and personality of a person. This belief prevailed for centuries, but was finally discredited by modern science.

What is spontaneous generation?

Spontaneous generation is the theory that living things can develop from nonliving things. One of the first scientists to test this theory, which originated in prehistoric times, was Italian physician Francesco Redi (1626–97). In 1668, Redi demonstrated that as long as meat was covered, maggots would not "form" on it. (When left uncovered, flies would land on the meat, lay eggs, and thus, produce maggots.)

The theory of spontaneous generation, which influenced scientists and physicians for centuries, was ultimately discredited with the experiments of Antoni van Leeuwenhoek (1632–1723), Louis Pasteur (1822–95), and Robert Koch (1843–1910), which together proved the existence of bacteria that cause disease.

During the Middle Ages, each of the humors was assigned certain characteristics. Someone of ruddy complexion was believed to have an excessive amount of blood in their system; that person would be sanguine (cheerful and optimistic) in character. (The word sanguine is derived from the Latin word for blood, *sanguis*.) Someone who had an imbalance resulting in more phlegm was considered to be phlegmatic, and would have a slow and impassive temperament. An individual who had excessive yellow bile was considered hot-tempered. And a person who had more black bile in their physiological system was believed to be melancholic.

What **advances** were made in **medicine during the Middle Ages**?

During the Middle Ages (A.D. 500 to 1485), medicine became institutionalized—the first public hospitals were opened and the first formal medical schools were established, making health care (formerly administered only in the home) more widely available, and improving the training of doctors. These developments had been brought on by necessity: Europe saw successive waves of epidemics during the Middle Ages. Outbreaks of leprosy began in the 500s and peaked in the 1200s; Black Death (the plague) killed about a quarter of the European population; and smallpox and other diseases afflicted hundreds of thousands of people. Consequently, many hospitals—meant to serve the poor—were established, as were the first medical schools, some of them associated with universities that were then forming, such as the University of Bologna (Italy) and the University of Paris (France). These institutions joined in Salerno, Italy, where in A.D. 900, the first medical school had been started.

European physicians during the period were greatly influenced by the works of Persian physician and philosopher Rhazes (or Razi; c. 865–c. 930). Considered the greatest doctor of the Islamic world, Rhazes's works accurately describing measles and smallpox were translated into Latin and became seminal references in the Christian world as well. Another prominent Islamic, the scientist Avicenna (or Ibn Sina; 980–1037), produced a huge philosophical-scientific encyclopedia, which included the medical knowledge of the time. In the West, the work became known as *Canon of Medicine* and with its descriptions of many diseases, including tetanus and meningitis, it remained influential in European medical education for the next six hundred years.

What **advances** were made in **medicine during the Renaissance**?

The chief advance of the Renaissance (1350 to 1600) was an improved understanding of the human anatomy. This knowledge was the direct result of dissection. Prohibited during the Middle Ages, the scientific spirit of the Renaissance saw those laws relaxed, and researchers were free to dissect human corpses for study.

Among those who practiced dissection was Leonardo da Vinci (1452–1519). While the Italian artist may be better known for the *Mona Lisa*, he also contributed greatly to the understanding of human anatomy, producing more than 750 anatomical drawings as a result of his studies in dissection.

What was the **first scientific textbook** on **human anatomy**?

It is a work titled *On the Structure of the Human Body*, written by Belgian physician and professor Andreas Vesalius (1514–64) and published in 1543, when he was a young man in his late-twenties. Like other anatomists during the Renaissance, Vesalius conducted numerous dissections of human cadavers. Publishing his findings and drawings, his textbook soon became the authoritative reference, overturning the works of Galen.

What is *Gray's Anatomy*?

It is the popular name for *Anatomy of the Human Body, Descriptive and Surgical*, written by English physician Henry Gray (1825 or 1827–1861). First published in 1858, the tome is still considered the standard work on anatomy, and is in print today in several editions, including *The Concise Gray's Anatomy*. Gray was a lecturer in anatomy at London's St. George's Hospital and was a fellow of the Royal College of Surgeons. He was thirty-three when he compiled the book, which went on to be used by medical students for more than a century.

MODERN MEDICINE

When did **modern medicine begin**?

The practices of modern medicine have their roots in the 1600s. It was early in the century when the work of English physician William Harvey (1578–1657) demonstrated to the science community that effective medicine depends on knowledge of the body's structure. From 1597 to 1602, Harvey had studied medicine at Padua (Italy) under Italian surgeon Fabricius (1537–1619) and went on to perform numerous experiments to learn how blood circulates through the body. In his studies, Harvey discarded the accepted method of studying parts of a problem and then filling in the gaps with theory; instead he aimed to understand the entire circulatory system, performing dissections on cadavers and studying the pulse and heartbeat. He accurately concluded that the heart pumps blood through the arteries to all parts of the body and that the blood returns to the heart through the veins. Putting his discovery into writing, Harvey published *An Anatomical Study of the Motion of the Heart and of the Blood in Animals* in 1628.

313

Another medical development during the 1600s came not at the hands of a physician or surgeon, but rather a naturalist, Antoni van Leeuwenhoek (1632–1723). A surveyor to the court of Holland, van Leeuwenhoek began making his own microscopes and used them to study organisms invisible to the naked eye—he had discovered microorganisms. Leeuwenhoek also observed (but did not name) bacteria, and he accurately described red blood corpuscles, striated muscle fibers, and the lens of the eye. This amateur scientist also disproved the theory of spontaneous generation (the belief that living organisms could be generated by lifeless matter).

When did **modern surgery begin**?

Modern surgical techniques were developed during the late Renaissance (1350 to 1600)—largely owing to the work of one man, Ambroise Paré (1510–90), called the father of modern surgery.

Prior to Paré's lifework, physicians had regarded surgery as something lowly. They left this "dirty work" to barber-surgeons. As a young man living in the French countryside, Paré became apprenticed to one such barber-surgeon. When he was only nineteen years old, Paré entered Paris' Hotel Dieu hospital to study surgery. Becoming a master surgeon by 1536, he later served as an army surgeon and then as physician to four French kings—Henry II, Francis II, Charles IX, and Henry III. Paré also built a flourishing surgical practice and authored works on anatomy, surgery, the plague, obstetrics, and the treatment of wounds. Opposing the common practice of cauterizing (burning) wounds with boiling oil to prevent infection, he introduced the method of applying a mild ointment and allowing the wound to heal naturally. Paré was renowned for his patient care, which he based on his personal credo, "I dressed him, God cured him."

How **old** are **hospitals**?

Hospitals date back to the third century B.C. when Buddhists established hospitals in India. Later, as Christianity spread, religious orders set up hospitals, but these facilities were intended to serve the poor—

When was anesthesia first used?

The first use, which was the subject of an embittered debate, was determined to have been in 1842, when Georgia physician Crawford Williamson Long (1815–78) became the first doctor to use ether as an anesthetic. He went on to use ether in seven more operations before 1846, when he made a public demonstration of anesthesia. Long published his accounts of the experiences in December 1849.

But Boston dentist William T. G. Morton (1819–68) disputed Long's claim to have been first in using anesthesia. Morton had begun experimenting with anesthetics at about the same time as Long and, on October 16, 1846, he had arranged the first hospital operation using ether as an anesthetic: A tumor was removed from the neck of a patient at the Massachusetts General Hospital in Boston. Nevertheless, it is Long who gets credit for being the first doctor to use ether in an operation.

since most people received a doctor's care in the privacy of their own home.

Paris' Hotel Dieu, founded during the seventh century, is the oldest hospital still in operation.

In 970, a hospital established in Baghdad divided physicians into the equivalent of the modern-day interns and externs. Its pharmacy disseminated drugs (and spices deemed to have medicinal value) from all over the known world.

In 1503, in the New World, the Spanish built the first hospital in the Western Hemisphere, at Santo Domingo in the Dominican Republic (then known as Hispaniola). It is no longer in existence (the ruins remain). The first Canadian hospital opened in Quebec in 1639. The first incorporated hospital in the United States was the Pennsylvania Hospital in Philadelphia, chartered in 1751 with the support of Benjamin Franklin (1706–90).

315

What was the "germ theory"?

The germ theory, established in the mid-1800s, posited that certain germs cause diseases, refuting the ages-old notion of spontaneous generation. The idea was first put forth by French chemist Louis Pasteur (1822–95) in a paper he published in 1861. His research, and that of German physician Robert Koch (1843–1910), eventually substantiated the germ "theory" as fact: They proved that the microbe, or germ, is a living organism that can cause disease. Koch was even able to isolate certain bacteria as the causes of particular diseases including anthrax (for which he published a method of preventive inoculation), tuberculosis, cholera, and rinderpest (a cattle disease). The anthrax germ was the first germ linked to a particular disease. By the end of the 1800s, researchers had discovered the kinds of bacteria and other microbes responsible for the plague, diphtheria, dysentery, gonorrhea, leprosy, malaria, pneumonia, tetanus, and other infectious diseases.

Who invented the vaccine?

English physician Edward Jenner (1749–1823) is credited with inventing the vaccine, however evidence suggests that vaccination (inoculation of a substance into the body for the purpose of producing active immunity against a disease) was used in China, India, and Persia (present-day Iran) in ancient times.

In modern times, Jenner pioneered the science of immunology by developing a vaccination against smallpox. The English physician was practicing medicine in rural Gloucestershire in 1796 when he observed that dairymaids who had been sick with cowpox did not contract smallpox, suggesting that they had developed an immunity to the often fatal disease, which then occurred in epidemics. Jenner must have been quite certain of his theory: He chose to test it on an eight-year-old schoolboy, James Phipps, whom Jenner vaccinated with matter from cowpox vesicles from the hands of a milkmaid, Sarah Nelmes. Jenner then allowed the boy's system to develop the immunity he had previously observed in the dairymaids. Several weeks later, Jenner inoculated Phipps with smallpox, and the boy did not become even the least bit ill. The experiment was a success. Jenner continued his experiments for two years and then published his findings, officially announcing his discovery of vaccination in 1798.

As Jenner had suspected, vaccines provide immunity by causing the body to manufacture substances called antibodies, which fight a disease. In this century, vaccination programs have greatly reduced disease, particularly in developed nations where childhood immunization programs are very effective. By 1977, vaccination had wiped out smallpox.

How old is the idea of **biological warfare**?

Biological or germ warfare has a long history. For example, in the year 1343, Tartars (originally a nomadic tribe of east-central Asia) became sick with bubonic plague. The disease, which is carried by fleas and rats, was called the Black Death since those who became afflicted with it were nearly all killed. Invading the Crimea (in present-day Ukraine), there the marauding Tartars encountered a group of Genoese merchants at a trading post. Besieging them, the Tartars even went so far as to catapult their dead at their "enemy," many of whom became infected, carrying the plague to Constantinople and to the Western European ports where they traveled.

In modern times, the use of microorganisms or toxins that produce sickness in people or in animals, or that cause destruction to crops, was outlawed by the Geneva Convention of 1925. Nevertheless, several nations have since conducted further research into not only defense against biological warfare, but into developing microorganisms suitable for military retaliation. The existence of such biological weapons—including anthrax—remains a concern today.

When were **antiseptics** introduced to **surgery**?

Antiseptics, which prevent infections, were introduced in the middle of the nineteenth century, and by the end of the century were in widespread use. The introduction in 1846 of anesthetics such as ether and chloroform handled the problem of pain during surgery. But even after successful operations, patients were dying or becoming permanently disabled from infections contracted while in the hospital. These infections, which often became epidemic inside the medical facilities, included tetanus, gangrene, and septicemia. In 1846, Hungarian obstetrician Ignaz Phillipp Semmelweiss (1818–65), who was practicing at a Vienna hospital, concluded that infection (in this case puerperal fever) was coming from inside the hospital ward; his analysis was met with strong rebuttal. While he began practicing antisepsis (cleanliness to reduce infection) and his statistics showed a decrease in mortality rates, the methods did not gain acceptance in the medical community, which remained unconvinced that disease can be contagious.

Nearly two decades later, in 1864, English surgeon Joseph L. Lister (1827–1912) became interested in Louis Pasteur's work with bacteria. While practicing surgery in Glasgow, Lister replicated Pasteur's experiments and concluded that the germ theory applied to hospital diseases. In order to stave off inflamation and infections in his patients, Lister began working with solutions containing carbolic acid, which kills germs. Observing favorable results, Lister reported his findings in 1867 in the British journal of medicine *Lancet*. Many physicians still rejected Lister's claims that antisepsis could reduce the danger of infection. Nevertheless, the medical community began adopting these methods. By the turn of the century, not only had these principles saved lives, they had transformed the way doctors practice medicine: Since doctors could not ensure necessary cleanliness in their patients' homes, hospitals became the preferred place to treat all patients—not just the poor or the very sick, as had been the case.

Who invented X-rays?

German physicist Wilhelm Conrad Roentgen (1845–1923) discovered X-rays in 1895—but did not understand at first what they were—which is how they got their name: In science and math, *X* refers to an unknown. By the end of the decade, hospitals had put X-rays to use, taking pictures (called radiographs) of bones and internal organs and tissues to help diagnose illnesses and injuries. Using the new technology, doctors could "see" the insides of a patient. In 1901, Roentgen received the first Nobel Prize for physics for his discovery of a short-wave ray.

Why is Florence Nightingale so famous?

The English nurse, hospital reformer, and philanthropist is considered the founder of modern nursing. The daughter of well-to-do British parents, Florence Nightingale (1820–1910) was born in Florence, Italy. Though she was raised in privilege on her family's estate in England, Nightingale had a natural and irrepressible inclination toward caring for others. Despite her parents' wishes, Nightingale—who, in accordance with the social standards of her set and day, had already been presented to the queen—entered a training program for nurses near Düsseldorf, Germany. She went on to study in Paris. In 1853, Nightingale became superintendent of a hospital for invalid women in London.

In 1854, Nightingale took thirty-eight nurses with her to the city of Üsküdar, near Istanbul, Turkey. There, despite great obstacles, she set up a barrack hospital to treat soldiers who were injured in the Crimean War (1853–56), then being fought between Russian forces and the allied armies of Britain, France, the Ottoman Empire (now Turkey), and Sardinia (now part of Italy). Nightingale set about cleaning the filthy hospital facility; established strict schedules for the staff; and introduced sanitation methods that reduced the spread of infectious diseases such as cholera, typhus, and dysentery. While her methods were considered controversial at first (doctors initially found Nightingale to be demanding and pushy), they got results. Before long, Nightingale was put in charge of all the allied army hospitals in the Crimea. By the end of the war, Nightingale had become a legend for her care of the sick and wounded: Known for walking the floor of the hospital at night, tending to her patients, Nightingale became known as the Lady with the Lamp. During the fighting, Nightingale had visited the front and caught Crimean fever—which threatened her life. Even at that time, she had become so well known that Queen Victoria was aware of—and deeply concerned about—Nightingale's illness.

After the war, Nightingale returned to London and in 1860, with fifty thousand pounds sterling, she established a training institution for nurses in London. In 1873, Massachusetts General Hospital in Boston, Bellevue Hospital in New York City, and New Haven Hospital in Connecticut opened the United States' first nursing schools; all of them were patterned after the London program founded by Nightingale.

Nightingale's fierce determination, which ran contrary to her parents' wishes for her, as well as, to the social standard of the day, became the stuff of legend. And rightly so: because of her concern for the sick, the standard of care of all patients improved.

What were **Pasteur's discoveries** on **disease**?

Louis Pasteur (1822–95) may be best known for developing the process that bears his name, pasteurization, but the French chemist and microbiologist made other important contributions to public health, including the discovery of vaccines to prevent diseases in animals and the establishment of a Paris institute for the study of deadly and contagious diseases.

It was in the 1860s that the hard-working Pasteur was asked to investigate problems that French wine-makers were having with the fermentation process: Spoilage of wine and beer during fermentation was resulting in serious economic losses for France. Observing wine under a microscope, Pasteur noticed that spoiled wine had a proliferation of bacterial cells that produce lactic acid. The chemist suggested gently heating the wine to destroy the harmful bacteria, and then allowing the wine to age naturally. Pasteur published his findings and his recommendations in book form in 1866. The idea of heating edible substances to destroy disease-causing organisms was later applied to other perishable fluids—chief among them, milk.

Pasteur later studied animal diseases, developing a vaccination to prevent anthrax in sheep and cattle. The deadly animal disease is spread from animals to humans through contact or the inhalation of spores. In 1876, Robert Koch had identified the bacteria that causes anthrax, and Pasteur weakened this microbe in his laboratory before injecting it into animals, which then developed an immunity to the disease. He also showed that vaccination could be used to prevent chicken cholera.

In 1881, Pasteur began studying rabies, an agonizing and deadly disease spread by the bite of infected animals. Along with his assistant, Pierre-Paul-Émile Roux (1853–1933), Pasteur spent long hours in the laboratory, and the determination paid off: Pasteur developed a vaccine that prevented the development of rabies in test animals. But on July 6, 1885, the scientists were called on to administer the vaccine to a small boy who had been bitten by a rabid dog. Pasteur hesitated to provide the treatment, but as the boy faced certain and painful death from rabies, Pasteur proceeded. Following several weeks of painful injections to the stomach, the boy did not get rabies: Pasteur's treatment was a success. The curative and preventive treatments for rabies (also called hydrophobia) we know today are based on Pasteur's vaccination, which has allowed officials to control the spread of the disease.

French chemist Louis Pasteur.

In 1888, the Institut Pasteur was established in Paris to provide a teaching and research center on contagious diseases; Pasteur was director of the institute until his death in 1895.

When were **antibiotics** invented?

The idea of antibiotics, substances that destroy or inhibit the growth of certain other microorganisms, dates back to the late nineteenth century, but the first antibiotics were not produced until well into the twentieth century.

321

The great French chemist Louis Pasteur (1822–95) laid the foundation for understanding antibiotics when, in the late 1800s, he proved that one species of microorganisms can kill another. German bacteriologist Paul Ehrlich (1854–1915) then developed the concept of selective toxicity—in which a specific substance can be toxic (poisonous) to some organisms but harmless to others. Based on this research, scientists began working to develop substances that would destroy disease-spreading microorganisms. A breakthrough came in 1928 when Scottish bacteriologist Alexander Fleming (1881–1955) discovered penicillin. Fleming observed that no bacteria grew around the mold of the genus *Penicillium notatum*, which had accidentally fallen into a bacterial culture in his laboratory.

But penicillin proved difficult to extract. It was not until more than a decade later (in 1941) that the substance was purified and tested—by British scientist Howard Florey (1898–1968). Another British scientist, Ernest Chain (1906–79) developed a method of extracting penicillin, and under his supervision, the first large-scale penicillin production facility was completed, making the antibiotic commercially available in 1945. That same year, Fleming, Florey, and Chain shared the Nobel Prize for physiology or medicine for their work in discovering and producing the powerful antibiotic, still used today in the successful treatment of bacterial diseases, including pneumonia, strep throat, and gonorrhea.

When was **insulin** discovered?

Insulin, a hormone that regulates sugar levels in the body, was first discovered in 1889 by German physicians Oskar Minkowski (1858–1931) and Joseph von Mering (1849–1908) who observed that the removal of the pancreas caused diabetes in dogs. Researchers set about isolating the substance but it was not until 1922 that insulin was used to treat diabetic patients. The first genetically engineered human insulin was produced by American scientists in 1978.

When was the **first kidney transplant**?

On December 23, 1954, Harvard physicians performed the world's first successful kidney transplant. The patient survived for seven years with a kidney from his identical twin brother.

When was the **first heart transplant**?

The world's first heart transplant took place on December 3, 1967, in Cape Town, South Africa. Surgeon Christiaan Barnard conducted the operation; the patient lived for eighteen days. The first U.S. heart transplant was performed four days later by New York surgeon Adrian Kantrowitz, whose patient survived for only a few hours. But surgeons have continued the practice with moderately improved results: While some heart recipients have lived as long as six years after the procedure, only 20 percent of the recipients survive more than one year.

How **old** is **animal experimentation**?

Scientific experimentation using animals—including mice, rats, rabbits, guinea pigs, monkeys, and dogs—dates back to ancient times. But the practice did not become widespread until late in the nineteenth century. Clinical experimentation, which includes vivisection (surgery on live animals), has yielded benefits to human health, but because it often results in the suffering and death of the animals, many people today are against the practice. Tens of millions of animals are used for experimentation in the United States today; official estimates cite that mice and rats account for some 90 percent of this number. The practice remains controversial as people grapple with the issues surrounding animal rights and weigh these considerations against improved scientific understanding of illnesses.

Does **yellow fever** still exist?

Yellow fever, an acute infectious disease, does still exist but for the most part is under control. Outbreaks still occur in jungle areas. The disease was once widespread—afflicting people in tropical climates such as Central and South American, Africa, and Asia. But with exploration during the 1500s and 1600s, and the opening of trade routes during the 1700s, the disease spread to North America by 1699, when there were epidemics in Charleston and Philadelphia; three years later, an epidemic broke out in New York City. Yellow fever first materialized in Europe in 1723. An epidemic in Philadelphia in 1793 was determined to have been carried there aboard a ship from the West Indies; nearly all of the city's people were afflicted by the fever, and more than four thousand people died in what has been called the worst health disaster ever to befall an American city.

Breakthroughs in controlling yellow fever came in the late 1800s and early 1900s. In 1881, Cuban physician Carlos Finlay (1833–1914) wrote a paper suggesting that yellow fever was transmitted by mosquitoes. This was proved to be true by U.S. army surgeon Walter Reed (1851–1902), who in 1900, headed a commission sent to Cuba to investigate the cause and mode of transmission of yellow fever. With this knowledge, U.S. army officer and physician William Gorgas (1854–1920) applied strict measures to destroy mosquitoes in Havana, eventually eliminating yellow fever from the Cuban port city. As chief sanitary officer of the Panama Canal Commission (1904–13), Gorgas implemented similar measures in the Panama Canal Zone, where the disease had been a menace. Again, his methods proved effective, greatly reducing the instances of yellow fever, which allowed the canal to be completed.

In 1937, the 17-D vaccine was developed by American physician and bacteriologist Max Theiler (1899–1972). The vaccine was found to be effec-

What is the plague?

The plague is a general term that refers to any contagious epidemic disease, but usually refers specifically to bubonic plague (which gets its name from the swelling of the lymph nodes, or buboes). A bubonic plague epidemic spread through Europe and Asia in the middle of the fourteenth century, killing as much as 75 percent of the population in twenty years; that epidemic came to be known as Black Death.

An acute infectious disease, the plague is carried to humans by fleas that have bitten infected rats and other rodents. Symptoms include high fever, chills, swelling of the lymph nodes, and hemorrhages. Once the bacteria spreads to the lungs, it is quickly fatal (this form of the disease is called pneumonic plague and can be transmitted from person to person via droplets).

Improved sanitation, chiefly in developed nations, has reduced the occurrence of the disease. Bubonic plague still occurs, but the development of antibiotics in the twentieth century has greatly reduced the mortality rate.

tive in combating yellow fever. In 1951, Theiler was awarded the Nobel Prize for medicine for his discoveries concerning the infectious disease. Conquering yellow fever was one of the great achievements of modern medicine.

When was **leprosy** first diagnosed?

Leprosy is an ages-old disease, described in many historical texts. Mentioned in the Bible, leprosy was introduced in Europe in the 400s B.C.—probably by the troops of the Persian ruler Xerxes (c. 519–465 B.C.) as they moved westward. By the twelfth century A.D., leprosy had reached epidemic proportions in western Europe, where it took hold, even claiming the lives of rulers (Portugal's Afonso II died from it in 1223, and Robert I, king of Scots, in 1329). Explorers and settlers from the Continent later carried the infectious chronic skin disease to the New World, where it had been unknown previously.

The cause of leprosy was unknown—and while some had theorized it was contagious, others asserted that it was hereditary or was caused by eating certain foods (even potatoes were at one time blamed for originating the affliction). The disease gradually disappeared from Europe, attributable to improved living conditions, better nutrition, and, later, the advent of drugs that are effective in treatment.

The first clinical description was not made until 1874 when Norwegian physician Gerhard Henrik Hansen (1841–1912) discovered the leprosy bacterium. Since then, the disease has been called Hansen's disease. Today, leprosy afflicts about five million people worldwide. It is endemic to tropical or subtropical regions, including Africa, Central and South America, India, and Southeast Asia. Most cases of leprosy that occur in the United States are among immigrants from areas where the disease is endemic. Beginning in the mid-1950s, Mother Theresa (1910–97) of Calcutta ministered to those afflicted with leprosy, setting up colonies for their care.

How **old** is the concept of **public health**?

Public health is an old concept—dating back to when people first began living in communities. Through the ages, governments have shown varying degrees of concern for the public health. The ancients Greeks, and the Romans after them, tried to ensure the health of their citizens by providing a supply of clean water (via aqueducts and pipelines), managing the disposal of waste, and working to control disease by hiring public physicians to treat the sick. These measures may have helped prevent the spread of certain diseases, but epidemics still occurred. After the fall of the Roman Empire (c. 496), Europe's civilizations largely ignored matters of public health: Once disease was introduced to a community, it would spread quickly. Epidemics of leprosy, the plague, cholera, and yellow fever ensued.

During the late 1800s, European governments began turning their attention to matters of public health in an effort to control the spread of disease. In the United States, the public health became an official con-

An outbreak of influenza.

cern when, in 1866, a cholera epidemic struck the nation—for the eighteenth consecutive year. It was part of a worldwide epidemic that persisted for twelve years. Though governments set up health facilities, including laboratories for the study of infectious disease, by 1893, another cholera pandemic began. During the twentieth century, the measures taken by national governments to safeguard their citizens from health risks have been strengthened by the establishment of regional and local laboratories, public education programs, and the research conducted at universities and other institutions. These combined efforts have made outbreaks of diseases such as diphtheria, dysentery, typhoid fever, and scarlet fever increasingly less common in developed nations. In developing nations, public health officials continue working with international agencies (such as the World Health Organization and other UN agencies) to reduce instances and the spread of infectious disease.

What was the **first disease** conquered by human beings?

Smallpox was the first disease eradicated by medicine. Caused by a virus spread from person to person through the air, smallpox was one of the most feared diseases and there was no treatment for it. Before the discovery of the New World, smallpox epidemics swept across Africa, Asia, and Europe, leaving victims scarred and/or blind, and killing countless millions. When explorers set out to find new trade routes and landed in North and South America, they brought the disease with them, infecting the indigenous peoples.

But once a person had the disease, they would not contract it again. This and other observations led British physician Edward Jenner (1749–1823) to develop a successful vaccine against the disease. (Prior to the vaccine, the only preventive method was inoculation of the disease itself, which sometimes led to further spread of the disease. For example, in 1777, General George Washington obtained congressional approval to inoculate the entire Continental army against smallpox, but the results were mixed.)

The use of Jenner's vaccine quickly spread. The first vaccine given in the United States was in 1799 by a Harvard physician. During the 1800s, many countries passed laws requiring vaccination. Improvements in the vaccine resulted in the elimination of smallpox from Europe and North America by the 1940s. When the World Health Organization was created by the United Nations in 1946, one of its aims was to reduce the instances of smallpox around the world. Immunization programs brought this about: The last natural occurrence of the disease was reported in October 1977 in Somalia, Africa. When no further cases were documented within the next two years, the disease was considered eradicated.

Why is **Jonas Salk** so well known?

American physician Jonas Edward Salk (1914–95) is familiar to many as the inventor of the polio vaccine. In 1952, more than twenty-one thousand cases of paralytic polio—the most severe form of polio—were reported in the United States. An acute viral infection, poliomyelitis (also called polio and infantile paralysis) invades the central nervous system; it is found worldwide and mainly in children.

In 1953, after years of research that included sorting through all the studies done on immunology since the mid-1800s, Salk announced the formulation of a vaccine—which contained all three types of polio known at the time. Salk tested it on himself first, and then on his wife and three children. He experienced no side effects and found the vaccine to be effective, so it was tested on 1.8 million schoolchildren in a program sponsored by the March of Dimes (then called the National Foundation for Infantile Paralysis). In April 1955, the vaccine was pronounced safe and effective. Salk was duly honored, including with a congressional gold medal and a citation from President Dwight D. Eisenhower (1890–1969). Four years later, American physician Albert B. Sabin (b. 1906) developed an effective polio vaccine that could be taken orally (versus via injection)—it is the sugar cube so well-known to people around the world. That vaccine contains live viruses (Salk's was a killed-virus vaccine). The two vaccines virtually eradicate polio from developed nations.

Who was **Typhoid Mary**?

Typhoid Mary was the name given to Mary Mallon (1870?–1938), the first known carrier of typhoid fever in the United States. Though Mallon had recovered from the disease, as a cook in New York City area restaurants, she continued to spread typhoid fever germs to others, infecting more than fifty people between 1900 and 1915. The New York state sanitation department connected her to at least six typhoid fever outbreaks there. Officials finally—and permanently—institutionalized her (in 1914) to prevent further spread of the acute infectious disease.

When was **AIDS** first diagnosed?

AIDS (acquired immunodeficiency syndrome) cases were first identified in 1981 by physicians in Los Angeles and New York City. But since that time, researchers have traced cases of the disease back to 1969. The human immunodeficiency virus (HIV), which severely damages the body's ability to fight disease, is transmitted through sexual contact, shared drug needles, and infected blood transfusions. While the disease was believed to have somehow been transmitted to humans from monkeys (since research shows HIV to be similar to simian immunodeficiency viruses), HIV has never been isolated in any wild animal. While the source of the deadly disease has not been definitively determined, scientists believe that infection began in Africa during the 1960s and 1970s when significant numbers of people migrated from rural areas to cities.

Marie Curie working with her husband, Pierre.

The overcrowding and unemployment that resulted contributed to the spread of sexually transmitted diseases.

Since AIDS was discovered, there have been millions of cases diagnosed and almost every country of the world has reported cases of AIDS to the World Health Organization. It is now considered endemic to many developing nations, where it is spread mostly among heterosexual men and women. In developed nations, public education programs have made people aware of how the disease is transmitted, which has helped control the spread of the HIV virus. Drug treatments are still being developed to treat HIV/AIDS; no cure has been discovered.

What were the **Curies'** contributions to medicine?

In 1898, French chemists-physicists and husband-and-wife team Pierre (1859–1906) and Marie Curie (1867–1934) discovered radium, the first radioactive element, which proved to be an effective weapon against cancer. They conducted further experiments in radioactivity, a word that Marie Curie coined, distinguishing among alpha, beta, and gamma radiation. Upon his death in 1906, Marie succeeded her husband as professor of

Why are Pavlov's dogs so well known?

Russian physiologist Ivan Pavlov (1849–1936) carried out famous experiments with dogs, which were intended to demonstrate conditioned reflex. Noticing that the laboratory dogs would sometimes salivate merely at the approach of the lab assistants who fed them, Pavlov, who was already a Nobel laureate for his research on digestion, set out to determine whether he could turn normally "unconditioned" reflexes or responses of the central nervous system into conditioned reflexes. He demonstrated that if a bell is rung every time a dog is fed, eventually the dog becomes conditioned to salivate at the sound of a bell—even if there is no food present. In this way, Pavlov substituted artificial stimulus (the ringing of the bell) for natural or environmental stimulus (food) to prompt a physiological reaction (salivation). Based on these experiments, Pavlov concluded that all acquired habits depend on chains of conditioned reflexes. This conclusion contributed to the development of behaviorism.

physics at the Sorbonne. During World War I (1914–18), Curie organized radiological services for hospitals. She went on to become director of the research department of the Radium Institute of the University of Paris (1918–34). The Curies's daughter, Irène (1897–1956), followed in her parents' footsteps, becoming a physicist, and marrying (in 1926) another scientist, Frédéric Joliot, who served as director of the Radium Institute for ten years beginning in 1946. The pair, who were known as the Joliot-Curies, contributed to the discovery and development of nuclear reactors. The Curies and the Joliot-Curies were all Nobel laureates.

What is **behaviorism**?

Behaviorism is a school of psychology that attempts to explain human behavior in terms of responses to environmental stimuli. Influenced by the conditioned reflex demonstrated by Ivan Pavlov, American psychologist John Broadus Watson (1878–1958), of Johns Hopkins University, codified and popularized the theory, which discards both the value of introspection and the concept of consciousness as influences on human behavior. Behaviorism was further studied by another American psychologist, Harvard professor B. F. Skinner (1904–90). Rejecting as stimuli that which cannot be observed, Skinner focused his work on patterns of responses to observable stimuli and external rewards. Applied to human learning, Skinner's theories on behaviorism affected educational methods.

What did **Freud** believe?

The Austrian neurologist believed that human behavior and all mental states are influenced by a complex of repressed and forgotten impressions, many of them from childhood. Sigmund Freud (1856–1939) further believed that by uncovering these impressions, he could effect a cure for his patient. Freud regarded infantile mental processes, including infantile sexuality, of particular importance to the unconscious.

While he initially used hypnosis as a method of revealing the unconscious, Freud later turned to a new form of treatment called free association. By this method, patients talk about whatever is on their minds, jumping from one idea to the next. The memories and feelings that surface through free association are then analyzed by the therapist to find the root of the patient's mental or emotional problem. Freud also interpreted his patients' dreams, which he believed are unconscious representations of repressed desires. Free association and dream analysis are the cornerstones of psychoanalysis.

In analyzing human behavior, Freud came to the conclusion that the mind (or psyche) is divided into three parts—the id, the ego, and the superego. The id is the source of instincts; the ego is the mediator between those instincts and reality; and the superego is the conscience. The superego functions to reward or punish through a system of moral attitudes and a sense of guilt. The theories of psychoanalysis hold that if the parts of the mind oppose each other, a mental or emotional disorder (called a neurosis) occurs.

Freud's theories revolutionized the fields of psychiatry and psychology. They also influenced methods and philosophies of child-rearing and education. While psychoanalysis has been credited with helping millions of mentally ill patients, Freud's theories have also been rejected or challenged by some.

What does the term **"Jungian"** mean?

Jungian refers to the analytical psychology founded by Swiss psychiatrist Carl Gustav Jung (1875–1961). Early in his career, Jung conducted experiments in mental association and, through this work, came into contact with famed psychoanalyst Sigmund Freud in 1907. While initially in harmony with each other, Jung later broke with Freud's theories, establishing his own doctrines of human behavior.

Like Freud, Jung believed that the unconscious (that part of the mind of which a person is unaware) effects human behavior. But unlike his Austrian colleague, Jung denied that neuroses have any sexual basis. Instead, Jung believed that many factors influence human behavior—including the personalities of one's parents. He also believed in something he described as the "collective unconscious": In his revolutionary work *Psychology of the Unconscious,* published in 1912, Jung asserted that there are two dimensions of the unconscious—the personal and the collective. The collective unconscious, according to Jung, is those acts and mental patterns that are shared by members of a culture or are perhaps universally shared by all humankind. He theorized that the collective unconscious manifests itself in archetypes—images, patterns, and symbols that appear in dreams and fantasies as well as in mythology, religion, and literature. Jung believed that the collective unconsciousness can serve as a guide to humanity, and therefore, he taught that therapy should make people aware of it. Jung's theories of archetypes, or universal symbols, have influenced such diverse fields as anthropology, art, filmmaking, and history.

Jung later developed a system for classifying personalities (into introverted and extroverted types) and distinguishing among mental functions (classifying them as thinking, feeling, sensing, or intuitive). Jung taught that therapists should help their patients balance introversion (relying only on oneself for personal fulfillment) with extroversion (relying on others for personal fulfillment). Jung's system of classifications, or "typology," has been used to develop theories of personality types and their influences on human behavior.

333

Who was **Dorothea Dix**?

Dorothea Lynde Dix (1802–87) was a philanthropist and she was among the first American women to become active in social reform. As head-mistress of her own school for girls in Boston, in 1841, Dix toured Mass-achusetts state correctional institutions, where she was shocked to see deplorable treatment of the mentally ill. Dix became an impassioned advocate for the mentally ill. Leading a drive to build hospitals for the specialized care of those afflicted with mental illnesses, Dix appealed to the consciences of legislators and philanthropists. She was successful in establishing mental hospitals throughout the United States, Canada, and Europe—many of which still bear her name.

Dix's campaign for humane treatment of the mentally ill transformed American attitudes and institutions in the two decades that led up to the Civil War (1861–65). During the war, she acted as superintendent of the U.S. Army nurses. She also worked to improve prison conditions during her lifetime.

When was the **Red Cross** founded?

The Red Cross was founded in Switzerland in October 1863 when the delegates from sixteen nations met in Geneva to discuss establishing "in all civilized countries permanent societies of volunteers who in time of war would give help to the wounded without regard for nationality." The idea had been described in a pamphlet published in 1862 by Swiss phil-anthropist Jean Henri Dunant (1828–1910), who in 1859 was touring Italy during the Austro-Sardinian War. Observing the suffering of the wounded, he immediately formed a group of volunteers to help them. After the Geneva conference in 1863, which had decided the organiza-tion symbol and name, European delegates met in August of the follow-ing year; they were joined by two American observers. This meeting gave rise to the First Geneva Convention, which determined the protection of sick and wounded soldiers and medical personnel and facilities during wartime, and adopted the Red Cross as a symbol for neutral aid.

The name of the organization comes from its flag showing a red cross on a white background—the inverse of the flag of Switzerland, where the organization was founded. In Muslim countries, the organization is known as the Red Crescent.

What is Clara Barton known for?

The American humanitarian was called the Angel of the Battlefield for her work during the Civil War (1861–65). Clara Barton (1821–1912) was a nurse in army camps and on battlefields, where she cared for the wounded. When the fighting ended, Barton formed a bureau to search for missing men. This demanding work left her exhausted. Recuperating in Switzerland in 1869, Barton learned of the newly formed Red Cross (established 1863). She soon rallied to the aid of that volunteer organization, tending to the needs of those wounded in the fighting of the Franco-Prussian War (1870–71), which German chancellor Otto von Bismarck (1815–98) had provoked in his attempt to create a unified German empire.

In 1877, Barton began working to form the American Red Cross. Her efforts came to fruition in 1881 with the establishment of the first U.S. branch of the Red Cross. She became the organization's first president, a post she held from 1882–1904. When Jamestown, Pennsylvania, experienced a devastating flood in 1889, Barton took charge of relief work there. She subsequently advocated a clause be added to the Red Cross constitution, stating that the organization would also provide relief during calamities other than war. She was successful. It is because of Barton that the red cross or red crescent has become a familiar and welcome site in times of disaster.

How did the **birth control movement** get started?

The decline in death rates, which has meant an overall increase in the world population, gave rise to the birth control movement. Scientific advances during the eighteenth and nineteenth centuries resulted in better food supplies, the control of diseases, and safer work environments for those living in developed countries. These improvements combined with progress in medicine to save and prolong human lives. During the 1800s, the birth rate, which in earlier times had been offset

335

by the death rate, became a concern to many who worried that population growth would outstrip the planet's ability to provide adequate resources to sustain life.

In 1798, British economist and sociologist Thomas Robert Malthus (1766–1834) published his *Essay on the Principle of Population*, arguing that populations tend to increase faster than do food supplies. He thereby concluded that poverty and suffering are unavoidable. Malthus viewed only war, famine, disease, and "moral restraint" as checks on population growth. In spite of or because of Malthus's assertions, during the 1800s, the idea of birth control as a practical method to keep population growth in check gained momentum.

Early in the 1900s, the movement found a leader in American Margaret Higgins Sanger (1883–1966), whose personal experience as a nurse working among the poor had convinced her that limiting family size is necessary for social progress. She became convinced that unwanted pregnancy should be avoided by using birth control methods. It was—and remains—controversial. Even though the distribution of birth control information was illegal at the time, Sanger advised people on the subject. In 1914, she founded a magazine, called *The Woman Rebel*, and she sent birth control information through the mail. She was arrested and indicted. But she was not deterred. In 1916 in Brooklyn, New York, Sanger founded the first birth control clinic in the United States. In 1921, she organized the first American Birth Control Conference, held in New York. That same year, she founded the American Birth Control League, which later became the Planned Parenthood Federation of America. As public support for the movement increased, Sanger succeeded in getting laws passed that allowed doctors to disseminate birth control information to their patients.

In other countries, Sanger's work inspired similar movements, but developed nations continue to have lower birth rates than do developing nations. With the world population exceeding 5.5 billion, the fear of overpopulation had prompted new interest in birth control.

RELIGION

How are **religions** classified?

Religion, which is a system of beliefs that usually centers on whatever is beyond the known or the natural, is commonly divided between elementary forms and higher religions.

Some elementary forms, or "traditional religions," are animism (the belief in spirits in nature or in natural objects), ancestor worship (revering the spirits of the dead), and totemism (belief in a mystical relationship between a group of people and an emblem). Animists might believe in spirits living in the sea or in the mountains. Believers in ancestor worship will both honor and fear the spirits of dead family members—for if they are neglected by the living, these spirits are believed to be able to bring harm to their descendants. Within clans, some tribal peoples adopt totems—such as a lion or a turtle. Totemists will be careful throughout their lives to not harm the animal or object that serves as their clan's emblem.

Higher religions are those that embody a concept of transcendence. Higher religions are classified as polytheistic (believing in many gods), dualistic (believing in equally powerful gods of good and evil), monotheistic (believing in one god), and pantheistic (believing in god as the forces and laws of the universe, or the worship of all gods). Religions are further classified as revealed or non-revealed. Revealed religions are those that followers know through divine agency; both Christianity and Islam are revealed religions. A non-revealed religion such as Buddhism, Brahmanism, or Taoism, are known only through inquiry.

What did **ancient civilizations** believe?

In the absence of scientific knowledge, ancient civilizations, including the Greeks, the Romans, the Egyptians, the Aztecs, and the Mayas, created mythologies to explain origination (how they came into existence as a people), the existence of good and evil, the natural cycle of the seasons, weather, and the motions of the sun, the moon, and the stars. Such natural phenomena were explained by a body of stories that centered around gods, goddesses, and heroes.

For example, the Romans, who largely adapted Greek mythology, believed that gods and goddesses had power not only over agriculture, but over all aspects of life. They worshiped Ceres as the goddess of the harvest, Vesta as the goddess of the hearth and home, and Jupiter as the god of the weather, who later became their supreme god and protector. These gods are traced to the Greek beliefs in Demeter as the goddess of the harvest and of fertility, Hestia as the goddess of the hearth (she symbolized security and happiness), and Zeus, the supreme Greek god who was believed to rule from his court on Mount Olympus, and was a symbol for power, rule, and law. The ancient Greeks were also the source of what is perhaps one of the most well-known myths of western civilization— Pandora's box. They believed that all that is bad or evil was once enclosed in a box, which was opened by Pandora (who, according to Greek mythology, was the first woman on earth), releasing evil into the world. Greek mythology was preserved in the works of Homer and Hesiod.

Other frequently studied mythologies include the Vedic (Indian), Egyptian, and Mesopotamian.

Why is **mythology** so widely studied?

The mythologies of various peoples are studied for their religious meanings, for their similarities to each other, and as a way of understanding the culture that originated them. Through the centuries, scholars have arrived at various conclusions about mythology. Scottish anthropologist Sir James Frazer (1854–1941) studied folklore and religion, and found parallel beliefs between the systems of primitive cultures and Christianity. He published his theories in the highly influential work *The Golden Bough* (1890), proposing that all myths center around the cycles of nature and birth, death, and resurrection. Polish-born English anthropologist Bronislaw Malinowski (1884–1942) asserted that myths are nothing more than the validation of accepted social behavior and patterns within a culture. While Swiss psychiatrist Carl Jung (1875–1961) posited that all cultures have unconsciously formed the same mythic symbols or motifs (called archetypes). To many theologians, mythologies are viewed simply as corruptions of the Bible.

Whatever their meaning or however they are interpreted, myths have figured prominently in literature–from the fifth-century B.C. works of Greek tragedian Aeschylus to the twentieth-century works of poets T. S. Eliot and Wallace Stevens.

When was the **Bible** written?

The Old Testament or Hebrew Bible, which is called "the Book of Books" because of its profound influence on humanity, was written over two thousand years ago. Scholars disagree about exactly when or how the books were written but it is generally accepted that parts of the Bible originated during the time of the Hebrew prophet and leader Moses (or Moshe)—about the fourteenth to the thirteenth century B.C. Moses is believed to be the author of the first five books of the Bible, called the Pentateuch or the Law of Moses: the books of Genesis, Exodus, Leviticus, Numbers, and Deuteronomy. These are believed to have been revealed to Moses by God.

Scholars believe that much of the material in the Bible was recited aloud as part of an oral tradition long before it was written down, which complicates the matter of assigning dates to the various books. The books of the prophets (Joshua, Isaiah, Samuel, Jeremiah, Ezekiel, etc.) are believed to have been written and collected during the kingdoms of Israel (c. 1020 B.C.–722 B.C.) and Judah (c. 933 B.C.–586 B.C.) and shortly thereafter.

Psalms, Proverbs, Song of Solomon (or Song of Songs), Ruth, Ecclesiastes, and Chronicles were written in the time of King David and King Solomon—during the tenth century B.C. or shortly after 1000 B.C. The books of Job, Lamentations, Esther, Daniel, Ezra, and Nehemiah are believed to have appeared between 600 B.C. and 100 B.C.

The twenty-seven books of the New Testament, upon which Christianity is based, were written on papyrus scrolls, none of which remain. Dating the writing of the New Testament is difficult but the historical events referred to in the books indicate they were written shortly after the time of Christ and probably before A.D. 100.

What are the **divisions** of the **Hebrew Bible**?

The Hebrew Bible is divided into three main sections called the Law (or Torah), the Prophets, and the Writings (or Hagiographa). The Hebrew Bible is accepted by Jews as sacred: Testaments comes from the ancient word *testamentum*, meaning covenant with God. Much of the Hebrew Bible recounts Jewish history, demonstrating faithful observance to their agreement with God.

The Law consists of those five books written by Moses, and these recount creation, early traditions, the lives of the patriarchs of Israel, early events of the Israelites, and entrance into the Promised Land. *Torah* translates as "teaching" and Jews (as do Christians) look to these first five books of the Bible for guidance. The Prophets consists of the books of the Former Prophets (books of Joshua, Judges, 1st and 2nd Samuel, and 1st and 2nd Kings) and the Latter Prophets (Isaiah, Jeremiah, Ezekiel, and the Twelve—the teachings of twelve other prophets). The books of the Prophets chronicle historical events, but according to the Jewish tradition, these books also teach that people must obey God's laws. The Writings consist of thirteen books, which are believed to have been written by poets and teachers.

What are the **Dead Sea Scrolls**?

The scrolls are ancient manuscripts of great historical and religious importance. They were found in dry riverbed caves situated on the northwestern side of the Dead Sea (a salt lake situated between Israel, the West Bank, and Jordan). More than eight hundred scrolls have been found, with the most famous discoveries made in 1947. The Dead Sea Scrolls were found miles apart at a number of different sites including Khirbat Qumran in the West Bank (formerly Israel). The texts date to different centuries but include fragments of every book of the Hebrew Bible (or Old Testament) except the Book of Esther. Some texts are almost identical to Bible texts used today, showing that much of the Old Testament is the same as it was two thousand years ago.

What is the difference between the Hebrew Bible and the Old Testament?

The Hebrew Bible is made up of twenty-four books; the Old Testament used by Christians consists of the same books as those of the Hebrew Bible, but they are arranged differently and many books are divided, resulting in more books in the Old Testament than in the Hebrew Bible.

Among Christians, the Old Testament varies between Protestantism and Roman Catholicsm: Protestants include thirty-nine books in the Old Testament while Roman Catholics add seven books, called the Apocrypha, to their version, for a total of forty-six books. The books of the Apocrypha resemble those of the Old Testament, but since they were written later than most of the Old Testament (probably 300 B.C.–A.D. 70), both Protestants and Jews treat them separately. The Bibles used by all three religions–Judaism, Roman Catholicism, and Protestantism—begin with the same seven books: Genesis, Exodus, Leviticus, Numbers, Deuteronomy, Joshua, and Judges. The first five of these were written by Moses.

What is **Golgotha**?

Golgotha is the Hebrew name for calvary—the site on a hillside outside ancient Jerusalem where Jesus Christ (c. 6 B.C.–c. 30 A.D.) was crucified. Though the exact site is unknown, it is believed to be where the church of the Holy Sepulcher is located.

What are the **Four Horsemen of the Apocalypse**?

The Four Horsemen of the Apocalypse are allegorical figures mentioned in chapter six of Revelations (also called the Revelation of St. John the Divine). The chapter describes a scroll held in God's right hand and which is sealed with seven seals. When the first four of the seals are opened, the four horsemen appear, each on a different colored horse. There are various interpretations of these allegorical figures but the rider on the white horse is believed to represent conquest (or the return of Christ); the rider on the red horse is believed to represent war; the rider on the black horse, famine; and the pale horse, death. Some believe these hardships to be signs of the end of the world. The four horsemen have appeared throughout art and literature.

Who wrote the **Koran**?

The Koran (or Qur'an) are the holy scriptures of Islam and were written by the followers of the prophet Muhammad (c. 570–632). It is not known whether these texts were written down during Muhammad's lifetime or after his death. It is known that the text was codified between 644 and 656. Muslims believe the angel Gabriel revealed the book to the Muhammad, beginning in 610 and continuing until the prophet's death in 632. The Koran, meaning "recitation," consists of 114 verses (*ayas*) that are organized in chapters (*suras*).

Muslims believe the beautiful prose of the Koran to be the words of God Himself—who spoke through Muhammad. Further, it is believed to be only a copy of an eternal book, which is kept by Allah. The Koran is also held up by Muslims as proof that Muhammad was indeed a prophet since no human is capable of composing such text. Among the most widely read texts today, the Koran is also taught orally so that even Muslims who are illiterate may know and be able to recite verses.

When did the **Sunni** and **Shiah sects** of Islam form?

It was during the 600s, not long after Muhammad's death, when Muslims split into two main divisions—Sunni and Shiah. Sunnite Muslims, which account for most of the Islamic world today, believe that Islamic leadership passed to caliphs (temporal and spiritual leaders) selected from the prophet Muhammad's tribe. The Shiites believe, however, that the true leaders of Islam descend from Ali (c. 600–61), husband of Muhammad's daughter, Fatima. Ali, who was the fourth caliph (656–61), is revered by Shiites as the rightful successor to the prophet Muhammad and are led by his descendants. Shiites form the largest minority group among the Muslims.

How old is Islam?

Islam, one of the world's largest religions, originated with the teachings of the prophet Muhammad (c. 570–632) during the early 600s A.D. Muhammad was born in Mecca (in present-day Saudi Arabia) and was orphaned at the age of six. He was raised by relatives who trained him as a merchant. When he was twenty-five years old, he married a wealthy widow, Khadijah, who bore him several children. In about 610, Muhammad began having visions in which he was called upon by God (Allah). More than six hundred of these were written down, becoming the sacred text known as the Koran (Qur'an). By 613, Muhammad had attracted followers with his messages of one God; Allah's power; the duty of worship and generosity; and the doctrine of the last judgment. Followers of this new religion became known as Muslims, an Arabic word meaning those who submit (to Allah); and the religion itself became known as Islam (submission).

Today, there are Muslims in every part of the world, but the largest Muslim communities in the world are in the Middle East, North Africa, Indonesia, Bangladesh, Pakistan, India, and central Asia. Additionally, most of the people of Turkey and Albania are Muslim.

There are other sects as well: the Wahhabi Muslims are a puritanical sect; the Baha'is emerged from the Shiites; and the Ismaili Khoja Muslims have been in existence almost from the beginning of Islam. While Islamic practices may vary somewhat among the sects, all Islamic people uphold the Five Pillars of Faith.

What are the **Five Pillars of Faith**?

Muslims practice adherence to the Five Pillars of Faith—belief in Allah as the only God and Muhammad as his prophet; prayer (five times daily—at dawn, at noon, in the afternoon, in the evening, and at nightfall); giving

343

alms to the poor; fasting from dawn until dusk during the holy month of Ramadan); and making the pilgrimage (*hajj*) to Mecca at least once.

What were the **Crusades**?

The Crusades were a series of nine Christian military expeditions that took place during the end of the eleventh century and throughout the twelfth and thirteenth centuries. The stated goal of the Crusades was to recover from the Muslims the Holy Lands of Palestine, where Jesus Christ (c. 6 B.C.–A.D. 30) had lived. The word "crusade" comes from the Latin word *crux* meaning cross, and Crusaders were said to have "taken up the cross."

The Crusades began with an impassioned sermon given by Pope Urban II (c. 1042–99) at Clermont, France, in November 1095. Earlier that year Byzantine Emperor Alexius Comnenus (1048–1118) had appealed to Urban for aid in fighting back the fierce Seljuk Turks (preceding the Ottomans, the Seljuks were named for their traditional founder, Seljuq). Seeing the expansion of the Turks, who were Muslim, as a threat to Christianity, the Pope agreed to help. Not only did Urban rally support for the Byzantines in staving off the further advances of the Turks, he also advocated the Holy Lands should be recovered from them. While the Arab Muslims who had previously controlled the Holy Land had allowed Christians to visit there, the Turks tolerated no such thing. Urban feared that if Palestine were not recovered, Christians would lose access to their holy places altogether.

But Urban also viewed the Crusades as a way of unifying Western Europe: The feudal nobility there had long fought against each other. He believed a foreign war would unite them behind a common cause as Christians. Further, he hoped the Crusades would unite Western with Eastern (Byzantine) Europe behind one goal. If successful, the expeditions would also have the effect of expanding the pope's moral authority across a greater region.

En route from Clermont to Constantinople (Istanbul, Turkey), where the Crusade was set to begin in August 1096, Urban continued to preach his message—at Limoges, Poitiers, Tours, Aquitaine, and Toulouse, France. The message found broad appeal—even if it appealed to something other than the people's religious sensibilities. Some of those who answered Urban's call took up arms not for the Christian cause, but for their own personal gain such as acquiring more land, expanding trade, or recovering religious relics. Many peasants "took up the cross" to escape hardships—northern France and the Rhineland had, in 1094, been the site of flooding and pestilence, which was followed in 1095 by drought and famine.

The First Crusade actually turned into two. A Peasants' Crusade (which had never been Urban's intent) had gone ahead of the official expedition, and many lives were lost. It ended in failure. But the planned expedition, called the Crusade of Princes, ultimately succeeded in capturing Jerusalem in 1099. Western Christian feudal states were established at Edessa, Antioch, and Tripoli—all of which were placed under the authority of the Kingdom of Jerusalem. But Urban did not live to see the recovery of the Holy Land. And the Christian hold on Palestine was not to last, as the Muslims refused to give up the fight for control of lands they too considered to be holy. The Second (1147–49), Third (1189–92), Fourth (1202–04), Fifth (1217–21), Sixth (1228–29), Seventh (1248–54), and Eighth (1270) Crusades were prompted by a mix of religious, political, and social circumstances. The Crusades ended in 1291—almost two hundred years after they had started—when the city of Acre, the last Christian stronghold in Palestine, fell to the Muslims, ending Christian rule in the East.

A ninth Crusade, in 1212, was particularly tragic: Called the Children's Crusade, the expedition was led by a young visionary who had rallied French and German children to believe they could recover Jerusalem—since, as poor and faithful servants, they would have God on their side. As the children marched south across Europe, many of them died even before reaching the Mediterranean coast. Some believe the Crusade was sabotaged, resulting in the children being sold into slavery in the East.

What **impact** did the **Crusades** have on **Western Europe**?

The goals of the Crusades were not accomplished: The Holy Land had been recovered, but the Christians were unable to keep control of it; and while the Western Europeans had joined with the Eastern (Byzantine) Christians in their fight against the Muslims, the two groups remained bitter toward each other, which likely contributed to the fall of Byzantium to the Ottoman Turks in 1453. Nevertheless, the Crusades had a lasting effect on the European economy: During the expeditions, trade routes had been established, new markets opened, and ship-building had been improved. Having fortified themselves for the fight, the Christian monarchies in

Western Europe emerged from the Crusades in 1291 as strong as—if not stronger than—before Pope Urban had first rallied the troops in 1095.

How does the **Catholic Church** determine who will be **pope**?

Present-day procedures for electing a pope, who serves the church until his death, vary from those of earlier times. Before the 300s, the clergy of Rome and the outlying areas cast votes in what was essentially a local papal election. Throughout history, some of Europe's powerful leaders tried to influence the outcome of papal elections in order to establish a pope who would be favorable to their leadership. This interference in the process sometimes resulted in disputes over who was the rightful pope, with more than one pope claiming authority based on the support of emperors or factions within the church. (Those claiming to be popes but who were considered illegitimate are called antipopes.)

The process observed by the Roman Catholic Church today was established over time. The first important decision came in 1059 when Pope Nicholas II (980?–1061) declared that papal electors must be cardinals. In 1179, the Third Lateran Council established that all cardinals have an equal vote and that popes may only be elected by a two-thirds majority; this came after Pope Alexander III (c. 1105–81) had been opposed by three antipopes. Pope Gregory X (1210–76), after being elected to the papacy following a three-year vacancy, convoked the Council of Lyon in 1274, which decreed that the cardinals must meet within ten days of a pope's death to determine the papacy. Further, the Council required that the cardinals remain together in strict seclusion until they have elected a new pope.

Today, when a pope dies, the dean of the Sacred College notifies all cardinals of the vacancy. The cardinals convene at Vatican City, in a meeting that is required to begin within twenty days of the pope's death. Any of three electoral processes may be used: ballot (which is most common), unanimous voice vote, or the unanimous decision of a committee of nine to fifteen delegates.

Four votes are taken a day (two in the morning and two in the afternoon) until there is a two-thirds majority vote. As soon as a decision is reached, the dean asks the pope-elect if he accepts the position. Once he accepts, he is considered pope and has full authority over the church. He then proceeds to select a name, which he announces to the cardinals.

Following these private meetings, the results of which are eagerly awaited by devoted Roman Catholics, white smoke is sent up a chimney of the Vatican palace, signaling to the crowd in St. Peter's Square that the election is complete. (The smoke is created by burning ballots; ballots from elections in which a two-thirds majority was not achieved are also burned, but in a way that creates black smoke. In this way, the public is apprised of the cardinals' decision-making process.) The oldest cardinal then has the honor of making the official announcement to the people in St. Peter's Square, who are then blessed by the new pope in his first official act. The coronation of the pope is held later.

How **many popes** have there been?

The accepted number is 264. Except for a few brief interruptions (when the papacy was vacant), the Roman Catholic Church has been headed by the pope as its visible head (and Jesus Christ as its invisible head) since Jesus said to the apostle Peter: "And I say also unto thee, That thou art Peter, and upon / this rock I will build my church; and the gates of hell / shall not prevail against it" (Matthew 16:18).

Peter, who was earlier called Simon, became the leader of the Christian community after the Crucifixion of Christ and he made Jerusalem the headquarters of his preaching in Palestine. According to second-century sources, Peter traveled to Rome about 55 A.D. and became the city's first bishop. During the persecution of Christians under Roman emperor Nero (37–68 A.D.), Peter was crucified on Vatican Hill in the year 64. He died a martyr and was canonized. St. Peter's Church, the principal church of the Christian world, is said to have been built over Peter's burial place. These events in Rome during St. Peter's time long after gave the city special status within the church. It further established the site of the papal palace in Vatican City (which is an independent state that lies within the city of Rome). And, almost all popes have been Italian: When John Paul II, who was born in Poland, was elected pope in 1978, he was the first non-Italian pope since 1523.

Where does the word **pope** come from?

The word *pope* is derived from the Greek word *pappas*, literally meaning papa (father).

347

What caused the **Reformation**?

The religious movement during the sixteenth century had religious, political, and cultural causes. As more and more people were converted to Christianity during the Middle Ages, the pope's sphere of influence gradually increased—giving him greater authority than many secular rulers. This supremacy was defended by Pope Innocent III (1160?–1216), one of the most prominent figures of the Middle Ages, who asserted that the church should rightly retain its full power—in both temporal and spiritual matters. But in Western Europe, the monarchs became increasingly powerful as peasants began moving away from their farms and villages and to the emerging cities, which were protected by kings and emperors rather than lords and princes. The European monarchs often opposed the pope, regarding him as a leader of a foreign state. This conflict continued for centuries.

In 1309, Pope Clement V did something that would later divide the Roman Catholic Church when he moved the papacy from Rome to Avignon, France (he was French), where it stayed for seventy years. When Pope Gregory XI moved it back to Rome in 1378, some French cardinals objected and elected a pope of their own (an antipope), installing him at Avignon. This resulted in two popes claiming supremacy, and in 1409, the situation grew more complicated when a third pope was added in Pisa, Italy. Not only had the power struggle divided the church, it had created tremendous confusion for the people, who further perceived that there were corrupt practices at work in the church. These included the selling of church positions and indulgences (pardons for sins), as well as, the lavish lifestyle enjoyed by the bishops and the pope (on a par with that of royalty). While these injustices were decried by critics, the abuses did not stop. As a remedy some began to think that the church should be led by church councils. Dissatisfaction with the church also extended to its message, which had turned away from God's mercy and the teachings of Jesus Christ, instead focusing on a life of good works as the way to salvation.

Europe was also in the midst of the Renaissance (1350–1600), which saw a proliferation in the number of universities, the circulation of printed materials (thanks to the advent of the movable type printing press), and broader study of classic texts, as well as, of the Holy Scriptures—in their original languages instead of how they had been handed

How did the Reformation begin?

The Reformation as a movement began on October 31, 1517, when the German monk and theology professor Martin Luther (1483–1546) nailed his Ninety-Five Theses to the door of the Castle Church at Wittenburg (Saxony, Germany). The theses questioned the value of indulgences (pardons that were disseminated by the church) and condemned the sale of them. Luther had already begun to preach the doctrine of salvation by faith rather than by works, and he went on to publicly defend his beliefs, which were in direct opposition to the church, during 1518. The following year he expanded his argument against the church by denying the supremacy of the pope. In 1521, Pope Leo X (1475–1521) declared Luther a heretic and excommunicated him. Ordered to appear before the Diet (council) of Worms in April 1521, Luther refused to retract his statements of his beliefs, saying "Unless I am convinced by the testimony of the Scriptures or by clear reason . . . I am bound by the Scriptures I have quoted and my conscience is captive to the Word of God." The following month, the Holy Roman Emperor Charles V (1500–58) issued the Edict of Worms, declaring Luther to be an outlaw and authorizing his death. The Prince of Saxony, known by history as Frederick the Wise (1463–1525), saw fit to protect Luther, whom he'd appointed as a faculty member at the University of Wittenburg (founded by Frederick the Wise in 1502). Luther continued the Protestant movement until his death in 1546.

down in translation by the church. Before long, a middle class of educated people had developed in Europe.

These circumstances combined to bring about a period of religious reform that lasted until 1648. The movement itself, however, continued to exert influence through its emphasis on personal responsibility, individual freedom, and the secularization of society.

What were the **results** of the **Reformation**?

The emergence of the Protestants (who got their name for protesting against the Catholic Church) was officially recognized by Holy Roman Emperor Charles V with the Peace of Augsburg (1555), which granted the people the right to worship as Lutherans (the church named for reformer Martin Luther). But the hostility between Catholic and Protestant countries erupted in 1618 with the Thirty Years' War. That series of conflicts, which had become increasingly political as it raged, was ended with the Peace of Westphalia, which, among other things, stipulated that Lutheranism and Calvinism (or Presbyterianism, founded by Frenchman John Calvin; 1509–64) be given the same due as Catholicism.

Through acts of state, both Catholicism and Protestantism took hold in Europe, with the northern countries, including those of Scandinavia, turning toward the "new" churches and the southern countries remaining Catholic. For the most part, the Reformation fostered an attitude of religious tolerance among Christians. Though conflict between Protestants and Catholics would continue (to the present day) in the British Isles where after Queen Elizabeth I adopted a moderate form of Protestantism (called Anglicanism) as the official religion of England, Protestants colonized Ulster Ireland, giving rise to hostilities with their Irish-Catholic countrymen to the south.

For its part, the Catholic Church, too, underwent a period of reforms (called the Counter Reformation), which rid the church of many of its pre-Reformation problems to emerge as a stronger religious body.

The Reformation had without question brought about greater religious freedom than had been known before. Among the churches that emerged during the Reformation are the Lutheran, the Anabaptist (ancestors to the Amish and Mennonite churches), the Presbyterian, the Episcopal, and the Puritan—all of which have strong followings today, both in Europe and in North America, where they were established by the colonists.

What is the **Protestant ethic**?

The Protestant ethic is a term describing a set of attitudes fostered by the leaders of the reformation—Martin Luther (1483–1546), John Calvin

(1509–64), John Knox (1513–72), Huldrych Zwingli (1484–1531), Conrad Grebel (c. 1498–1526), and their Protestant successors such as Methodist Church founders John (1703–91) and Charles Wesley (1707–88). These church leaders stressed the holiness of a person's daily life; the importance of pastors to lead family lives (versus the celibacy of Catholic monks and nuns); education and study; and personal responsibility. According to these beliefs, the person who is hard-working, thrifty, and honest is a good person—of value to their community and to God.

In 1904–05, German sociologist Max Weber (1864–1920) wrote an essay called "The Protestant Ethic and the Spirit of Capitalism," asserting that Protestant principles contributed to the growth of industry and commerce during the 1700s and 1800s since the hard work, investment, and savings of individuals help build a capitalist economy.

When did **artwork** begin?

The first true art was originated by *Homo sapiens sapiens* (called "man the double wise") in Europe about 35,000 years ago (during the Stone Age). Man the double wise painted his own hand prints, warrior images, and animals (including bison, horses, and reindeer) on the walls and ceilings of uninhabited caves in France and Spain between 35,000 B.C. and 8,000 B.C. He used red, black, and yellow paints, which he made by mixing powdered earth and rock pigments with water. Among the most famous paintings are those in the caves at Lascaux (in Dordogne, France), Niaux (Ariège, France), Pech-Merle (Lot, France), Gasulla (Castellón, Spain), and Altamira (Cantabria, Spain).

These early modern humans—who, if dressed in contemporary clothing, would be indistinguishable from anyone on a modern city street—also decorated tools, and created lifelike sculptures of animals and of women. European man of this period, who had fully developed human brains, is also referred to as "Cro-Magnon man" for a shallow rock shelter near Les Eyzies in the Dordogne region of southwestern France, where the first fossils from this period were found in 1868.

When did **human beings begin** to write?

That depends on how one defines writing. If it is viewed as a means of communicating between humans, using conventional, visible marks, then writing spans the entire history of visual communication—from early pictographic beginnings to alphabetical writing. The oldest picture writing identified was found in Mesopotamia and dates back to about 3500 B.C. The finding consisted of about a dozen pictures, inscribed on both sides of a limestone tablet. The value of writing is immeasurable; historian James Henry Breasted called it "the greatest influence in uplifting the human race."

When was the **first alphabet** created?

The earliest form of the alphabet was developed between 1800 and 1000 B.C. by Semitic peoples of unknown identity. In 1928 in the northern Syria city of Ras Shamra, a cuneiform (wedge-shaped) alphabet of characters used in writing on clay tablets was discovered.

According to most scholars, these early Semitic inventors got the idea of developing an alphabet because of their contact with Egyptian hieroglyphics. Although some of the Semitic symbols were Egyptian, the system of writing was distinctly their own, consisting of twenty-two characters representing only consonants. (There were no written directions for vowels; the reader had to supply the vowels from his knowledge of the language.)

The characters were developed this way: Important Semitic words were selected so that each would begin with a different consonant. Then, stylized pictures portraying the words (mostly nouns) were assigned the phonetic value of the initial sound of each word. For example, the first character in the Semitic (Hebrew) alphabet, *aleph*, originally meant and was the symbol for an oxhead. The second, *beth*, which came to represent the sound "b," meant "house" and renderings of the symbol in early Phoenician writing reveal a shelter with a roof. The third character, *gimel*, was used for the initial sound of the word describing "camel," and all early symbols show a hump.

How did **paper** develop?

The oldest writing surfaces in existence include Babylonian clay tablets and Indian palm leaves. Around 3000 B.C., the Egyptians developed a writing material using papyrus, the plant for which paper is named.

Egyptian hieroglyphics illustrating man's early attempt at writing.

Early in the Imperial period of the Holy Roman Empire, the long manuscript scrolls used by Egyptians, Greeks, and Romans, and which were made of fragile papyrus, were replaced by the codex, separate pages bound together at one side and having a cover (like the modern book). Eventually, papyrus was replaced by vellum (made of a fine-grain lambskin, kidskin, or calfskin) and parchment (made of sheepskin or goatskin), both of which provided superior surfaces for painting.

The wood-derived paper we know today was developed in A.D. 105 by the Chinese who devised a way to make the bark of the mulberry tree into paper. The process used then contained the basic elements that are still

355

found in paper mills today. But it was not until around the turn of the eighteenth century that paper was produced in continuous rolls. In 1798, a French paper mill clerk invented a machine that could produce a continuous sheet of paper in any desired size from wood pulp. The machine was improved and patented by English paper-makers Henry and Sealy Fourdrinier in 1807. The invention spurred the development of newspapers.

What was the **first book** ever printed?

It was *The Diamond Sutra*, published in the year A.D. 868. Archeologists discovered it in the Caves of the Thousand Buddhas, at Kansu, China.

Who **developed** printing?

If printing is defined as the process of transferring repeatable designs onto a surface, then the first known printing was done by the Mesopotamians, who as early as 3000 B.C., used stamps to impress designs onto wet clay.

Printing on paper developed much later; Chinese inventor Ts'ai Lun (50?–118? A.D.) produced the first paper in 105 A.D. During the T'ang Dynasty (618 A.D.–907 A.D.) Chinese books were printed with inked wood blocks, and it was the Chinese—not German printer Johannes Gutenberg, as is widely believed—who developed movable type, allowing printers to compose a master page from permanent, raised characters. However, movable-type printing did not catch on in medieval China since the Chinese language has some 80,000 characters; printers found it more convenient to use carved blocks.

Who was **Gutenberg** and why was he considered the pioneer of **modern printing**?

Johannes Gutenberg, a German (c. 1390–1468) who built his first printing press around 1440–50, is considered the inventor of a lasting system of movable-type printing. Printing technology had only a brief existence in Europe before Gutenberg, whose printing process helped spread the ideals of the Renaissance throughout Europe.

How old is the oldest illuminated manuscript?

The oldest painted manuscript known is the *Vatican Vergil*, which dates back to the early fifth century A.D. The content is pagan, representing a scene from Virgil's *Georgics*, his poem idealizing country life and nature. But illuminated manuscripts such as this one were typically renderings of sacred texts. When the great fathers of the Eastern Church advised that pictures could be used in books and art to teach the people, the pictures (or illuminations) took on great importance. Sacred books became increasingly decorative and ornamental, as the material beauty of the manuscript served as a vehicle for the spiritual beauty of the text.

When was the **first newspaper** published?

In 1605 in Antwerp, Belgium. It was published by local printer Abraham Verkoeven, who was reputed to have been a drunkard. In 1621, the first London newspaper was published on September 24 (called the *Corante or newes from Italy, Germany, Hungarie, Spaine, and France*). Newspapers proliferated in the 1800s after the development of a machine that allowed paper to be produced in sheets of any size.

What was the **first American** newspaper?

America's first regular newspaper was the weekly *News-Letter* published by Boston postmaster John Campbell. It began publication in 1704 and consisted of a single 7-by-11½-inch sheet of paper covered on both sides with news and rumors received from post riders, sea captains, and sailors.

EDUCATION

PUBLIC EDUCATION

When were the **first schools** established?

In about the fifth century B.C. In ancient Greece, it is believed that Spartan boys who were being trained for the military also learned reading and writing, and studied music. In Athens, boys learned to read and write, memorized poetry, and learned music as well as training in athletics. In the second half of the fifth century B.C., the Sophists (ancient Greek teachers of rhetoric and philosophy), trained young men in the social and political arts, hoping to mold them into ideal statesmen.

How **old** is the concept of **public schools**?

It dates at least as far back as ancient China. The philosopher Confucius (551–479 B.C.) was among the first in China to advocate that primary school education should be available to all. He averred that "in education there should be no class distinctions." He never refused a student, "even though he came to me on foot, with nothing more to offer as tuition than a package of dried meat." Confucius asserted that any man—including a "peasant boy"—had the potential to be a man of principle.

However, it was not until the Scientific Revolution and Age of Enlightenment that public schools were widely instituted. In Prussia (present-day Germany), Frederick the Great was considered an enlightened ruler for, among other things, having started a public education system.

How **long** have children attended **kindergarten**?

For about one and a half centuries: It was in 1837, that the world's first kindergarten opened at Blankenburg, Germany, under the direction of educator Friedrich Froebel (1782–1852). Froebel went on to establish a training course for kindergarten teachers and he introduced the schools throughout Germany. Such schools and classes for kids age four to six are the norm today in much of the world.

How did **Montessori** schools get started?

The schools, evident throughout the United States, as well as Great Britain, Italy, The Netherlands, Spain, Switzerland, Sweden, Austria, France, Australia, New Zealand, Mexico, Argentina, Japan, China, Korea, Syria, India, and Pakistan, carry the name of their founder—Marie Montessori (1870–1952). She was the first woman in Italy to earn a medical degree and to practice medicine. In 1900, Montessori pioneered teaching methods to develop sensory, motor, and intellectual skills in retarded kindergarten and primary school students. Under her direction, these "unteachable" pupils not only mastered basic skills including reading and writing, but they passed the same examinations given to all primary-school students in Italy.

Montessori then spent time in normal primary-schools, where she observed the educators' practice of teaching by rote (by using repetition and memory) and their reliance on restraint, silence, and a system of reward and punishment in the classroom. She believed her system, called "scientific pedagogy," which was based on non-coercive methods and self-correcting materials (such as blocks, graduated cylinders, scaled bells, and color spectrums), would yield better results in students. Montessori theorized that children possess a natural desire to learn, and that if put into "a prepared environment," their "spontaneous activity" would prove educational. Instead of lecturing to their students, Montessori encouraged educators to simply demonstrate the correct use of materials to students who would then teach themselves and each other. She also believed in community involvement in schools, encouraging parents and other community members to take active roles in the education of the children. When Montessori put these principles into action, it was to highly favorable results.

In 1909, Montessori published the original, Italian edition of *The Montessori Method*, which was published in English three years later, and became an instant best-seller in the United States. Her method, which she believed "would develop and set free [a child's] personality in a marvelous and surprising way," caught on. For Montessori, called a "triumph of self-discipline, persistence, and courage," spreading the message about her teaching method became her life's work. She was still traveling, speaking to enthusiastic crowds the world over, when she died in The Netherlands at the age of eighty-one. Montessori's beliefs—

How has the U.S. separation of church and state effected the public schools?

Religion in American public schools continues to be a hot topic in the 1990s. But the Supreme Court rulings in the middle of the twentieth century proved to have the most bearing on religious practices in state-supported schools. On June 17,1963, the Supreme Court ruled (eight to one) that prayer and Bible-reading in the U.S. public schools were unconstitutional. The decision in the case of *Schempp v. Abington Township* culminated a series of Supreme Court rulings over the course of almost twenty years, which gradually removed the practice of religious activities from state-supported schools.

The rulings began in 1947 with the New Jersey case of *Everson v. Board of Education*, in which the Supreme Court defended the use of state funds to bus children to parochial schools, but warned that "a wall of separation between church and state" must be maintained. In 1948, in *McCollum v. Board of Education*, the Court banned a program of religious instruction from the schools of Champaign, Illinois. In *Engel v. Vitale* (1962) the justices of the Supreme Court ruled that the state-composed prayer recited in New York classrooms was unconstitutional.

which were both scientific and spiritual—had a profound effect not only on students in Montessori Schools, but on primary education in general.

When were **schools** in the U.S. **desegregated**?

On May 17, 1954, in the case of *Brown v. Board of Education*, the Supreme Court ruled (nine to zero) that racial segregation in public schools is unconstitutional. The court overturned the "separate but equal" doctrine laid down in the 1896 case *Plessy v. Ferguson*. Chief Justice Earl Warren ordered the states to proceed "with all deliberate speed"

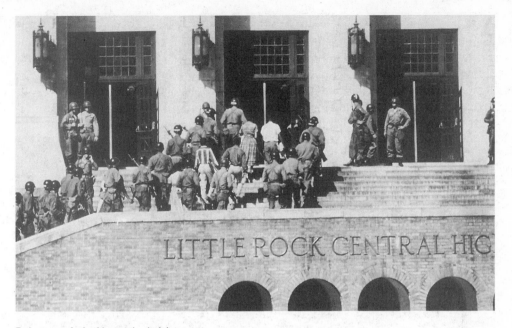

Early stages of school integration in Arkansas.

to integrate educational facilities. In the aftermath of this ruling, desegregation proceeded slowly and painfully. In the early 1960s, sit-ins, "freedom rides," and similar expressions of nonviolent resistance by blacks and their sympathizers led to a lessening of segregation practices in public facilities.

On November 7 of the same year, the Supreme Court also ordered desegregation of public golf courses, parks, swimming pools, and playgrounds.

HIGHER EDUCATION

When did **higher education** begin?

About the sixth century B.C. schools of medicine existed on the island of Cos, Greece, and there philosophers theorized on the nature of man and the universe. The Pythagoreans (followers of the Greek philosopher and mathematician Pythagoras, c. 580–500 B.C.) began the first schools of

361

What was the first American university?

It was Harvard, chartered on October 28, 1636, by the Massachusetts General Court, which passed a legislative act to found "a schoale or colledge." It was not until November of the following year, however, that there was further action; it was then that the General Court decreed that the college be built in New Town, Massachusetts, which was later renamed Cambridge. In fall of 1638, Harvard's first professor, Nathaniel Eaton, began classes, at which time the first building was under construction and a library was being assembled. The university got its name not from a founder, but from a newly arrived British philanthropist and colonial clergyman, John Harvard (1607–38), who left the library some four hundred volumes and donated about eight hundred pounds sterling to the college at New Town. The institution was named in his honor in 1639, the year after he died.

The first state university was the University of North Carolina at Chapel Hill—it was founded in 1789. And in 1795, it became the first public institution of higer education in the United States to begin enrolling students.

higher education in southern Italy, where they taught philosophy and mathematics in Greek. The great philosophers Socrates, Plato, and Aristotle carried on the Pythagoreans' tradition, as did Epicurus and Zeno in the fourth century B.C.

However, it was not until the Scientific Revolution and the Enlightenment (1500–1800) that modern education developed. The academies attended by great scientists and philosophers led to the founding of the first modern universities. Among those established during this period were the French Academy of Sciences (founded in 1666) and the Academia dei Lincei in Rome, which was attended by Galileo. The scientific methods and experimentation techniques developed in these institutions of higher learning set standards of academic inquiry that remain part of higher education in the world today.

When was the **first university** established?

The first modern university was established in the Middle Ages—1158 to be exact—in Bologna, Italy. It was in that year that Frederick I (1123–90), Holy Roman Emperor, asserted his authority in Lombardy. He granted the first university charter when he proclaimed the existence of the University of Bologna, authorizing its students to organize. The universities that were set up in Europe during that time were not places or groups of buildings; they were groups of scholars and students who organized themselves. The University of Paris, also founded in the 1100s and today known as the Sorbonne, soon became the largest and most famous university in Europe. But by 1500, universities had been founded throughout the continent. Of these, the ones that survive today include the universities of Cambridge and Oxford in England; Montpellier, Paris (the Sorbonne), and Toulouse in France; Heidelberg in Germany; Bologna, Florence, Naples, Padua, Rome, and Siena in Italy; and Salamanca in Spain.

AUTHORS WHO HAVE
STOOD THE TEST OF TIME

How **old** are **Aesop's** *Fables*?

They date back to the sixth century B.C. However it was not until the late 1600s that English-language versions appeared: In 1692, a complete translation of the stories, which are believed to have been written by a Greek slave, were published in London by Sir Roger L'Estrange, a journalist, who was also a translator. Among the lesser works of English philosopher John Locke (1632–1704) is a 1691 edition of Aesop's *Fables*, which was printed in English and Latin with the idea that the book would help children learn Latin.

Since some of the timeless fables have been traced to earlier literature, many believe it is almost certain that Aesop is a legendary figure.

Who were the **Brothers Grimm**?

The German brothers, Jacob (1785–1863) and Wilhelm (1786–1859), best known for their fairytales, were actually librarians and professors who studied law, together wrote a dictionary of the German language, and lectured at universities.

In 1805, Jacob traveled to Paris to do research on Roman law, and in a library there he found medieval German manuscripts of old stories that were slowly disintegrating; he decided the tales were too valuable to lose and he vowed to collect them. The brothers' interest in fairytales also led them to search for old traditions, legends, and tales, especially those meant for children. They traveled the German countryside, interviewing villagers in an effort to gather stories—most of which were from the oral tradition and had never been written down. The brothers were diligent in their efforts, recording everything faithfully so that nothing was added and nothing was left out. When the first volume of *Kinder- und Hausmärchen (The Children's Household Tales)* was published in 1812, children loved it. Subsequent volumes were published in German through 1815. The fairytales collected in the multi-volume work included such classics as "The History of Tom Thumb," "Little Red Riding-Hood," "Bluebeard," "Puss in Boots," "Snow White and the Seven Dwarfs," "Goldilocks and the Three Bears," "The Princess and the Pea," "The Sleeping Beauty in the Wood," and "Cinderella."

What is **"the Homeric Question"**?

During the eighteenth and nineteenth centuries, scholars became involved in a debate—referred to as "the Homeric question"—about whether both the *Iliad* and the *Odyssey* were written by the same author. The dispute continues today: scholars believe that the *Iliad* was probably written much earlier than the *Odyssey*, though there is not enough evidence to prove that Homer did not write both poems.

Several other poems, including the *Margites* and the *Batrachomyomachia*, have also been attributed to Homer, but they were most likely written by his successors.

Was **Homer** a Greek scholar?

No, it is most likely that he was an oral poet and performer. Though little is known about Homer, it's believed that he was an Ionian Greek who lived circa the eighth century B.C. In the 1920s, scholar Milman Parry proved that Homer's poems were "formulaic in nature, relying on generic epithets (such as 'wine-dark sea' and 'rosy-fingered dawn'), repetition of stock lines, and descriptions and themes typical of oral folk poetry." All of this suggested that Homer was most likely a bard or rhapsode—an itinerant professional reciter—who improvised pieces to be sung at Greek festivals.

Why is the *Iliad* so important today?

Homer's *Iliad* and *Odyssey* (both works credited to him) are considered to be among the greatest European works of literature and have had a profound influence on Western poetry, serving as the primary models for subsequent works, including the *Aeneid* (Virgil) and the *Divine Comedy* (Dante).

The *Iliad* in particular can be seen as both the beginning of Western literature as we know it and the culmination of a long tradition of oral epic poetry that may date as far back as the twelfth and thirteenth centuries B.C. The *Iliad* has been a part of Western education for nearly three thousand years. The epic poem, telling the story of the ten-year Trojan War, reveals the author's keen understanding of human nature.

Is Virgil's *Aeneid* really **an unfinished work**?

Yes, the *Aeneid* was technically unfinished by its author, Virgil (70–19 B.C.), who is considered the greatest Roman poet. Virgil spent the last ten years of his life working on the *Aeneid*, and he planned to devote three more years making revisions to this epic when, during his travels to gather new material for the poem, he became ill with fever and died. On his deathbed, Virgil had requested that his companions burn the *Aeneid*. However, Augustus, the Emperor of Rome, countermanded the request, asking Virgil's friends to edit the manuscript. Augustus did specify that the writers not add, delete, or alter the text significantly.

The *Aeneid*, Virgil's great epic about the role of Rome in world history, was published in 17 B.C. The work consists of twelve books, each between seven hundred and one thousand lines long.

What **innovations** is **Virgil** credited with?

Scholars acclaim Virgil for transforming the Greek literary traditions, which had long provided Roman writers with material, themes, and styles. Virgil populated his pastoral settings (always idealized by other writers) with contemporary figures; he combined observation with inquiry; employed a more complex syntax than had been in use; and developed realistic characters. These technical innovations informed all subsequent literature.

However, writing was not supposed to have been Virgil's occupation: In his youth, he studied rhetoric and philosophy, and he planned to practice law, but proved too shy for public speaking. So he returned to the small family farm his mother and father operated, where he studied and wrote poetry.

In addition to the *Aeneid*, Virgil wrote *Eclogues*, pastoral poems written as a response to the confiscation of his family's lands, and *Georgics*, a four-volume work glorifying the Italian countryside.

Within fifty years of his death in 19 B.C., Virgil's poems became part of the standard curriculum in Roman schools, ensuring the production of numerous copies. Virgil's works have remained accessible to scholars and students ever since.

Who was **Dante's Beatrice**?

In Dante's masterpiece the *Divine Comedy*, the central figure is led to redemption by a character named Beatrice. Dante Alighieri (1265–1321) was born and lived in Florence, Italy. In 1274, at the age of nine, he was introduced to Beatrice Portinari; they met again nine years later, and Dante was profoundly effected by her beauty and grace. When she died in 1290, Dante was inspired to commemorate her in several works, most notably *The Divine Comedy* (c. 1313–21). Beatrice is also depicted in Dante's *The New Life* (c. 1293), a collection of love poems. He wrote *The*

Why is *The Divine Comedy* so widely studied?

Simply put, *The Divine Comedy*, which consists of three books (or *cantos*), is studied not only for the beauty of its verse, but for its timeless message.

In a letter to his benefactor, Dante explains that by writing *The Divine Comedy* he would attempt "to remove those living in this life from the state of misery and lead them to the state of felicity." While the subject of the poem, according to Dante, is "the state of souls after death," allegorically, the poem is about humankind, who can exercise free will to bring "rewarding or punishing justice" upon themselves.

Dante's masterpiece is considered the seminal work of Italian literature: At the time that he wrote *The Divine Comedy*, Latin was the undisputed language of science and literature. Italian, on the other hand, was considered vulgar. By skillfully writing this poem in the vernacular rather than Latin, Dante broadened the horizons of the Italian language.

The Divine Comedy is a point of reference for writers in any language. Scholars and students agree Dante expresses universal truths in this work, which is also a finely crafted piece of literature.

Banquet (c. 1304-07), another collection of lyrical poems, to commemorate Beatrice's death.

Who did **Shakespeare** study?

It is thought that Shakespeare attended the King's New School, the local grammar school in Stratford-upon-Avon, England, where the main course of instruction was in Latin. There, students were taught rhetoric, logic, and ethics and studied works by classical authors Terence, Plautus, Cicero, Virgil, Plutarch, Horace, and Ovid. It is believed that this

Playwright William Shakespeare.

was the extent of Shakespeare's education; there is no evidence that he attended any university.

Why is **Shakespeare** so **widely studied**?

English dramatist Ben Jonson (1572–1637) said it best when he proclaimed that Shakespeare "was not of an age, but for all time." Most teachers and students, not to mention critics and theater-goers throughout the ages, likely agree with Jonson's remark: Shakespeare's canon (consisting of thirty-seven plays, plus poems and sonnets) expresses universal and unchanging human concerns—as no other works have. Shakespeare's words are familiar even to those who have not studied them, not simply because of the many contemporary adaptations of his works, but because Shakespearean phrases and variations of phrases have, through the years, fallen into common usage. Consider these few examples from *Hamlet* alone: "Neither a borrower nor a lender be" (Act I, scene iii); "to thine own self be true" (Act I, scene iii); and "The play's the thing" (Act II, scene ii).

Was **Shakespeare** famous in **his own time**?

Yes, beginning in 1592, he was well known as a dramatist. William Shakespeare (born 1564) was the son of John Shakespeare, who belonged to the merchant class, and Mary Arden, who came from a family of slightly higher social standing. His first plays, the three parts of the Henry VI history cycle, were presented in London in 1589–91. The first reference to Shakespeare in the London literary world dates from 1592, when dramatist Robert Greene alluded to him as "an upstart crow."

The critical remark notwithstanding, Shakespeare's literary reputation and his acclaim grew over the next few years. He experimented with classical dramatic forms in the early tragedy *Titus Andronicus* (1593–94), issued a pair of narrative poems *Venus and Adonis* (1593), and wrote *The Rape of Lucrece* (1594). These works, which played to the fashion for poems on mythological themes, were immensely successful, establishing "honey-tongued Shakespeare"—as his contemporary Francis Meres called him—as a prominent writer.

Shakespeare further established himself as a professional actor and playwright when he joined the Lord Chamberlain's Men, an acting company formed in 1594 when they began performing at theaters in London. They became the foremost London company, largely attributable to the fact that after joining the group in 1594, Shakespeare wrote for no other company.

What is a **"poet laureate"**?

A poet laureate is someone who is recognized by their country (or region) as its most eminent and representative poet. Officially, a poet

How did the word "Machiavellian" get its meaning?

Machiavellian is defined as "characterized by cunning, duplicity, or bad faith." It's based on the theory of Italian diplomat Niccolò Machiavelli (1469–1527), who developed a code of political conduct that operates independent of ethics, thus disregarding moral authorities such as classical philosophy and Christian theology.

In 1513, after having been exiled from Florence, Italy, by the Medici family, Machiavelli abruptly turned his attention to writing *The Prince*, which puts forth a calm and uncompromising analysis of techniques and methods that the successful ruler must use in order to gain—and keep—power. Written in the form of advice to the ruler, Machiavelli advises the Prince that only one consideration should govern his decisions: the effectiveness of a particular course of action, regardless of its ethical character. The book had little immediate impact in Italy, although it soon became legendary throughout Europe and its major ideas are familiar today even to people who have never read the book.

laureate is appointed or named by the government. The first poet laureate of England was Ben Jonson (1572–1637), a contemporary of Shakespeare. (Shakespeare acted a leading role in the first of Jonson's great plays, *Every Man in His Humor*.)

In 1605, Jonson began writing a series of masques (short, allegorical dramas that were performed by actors wearing masks) for the court. Years later, in 1616, he was appointed poet laureate and in that capacity received a "substantial pension." Among Jonson's works are *Volpone* (1606), *Works* (a collection of poetry published in 1616), and *Pleasure Reconciled to Virtue* (1618).

However, the title of poet laureate was not conferred on an English writer until John Dryden, who received the official distinction in 1670. Other poet laureates of England included William Wordsworth (1770–1850) and Lord Alfred Tennyson (1809–92).

Why is **Milton** considered so important to **English literature**?

Except for Shakespeare, the works of John Milton (1608–74) have been the subject of more commentary than those of any other English writer. Milton is considered one of only a few writers to take their place in "the small circle of great epic writers." According to *Norton Anthology of English Literature*, in Milton's writings "two tremendous intellectual and social movements come to a head." The movements referred to are the Renaissance and the Reformation. Scholars point to Milton's use of classical references and the rich tapestry of his works as being Renaissance in nature, while his "earnest and individually-minded Christianity" are resonant of the Reformation. For example, in his masterpiece *Paradise Lost* (1667), Milton, like Homer and Virgil before him, takes on humankind's entire experience—war, love, religion, hell, heaven, and the cosmos. But rather than having Adam triumph over evil through an act of heroism, he "accepts the burden of worldly existence, and triumphs over his guilt by admitting it and repenting it."

In addition to his famous epics, Milton wrote sonnets and other short poems, including "On Shakespeare," "L'Allegro," "Il Penseroso," and "Lycidas." His writings also include political discourse, chief of which is the essay *Areopagitica* (1644). Among the ideas that Milton championed were the limitation of the monarchy, dethroning of bishops, freedom of speech, and the institution of divorce. One commentator mused that "the guarantees of freedom in the United States Constitution owe more to Milton's *Areopagitica* than to John Locke." In *Areopagitica*, Milton sets forth the notion that untested virtue is no virtue at all—that humankind is purified by trial, that we "might see and know, and yet abstain."

Why was **Voltaire** exiled from France?

Voltaire, born Francois-Marie Arouet in 1694, was actually exiled twice during his lifetime—once within France and once outside of France. A principal figure of the French Enlightenment, Voltaire was a prolific writer. To the European literary world, he embodied the highest ideal of the Age of Reason. Yet victims of his biting wit both feared and denigrated him, which twice led to his exile.

The son of a prosperous solicitor, Voltaire studied at the College Louis-le-Grand (1704–11). As a young man in Paris, he wrote and circulated verse criticizing the regent, Phillipe d'Orleans. As a result of these offensive works, Voltaire was subjected to a state-mandated internal exile.

Voltaire's epic about Henri IV, infused with indictments of fanaticism as well as praise for religious toleration, were highly controversial for their time. These anti-establishment protests eventually led Voltaire to have an argument with the chevalier de Rohan, a member of one of the most powerful families of France. This conflict resulted in Voltaire's arrest, imprisonment, and exile to England in 1726.

What were **Voltaire's beliefs**?

While Voltaire wrote several masterpieces, including *Candide*, *Letters concerning the English Nation*, and the *Philosophical Dictionary*, he may well be known more for his beliefs than for his body of works. He believed in God, but abhorred "priestly" traditions, even though he was educated by Jesuit teachers whom he always admired. Voltaire spread the doctrines of rational skepticism to the world, strongly advocated religious and political tolerance, and seemed to have great faith in humankind's ability to strive for perfection.

Why do economists still regard **Adam Smith** so highly?

Scottish economist Adam Smith (1723–90) is popular with conservative economists today because of his work *The Wealth of Nations* (written in 1776), which proposes a system of natural liberty in trade and commerce—in other words, a free market economy. Smith, who was teaching at the University of Glasgow at the time, wrote "Consumption is the sole end and purpose of all production, and the interest of the producer ought to be attended to, only so far as it may be necessary for promoting that of the consumer."

The Wealth of Nations established the classical school of political economy but has been faulted for showing no awareness of the developing industrial revolution. While Smith advocated both free-market competition and limited government intervention, he also viewed unemployment as a necessary evil to keep costs—and therefore prices—in check.

What was Goethe's contribution to world literature?

Johann Wolfgang Goethe (1749–1832) is considered Germany's greatest writer. He also was a scientist, artist, musician, and philosopher. As a writer, Goethe experimented with many genres and literary styles, and his works became a shaping force in the major German literary movements of the late eighteenth and early nineteenth centuries. His drama *Faust* ranks beside the works of Dante and Shakespeare, and in so doing is the embodiment of his own humanistic ideal of a world literature—that it transcends the boundaries of nations and historical periods.

How did a **Frenchman** come to be one of the earliest and most astute observers of **American democracy**?

Aristocrat Alexis de Tocqueville (1805–59) was only twenty-six years old when he traveled to New York with his colleague and a friend, Gustave de Beaumont, to study and observe American democracy.

Though Tocqueville set out with the pretext of studying the American penal system on behalf of the French government (both he and Beaumont were magistrates at the time), he had the deliberate and personal goal of conducting an on-site investigation of the world's first and (then) only completely democratic society: the United States. Tocqueville and Beaumont traveled for nine months through New England, eastern Canada, New York, Philadelphia, Baltimore, Washington, Cincinnati, Tennessee, and New Orleans.

The pair returned to France in 1832 and the following year published their study, *On the Penitentiary System in the United States and Its Application in France*. Once this official obligation was behind him, Tocqueville left his post as magistrate, and moved into a modest Paris apartment. There he devoted two years to writing *Democracy in America* (1835, 1840). The work was soon proclaimed the classic treatment of its subject throughout the Western world and secured Tocqueville's fame as political observer, philosopher, and, later, sociologist.

Tocqueville proclaimed that during his travels "Nothing struck me more forcibly than the general equality of conditions . . . All classes meet continually and no haughtiness at all results from the differences in social position. Everyone shakes hands. . . ." But he also foresaw the possibility that the principles of economic equality would be undermined by the American passion for equality, which not only "tends to elevate the humble to the rank of the great," but also "impels the weak to attempt to lower the powerful to their own level." While he warned against the possible tyranny of the majority as a hazard of democracy, he also added that law, religion, and the press provide safeguards against democratic despotism.

Which came first—the word **"scrooge"** or **Charles Dickens's character Ebenezer Scrooge**?

The character Ebenezer Scrooge came first, brought to life in Dickens's extremely popular story *A Christmas Carol*, published in 1843. By 1899, "scrooge," meaning a miserly person, had entered into usage.

Dickens (1812–70) created many memorable characters: Oliver Twist, Tiny Tim, and Little Nell, to name a few. Among the English writer's most notable works are *Oliver Twist* (1838), *The Old Curiosity Shop* (1841), *A Tale of Two Cities* (1859), *Bleak House* (1853), and *Great Expectations* (1861). Dickens was popular during his own time, and is still popular today—attributable not only to the vivid characters he created, but for his expression of social concerns. Though he grew more pessimistic in his later works, Dickens continued to demonstrate his profound sympathy for the oppressed and his belief in the dignity of man.

Who was the **first** to write a **modern novel**?

While there are differing opinions on the answer to this question, it is generally accepted that the credit for the novel as we know it belongs to Spanish writer Miguel de Cervantes (1547–1616). Cervantes wrote *Don Quixote* (1605, 1616): it was the first extended prose narrative in European literature in which characters and events are depicted in what came to be called the modern realistic tradition. Considered an epic masterpiece, *Don Quixote* had an undeniable influence on early novelists, including Henry Fielding (who wrote *Tom Jones*). *Don Quixote* is also said to have anticipated later fictional masterpieces, including Gustave Flaubert's *Madame Bovary* (1857), Fyodor Dostoevsky's *The Idiot* (1868), and Mark Twain's *Tom Sawyer* (1876) and *Huckleberry Finn* (1884).

Critics and scholars agree that it is French writer Flaubert (1821–80) who developed the modern novel into a "conscious art form." Flaubert's *Madame Bovary* is recognized for its objective characterization, irony, narrative technique, and use of imagery and symbolism. American writer Henry James (1843–1916) is acknowledged for having enlarged the scope of the novel, introducing dramatic elements to the narrative, developing point of view technique, and advocating realism in literature. James's works include *The American* (1877), *Daisy Miller* (1879), and *The Ambassadors* (1903).

It is Irish writer James Joyce (1882–1941), considered the most prominent English-speaking literary figure of the first half of the twentieth century, who is often credited with redefining the modern novel. Joyce experimented with the form—and revolutionized it—through his first novel, *A Portrait of the Artist as a Young Man* (1916) and with his masterpiece *Ulysses* (1922).

What is **Proust's** claim to literary fame?

Marcel Proust (1871–1922) is generally considered the greatest French novelist of the twentieth century and is credited with introducing to fiction the elements of psychological analysis, an innovative treatment of time, and manifold themes. Proust is primarily known for his multi-volume work *A la recherche du temps perdu* (1954), which was published in English as *Remembrance of Things Past*. Proust was an imaginative stylist as well as shrewd social observer.

In the mid–1890s, Proust joined other prominent artists, including the great French novelist of the nineteenth century, Emile Zola (1840–1902), to form the protest group known as the Revisionists or Dreyfusards. The artists were staunch supporters of Alfred Dreyfus (1859–1935), and therefore vocal critics of the French military, whom they accused of anti-Semitism for keeping Dreyfus, wrongly accused of treason, imprisoned on Devil's Island.

When did American poetry begin?

As the self-described poet of democracy, Walt Whitman (1819–92) was the first to compose a truly American verse—one that showed no references to European antecedents and that unequivocally articulated the American experience. He is credited with liberating poetry from its narrative and ode forms.

His first published poetry was the collection *Leaves of Grass* (1855). In an effort to gain recognition, Whitman promptly sent a copy to the preeminent man of American letters Ralph Waldo Emerson (1803–82), who could count as his acquaintances and friends the great British poets William Wordsworth and Samuel Taylor Coleridge, the renowned Scottish essayist Thomas Carlyle, as well as prominent American writers Henry David Thoreau and Nathaniel Hawthorne. It was a bold move on Whitman's part, but it paid off: While *Leaves of Grass* had been unfavorably received by American reviewers, Emerson composed a five-page tribute, expressing his enthusiasm for the poetry and remarking that Whitman was "at the beginning of a great career." Thoreau, too, praised the work. More than a century later, biographer Justin Kaplan acclaimed that in its time *Leaves of Grass* was "the most brilliant and original poetry yet written in the New World, at once the fulfillment of American literary romanticism and the beginnings of American literary modernism."

Whitman's well-known and frequently studied poems include "Song of Myself," "O Captain! My Captain!", "Song of the Open Road," and "I Sing the Body Electric."

While she was virtually unknown for her poetry during her lifetime, Emily Dickenson (1830–86) was writing at about the same time as Whitman, publishing only a handful of poems before her death. Collections of Dickenson's works were published posthumously and today she, too, is regarded as one of the great American poets. Had more of her poems been brought out in print, perhaps Dickenson would have been recognized as the first truly American poet.

Why was **James Joyce's *Ulysses*** banned in the United States?

James Joyce's masterpiece was originally published in 1922 (it had been serialized prior to then) by the Paris bookstore Shakespeare and Company. By 1928, it was officially listed as obscene by the U.S. Customs Court. The reason was twofold: the use of four-letter words and the stream-of-consciousness narrative of one of the characters, which reveals her innermost thoughts. When the official stance on the book was challenged in U.S. court in 1933, the judge (John Woolsey) called it a "sincere and honest book," and after long reflection he ruled that the book be openly admitted into the United States.

Random House, the American publisher who had advocated the obscenity charge be challenged in court, promptly began typesetting the work in order to release a U.S. edition. But the decision had important and lasting legal impact as well: it was a turning point in reducing government prohibition of obscenity. Prior to the case, laws that prohibited obscenity were not seen to be in conflict with the First Amendment of the U.S. Constitution (which is most often interpreted as a guarantee of freedom of speech), and the U.S. Post Office and the Customs Service alike both had the power to determine obscenity. The government appealed the decision to the Circuit Court of Appeals, but Judge Woolsey's decision held.

Writer William Faulkner (1897–1962) was the beneficiary of—or American counterpart to—Joyce's experimentation with the form of the novel. The author of *The Sound and the Fury* (1929), *Light in August* (1932), and *Absalom! Absalom!* (1936), Faulkner, in his acceptance speech for the Nobel Prize for literature in 1949, stated that the fundamental theme of his fiction is "the human heart in conflict with itself." This he explored by employing a variety of narrative techniques, which, like Joyce's, departed radically from normal methods.

What were the lasting effects of the **Harlem Renaissance**?

The Harlem Renaissance (1925–35) marked the first time that white Americans (principally intellects and artists) gave serious attention to the culture of African Americans. The movement, which had by some accounts begun as early as 1917, was noted in a 1925 *New York Herald Tribune* article that announced, "we are on the edge, if not in the midst, of what might not improperly be called a Negro Renaissance." The first African American Rhodes scholar, Alain Locke (1886–1954), who was a professor of philosophy at Howard University, led and shaped the movement during which Upper Manhattan became a hotbed of creativity in the post-World War I era.

Not only was there a flurry activity, but there was a heightened sense of pride as well. The movement left the country with a legacy of literary works including those by poets Jean Toomer (his 1923 work *Cane* is generally considered the first novel of the Harlem Renaissance), Langston Hughes (*The Weary Blues*, 1926; *Fine Clothes to the Jew*, 1927), and Countee Cullen (*Color*, in 1925; *Copper Sun*, 1927); as well as those by writers Jessie Fauset (editor of *The Crisis*, the journal of the NAACP, by the time of her death in 1961, she had published more novels than any other Harlem Renaissance writer), Claude McKay (whose 1928 novel *Home to Harlem* evoked strong criticism from W. E. B. Du Bois and Alain Locke for its portrayal of black life), and Zora Neale Hurston (the author of the highly acclaimed 1937 novel *Their Eyes Were Watching God*, she was the first black woman to be honored for her creative writing with a prestigious Guggenheim fellowship).

The Harlem Renaissance was not only about literature however: jazz and blues music also benefitted during the prosperous times of the postwar era, and continued to develop during the Great Depression. It was during these decades that the likes of Louis Armstrong, Jelly Roll Morton, Duke Ellington, Bessie Smith, Ethel Waters, and Josephine Baker rose to prominence, and their contributions to music performance are still felt by artists and audiences, regardless of color.

FINE ART

What are the hallmarks of **Botticelli's** paintings?

The works of Sandro Botticelli (1445–1510), one of the early painters of the Italian Renaissance, are known for their serene compositions, refined elegance, and spirituality. A student of Florentine painter Fra

Filippo Lippi (1406–69), Botticelli refined Lippi's method of drawing such that he is considered one of the great "masters of the line."

Botticelli's work was soon eclipsed by that of Leonardo da Vinci, who was just a few years younger than he, but whose range of talents made Botticelli's work seem dated. Nevertheless, late in the nineteenth century, Botticelli began to be revered again by artists and critics alike. The English Pre-Raphaelites hailed his works for their simplicity and sincerity. English art critic and Pre-Raphaelite defender John Ruskin (1819–1900) held Botticelli up as an example of an artist who presented nature as an expression of a divinely created world.

Why is **Botticelli's *The Birth of Venus*** so well known?

This immediately recognizable painting (c. 1482) is most likely known for its elegant figures, use of pictorial space, and decorative detail, which give the painting a tapestry effect. At the time it was painted, the presentation of a nude Venus was an innovation since the use of unclothed figures in art had been prohibited during the Middle Ages. Botticelli, however, felt free to render Venus in this way since the work was commissioned by Florence's powerful Medici family, who were his patrons. Under their protection, Botticelli could pursue the world of his imagination without fearing charges of paganism and infidelity.

Though *The Birth of Venus* is extremely well known, *The Magnificat* (1483), Botticelli's round picture of the Madonna with singing angels, is his most copied work.

Why was the **Medici family** so important to **Renaissance art**?

The Medici family was powerful in Florence and Tuscany, Italy, between the fourteenth and sixteenth centuries. The founder of the family was Giovanni di Bicci de' Medici (1360–1429), who had amassed a large fortune through his skill in trade and who virtually ruled Florence between 1421–29.

Later, Lorenzo de' Medici (1449–92), ruled Florence from 1478–92. Though he was tyrannical, he was a great patron of the arts and letters. Lorenzo (also called "The Magnificent") maintained Fiesole, a villa out-

379

side Florence, where he surrounded himself with the great talents and thinkers of Florence, including a young artist named Sandro Botticelli. Lorenzo was also a patron of Michelangelo.

Why is **da Vinci** referred to as the **"universal man"**?

Leonardo da Vinci (1452–1519) possessed an intensely curious mind and an inventive imagination. He is known by students both for his famous works of art including *The Last Supper* (1495–98) and *Mona Lisa* (1503–05), as well as for his scientific notes and drawings dealing with matters of botany, anatomy, zoology, hydraulics, and physiology. By his own claim, he pursued scientific investigations only to make himself a better painter. Nevertheless, he clearly endeavored to understand the laws of nature. Consequently, he made a study of man, contributing to our understanding of physiology and psychology.

Leonardo da Vinci's body of work provided the foundation of High Renaissance sculpture, painting, drawing, and architecture. As an artist-genius, da Vinci earned the epithet "universal man," and has become a wonder of the modern world, for having stood at the beginning of "a new epoch like a prophet and a sage" (*Gardner's Art through the Ages*).

Did **Michelangelo** study anatomy?

Yes: In 1492, Michelangelo Buonarroti (1475–1564), a master sculptor of the human form, undertook the study of anatomy based on the dissection of corpses from the Hospital of Santo Spirito.

Perhaps most well known for his sculptures of *David* (1501–04) and *Moses* (1515–15), as well as his frescoes on the ceiling and walls of the Sistine Chapel, Michelangelo was also an architect who believed that architecture should follow the form of the human body "to the extent of disposing units symmetrically around a central and unique axis, in a relationship like that of the arms to the body." He also wrote poetry—a true Renaissance man.

Michelangelo was totally absorbed in his work and was known to be impatient with himself and with others. He has been likened to Beethoven since the personal letters of both men reveal a "deep sympa-

Michaelangelo's *David*.

thy and concern for those close to them, and profound understanding of humanity informs their works" (*Gardner's*).

Of the great trio of **High Renaissance artists**—Leonardo, Michelangelo, and Raphael—who is considered *the* master?

Most historians and critics agree that it was Raphael Sanzio (1483–1520) who most clearly stated the ideals of the High Renaissance. Though archrivals Leonardo and Michelangelo influenced the younger Raphael, 381 he developed his own style. A prolific painter, he was also a great technician whose work is characterized by a seemingly effortless grace.

His most well-known work is *The School of Athens* (1509–11), which has been called "a complete statement of the High Renaissance in its artistic form and spiritual meaning." The painting, which projects a stage-like space onto a two-dimensional surface, reconvenes the great minds of the ancient world—Plato, Aristotle, Pythagoras, Herakleitos, Diogenes, Euclid—for an exchange of ideas. Raphael even included himself in this gathering of greatness. But it seems only appropriate for the master to be in such company: In this work, Raphael has achieved the art of perspective, bringing the discipline of mathematics to pictorial space where human figures appear to move naturally.

Why is **Titian** thought of as the father of modern painting?

During Titian's time (1490–1576), artists began painting on canvas rather than on wood panels. A master of color, the Venetian painter was both popular and prolific. His work was so sought after that even with the help of numerous assistants, he could not keep up with demand.

His body of works established oil color on canvas as the typical medium of Western pictorial tradition. Among his most well known paintings are *Sacred and Profane Love* (c. 1515) and *Venus of Urbino* (1538).

Which **van Eyck**—Hubert or Jan—painted *The Ghent Altarpiece*?

The large, multi-paneled altarpiece is as controversial as it is admired. The controversy stems from an 1832 discovery (under a coat of paint on one of its outside panels) of a Latin poem that indicated that Hubert had begun the work and Jan had completed it. So it was believed that *The Ghent Altarpiece*, (1432) was a collaboration between the Flemish brothers.

But the question of attribution continued to puzzle art historians for a century and a half as attempts to assign different parts of the polyptych to either of the brothers failed to gain acceptance. One art historian suggested that Hubert, the elder of the two, may not have been a painter at all, but rather a sculptor. This theory posited that Hubert's contribution was only in crafting the frames—from which the paintings had been removed in 1566 and which were subsequently lost. However, scholars seem to have now reached the consensus that Hubert was largely responsible for the design of the altarpiece and for much of its execution, while Jan was the designer and painter of most of the figures. This elaborate altarpiece, which is composed of twenty folding panels, was typical of northern European art during the Middle Ages. However, both van Eycks contributed to the flowering of Renaissance art in northern Europe as well.

In Jan's works, which are finely detailed and ornamental (he was originally a miniaturist and illuminator), the progression from Medieval to Renaissance art can be seen. In particular, his painting *Man in a Red Turban* (1433), which may be a self portrait, marks an important step in the humanization of art: Prior to this, the artist's subjects had been religious in nature; here the painting is simply a record of a living individual. This kind of portraiture began to multiply as artists and patrons alike became increasingly interested in the reality revealed by them. Through such portraits, man began to confront himself—rather than the "otherworldly anonymity of the Middle Ages." Renaissance art—in Italy as well as in northern Europe—marks the "climax of the slow but mighty process that brings man's eyes down from the supernatural to the natural world" (*Gardner's*).

Why is **Rembrandt** considered the archetype of the modern artist?

To understand the similarities between Rembrandt (1606–69) and the modern artist, it's important to note that this master portrait-painter, who broke ground in his use of light and shadow, was in his own time criticized for his work: Some thought it too personal or too eccentric. An Italian biographer asserted that Rembrandt's works were concerned with the ugly, and he described the artist as a tasteless painter. Rembrandt's subjects included lower-class people, the events of everyday life and everyday business, as well as the humanity and humility of Christ (rather than the choirs, trumpets, and celestial triumph that were the nature of other religious paintings at the time). His portraits reveal his interest in the effects of time on human features—including his own. In summary, the Dutch artist approached his work with "psychological insight and . . . profound sympathy for the human affliction." He was also known to use the butt end of his brush to apply paint. Thus, he strayed outside the accepted limits of great art at the time.

383

Art critics today recognize Rembrandt as not only one of the great portrait painters, but as a master of realism. The Dutch painter, who also etched, drew, and made prints, is regarded as an example for the working artist; he showed that the subject is less important than what the artist does with his materials.

Among his most acclaimed works are *The Syndics of the Cloth Guild* (1662) and *The Return of the Prodigal Son* (c. 1665). The first painting shows the board of directors going over the books, and Rembrandt astutely captures the moment when the six businessmen are interrupted, thus showing a remarkably real everyday scene. *The Return of the Prodigal Son* is one of the most moving religious paintings of all time. Here Rembrandt has with great compassion rendered the reunion of father and son, capturing that moment of mercy when the contrite son kneels before his forgiving father.

Through his series of self-portraits, Rembrandt documented his own history—from the confidence and optimism of his youth to the "worn resignation of his declining years."

So much art is called impressionistic today—**what is impressionism**?

The term "impressionism" was derived by a rather mean-spirited art critic from the title of one of Claude Monet's (1840–1926) early paintings, *Impression, Fog (La Havre*; 1872). The painters were interested in the experience of the natural world and in rendering it exactly as it is seen—not fixed and frozen with an absolute perspective, but rather as constantly changing and as it is glimpsed by a moving eye.

George Seurat and Paul Signac are also typically thought of as impressionists, however they are more appropriately dubbed "neo-impressionists" since they, along with Pisarro, advanced the work of the original group through more scientific theories of light and color, introducing deliberate optical effects to their works. Seurat and Signac are commonly referred to as "pointalists" for the technique, pioneered by Seurat, of using small brush strokes to create an intricate mosaic effect. The "post-impressionists," artists representing a range of explorations but all having come out of the impressionist movement, included both Seurat and Signac, as well as Henri de Toulouse-Lautrec, Paul Gaugin,

Was Monet the father of (French) impressionism?

Though the movement was named for one of Claude Monet's paintings and his *Water Lilies* (1905) are arguably the most well-known and highly acclaimed impressionist works, impressionism is actually rooted in the works of the group's spiritual leader Edouard Manet (1823–83), who first began experimenting with color and light to bring a more naturalistic quality to painting. Thus, one could argue that Manet was the father of French impressionism.

In 1863, Manet exhibited two highly controversial and groundbreaking works: *Déjeuner sur l'herbe* and *Olympia*. Both paintings were based on classic subjects, but Manet rendered these pastoral scenes according to his own experience, giving them a decidedly more earthy and blatantly erotic quality than the Parisian critics and academicians could accept. He was roundly criticized for his scandalous exhibition. Nevertheless, Manet persevered and in 1868, with his portrait of the French writer Emile Zola, he again challenged the art world and its values. A critic for *Le National* denounced the portrait and cited among his complaints that Zola's trousers were not made of cloth. This was both truth and revelation: the pants were made of paint. A few years later, in 1870, Manet began experimenting with painting outside, in the brilliance of natural sunlight. Thus, Manet pioneered many of the ideas taken up by the impressionists.

Vincent Van Gogh, and Paul Cézanne (who was also associated with the original impressionists).

Together the impressionists paved the way for the art of the twentieth-century, since as a group they "asserted the identity of a painting as a thing, a created object in its own right, with its own structure and its own laws beyond and different from . . . the world of man and nature" (*History of Modern Art*).

How does one characterize **Picasso's** work?

It's impossible to characterize the work of Spaniard Pablo Picasso (1881–1973) since his career as an artist spanned his entire life and he experimented with many disciplines. Picasso often claimed that he could draw before he could speak, and by all accounts, he spent much of his childhood engaged in drawing. He was only fifteen years old when he submitted his first works for exhibition. And by the turn of the century, when he was but a young man, he began exploring the blossoming modern arts movement. The rest of his career breaks into several periods:

His Blue period (1901–04) was named for the monochromatic use of the color for its subjects, and was likely the result of a despair brought on by the suicide of a friend. Next came his Rose period (beginning 1905), when images of harlequins and jesters appear in his works—all to a somewhat melancholic effect. He soon began to incorporate aspects of primitive art, and later experimented with geometric line and form in his works, which were constructions—or deconstructions—sometimes only identifiable by their title.

In the spring of 1912, Cubism exploded and Picasso was on its forefront. In 1923, he broke new ground with Surrealism. The key masterpiece in his body of works came in 1937 when he painted *Guernica*, his rendering of the horror of the German attack (supported by the Spanish fascists) on the small Basque town in Spain. His career reached its height during the 1940s, during which he lived in (Nazi-occupied) Paris.

Biographer Pierre Cabbane summed up the last period (1944–73) of Picasso's work: "(H)e invented a second classicism: autobiographical classicism. . . . (H)is final thirty years were to be a dizzying, breakneck race toward creation." During this time, Picasso did not chart any new artistic territory, but simply created art at an amazing rate. After his death in 1973, his estate yielded an inventory of thirty-five thousand remaining works—paintings, drawings, sculpture, ceramics, prints and woodcuts.

He left an enormous—even mind-boggling—legacy to the art world. In a 1991 article in *Vanity Fair*, Picasso's friend and biographer John Richardson observed, "Almost every artist of any interest who's worked in the last fifty years is indebted to Picasso . . . whether he's reacting against him knowingly or is unwittingly influenced by him. Picasso sowed the seeds whose fruits we are continuing to reap."

Why were **Matisse's** paintings considered so shocking when they were debuted?

Even if they seem commonplace to art today, the color and style of the paintings of French expressionist Henri Matisse (1869–1954) were revolutionary in their day.

In 1905, Matisse, along with several other artists, exhibited works at Paris's Salon d'Automne. The wildly colorful paintings on display there are said to have prompted an art critic to exclaim that they were *fauves*, or "wild beasts." The name stuck: Matisse and his contemporaries who were using brilliant colors in an arbitrary fashion became known as the Fauves. His famous work *Madame Matisse*, or *Green Stripe* (1905), showed his wife with blue hair, and a green stripe running down the middle of her face, which was colored pink on one side and yellow on the other. Matisse was at the forefront of a movement that was building new artistic values. The Fauves were not using color in a scientific manner (as George Seurat had done), nor were they using it in the non-descriptive manner of Paul Gaugin (1848–1903) and Vincent Van Gogh (1853–90). The Fauves were developing the concept of abstraction.

Throughout his career, Matisse continued to experiment with various art forms—painting, paper cutouts, and sculptures. All of his works indicate a progressive elimination of detail and simplification of line and color. So influential was his style on modern art that some seventy years later, one art critic commented that it was as if Matisse belonged to a later generation—and a different world.

ARCHITECTURE

When did **modern architecture begin**?

The term "modern architecture" is used to refer to the architecture that turned away from past historical designs in favor of designs that are expressive of their own time. As such, it had its beginnings in the late nineteenth century when architects began reacting to the eclecticism

387

that was prevalent at the time. Two "schools" emerged: Art Nouveau and the Chicago School.

Art Nouveau, which had begun about 1890, held sway in Europe for some twenty years, and was evident not only in architecture and interiors, but in furniture, jewelry, typography, sculpture, painting, and other fine and applied arts. Its proponents included Belgian architects Victor Horta (1861–1947) and Henry Van de Velde (1863–1957), and Spaniard Antoni Gaudi (1852–1926).

But it was the Chicago School that, in the rebuilding days after the Great Chicago Fire (1871), created an entirely new form. American engineer and architect William Le Baron Jenney (1832–1907) led the way. Four of the five younger architects who followed him had at one time worked in Jenney's office: Louis Henry Sullivan (1856–1924), Martin Roche (1855–1927), William Holabird (1854–1923), and Daniel Hudson Burnham (1846–1912). Burnham was joined by another architect, John Wellborn Root (1850–91). Together these men established solid principles for the design of modern buildings and skyscrapers where "form followed function." Ornament was used sparingly and the architects fully utilized iron, steel, and glass.

By the 1920s, modern architecture had taken firm hold and in the mid-twentieth century was furthered by the works of Walter Adolf Gropius (1883–1969), Le Corbusier (Charles-Édouard Jeanneret; 1887–1965), Ludwig Mies van der Rohe (1886–1969), and Frank Lloyd Wright (1867–1959). For practical purposes, modern architecture ended in the 1960s with the deaths of the aforementioned masters.

Examples of modern architecture include Chicago's Monadnock Building (1891), Reliance Building (1895), Carson Pirie Scott Store (1904), and Robie House (1909); New York City's Rockefeller Center (1940), Lever House (1952), and Seagram Building (1958); as well as Taliesin West (1938–59) in Arizona, Johnson Wax Company's Research Tower (1949) in Wisconsin, and the Lovell House (1929) in Los Angeles.

Who **invented** the **skyscraper**?

The credit is usually given to American architect William Le Baron Jenney (1832–1907) who designed the ten-story Home Insurance Building, erected on the corner of LaSalle and Monroe streets in Chicago in 1885. The building was the first in which the entire structure was of skeleton construction—of cast iron, wrought iron, and Bessemer steel. However, some experts believe the first skyscraper to have been designed was one by the American firm Holabird and Roche, also in Chicago. The firm, founded by two former students of Jenney, designed the skeleton-framed Tacoma Building, which was actually not completed until 1889. Both the Home Insurance Building and the Tacoma Building were demolished in the 1920s.

It was the use of steel, the innovation of a safe elevator, and the use of central heating that combined to make possible the construction of tall buildings toward the end of the nineteenth century. Once the trend had started, it quickly took off: Another Chicago firm, Burnham and Root (Burnham, too, had been a student of Jenney), completed the fourteen-story Reliance Building in 1895; it had a steel skeleton frame. The further development of the skyscraper is visible in the Gage Buildings (in Chicago)—two of which were designed by Holabird and Roche, and one by Louis Henry Sullivan (1856–1924), the Chicago architect often credited for mastering the skyscraper. Other Chicago skyscrapers built by Holabird and Roche during the early days of modern architecture include the Marquette Building (1894) and the Tribune Building (1901).

When New York's Chrysler Building (William Van Alen, architect) went up in 1930, its seventy-five stories broke the record for tallest building—the next tallest was only twenty stories. But the Chrysler Building held that distinction for only a year: In 1931, the 102-story Empire State Building (designed by Shreve, Lamb, and Harmon) was completed. That New York City landmark held on to the tallest building title for more than forty years, losing it in 1973 to the World Trade Center (NYC), which was equaled—or at least rivaled by—the Sears Tower in Chicago, completed in 1974.

When was **photography** established as an art form?

In the early 1900s. Alfred Stieglitz (1865–1946) is the acknowledged pioneer of modern photography. His interest in photography began when he was but a toddler: At the age of two, he had become obsessed with a photo of his cousin, carrying it with him at all times. When he was nine

389

years old, he met his first photographer. He took exception to the professional's practice of using pigment to color the black-and-white photo, citing that this spoiled the quality of the print.

Between 1887 and 1911, Stieglitz worked to establish photography as a valid form of artistic expression, a pursuit for which he was sometimes publicly derided. He believed that photography should be separate from painting, but on an equal footing as an art form. He also strove to differentiate photography by instilling it with an American essence. Thus the streets of New York City became his subject. By the time Stieglitz founded the Photo-Secession Group in 1902, he had developed a uniquely American art form. Stieglitz also published and edited photography magazines, most notably *Camera Work* (1903–17). After an unhappy first marriage, in 1924, Stieglitz married American artist Georgia O'Keefe (1887–1986), who became the subject of one of his best-known series of works.

THEATER

What is *No* drama?

It is a form of Japanese drama dating back to A.D. 1383. It has at its roots the principles of Zen Buddhism, which emphasizes rigorous meditation and discipline and the transition of truth from master to disciple. *No* dramas were traditionally performed on a bare, wooden stage by male actors who wore masks to portray women, supernatural beings, or old men. The art form was pioneered by actor-dramatist Motokiyo Zeami when he was twenty years old. Zeami had begun acting at age seven and went on to write more than 240 *No* plays before he died in 1443.

What are the elements of Japanese *Kabuki*?

In 1603, the Japanese embraced *Kabuki*, a popular new theater form where the actors dressed in colorful costumes, wore heavy makeup, and used exaggerated movements. The drama had its beginnings in April 1603 at Kyoto, where women danced at the Kitani shrine, playing men's roles

Actor in a Kabuki play.

as well as women's. In October 1629, Kabuki became an all-male affair by order of the shogun Iemitsu who decided that it was immoral for women to dance in public. Just as in Elizabethan England, women's roles were then performed by men. In 1652, Theater Regents of the Japanese shogun Ietsuna prohibited young boys from taking roles in the Kabuki theater.

Why is the **Globe Theatre** so well known?

The Globe is known because of William Shakespeare's involvement in it. In the 1590s, an outbreak of the plague prompted authorities to close

London theaters. At the time Shakespeare was a member of the Lord Chamberlain's Men, an acting company. With other members of the troupe, he helped finance the building of the Globe (on the banks of the Thames River), which opened in 1599 as a summer playhouse. Plays at the Globe, then outside of London proper, drew good crowds and the Lord Chamberlain's Men also gave numerous command performances at court for King James. By the turn of the century, Shakespeare was considered London's most popular playwright, and by 1604 the acting group, whose summer home was the Globe Theatre, were known as the King's Men.

What is a **passion play**?

A passion play is a dramatization of the scenes connected with the passion and crucifixion of Jesus Christ. The art form first appeared in the Middle Ages when liturgical dramas were performed. Toward the end of the tenth century, the Western Church began to dramatize parts of the Latin Mass, especially for holidays such as Easter. These plays were performed in Latin by the clergy, inside the church building. Eventually the performances became more secular, with laymen acting out the parts on the steps of the church or even in marketplaces. The liturgical dramas developed into so-called miracle plays or mystery plays. As a symbol of gratitude or as a request for a favor, Villagers would stage the life story of the Virgin Mary or of a saint.

When the plague (also called the Black Death) ravaged Europe, the villagers at Oberammergau, Germany, in the Bavarian Alps, vowed to enact a passion play at regular intervals in the hope that by so doing they would be spared the Black Death. They performed this folk drama, which had anti-Jewish slurs, every ten years for centuries.

MUSIC

How many musical **Bachs** were there?

Johann Sebastian Bach (1685–1750) was only one of a long and extended line of competent musicians—some fourteen of them. The Bach fam-

How old was Mozart when he composed his first work?

A child prodigy, Wolfgang Amadeus Mozart (1756–91) was composing at the age of five. He had been playing the keyboard (harpsichord) since the age of three. His father, Leopold (1719–87), was a composer and violinist who recognized his son's unusual music ability and encouraged and taught young Mozart. In 1762, Leopold took the boy, along with the boy's sister Maria Anna ("Nannerl"; 1751–1829), on tour to Paris. While there, young Mozart composed his first published violin sonatas and improvisations.

However, the image of the effortless and "artless child of nature" is not altogether true. Contrary to the reports that the gifted composer never revised first and only drafts, he did work at his craft. In a letter to his father, he wrote, "It is a mistake to think that the practice of my art has become easy to me—no one has given so much care to the study of composition as I have. There is scarcely a famous master in music whose works I have not frequently and diligently studied." The fact is that he did make revisions to his works, though it is also true that he composed at a rapid pace. The result is an impressive body of works, unequaled in beauty and diversity. The complete output—some six hundred works in every form (symphonies, sonatas, operas, operettas, cantatas, arias, duets, and others)—would be enough to fill almost two hundred CDs. And he achieved all of this within the span of roughly two decades.

Among his most cherished works are *The Marriage of Figaro* (1786), *Don Giovanni* (1787), *Così fan tutte* (1790), and *The Magic Flute* (1791).

ily was a musical dynasty. His father, Johann Ambrosius Bach (1645–1695), was a court musician for the Duke of Eisenach, and several of J. S. Bach's close relatives were organists in churches. His eldest brother, Johann Christoph Bach (1671–1721) was apprenticed to the famous German composer Johann Pachelbel.(1653–1706).

J. S. Bach left a musical legacy even beyond the vast body of church, vocal, and instrumental music that he composed: Four of his sons and one grandson were also accomplished musicians. "The English Bach" refers to J. S.'s son Johann Christian Bach (1735–82), who composed operas, oratorios, arias, cantatas, symphonies, concertos, and chamber music. A proponent of Rococo style music, J. C. Bach influenced Mozart.

Why do music historians talk about **"before Bach"** and **"after Bach"**?

Some scholars use these terms to classify music history since the life work of Johann Sebastian Bach (1685–1750) was so substantial, consisting of some eleven hundred works, and has had lasting and profound influence on music composition. While he was not famous during his lifetime and had disagreements with employers throughout his career, J. S. Bach's works and innovations in many ways defined music as we now know it. The tempered scale is among his inventions, and he initiated a keyboard technique that is considered standard today. Chronologically, J. S. Bach marks the end of "the prolific and variegated" Baroque Era, which began about 1600 and ended the year of his death, 1750.

A devout Christian, J. S. Bach believed that all music was to "the glory of God and the re-creation of the human spirit." As a spiritual person and true believer in eternal life, he left behind an impressive body of church music including three hundred cantatas (or "musical sermons") as well as passions and oratorios. As a devoted family man who believed all his children were born musicians (and therefore, the Bachs could stage drawing room music at any time), J. S. Bach also wrote chamber music, including instrumental concertos, suites, and overtures. Among his most well known and beloved works are *The Saint Matthew Passion*; *Jesu, Joy of Man's Desiring*; *Sheep May Safely Graze*; and his *Christmas Oratorio*.

Was **Beethoven** really deaf for much of his life?

Yes, Ludwig van Beethoven (1770–1827) suffered a gradual hearing loss during his twenties, and eventually lost his hearing altogether (in his early thirties). The loss was devastating to the German composer: In a letter to his brother he wrote, "But how humbled I feel when someone near me hears the distant sound of a flute, and I hear nothing; when

Ludwig van Beethoven.

someone hears a shepherd singing, and I hear nothing!" At one point he even contemplated suicide but, instead he continued with his work.

He had studied briefly with Mozart (in 1787) and Joseph Haydn (in 1792), and appeared for the first time in his own concert in 1800. While the loss of his hearing later prevented him from playing the piano properly, it did nothing to hold back his creativity. Between 1800 and 1824, Beethoven wrote nine symphonies, and many believe that he developed the form to perfection. His other works include five piano concertos, thirty-two piano sonatas, as well as string quartets, sonatas for piano and violin, opera, and vocal music, including oratorios. It was about the time that he completed his work on his third symphony, the *Eroica* (1804), that he went completely deaf. Though he was himself a classicist, music critics often refer to a turning point marked by the *Eroica*, which shows the complexity of the Romantic age of music.

A true genius, Beethoven's innovations include expanding the length of both the symphony and the piano concerto, increasing the number of movements in the string quartet (from four to seven), and adding instruments—including the trombone, contrabassoon, and the piccolo—to the orchestra, giving it a broader range. Through his adventurous piano compositions, Beethoven also heightened the status of the instrument, which was a relatively new invention (1710). Among his most well-known and most-often-performed works are his third (*Eroica*), fifth, sixth (*Pastoral*), and ninth (*Chorale*) symphonies, as well as the fourth and fifth piano concertos.

It is remarkable—even unfathomable—that these works, so familiar to so many, were never heard by their composer. A poignant anecdote tells of Beethoven sitting on stage to give tempo cues to the conductor during the first public performance of his ninth symphony. When the performance had ended, Beethoven—his back to the audience—was unaware of the standing ovation the work had received until a member of the choir turned his chair around so he could see the tremendous response.

In many ways, Johannes Brahms (1833–97) was the inheritor of Beethoven's genius: Music historians sometimes refer to Brahms's first symphony as "Beethoven's tenth." This is not to diminish the work of the great nineteenth-century composer, who left an enduring corpus of works. Brahm also demonstrated that classicism continued to have artistic validity and was not incompatible with Romanticism of the late nineteenth century.

What does **Wagnerian** mean?

It's a reference to anything that is in the style of German composer Richard Wagner (1813–83). Wagner was an enormously creative composer, conductor, and artistic manager who is credited with no less than originating the music drama. His interest in theater began in his boyhood, and by his teens he was writing plays. So that he could put music to these works, he sought out composition teachers. It is no surprise then that Wagner would conceive of the idea of the "total work of art," where music, poetry, and the visual arts are brought together in one stunning performance piece.

As an adult, Wagner led a scandalous life—challenging the music-listening public to separate his life from his art even today. He was someone modern audiences would recognize as a truly gifted and charismatic—if amoral—artist, working on a grand scale. Were he alive now, Wagner might well be creating blockbusters. In fact his musical compositions are heard in movies (including Francis Ford Coppola's *Apocalypse Now*) and are familiar to even the youngest audience today—or at least those who watch Bugs Bunny cartoons.

But this is not to take away from Wagner's serious accomplishments: His most widely recognized operatic works include *Lohengrin* (1848), *Ring of the Nibelun* (the Ring cycle; 1848–74), and *Tristan und Isolde* (1859). In the decades after his death, Wagner's reputation grew to the point that through the end of the nineteenth century, his influence was felt by most every composer, who often referred to Wagner's works in measuring the value of their own.

Why did **Schoenberg** face so much hostility during his lifetime?

The Vienna-born American composer Arnold Schoenberg (1874–1951), now considered one of the great masters of the twentieth century, was derided for having thrown out the rules of composition—for working outside the confines of traditional harmony.

In his youth, he was a fan of Wagner's compositions, seeing each of his major operas repeatedly. A series of Schoenberg's early works reflects the Wagnerian influence. But just after the turn of the century, Schoenberg set out on his own path. The result was the 1909 composition *Three Pieces* for piano, which some music historians argue is the single most important composition of the twentieth century. The work is atonal, which is to say it is organized without reference to key. Schoenberg had abandoned the techniques of musical expression as they had been understood for hundreds of years. This was no small moment for the music world, and many reacted with vocal and vehement criticism. (Of the outcry Schoenberg remarked in 1947 that it was as if "I had fallen into an ocean of boiling water.")

But he had his followers, too, among them his students. Though he was essentially self-taught as a composer, he became one of the most influential teachers of his time. It's interesting to note, however, that his teaching approach was grounded in the traditional practices of tonal harmony.

He later brought order to the chaos of atonalism by developing a twelve-tone serialism, showing how entire compositions could be organized around an ordained sequence of twelve notes. However, he never taught the method and rarely lectured or wrote about it.

Why does the music of **Bartók** figure prominently in concert programs today?

Béla Bartók (1881–1945) is revered today not only for his ability as a pianist (his teacher compared him to Franz Liszt, who was perhaps the greatest pianist of the nineteenth century), but for his compositions, which are steeped in the tradition of Hungarian folk music. Bartók studied and analyzed Hungarian, Romanian, and Arabian folk tunes, publishing thousands of collections of them in his lifetime. While ethnic music had influenced the works of other composers, Bartók was the first to make it an integral part of art music composition. His works were unique in that the folk music provided the sheer essence and substance of the music, lending the compositions a primitive quality. Among his masterpieces are his three stage works—the ballets *The Wooden Prince* and *The Miraculous Mandarin*, and the one-act opera *Duke Bluebeard's Castle*.

The introduction of folk music as the core of a musical composition has had far-reaching influence, which must have been felt by American composer Aaron Copland (1900–90) whose *Appalachian Spring* (1944) features a simple Shaker tune, front and center.

Is **Stravinsky** the twentieth century's foremost composer?

The Russian-born American composer Igor Stravinsky (1882–1971) is certainly one of the greatest composers of the twentieth century. Stravinsky wrote concerts, chamber music, piano pieces, and operas, as well as three ballets, for which he may be most well known.

Between 1903 and 1906, Stravinsky studied under the great Russian composer Nikolay Rimsky-Korsakov (1844–1908). In 1908, Stravinsky wrote his first work of note, the orchestral fantasy *Fireworks*, which was in honor of the marriage of Rimsky-Korsakov's daughter. The piece caught the attention of Sergei Diaghilev of the Ballets Russes, who invited the young composer to participate in the ballet company's 1910 season (Ballets Russes had dazzled audiences the year before and had brought new energy to the art form). In collaboration with Diaghilev, Stravinsky went on to create masterpieces—*The Firebird* (1910), *Petrushka* (1911), and *The Rite of Spring* (1913) among them. The partnership served to elevate the role of the ballet composer in the art world.

Rite of Spring is either Stravinsky's most famous or most infamous work. It was first performed by the Ballets Russes in the third week of its 1913 season. The choreography was arranged by the famous dancer Vaslav Nijinsky (1890–1950). But the performance stunned both the music and dance worlds. So extreme was the audience's reaction to this premier work that a riot nearly broke out inside the theater. Stravinsky had composed his music not to express spring's idyllic qualities but rather its turmoil and dissonance—similar to childbirth. Unfortunately, Nijinsky had decided to pair the composition with complicated and visually frenzied movements, characterized by the composer as a jumping competition. Though many thought it a disastrous performance, when the Ballets Russes continued on to London, *Rite of Spring* was more widely accepted there—largely because the audience had been duly prepared for it.

The following year, *Rite of Spring* was performed in concert in Russia, but again the reaction was mixed. The young composer Sergei Prokofiev

(1891–1953) was in the audience and later wrote that he had been so moved by the work that he could not recover from the effects. Listeners today are still moved by the elevated rhythm of *Rites of Spring*, which makes an entire orchestra into a kind of sustained percussion instrument. Ultimately, most musicians and critics came to regard the watershed work as one of the finest compositions of the twentieth century.

Who **invented jazz**?

Ferdinand "Jelly Roll" Morton (1885–1941), a New Orleans pianist, claimed credit for having invented jazz. And to some degree, it was fair of him to think so—after all, his recordings with the group the Red Hot Peppers are among the earliest examples of disciplined jazz ensemble work. But in truth, the evolution of jazz from ragtime and blues was something that many musicians, in several cities, took part in. Most regard Morton as *one* of the founders of jazz, the other founders include Bennie Moten (1894–1935), Eubie Blake (1883–1983), Duke Ellington (1899–1974), and Thomas "Fats" Waller (1904–43).

Some would go back even farther to trace the roots of jazz: From 1899 to 1914, Scott Joplin (1868–1917) popularized ragtime, which was based on African folk music. Even astute music critics may not be able to draw a clear-cut distinction between ragtime and early jazz. Both musical forms rely on syncopation (the stressing of the weak beats), and either style can be applied to an existing melody and transform it. The definitions and boundaries of the two terms have always been subject to debate, which is further complicated by the fact that some musicians of the time considered ragtime to be more or less a synonym for early jazz.

But there are important, albeit not strict, differences between the two genres as well: Rags were composed and written down in the European style of notation while early jazz was learned by ear (players would simply show one another how a song went by playing it); jazz encourages and expects improvisation, whereas ragtime, for the most part, did not; the basic rhythms are also markedly different, with jazz having a swing or "hot" rhythm that ragtime does not.

Whatever its origins, jazz became part of the musical mainstream by the 1930s and influenced other musical genres as well—including classical. American composer George Gershwin (1898–1937) was both a song-

Is blues music older than jazz?

Only slightly (and only if your definition of jazz doesn't include ragtime). Really, the two musical traditions developed side by side, with blues emerging about the first decade of the 1900s and hitting the height of its early popularity in 1920s Harlem, where the songs were seen as an expression of African American lives. Great blues singers like Ma Rainey (1886–1939) and Bessie Smith (1894 or 1898–1937) sang of the black reality—determined but weary. During the Harlem Renaissance, the music was a symbol for African American people who were struggling to be accepted for who they were. Poet Langston Hughes (1902–67) saw the blues as distinctly black, and as helping to free blacks from American standardization.

As the first person to codify and publish blues songs, American musician and composer W. C. Handy (1873–1958) is considered the "Father of the Blues." The Florence, Alabama, native produced a number of well-known works, including "Memphis Blues," "St. Louis Blues" (which is one of the most frequently recorded songs in popular music), "Beale Street Blues," and "Careless Love."

writer and composer of rags as well as a composer of symphonic works. Many of his works, including *Rhapsody in Blue* (1924) and his piano preludes, contain ragtime and jazz elements.

Perhaps more than any other composer and musician, Miles Davis (1926–91) expanded the genre: Through decades of prolific work, Davis constantly pushed the boundaries of what defines jazz and in so doing set standards for other musicians.

How **old** is **country music**?

Old-time music or "hillbilly music," both early names for country music, emerged in the early decades of the 1900s. By 1920, the first

401

country music radio stations had opened and healthy record sales in rural areas caused music industry executives to take notice. But it was an event in 1925, in the middle of the American Jazz Age, that put country music on the map: On November 28, WSM Radio broadcast *The WSM Barn Dance*, which soon became known as *The Grand Ole Opry* when the master of ceremonies, George D. Hay, took to introducing the program that way—since it was aired immediately after an opera program. The show's first performer was Uncle Jimmy Thompson (1848–1931). Early favorites included Uncle Dave Macon (1870–1952), who played the banjo and sang, and Roy Acuff (1903–92), who was the Opry's first singing star. Millions tuned in and soon the Nashville-based show had turned Tennessee's capital city into Music City U.S.A. In the 1960s and again in the late 1980s and 1990s, country music reached the heights of popularity, while holding on to its small-town, rural-based audience who were the show's first fans.

Is **bluegrass** music a distinctly American genre?

Yes: the style of music developed out of country music during the late 1930s and throughout the 1940s. Bill Monroe (1911–96), a country and bluegrass singer-songwriter, altered the tempo, key, pitch, and instrumentation of traditional country music to create a new style—named for the band that originated it, Bill Monroe and the Blue Grass Boys (Monroe's home state was Kentucky). Bluegrass was first heard by a wide audience when in October of 1939, Monroe and his band appeared on the popular country music radio program *The Grand Ole Opry*.

Although bluegrass evolved through several stages and involved a host of contributors, through it all, Bill Monroe remained the guiding and inspirational force, and therefore merits the distinction of being the "Father of Bluegrass."

Who was **more important** to rock-and-roll—**Elvis Presley** or **The Beatles**?

While music historians—and fans of either or both—may be willing to offer an opinion, the question cannot be definitively answered. The fact is that popular music today would not be what it is had it not been for

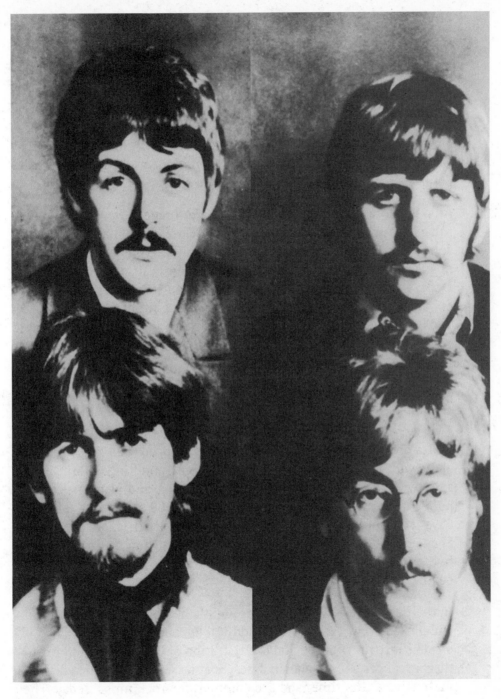

The Beatles.

both Elvis Presley and The Beatles. And the influences of both are still felt.

Elvis Presley (1935–77) brought to music an exciting combination of country, gospel, blues, and rhythm & blues music, and topped it all off with a style and sense of showmanship that dazzled young audiences. His first commercial recording was "That's All Right, Mama" in 1954, which was followed in 1956 by the success of "Heartbreak Hotel." Between 1956 and 1969, he had seventeen number-one records. Presley defined a new musical style—and an era.

Among those the American Presley had influenced were four English musicians who called themselves The Beatles. Originally founded by John Lennon in 1956 (as The Quarrymen), the group became the most popular rock-and-roll band of the 1960s. Their first single was "Love Me Do," released on October 5, 1962, and producer George Martin was encouraged that The Beatles could produce a number-one record. In 1963, they did: "Please Please Me" was released in Britain on January 12 and was an immediate hit. Other hits off their first album included "She Loves You" and "I Want to Hold Your Hand." The follow up album, *With the Beatles*, was released in 1964 and established them as Britain's favorite group.

Already popular in their homeland, "Beatlemania" began in the United States on February 7, 1964, when the mop-topped "Fab Four" (Lennon along with Paul McCartney, George Harrison, and Ringo Starr) arrived at New York's Kennedy International Airport and were met by 110 police officers and a mob of more than 10,000 screaming fans. Two days later, on February 9, The Beatles made their legendary appearance on *The Ed Sullivan Show*. By April the group held onto the top five positions on the U.S. singles charts. The British Invasion had begun.

In their early years, The Beatles brought a new energy to rock-and-roll, and picked up where Presley, Buddy Holly, and Little Richard had left off. The instrumentation and orchestration of Beatles songs (for which their producer George Martin deserves at least some of the credit) were innovative at the time, and are common for rock music today. Their rock movies, *A Hard Day's Night* (1964) and *Help!* (1965) were a precursor to the music videos of today. When the band decided to break up, the April 10, 1970, announcement proved to be the end of an era.

DANCE

Why is the **Ballets Russes** so famous?

The notoriety of the Ballets Russes began on a May night in 1909. It was then that the company, created by Russian impresario Sergei Diaghilev (1872–1929), performed innovative ballet choreographed by Michel Fokine (1880–1942). The Parisian audience, made up of the city's elite, was wowed by the choreography, set design, and musical scores, as well as the performances of the lead dancers—the athletic vigor of Vaslav Nijinsky, the delicate beauty of Tamara Karsavina, the expressiveness of Anna Pavlova, and the exotic quality of Ida Rubinstein. Ballet had been freed of the constraints and conventions that had held it captive. The art form was reawakened.

The reforms were on every level: choreography, performance, costuming, and design. The company's chief set designer was Léon Bakst, whose sense of color had influenced not only stage designs but even women's fashions. Soon Diaghilev and the Ballets Russes were at the center of the art world: Major twentieth-century painters, including Robert Edmond Jones, Pablo Picasso, Andre Derain, Henri Matisse, and Joan Miró, created set and costume designs for the dance company. And Diaghilev commissioned music that could match the spectacular dancing, choreography, and decor of his ballets. History's most celebrated composers, including Maurice Ravel, Claude Debussy, Richard Strauss, Sergei Prokofiev, and Igor Stravinsky, provided the scores for the ballets performed by Ballets Russes. The company, under Diaghilev's direction, had created a completely different kind of dance drama, bringing ballet out of the shadows of opera and asserting it as an art form unto itself.

The ballet companies of today are the lasting legacy of the Ballets Russes. Diaghilev illustrated that through a collaborative process, excellent art could be created outside the traditional academy. The Ballets Russes provided twentieth century dance with the model of the touring ballet company and seasonal repertory.

Who or what is **Balanchine**?

"Balanchine" is both a "who" and a "what": The name of the Russian-born choreographer is synonymous with modern American ballet.

George Balanchine (1904–83) was one of the most influential choreographers of the twentieth century, creating more than two hundred ballets in his lifetime and choreographing nineteen Broadway musicals as well as four Hollywood films. He co-founded three of the country's foremost dance institutions: the School of American Ballet (in 1934); the American Ballet Company (1935); and the New York City Ballet (1948), the first American ballet company to become a public institution.

His entrance into the world of dance was entirely accidental: In August 1914, Balanchine accompanied his sister to an audition at the Imperial School of Ballet and was invited to audition as well. Though his sister failed, he passed and, against his own wishes, was promptly enrolled. However Balanchine remained uninterested in the art form, even running away from school shortly after starting. The turning point for the young dancer came with a performance of Tchaikovsky's ballet *The Sleeping Beauty* (1890). He was dazzled by the experience, and chose to stay with the school's rigorous training program.

Serenade (1935; music by Tchaikovsky) is considered by many to be Balanchine's signature work. His other well-known works include *Apollo* (1928), *The Prodigal Son* (1929), *The Nutcracker* (1954), and *Don Quixote* (1965), as well as *Jewels*, the first full-length ballet without a plot.

Remembering the opportunity he had been given as a child, Balanchine was known for choreographing children's roles into many of his ballets. His outreach did not end there: he organized lecture-demonstration tours for schools, gave free ballet performances for underprivileged children, conducted free annual seminars for dance teachers, and gave free advice and use of his ballets to other ballet companies. Balanchine's unparalleled body of work was instrumental in establishing the vibrant style and content of contemporary ballet in America, where he established a training tradition and brought ballet to the forefront of the performing arts.

Why is **Dame Margot Fonteyn** so important to dance?

Fonteyn (1919–91) has been called an "international ambassador of dance." The British-trained ballerina achieved worldwide fame and recognition during her thirty years with the Royal Ballet, expanding the company's female repertoire and becoming the model for the modern ballerina. In 1962, at the age of forty-three, Fonteyn formed a dance

How did modern dance begin?

American dancer and choreographer Martha Graham (1894–1991) is the acknowledged creator of modern dance. She was thirty-five years old when the Martha Graham Dance Group made its debut on April 14, 1929, ushering in a new era in dance performance. The new form of dance dissolved the separation between mind and body and relied on technique that was built from within.

Graham's interest in dance had begun in her youth, and as an astute observer and manipulator of light and space, she came to be regarded later in life as one of the masters of the Modernist movement—on a par with artist Pablo Picasso. She is credited with revolutionizing dance as an art form; in her hands it had become nonlinear and nonrepresentational theater. Choreographing some 180 works in her lifetime, she also taught many students who rose to prominence as accomplished and masterful dancers, including Merce Cunningham and Paul Taylor.

partnership with Soviet defector Rudolf Nureyev (1938–93), challenging traditional assumptions about the ability of mature dancers to continue vigorous performance careers. In her later years, she continued to be active in the world of dance, helping to set up dance scholarships, fostering international artistic relations, and encouraging the growth of dance institutions around the world.

Who founded the **Dance Theatre of Harlem**?

The Dance Theatre of Harlem, the first world-renowned African American ballet company, was founded by Arthur Mitchell (b. 1934), a principal dancer with the New York City Ballet, along with Karel Shook (1920–85), a dance teacher and former director of the Netherlands Ballet. The impetus for the creation of the company came on April 4, 1968, while Mitchell was awaiting a plane from New York City to Brazil (where he was establishing that country's first national ballet company) and heard that Martin Luther King Jr. (1929–68) had been assassinated. Mitchell later said that as he sat thinking about the tragic news, he wondered to himself, "here I am running around the world doing all these things, why not do them at home?" Mitchell had spent his youth in Harlem and he felt he should return there to establish a school to pass on his knowledge to others and to give black dancers the opportunity to perform. The primary purpose of the school was "to promote interest in and teach young black people the art of classical ballet, modern and ethnic dance, thereby creating a much-needed self-awareness and better self-image of the students themselves."

The idea was a success: During the 1970s and 1980s the company toured nationally and internationally, often performing to sell-out crowds, and participating in prestigious events including international art festivals, a state dinner at the White House, and the closing ceremonies of the (1984) Olympic Games.

Today, the Dance Theater of Harlem is acknowledged as one of the world's finest ballet companies. Not only did Mitchell succeed in giving black dancers the opportunity to learn and to perform, he effectively erased color barriers in the world of dance, testimony to the universality of classical ballet.

How long has the waltz been danced?

Considered the quintessential ballroom dance, the waltz first became popular in Europe in 1813. But it dates as far back as the mid–1700s (the first written occurrence of the word *waltz* was in 1781). In the 1850s, the dance captivated Vienna, and the prolific Johann Strauss (1825–99), also known as "The Waltz King," produced scores of new waltzes to meet the increasing demand. Many of the compositions were named for professional associations and societies.

One of the most well-known waltzes is "The Blue Danube," first performed by Strauss on February 15, 1867, in Vienna. The lyrics, from a poem by Karl Beck, were sung by the Viennese Male Singing Society. The new waltz created an immediate sensation. It is an Austrian tradition, whenever "The Blue Danube" is played that the opening strain is played first, followed by a pause before the work is played by the full orchestra. The pause is so that the audience may applause.

How did the **Charleston** get started?

The Charleston, a lively ballroom dance, is named for the South Carolina city where it originated. The dance, which emerged in 1923, is one of the flashy elements of the period in American history that writer F. Scott Fitzgerald dubbed the Jazz Age. Other hallmarks of the Jazz Age, also called the Roaring Twenties, were speakeasies (since the country was in the midst of Prohibition), flappers, roadsters, raccoon coats, hedonism, and iconoclasm. The optimism of the Jazz Age came to a screeching halt on October 29, 1929, when the U.S. stock market crashed.

When did the **Big Band Era** begin?

On December 1, 1934, Benny Goodman's *Let's Dance* was broadcast on network radio, which effectively launched the Swing Era, in which big-band music achieved huge popularity. Goodman (1909–86) was a virtuoso clarinetist and bandleader. His jazz-influenced dance band took the lead in making swing the most popular style of the time.

How did the **jitterbug** get started?

During the height of swing music's popularity in the late 1930s and early 1940s, there were at least fifty dance bands with national reputations and significant followings. Dance styles such as the jitterbug were based on swing music, which was the dominant form of American musical entertainment during those decades. The dance itself is a variation of the two-step; couples swing and twirl in standardized patterns, which sometimes include acrobatics.

GAMES

When was **poker** invented?

The card game, in which a player bets that the value of his/her hand is higher than those held by the other players, was invented in the 1820s by sailors in New Orleans. (Webster's Dictionary cites the word "poker"

409

What is contract bridge?

It's the game most people are referring to when they talk about playing bridge—a card game (dating back to the mid–1800s) for four players in two partnerships who bid to name the trump suit. Auction bridge was invented in 1904 as a variation on the card game whist, which had been played since the early sixteenth century, if not longer. Auction bridge differs from contract bridge in that tricks made in excess of the contract are scored toward game; in contract bridge they are not. It's believed that contract bridge originated in 1925 when railroad heir and yachtsman Harold S. Vanderbilt invented the variation while on a Caribbean cruise. The variation did not catch on until 1930 though when Romanian-American expert Eli Culbertson defeated Lieut. Col. W. T. M. Butler in a challenge match at London's Almack's Club; the match was highly publicized.

originating in 1834.) The sailors combined the ancient Persian game *As Nas* with the French game poque, which itself was a derivation of the Italian game *Primiera*, and a cousin of the English game *Brag*.

Poker was originally played with three cards from a deck of only thirty-two, and included combinations such as pairs and three of a kind. The game was later played with five cards from a deck of fifty-two cards and the draw was also added.

Stud poker, where each player is dealt their first card face-down and the next four cards face-up, didn't come into existence for many years (until about 1864). Other later additions to the game were the straight (a hand consisting of five cards in sequence but not of the same suit) and the flush (a hand consisting of five cards of the same suit but not in sequence).

Who was **Hoyle**?

Edmond Hoyle was an English card-player, who in 1742 at the age of seventy, published *Short Treatise on Whist*, which provided the rules for a game that developed into auction bridge and later into contract bridge. Hoyle's name has survived among bridge-players in the phrase "according to Hoyle. . . ."

How old is **chess**?

It dates back to the Middle Ages: In 1283, Alfonso X (1221–84), King of Castile and León (Spain), commissioned the *Libro de ajedrez, dados y tablas* (Book of Chess, Dice, and Backgammon), based on an Arabic text. This book is still considered an important source on leisure activities in the Middle Ages.

How old is the game of **billiards**?

The Italians were the first to play this table-game, in the 1550s. It's different than pool, since billiards requires the players to cause the cue ball to hit two object balls in succession. There are no pockets, as there are in pool.

MOVIES

When was the **first movie shown**?

On March 22, 1895, the first in-theater showing of a motion picture took place in Paris, when the members of the Société d'Encouragement à l'Industrie Nationale (National Society for the Promotion of Industry) gathered to see a film of workers leaving the Lumière factory at Lyons for their dinner hour. The cinematography of inventors Louis and Auguste Lumière, ages thirty-one and thirty-three respectively, was a vast improvement over the kinetoscope, introduced in 1894 by Thomas Edison, whose film could only be viewed by one person at a time. The sixteen-frame-per-second mechanism developed by the Lumière brothers became the standard for films for decades.

The following year, on April 20, 1896, the first motion picture showing in the United States took place in New York; the film was shown using Thomas Edison's Vitascope, which was an improvement on his kinetoscope, and a projector made by Thomas Armat.

What are considered *the* milestones for the **motion picture industry**?

Motion pictures continue to develop as new, sophisticated technologies are introduced to improve the movie-going experience. In the decades following their rudimentary beginnings, there were many early milestones, including not only advancements in technology but improvements in conditions for those working in the then-fledgling industry:

1903: Edwin S. Porter's *The Great Train Robbery* was the first motion picture to tell a complete story. Produced by Edison Studios, the twelve-minute epic established a pattern of suspense drama that was followed by subsequent movie-makers.

1907: Bell & Howell Co. was founded by Chicago movie projectionist Donald H. Bell and camera repairman Albert S. Howell with $5,000 in capital. The firm went on to improve motion picture photography and projection equipment.

1910: *Brooklyn Eagle* newspaper cartoonist John Randolph Bray pioneered animated motion picture cartoons, using a "cel" system he invented and which was subsequently used by all animators.

1912: *Queen Elizabeth*, starring Sarah Bernhardt, was shown July 12 at New York's Lyceum Theater and was the first feature-length motion picture seen in America.

1926: The film *The Battleship Potemkin* revolutionized the making of motion pictures around the world by using a new editing technique called a *montage*. Soviet film director Sergei Eisenstein created his masterpiece by splicing film shot at many locations, an approach subsequently adopted by most film directors.

1926: The first motion picture with sound ("talkie") was demonstrated.

1927: The Academy of Motion Picture Arts and Sciences was founded by Louis B. Mayer of MGM Studios. The first president of the Academy was Douglas Fairbanks Sr.

A scene from *Birth of a Nation*, a film that began to popularize motion pictures.

1927: The first full-length talking picture, *The Jazz Singer*, starring vaudevillian Al Jolson was released. By 1932, all movies talked.

1928: The first Academy Awards were held: winners were William Wellman for *Wings*, Emil Jannings for best actor (in *Last Command*), and Janet Gaynor for best actress (in *Sunrise*). It was movie columnist Sidney Skolsky who dubbed the awards "the Oscars."

1928: Hollywood's major film studios signed an agreement with the American Telephone & Telegraph corporation (AT&T) to use their technology to produce films with sound, leading to an explosion in the popularity of motion pictures.

1929: Eastman Kodak introduced sixteen-millimeter film for motion picture cameras.

1933: The Screen Actors Guild (SAG) was formed when six actors met in Hollywood to establish a self-governing organization of actors. The first organizing meeting yielded eighteen founding members.

1935: The first full-length Technicolor movie was released, *Becky Sharpe*. The technology, however, was still in development and the colors appeared garish.

413

When was Hollywood's Golden Age?

Hollywood had its heyday in the 1930s: In the same decade that the Great Depression crippled the world economy, the American film industry enjoyed its Golden Age. The era was marked by technical innovations: "talking movies" had made their debut in 1927 with the first full-length film with sound, *The Jazz Singer*, and by 1932 all films were "talkies"; the first Technicolor film, *Becky Sharpe*, debuted in 1935, and by 1939 was perfected when *Gone with the Wind* was released; and special effects were brought to the screen in 1933 with *King Kong*, which was the result of painstaking stop-motion and rear-projection photography.

During this same time, movie stars such as Clark Gable, Claudette Colbert, Greta Garbo, and the Marx Brothers achieved public followings that were "the envy of political and business leaders."

The MGM, Warner Bros., and RKO studios were the head of the class, but other movie production companies fared well during these difficult times—including 20th Century Fox, Paramount, Universal, Columbia, and United Artists. Though many of the movies produced during this time might be described as "entertaining escapism," Hollywood had nevertheless become a "major contributor to popular culture, an occasional contributor to high culture, and a dynamic, if unsteady, force in the nation's economy."

1939: *Gone with the Wind* was released in Technicolor, which had come along way since its 1935 debut.

What was the **Hollywood Black List**?

In 1947, studio executives assembled at the Waldorf-Astoria Hotel in New York put together a list of alleged Communist sympathizers, naming some three hundred writers, directors, actors, and others known or suspected to have Communist party affiliations or of having invoked the Fifth Amendment against self-incrimination when questioned by the House Committee to Investigate Un-American Activities.

The "Hollywood Ten" who refused to tell the committee whether or not they had been Communists were Alvah Bessie, Herbert Biberman, Lester Cole, Edward Dmytryk, Ring Lardner Jr., John Howard Lawson, Albert Maltz, Samuel Ornitz, Adrian Scott, and screenwriter Dalton Trumbo. The film industry blacklisted the "Hollywood Ten" on November 25 and all of them drew short prison sentences for refusing to testify.

How did **newsreels** get started?

Newsreels got their start in 1910 when the pioneer film newsreel *Pathé Gazette* was shown in Britain and the United States. French cinematographer Charles Pathé and his brother Emil, were Paris agents for the Edison phonograph. They visited London to acquire filmmaking equipment and secured financial support in order to set up production units in Britain, the United States, Italy, Germany, Russia, and Japan.

These short movies, covering current events, were predominately used during wartime and were shown before motion pictures in theaters. They were superceded by television newscasts. The last newsreels were screened in 1967.

TELEVISION

What was the immediate **impact** of **television**?

The publicity surrounding the World's Fair television broadcast (April 30, 1939) inspired a flurry of broadcasting activity, but reached limited audiences. On May 17, NBC televised a baseball game between Princeton University and Columbia University, which NBC billed as the world's first televised sporting event. On August 26, NBC telecasted a professional baseball game between the Brooklyn Dodgers and the Cincinnati

The television in its early days.

Reds. More NBC broadcasts from Radio City featured live opera, comedy, and cooking demonstrations. Crowds waiting outside the 1939 New York premiere of *Gone with the Wind* were also televised. Feature films were aired, including a dramatization of *Treasure Island, Young and Beautiful*, and the classic silent film *The Great Train Robbery* (1903). Soon television stations had proliferated: by May 1940, twenty-three stations were broadcasting.

In 1941, after considerable deliberation on its part and that of the industry itself, the Federal Communications Commission (FCC) adopted transmission standards. Commercial operations were approved effective

416

July 1, and two New York stations, NBC and CBS affiliates, went on the air. By the end of that year, the first commercial on television, financed by watch-manufacturer Bulova, was aired. In December, with the bombing of Pearl Harbor and the entrance of the United States into World War II, commercial development of television was put on hold while American industry devoted its resources to the war effort.

But the television industry was eager, and as soon as allied victory was ensured, RCA reopened its television studio on April 10, 1944. CBS followed suit, reopening its operations on May 5. At the war's end in 1945, nine part-time and partly commercial television stations were on the air, reaching about seventy-five hundred set owners in the New York, Philadelphia, and Schenectady, New York, areas.

By 1947, the four networks that then existed—ABC, CBS, NBC, and DuMont (a short-lived competitor to ABC)—could still provide only about ten hours of prime-time programming a week, much of it sporting events. In late 1948, it was estimated that only 10 percent of the population had even seen a television show. However, as the networks stepped up their programming with live-drama programs, children's shows, and variety shows (a format that was familiar and popular to the American radio-listening audience), the interest in television grew rapidly. By the spring of 1948, industry experts estimated that 150,000 sets were in public places (such as bars and pubs), accounting for about half of the total number of sets in operation. Just a year later, 940,000 homes had televisions. And by 1949, production of sets had jumped to three million.

Which was the **first network**—ABC, CBS, or NBC?

It was NBC, the National Broadcasting Company, founded November 11, 1926, by David Sarnoff (1891–1971), who was then president of RCA. Sarnoff , considered one of the pioneers of radio and television broadcasting, created NBC to provide a program service to stimulate the sale of radios. In the 1940s, he reorganized the network to provide TV programming, again to stimulate sales of RCA products—this time, televisions. It was Sarnoff who demonstrated television at the World's Fair in New York in 1939.

Next came CBS (Columbia Broadcasting System), on September 26, 1928, which was established by William S. Paley (1901–90), an advertising manager for Congress Cigar Company. Paley sold some of his stock in the cigar company in order to raise $275,000 to buy into the beleaguered United Independent Broadcasters (which controlled Columbia Phonograph, hence the name). He built the floundering radio network into a powerful and profitable broadcasting organization.

The ABC (American Broadcasting Corporation) television network was last, in 1943. It was only by government order that the third network, ABC, was created at all. In 1943, when the RCA was ordered to give up one of its two radio networks, it surrendered the weaker of the two (NBC Blue), which was bought by Edward J. Noble, the father of Life Savers candy. In 1945 Noble formally changed the name to the American Broadcasting Company, which three years later began broadcasting television from its New York flagship station.

Is there a **Golden Age of television**?

Yes, people commonly refer to the 1950s as TV's Golden Age, which is the decade when Americans embraced television and the networks responded with a rapid expansion of programming. Critics still hail the programs of TV's Golden Age to be the most innovative programming in television history.

It was during this decade that anthology programs such as *Kraft Television Theatre*, *Playhouse 90*, and *Studio One* made live drama part of the nightly fare on prime-time television. Americans could tune in to watch original screenplays such as *Twelve Angry Men* (1954), *Visit to a Small Planet* (1955), and *The Miracle Worker* (1957). And tune in they did, prompting the production of more than thirty anthology programs—sponsored by the likes of Goodyear, Philco, U.S. Steel, Breck, and Schlitz. Since the production work was based in New York, the anthologies drew young playwrights including Gore Vidal, Rod Serling, Arthur Miller, and A. E. Hotchner. A new group of prominent television directors and producers emerged. And the studio dramas attracted the talents of actors George C. Scott, James Dean, Paul Newman, Grace Kelly, Eva Marie Saint, Sidney Poitier, Lee Remick, and Jack Lemmon.

The other cornerstone of 1950 television programming was the variety show—also done live. Comedians Jack Benny, Red Skelton, Jackie Gleason, George Burns, Sid Caesar, and "Mr. Television" Milton Berle thrived in the format.

But the cost of producing live programs and the growing popularity of television (which created a new mass market that demanded even more programming), combined to spell the end of television's Golden Age. Soon, live dramas and variety shows were replaced by situation comedies, Westerns, and other set-staged programs that could be taped in advance, and could be produced in quantity.

What was the **impact** of **network television**?

The Big Three networks rose to power in the 1950s and dominated television for the next two decades. During much of this period, they captured more than 90 percent of the total viewing audience. Americans had turned away from the radio and films that had diverted them in the postwar 1940s, and were tuning in to television—"the tube"—to the tune of an average twenty-five hours per week, leaving little time for any other recreational pursuits. In short, television had become not only an American pastime, but an American obsession.

Radio, which had given birth to television (both NBC and CBS were radio networks before they began developing TV programming), saw its revenue cut in half almost overnight. It not only lost audiences and advertisers to TV, but lost popular programs and stars as well. Radio turned its attention to an emerging new art form: rock and roll. The move was a success, as young listeners tuned in to hear the music that was considered too raw to be included in the evening TV line-up.

Film felt the effects of television as well, as audiences stayed home to be entertained. Movie-makers attempted to lure audiences back into the theaters with gimmicks including 3-D movies, Panavision, Cinemascope, and Circle-Vision. Hollywood abandoned the Western and other B-movies, in favor of big-budget blockbusters, many of which were filmed on location rather than at studios or on back lots. Studios even forbade their stars from appearing on TV, but they soon relented. Cooperation between the two industries is what saved film: studios sold old movies to the networks for broadcast and provided production talent and facilities to television.

When was public broadcasting started?

In the United States, it was started in 1967 when the Public Broadcasting Act was signed into law by President Lyndon B. Johnson on November 7, creating a Corporation for Public Broadcasting to broaden the scope of noncommercial radio and TV beyond its educational role. Within three years, and as a result of federal grants, plus funds from foundations, business, and private contributions, PBS rivaled the big three networks, NBC, CBS, and ABC, for viewers.

In England, The BBC (British Broadcasting Corp.) took control of the development of television in 1932, launching BBC-TV. The BBC, which had been broadcasting radio prior to getting involved in television, was founded under the leadership of English engineer John Charles Reith (1889–1971), in 1922. Reith remained at the helm of the BBC for sixteen years after its founding and under his guidance, it became one of Britain's most revered institutions, supported by the public with license fees.

Newspapers were least effected by the tremendous popularity of television, since programming time was at first limited to 8 p.m.–11 p.m., which still left time to read the paper. As soon as television expanded programming beyond that three-hour window, however, newspapers felt the pinch—more sharply in 1963, when both CBS and NBC began airing news shows. The daytime programming spelled the demise of the evening paper.

While television had no impact on the number of books published, it did prompt a decrease in the number of fiction titles that were published (and a corresponding increase in the number of nonfiction titles). The upward tend of nonfiction titles is a lasting effect of television on the publishing industry.

Today experts disagree over the impact of television on our lives. Some argue that increased crime is a direct outcome of television since programs show crime as an everyday event and advertisements make people aware of what they don't have. Critics also maintain that television stimulates aggressive behavior, reinforces ethnic stereotyping, and leads to a decrease in activity and creativity. Proponents of television counter, citing increased awareness in world events, improved verbal abilities, and greater curiosity as benefits of television-viewing.

THE EMERGENCE OF CABLE TV

How did cable TV develop?

The industry had its beginnings in the 1970s when Home Box Office (HBO) started to beam its signal to customers on a subscription basis. It was a radical concept: Let audiences pay direct for the programming (in this case, movies) rather than having it wholly supported through advertising and, in some cases, syndication fees. Another development during that decade proved to have lasting effect: Southern businessman Ted Turner bought an independent TV station based in Atlanta, and dubbed it a "superstation." WTBS was soon made available to some ten million subscribing households and was the beginning of Turner's cable TV empire, which would later include CNN (Cable News Network), CNN's Headline News, Turner Network Television (TNT), and, briefly, the music network VH-1.

Soon there were a number of niche-based cable networks airing programming around the clock: MTV was reaching teens and twenty-somethings; Lifetime targeted the women's audience; ESPN focused on sports; Black Entertainment Television catered to the African American audience; and All Movie Classics (AMC) appealed to a cross-section of American viewers who share a fondness for old movies, mostly black and white.

By the 1980s, the three major television networks, which had risen to power in the 1950s and had remained on the top of their game for the next two decades, found their audience share was dropping. This was aided by the introduction of the upstart Fox television network, backed by media mogul Rupert Murdoch. Fox's programming, geared toward a young, hip, and increasingly multicultural audience, found its own following.

421

Soon Americans had more choices than ever before—and for a relatively low subscription cost. By the 1990s, the Big Three networks (NBC, ABC, and CBS) were reaching only 61 percent of the television audience. Not to be beaten at their own game, the networks responded to the new competition by producing more cutting-edge shows—programs that likely would not have made it on the air before the advent of cable. Further, they began charging their affiliate stations for programming—a trend begun by CBS in 1992.

How did **CNN** change **television news**?

When Ted Turner's Cable News Network went on the air June 1, 1980, it was amid a fair amount of skepticism. Some thought the maverick businessman was ill-advised to air news around-the-clock to cable television subscribers. History would soon prove Turner's detractors wrong.

Twenty-four hours of air time brought CNN something other news entities didn't have—the time to do more in-depth news stories. The American public embraced the concept and soon began to rely on CNN not only to provide more information than other TV news sources, but for breaking news and up-to-the minute updates on top stories. In 1991, during the CNN coverage of the Persian Gulf War (which CNN had more or less aired live), newspapers reported a phenomenon—Americans couldn't turn the news station off.

Gone were the days of planning dinner around the evening network news or waiting up until 11 o'clock to learn the latest. CNN, and it's sister company, Headline News Network, were news at the ready. At a time when the term "global marketplace" was quickly becoming part of the vocabulary of every working American, CNN was uniquely able to capitalize on the growing sensibility of a world community. In 1985, CNN International was launched as a twenty-four-hour global news service. At first reaching only to England, by 1989, the signal was beamed to Africa, Asia, and the Middle East via satellite.

Since its early days, CNN has continued to evolve its programming to cover news in every area of endeavor with programs such as *Business Day, Larry King Live, Style, Special Report, World Today*, and *Science and Technology Week*, proving that the concept has staying power. The network, which began turning a profit after five years, has picked up multiple journalism awards, including the coveted Peabody award. One of the early harbingers of CNN's success came in April 1982 when CNN won the right to be on equal footing with the major network news organizations in the White House Press pool.

When did **MTV** first air?

MTV (Music Television) made its debut August 1, 1981, when it was made available to 2.1 million cable-subscribing households in the United States. The format was all music, twenty-four hours a day. Audiences could tune in any time to watch popular rock artists performing hit songs.

The notion of pairing music with video was not without precedent, the most obvious of which is The Beatle's 1964 critically-acclaimed pseudo-documentary, *A Hard Day's Night*. However, what was new was the idea of airing music videos around the clock. MTV was the brainchild of John Lack, vice president of Warner-Amex-Satellite Entertainment, which owned the cable station Nickelodeon. He'd taken interest in the Nickelodeon program *Popclips*, a music and video show developed by Michael Nesmith, a former member of the pop group the Monkees. Lack thought the format had potential and soon a young executive, Robert Pittman, just twenty-seven years old, was given charge of the project. MTV was launched with thirteen advertisers and a meager video library of only 125 videos, all provided by the record labels. But MTV caught on and by 1984, it had captured an audience of more than twenty-four million viewers, was showing a profit, and was soon spun off into a separate company by parent company Warner.

The video colossus thrived during the 1980s, helping launch more than a few music careers, including those of Madonna, Australia's Men at Work, and England's Culture Club. However, in the following decade, "veejays" (video jockies) had to make way for alternate programming on the music channel in order to keep audiences interested. In addition to the standard video programs (including theme shows such as *Yo! MTV Raps*), the cable channel broadened its offerings to include specials (*MTV Spring Break* and *MTV Beach House*) as well as series such as *Real Life*, *Road Rules*, and *My So Called Life* (which was bought in syndication). All of the new programming was aimed at the "Generation-X"

MTV's original VJs.

audience—the very group of teens and twenty-somethings who, in the 1990s, couldn't remember *not* watching MTV.

In the 1990s, even though its audience was estimated to have declined by more than half since its peak, MTV remained a going—and profitable—concern, as advertisers continued to rely on the medium to reach the youth market.

How has **MTV effected the music industry**?

MTV's almost immediate impact was to launch the music careers of fledgling artists. Some critics believe that superstar Madonna (1958–), who showed up on the music scene at about the same time as MTV, would not have risen to the heights of fame that she has were it not for Music Television. Or at least her star might not have risen so quickly. But she, and other media-savvy artists, exploited the new format to reach the music-buying public—the world over, for soon MTV had a global presence.

The video colossus also gave established artists a boost by airing more than one single off a given album—resulting in several hits

What impact have VCRs had on television viewing?

Since VCRs afford viewers the ability to tape TV programming and watch it at their choosing, a phenomenon known as "time-shifting" emerged. As Americans sat down to watch taped programming, they missed the prime-time programming being broadcast as they were viewing. Viewers who watched taped TV programs also enjoyed the ability to fast-forward through advertisements, or "zapping." Commentators mused that Americans were losing a sense of community—they posited that gone were the days when office workers would stand around the water cooler to chat about last night's episode of a certain program.

While the price of videocassette recorders was dropping, video rental outlets proliferated during the 1980s. The motion picture industry feared audiences would stay at home to watch movies rather than go out to the theater. But just as with television, the two industries soon found they could prosper side by side. Movie studios began reaping the rewards of video sales, and a whole new movie market emerged as companies like Disney began producing "direct-to-video," creating a whole new category of films that were neither shown on television or on the big screen.

from any one recording. Such was the case for artists like Billy Joel, Bruce Springsteen, U2, and Peter Gabriel. Increasingly creative videos gave the works of album-oriented musicians longer lives and steady sales.

MTV quickly established itself—and the format—as an integral part of the music industry. Once the format was proven viable, other music television channels emerged—including VH-1 (which was begun by media mogul Ted Turner and was later bought by MTV and molded into a more adult-oriented music station), TNN (The Nashville Network, showing country music videos and programming), and CMT (Country Music Television). Today, a new artist whose video is aired on any one of these cable music channels is given a major break.

Media analysts also believe MTV has had an impact on modern culture. Since the channel relies on interesting visuals to capture viewing audiences, MTV is constantly upping the creative ante for artists who freely experiment with bright colors, images, rapid-fire editing, motifs, dreamlike imagery, and other visual techniques, which began showing up on other television shows, in movies, and in advertising. Some observers believe the phenom has ushered in a new visual order.

Still, MTV has its detractors: Critics argue that the MTV aesthetic is superficial and that it is accelerating the movement away from traditional forms of literacy. While MTV is praised and panned in the worldwide media, there's no arguing that the music channel continues to be a window on what's hip and hot among American youths.

How **old** is the **VCR**?

Videocassette recorders (VCRs), certainly a familiar site in most households, were introduced by Sony in 1975 when the Japanese company debuted its Betamax, a small home "videocorder." But because of formatting issues (Beta vs. VHS) and the high per-unit cost to the consumer, sales of VCRs were lackluster at first. Nevertheless, the formatting issue resolved (VHS emerged the winner) and the prices coming into reach of the average consumer, sales took off. At the beginning of the 1980s less than 1 percent of American households owned a VCR, but by the end of the decade that figure had risen to 70 percent. Since that time, the VCR has become virtually ubiquitous.

THE OLYMPICS

When were the **first Olympic Games**?

The Olympics date back to about 900 B.C., when, in Ancient Greece, tens of thousands of sandal-wearing spectators descended on Olympia to cheer the runners, wrestlers, and bare-skinned boxers competing there. The games at Olympia were one of four athletic festivals in Greece, the others being the Isthmian games at Corinth, the Nemean games, and the Pythian games at Delphi, all of which alternated to form the *periodos*, or circuits, which guaranteed sports fans the opportunity to attend an athletic festival every year.

Winning was everything then: Athletes were required to register in order to compete and rumors of Herculean opponents sometimes prompted competitors to withdraw. Victors were awarded crowns of olive leaves, and the second- and third-place finishers returned home undecorated.

The modern Olympic Games, begun by diminutive Frenchman Baron de Coubertin, possess a decidedly different spirit than did their ancient counterpart where the only rules were that participants were not allowed to gouge, bite, put a knee to the groin, strangle, or throw sand at their opponent. The modern Games, publicly proposed by Coubertin on November 25, 1892, in Paris, and first held in Athens, Greece, in 1896, are based on their initiator's vision of the Olympic competition as an occasion to promote peace, harmony, and internationalism.

In April 1896, some forty thousand spectators pressed into the Panathenean Stadium, which had been constructed on the site of an ancient stadium in Athens, to witness the athletic feats of the first Modern Olympic heroes. Thirteen nations participated; only male athletes (just over three hundred of them) competed; and Greece received the most medals (forty-seven). The second Olympic Games were held in 1900 in Paris.

When were the **first Winter Games** held?

The Winter Olympic Games had a slow birth—making their first official appearance almost three decades after the first modern Games were held in Athens (1896).

In 1901, Nordic Games were held in Sweden. However, only Scandinavian countries participated in the events, which organizers intended to hold every four years. The Nordic Games constituted the first organized international competition involving winter sports. Then, as part of the Summer Olympic Games in 1908, host-city London held a figure skating competition that October. Three years later, an Italian member of the International Olympic Committee (IOC) encouraged Sweden, the next host of the Summer Games, to include winter sports in 1912 or hold a separate event for them. Since Sweden already played host to the Nordic Games, they declined to pursue the IOC suggestion. The sixth Olympiad was slated to be held in 1916 in Berlin, and Germany vowed to stage winter sports competition as part of the event. But in 1914, World War I began, and the Berlin Games were canceled altogether.

After an eight-year hiatus, the Olympics resumed in 1920: Antwerp, Belgium played host to athletes, which included figure skaters and ice hockey players along with the usual contingency of gymnasts, runners, fencers, and other summer sports competitors. The first IOC-sanctioned competition of winter sports was held in Chamonix, France, from January 25 to February 4, 1924. When the Games were staged next, in St. Moritz, Switzerland, in 1928, they were formally designated the second Winter Olympics.

From that year on, the Winter Games were held every four years in the same calendar year as the Summer Games—until 1994. In 1986, IOC officials voted to change the schedule. The result was that the 1992 Winter Olympics in Albertville, France, were followed only two years later by the Games in Lillehammer, Norway. The Winter and Summer Games are now each held every four years, alternating in even-numbered years.

Have the **Olympic Games** been held **regularly** since 1896?

No. In spite of the fact that international harmony ("Truce of God") is one of the hallmarks of the Modern Olympic Movement, the Games have been canceled by the governing body, the International Olympics Committee (IOC), due to world events: In 1916, the Games were canceled because of World War I; the 1940 and 1944 Games were called off due to World War II.

The Games have been effected by international politics, occasional boycotts, and demonstrations as well. Though the 1980 Summer Games continued as planned, the U.S. and as many as sixty-two other non-communist countries (including Japan and the Federal Republic of Germany) boycotted them in protest of the 1979 Soviet invasion of neighboring Afghanistan. The following Summer Games, held in Los Angeles in 1984, the Soviets took their turn at boycotting. The official reason was cited as "fear," though some skeptics believed the reason to be more specific: a fear of drug-testing. In 1968, in Mexico City, two black-socked American track medalists rose gloved-and-clenched fists of support for Black Power, which earned them suspension and expulsion from the Olympic Village.

Olympic history turned dark when in 1972 at the Summer Games in Munich, eleven Israeli athletes were killed in the Olympic Village by the Arab terrorist group, Black September.

A 1996 bombing at Olympic Park in Atlanta, Georgia, also cast shadows over the Games.

References

Aranson, H. H. *History of Modern Art.* New York: Harry N. Abrams, 1977.

Boyden, Matthew, Matthew Rye, Simon Broughton, Joe Staines, Gavin Thomas, Jonathan Webster, Sophie Fuller, Stephen Jackson, Mark Prendergast, David Doughty, Jonathan Buckley, and Kim Burton. *The Rough Guide to Classical Music on CD.* Edited by Jonathan Buckley. London: Rough Guides, 1994.

Brown, Les. *Les Brown's Encyclopedia of Television.* 3rd edition. Detroit: Visible Ink Press, 1992.

Cantor, George. *North American Indian Landmarks.* Detroit: Visible Ink Press, 1993.

———. *Pop Culture Landmarks.* Detroit: Visible Ink Press, 1995.

Dauphinais, Dean, and Peter M. Gareffa. *Car Crazy.* Detroit: Visible Ink Press, 1996.

de la Croix, Horst, and Richard G. Tansey. *Gardner's Art through the Ages,* 7th (revised) edition. New York: Harcourt Brace Jovanovich, 1980.

DISCovering U.S. History. Detroit: Gale Research, 1997.

DISCovering World History. Detroit: Gale Research, 1997.

Graff, Gary (ed.). *MusicHound Rock: The Complete Album Guide.* Detroit: Visible Ink Press, 1997.

Hunt, William Dudley. *Encyclopedia of American Architecture.* New York: McGraw-Hill, 1980.

Knappman, Edward. W. (ed.). *Great American Trials.* Detroit: Visible Ink Press, 1994.

Levey, Judith S., and Agnes Greenhall (eds.). *The Concise Columbia Encyclopedia.* New York: Avon Books, 1983.

Nelson, Rebecca, and Marie MacNee (eds.). *The Olympic Factbook: A Spectator's Guide to the Summer Games.* Detroit: Visible Ink Press, 1996.

Smith, Jessie Carney (ed.). *Black Heroes of the Twentieth Century.* Detroit: Visible Ink Press, 1998.

Index

F

Fabricius 313
Fahrenheit, Daniel 292
Fairbanks Sr., Douglas 412
Fall, Albert Bacon 177
Fallen Timbers 92
Far East 129
Farnsworth, Philo 303
Fatima 342
Faulkner, William 377
Fauset, Jessie 378
Faust (book) 373
Fawkes, Guy 85
Federal Bureau of Investigation (FBI) 236
Federal Communication Commission (FCC) 233, 416
Federal Deposit Insurance Corporation (FDIC) 180
Federal Emergency Management Agency (FEMA) 237
Fenian movement 207
Ferdinand, Archduke Francis 118–119
Ferdinand II 44, 46, 85, 151–152
Fermi, Enrico 282
fermium 282
Fessenden, Reginald Aubrey 301
Feudalism 21, 83
Fielding, Henry 375
Fiesole 379
Fifth Amendment 165, 415
Fillmore, Millard 173
Fine Clothes to the Jew (book) 378
Finland 118, 124–25, 131
Finlay, Carlos 324
Firebird, The (symphony) 399
Fireworks (symphony) 399
First Amendment 165
First Geneva Convention 334
First Home Rule Bill 207

First Land Act 207
First Triumvirate 143
Fisk University 197
Fitzgerald, F. Scott 409
Flanders 83
Flaubert, Gustave 32, 375
Fleming, Alexander 322
Florence, Italy 25, 26, 47, 370
Florey, Howard 322
Florida 50, 106, 112, 200, 212
Florida Keys 213
Florida Panhandle 215
Fog (painting) 384
Fokine, Michel 405
Fonteyn, Dame Margot 406
Ford, Gerald R. 204
Ford, Henry 293–295
Ford Motor Company, see Henry Ford
Fort Hood, Texas 197
Fort Riley, Kansas 197
Fort Sumter 107
Föster, Bernhard 268
Föster-Nietzche, Elizabeth 268
Four Horsemen of the Apocalypse 341
"four humors" 310
Fourteenth Amendment 166, 195–96
Fourth Amendment 165
France 15, 16, 17, 19, 20, 27, 33, 35, 58, 81–83, 86, 93–99, 112, 119, 121, 123, 262, 371–372
Francis I 153, 169
Francis II, Emperor 21, 314
Franco-Prussian War 34, 335
Frank, Anne 132–33
Frank, Otto 132
Franklin, Benjamin 112, 167, 315
Franks, the 17, 19, 150
Frazer, Sir James 338
Frederick I 363

Frederick II 274
Frederick the Great 87, 358
Frederick the Wise 349
freedom rides 361
French Academy of Sciences 362
French and Indian War 87–88
French Revolution 33, 93–95, 161, 168, 170
Freud, Sigmund 32, 332
Friendship 7 (spacecraft) 64
Frobisher Bay 52
Froebel, Friedrich 358
Fulton, Missouri 191

G

Gable, Clark 414
Gagarin, Yuri A. 64
Galapagos 284
Gale, Leonard 298
Galen 310
Galilei, Galileo 271–274, 291, 362
Galveston, Texas 212
Gandhi, Feroze 187
Gandhi, Indira 187–88
Gandhi, Mohandas 184–186
Gandhi, Rajiv 188, 246
Gapon, Father Georgi 114
Garbo, Greta 414
Garden School 257
Gargantua and Pantagruel (book) 27
Gates, Bill 306
Gaudi, Antoni 388
Gaugin, Paul 384
Gaul 17, 19, 80, 144
Gauls, the 20
Gaynor, Janet 413
Gaza Strip 189–90
General Assembly 184
General History of Connecticut, A (book) 166
Genesis 70, 339
Geneva 135

452